Rama Janamabhoomi:

Professor B.R. Grover's Analysis of Revenue Records and Historical Facts

Rama Janamabhoomi: Professor B.R. Grover's Analysis of Revenue Records and Historical Facts

Edited by

Amrita Grover

Dr. Anju Grover Chaudhary

Originals

Delhi-110052

First Published 2015

ISBN 10: 81-8454-156-2
ISBN 13: 978-81-8454-156-4

Published by
ORIGINALS
(an imprint of Low Price Publications)
A-6, Nimri Commercial Centre,
Ashok Vihar Phase-IV, Delhi-110052
Phone: +91-11-27302453 Fax: +91-11-47061936
e-mail: info@Lppindia.com
website: www.Lppindia.com

Printed at
D K Fine Art Press P Ltd.
Delhi-110052

PRINTED IN INDIA

Dedication:

At the Lotus Feet of Lord Rama

and

To the Memory of My Esteemed Brother

Professor B.R. Grover

Amrita Grover

Table of Contents

List of Maps

List of Plates

List of Exhibits

About the Author

(b. 1923- d. 2001)

Professor B.R. Grover, former Chairman of the Indian Council of Historical Research, with an academic and administrative career spanning more than 55 years, has left an indelible mark as one of India's most eminent and dedicated historians. He has left behind a massive wealth of historical research based on original Persian, Urdu, Ottoman Turkish, Punjabi and English sources. Known for doing intensive research in the archives and libraries of India, several European countries and the United States of America, Professor Grover had carved out a distinct position for himself as a moving encyclopaedia of source material on the land revenue administration of the Mughals.

Upon his death on May 10, 2001, the then Prime Minister Atal Behari Vajpayee paid him a rich tribute, stating: "He would always be remembered for his formidable legacy of excellence, erudition, and dedication to historical research and academic administration." Dr. Murli Manohar Joshi, then Minister of Human Resources and Scientific Research, paid him a personal homage and called him a real "Karma Yogi". He said, "He lived like a Yogi and died like a Yogi." Former Vice President of India, Justice Hidayatullah, had also applauded him for his research. His colleagues described him as "a man of sterling qualities of head and heart"; and "a dynamic and objective head of country's premier historical Institute who has left a rich legacy of his outstanding achievements in the world of historical research," among other things.

Born on February 10, 1923, Professor Grover started his career in teaching in 1946 in Lahore and later taught at the University of Punjab and various universities in Delhi until 1974, including Delhi University, Jawahar Lal Nehru University and Jamia Milia Islamia, where he also served as head of the Department of Indian History and Culture. In 1974, he was called upon to join as Director cum Member-Secretary of the newly established Indian Council of Historical Research (ICHR), a premier historical research Institute, where he served from 1974 to 1985 as Director and was later appointed as Chairman in 1999. For his long association with ICHR, his colleague, Prof. A.R. Khan, wrote in his obituary: "On account of his long association with the Council and the services rendered by him to it, Professor Grover became an institution by himself and he and the Council became a synonymy, as the latter came to be identified, both in India and abroad, with Professor Grover, even when he was not holding any office in the Council."

Initially having received training at Paris under the auspices of UNSCO for the promotion of history as a means of international understanding, Professor Grover wrote and published books in British history. Later, because of his deep interest in the study of original sources and his proficiency in Persian language, his research interests shifted to the medieval period of Indian history. As an avid researcher, Professor Grover wrote and published copiously on various aspects of the Mughal Agrarian System, Patterns of Rural Trade, the Concept of Village Community and a host of other topics including the Ramjanambhoomi/'Baburi Masjid' controversy. To determine whether a temple or a mosque existed at the Ramjanambhoomi site, he made a critical scientific and historical analysis of extensive data. He examined original land revenue documents, maps of Ayodhya, judicial records, recorded eyewitnesses of travels to Ayodhya in the earlier period as well as Babur's Memoirs and other documents and manuscripts at various libraries in Persian Arabic, Chaghatay-Turkish, Urdu, Sanskrit, Punjabi and English to arrive at conclusions about the exact location of Janmasthan, the location of the ancient city of Ayodhya, and the ownership/occupation of the land, among other things. For example, he studied the *abadi* maps, *hadbast* maps and the revenue settlement maps of 1851, 1893 and 1936-37 A.D. to examine the Janamsthan site. He spent numerous months at the district office of Faizabad and various other locations to examine the earliest revenue documentary evidence that was traceable to the early 18th century as well as the revenue documents of the Nawabi period and the British phase (from 1856 onwards) during the latter half of the 19th and early 20th centuries that have a direct linkage with the Mughal pattern of revenue administration. Moreover, during the "Janmasthan versus 'Baburi Masjid'" controversy in the 1990s, Professor Grover's expert advice as a leading historian was sought by the Government of India. On behalf of the Vishwa Hindu Parishad, Professor Grover was officially invited to submit a detailed report on "Janmasthan versus 'Baburi Masjid'" to present to the then Hon'ble Prime Minister Shri Chandra Shekhar and later to Hono'ble Prime Minister Shri P.V. Narasimha Rao. (Then from July 4th through July 18, 1992, Professor Grover camped at Ayodhya to examine the actual site and artifacts during the time when the ground acquired by UP Government at the Janmasthan site was being leveled and discovered large floor areas, in the pre-Islamic period, which was carefully paved with burnt bricks. Based on his findings, the Historians' Forum sent an investigative team of archaeologists to examine the site who concluded that "the archaeological findings of burnt-brick pillar bases a few metres from the mosque indicated that a large building stood in alignment with the Babri Mosque since the 11th century.")

Because of his expertise in historical manuscripts/documents and objects, Professor Grover was nominated by the Government of India for several honorary positions such as member of the Indian Historical Records Commission, member of the Historical Documents Purchase Committee of the National Archives of India, member of the Committee on Preservation and Development of Cultural Heritage of Delhi, and an expert member of the Verification Committee of National Museum, India. Professor Grover was also a member of the Publication Committee of the "Comprehensive History of India". For the Indian History Congress, he served intermittently as a Joint Secretary, a Treasurer and Sectional President (Medieval India). Professor Grover also edited the well-known Time Capsule in 1978, and advised the Government to display it in the National Museum instead of inserting it again underground. He also served on the Editorial Board constituted by the Government of India for the production of documentaries on "Freedom Struggle for India's Independence, 1984-2001." Under this scheme, more than 75 documentaries were published by the Films Division, Ministry of Information and Broadcasting.

Professor Grover represented India at several international organizations, including UNESCO in 1951; Indian delegate to West Germany, 1957; delegate to the International Conference in History, Bucharest, 1980; delegate to the International Conference on the Bulgarian Studies, Sofia, 1986; and delegate to the World Archaeological Congress, Croatia, 1998, among others. Besides participating in numerous Indo-European cultural exchange programmes, presiding over innumerable regional/national/international seminars and conferences and contributing papers to various national/international seminars and conferences, he also lectured widely in West Germany (1957), Bulgaria (1986), Zagreb (1998), UK (1998), Holland (1998), and United States (1998 and 2000).

Professor Grover received several honours and awards for his historical research. For his writings on Georgi Dimitrov, the "Role of the Indian Immigrants in the Culture and Economy of the West Asian and East European Countries During the Medieval Age," and "The Social, Religious and Agrarian Aspects in East Europe, especially Bulgaria under the Ottoman-Turkish Rule (14th-19th centuries)," he was awarded Georgi Dimitrov Gold Medal by the Peoples Republic of Bulgaria. For his work on Punjab History, Professor Grover was awarded Saropa Roll of Honour by the Punjabi University, Patiala, in 1996. A life-long scholar of medieval and Islamic India, Professor Grover again came in limelight in 2001 when (upon the demolition of Buddhist statues at Bamiyan by the Taliban government), his expert opinion was sought by the Indian media to determine whether there was any parallel between Bamiyan and Ayodhya.

As a distinguished historian and a scholar with an integrated and scientific approach to the analysis of historical process, Professor Grover played a tremendous role in dispelling several earlier fallacious theories on the Ayodhya controversy. Moreover, as a liberal thinker, he was a great believer in the social cohesion and national integration in India and made an immense contribution in this regard.

Preface

Ever since the demolition of the disputed structure ('Baburi Masjid') at Ayodhya on December 6, 1992, a stormy controversy has raged over the presidential reference to Supreme Court on 14th January 1993 about whether a Hindu temple or any Hindu religious structure existed prior to the construction of the 'Ramjanmabhoomi-Baburi Masjid' (including the premises of the inner and outer courtyards of such construction) in the area on which the structure stood. Moreover, controversies have also arisen about a number of other related issues, including the location of the ancient ciyt of Ayodhya; the tradition of the exact site of the birth-place of Lord Rama; whether the temple was replaced with a mosque by the orders of Sultan Ibrahim Sharqi of Jaunpur or under the orders of the first Mughal monarch, Zahiruddin Muhammad Babur; and whether a mosque was constructed on a vacant plot of land or after the demolition of temple, if any, on the site of the Janamsthan temple. In fact, BMAC contention before the court of law is that the 'mosque' was constructed on an absolutely plain and vacant piece of land. As a result of the Ayodhya controversy, numerous books and articles have been and continue to be written by several scholars. On this subject, in fact, we have been inundated with so much controversial literature by various scholars offering a variety of viewpoints that the entire issue has become politicized and communalised, resulting in polarisation of historians.

This book, however, is not just another book on the topic of Ramjanambhoomi. It is a part of India's contemporary history written in the form of memoirs, rejoinders, articles, legal notes, reviews of published documents, etc. by one who actively participated in the deliberations initiated by the Government of India. It is also an authentic eyewitness account of the happenings before and after the demolition of the disputed structure, popularly called 'Baburi Masjid'.

After the issue was raised at The Indian History Congress session at Gorakhpur, Professor Grover's curiosity for research was raised and he went straight from Gorakhpur to Faizabad and Ayodhya to examine to original records pertaining to the subject. He spent several months making an intensive study of the original land revenue records at Faizabad district offices and also visited the disputed site.

The material presented in this book is also based on critical historical analysis and scientific study of the land right of *Janmasthan* versus 'Baburi Masjid' and dispels several earlier fallacious theories on the said subject. He was of the view that "for matters relating to land rights during the medieval or modern periods, the importance of the original revenue documents, for whatsoever region, available in series or in fragments, cannot be underestimated. They command primacy over the literary sources or archaeological theories". Therefore, in tracing the history of the Muslim and Hindu Kingdoms in North India during the 11th and 12th centuries and establishing the position of Ayodhya/Awadh vis-a-vis Manhaich/ Jaunpur in the administrative territorial set-up from the mid-12th century to 16th century, Professor Grover not only critically analysed the history of the time prior to the building of the *Janmasthan* temple in Ayodhya by a local ruler named Nayachandra around mid-12th century, he also relied upon his examination of original land revenue documents, maps of Ayodhya, recorded eyewitness accounts of travelers to Ayodhya as well as Babur's Memoirs and other original documents and manuscripts in Sanskrit, Persian, Arabic, Chaghatai-Turkish, Urdu, Punjabi and English available in various libraries all over India.

To begin with, in the articles presented herein, Professor Grover set the record straight regarding the location of the ancient city of Ayodhya. According to him, some earlier historians had been wrongfully considering Ayodhya as a part of the Jaunpur territorial division. In his research, Professor Grover found that although the territorial divisions of Ayodhya and Jaunpur became an integral part of the Mughal kingdom after Babur won the battle of Panipat in 1526, they were separate and distinct territorial divisions with their respective revenues and were governed by separate *jagirdars*-cum-governors. As such, till at least the establishment of the Sharqi Kingdom of Jaunpur (1399), Ayodhya was never a part of the neighbouring administrative territorial division of Jaunpur, concluded Professor Grover.

Regarding the exact location of *Janmasthan,* Professor Grover examined the map of Ayodhya and the earliest revenue documentary evidence that was traceable to the early 18th century. An examination of the map of Ayodhya (painted on a large white cotton fabric, as wall hanging, that forms a part of the Kapad-Dwara Collection—private collection of the rulers of Ajmer/Jaipur State in Jaipur that depicts *Janmasthan* along with various other religious places of Ayodhya reveals that the structure of the *Janmasthan*/ Masjid temple with three spirals or *shikharas* of the tort, i.e., Kot Ramchandra. Upon an examination of this picturial map and the revenue documents of the Nawabi period and the British phase (from 1856 onwards) during the latter half of the 19th and early 20th centuries, that have a direct linkage with the Mughal pattern of revenue administration, Professor Grover was able to determine that Kot Ramchandra was one of the villages (*mauzas*) of the suburban mahal/pargana of Ayodhya and was quite distinct from the city (*shahar*) of Ayodhya. He further established that the identity of *mauza* Kot Ramchandra as a distinct separate revenue village was maintained right from the inception of the British Raj (1856) till 1947 and, in fact, continued to do so even till date. In the records, he further found that Kot Ramchandra was decreed to the Government in 1869, and ordered to be assessed to revenue in 1872 as a *'Nazul'* or Government property. As such, complete records of rights along with maps of Kot Ramchandra were prepared. He explained further that *'Janmasthan'* is the name used both by the 19th century revenue records and literary sources, being a large complex comprising the palace, inclusive of the birth-place (*Janmabhoomi*) area of Sri Ram Chandra, temple kitchen (*Sita-ki-Rasoi*), etc., that was situated in Kot Ramchandra. The revenue records relating to village Ram Kot, Haveli Awadh, District Faizabad, which Professor Grover personally examined at the District Records

Office, Tehsil Office and *Nazul* Office in Faizabad, thus clarify the factual proprietary position of *Janmasthan* versus 'Baburi Masjid'.

As per land revenue procedure, the records offer details of the numbered plots of the entire village of Ram Kot in respect of the nature of land rights. Professor Grover found that the *hadbast* map appended to the Settlement Report (1861) as well as the *abadi* map of Kot Ramchandra (1866) show only the *Janmasthan* in the *abadi Janmasthan* comples Plot No. 163. Moreover, the revenue settlement maps of 1861, 1893 and 1936-37 A.D. do not bear any indication of a 'mosque' at the *Janmasthan* site and indicate only the *Janmasthan* temple at the site. Also, the settlement reports of 1893 and subsequent settlement reports of 1936-37 and 1989-90 distinctly mention the sub-plot, on which the mosque is situated, as *Sita-ki-Rasoi,* observed Professor Grover. According to Professor Grover, "None of the revenue maps mention the disputed structure as a 'masjid' or any land in Ramkot attached to it as *'waqf'*".

Further, Professor Grover made it clear that the 'superior ownership' of the land had been declared in the name of *Sarkar Bahadur Nazul,* and the Hindu priests (*mahants*) were declared as the 'under proprietors' (*malkan-i-matahit*) in the entire *Janmasthan* complex. He wrote: "As per *khasra bandobast* and *khatauni* documents of the 1893 settlement, the core area of the *Janmasthan* complex was under *Mahal Nazul Sarkar* comprising two *khasras,* Nos. 163/1 and 163/2, with an area of 2 *bighas,* 14 *biswas* and 2 *biswansies,* respectively. These were shown as *abadi,* i.e., habitation, and were vested in the subordinate ownership and occupation of the Hindu *Mahants* Raghubir Das, Gopal Das and *Thakurdwara* Sita Ram." Hence, the theory that the *Janmasthan* complex falls in the category of *waqf* or that there was a graveyard on this plot is hardly borne out by the government records. Professor Grover wrote: "As per revenue records, no part of *khasra kishtwar* plots...comprising the disputed structure, i.e., *Ramjanmabhoomi*-'Baburi Masjid' (including the premises of both the inner and outer courtyards) has been shown in *waqf* or *maufi* or associated with any *qabristan* (graveyard)." According to Professor Grover, "The settlement report provides a separate detailed list of the *khasra* plots along with their respective areas which are declared graveyards under *waqf* but there is no *khasra* plot/sub-plot of the *Janmasthan* complex which falls in this category". Thus it is clear that the area on which the structure of the 'Baburi Masjid' stood is a part of the *Janmasthan* and was under the subordinate ownership of Hindu *Mahants*.

Professor Grover further observed that the same is well borne out by documentary evidence since the Mughal age. He emphatically said that "the land comprising the outer courtyard and covering Ram Chabutra/platform and *Sita-ki-Rasoi/Kaushilya Rasoi* with *Pacca Chula, Chakla* and *Belan* as well as footprints of Ram, Lakhan, Bharat and Shatrughan – have never been disputed and have always remained in the ownership and possession of the Hindu *Mahants*" and the Hindus have been worshipping there all through the ages.

Professor Grover said that this is further confirmed by the European traveler, Joswph Tieffenthaler, a Jesuit Austrian, who visited the Ayodhya region around 1766-71 A.D. and narrated the past facts about the demolition of the birth-place temple of Rama and the utilization of its pillars for the construction of the 'masjid' by Babur. Tieffenthaler stated that 'despite the prohibitive efforts of the Mughals, the Hindus continued to visit the place for worship and consequently they had constructed a *vedi* Ram *Chabutra* in the main courtyard of the Janmasthan/Masjid Complex'. Professor Grover further wrote: "That the Hindus had been not only been worshipping at the *Chabutra* for hundreds of years but the *Bairagis* would even enter the premises of the 'masjid' structure and write the words 'Ram, Ram' with charcoal on the inner walls of the main structure is further confirmed by Muhammad Asghar, the *Khatib* and *Muazzan* of the Baburi Masjid in his representation, dated 30.11.1858, to the British government for alleged interference in the Baburi Masjid. All this well confirms that despite the construction of the 'mosque' on the *Janmasthan* site, the Hindus never surrendered their claims of worship at this site all through the centuries".

Further, Professor Grover discovered that it was also recorded that "Before the British occupation of Awadh (1846), for most of the period since its very construction (1528), the disputed structure comprising the so-called 'masjid' was regarded as *'masjid-i-nazar'* wherein prayers could not be offered by the Muslim community as it was built on the very site of the place of worship of another community and was rather deserted."

Another viewpoint of some earlier writers that Professor Grover challenged was that the Janmasthan temple at Ayodhya had already been demolished and replaced by a 'mosque' on the same site by either Sultan Ibrahim Sharqi of Jaunpur or Sikandar Lodhi and that Mir Baqi simply carried out repairs and renovation under the orders of Babur. This viewpoint, Professor Grover observed, is not at all correct. Nor has the view that the "mosque" at the old site of *Janmasthan* at Ayodhya was built by the Sharqi ruler, Sultan Hussain Shah in 1467-68 A.D. on an open plot unoccupied by any previous structure any valid justification". Professor Grover iterated that such versions are contradictory to the text of the inscriptions installed on the "mosque" which clearly put the date of construction/ completion in the year 1528-29 A.D. He wrote that "One of the verses of the Persian inscription specifically mentioned the year of construction (*sal-i-banaish*) coverable in the chronogram *"Bavad Khair Baqi"* which comes to 935 AH/1528-29 A.D." Moreover, Professor Grover stipulated that if the theory of the destruction of the temple and construction of the "mosque" thereupon prior to Babur's reign were to be true, there would have been no inscription slab (*Shila-lekh*) embedded in the disputed structure demolished on 6th December, 1992. He wrote that "The text of the Sanskrit inscription discovered in the rubble in the aftermath of the demolition of the disputed structure clearly states that the inscription was intended to be a foundation stone giving detials about the sanctity of the Vaishnava temple as well as the builder of the temple around mid-12th century. As per the Sanskrit inscription discovered on 6th December 1992, Nayachandra, the feudatory of Govind Chandra, the ruler of Kanauj, built the *Janmasthan* temple at Ayodhya." However, a fresh decipherment of the same inscription by Dr.

Ramesh, former Jt. Director General, Archaeological Survey of India, has found it was Meghasut who, in fact, effected the construction of the temple.

While researching the topic, Professor Grover also found that many scholars have misread Mir Baqi, Asif Saani, as recorded in the inscription installed on one of the walls of the demolished disputed structure as Mir Baqi Isfahani. He stated that Saiyyed Shihabuddin Abdul Rehman, for example, in his well-known book on "Baburi Masjid" published by Darul Musanfin (National Academy, Azamgarh, 3rd ed., 1987, pp. 1-3) has misread/deciphered the word *'Asif Saani'* as *'Isfahani'*. He further stipulated that "Such an erroneous version of Mir Baqi as 'Isfahani' has already found currency in many other popular books on Ramjanmabhoomi/"Baburi Masjid". Professor Grover concluded that "Baqi Tashkindi', as recorded in Babur's Memoirs, could not be 'Mir Baqi Isfahani' as Tashkind/Tashkand is in Central Asia whereas Isfahan is in Iran. He quoted the work of Late Maulavi Ashraf Hussain in "Archaeological Survey of India", volume, titled, "Biographica Indica-Arabic and Persian" (Supplement, 1965, pp. 50-51) for the absolutley correct reading and decipherment of the word 'Asif Saani'."

Another theory that Professor Grover challenged was that the Hindu *Janmasthan* temple was demolished in the course of war in Ayodhya. "There is no authentic evidence to show that any battle was fought between the Mughal forces and the local Raja of Ayodhya," wrote Professor Grover, "by the time the administration of Ayodhya was entrusted to Mir Baqi on 28th April, 1528 A.D. or so, Afghan menace had been stamped out from the Ayodhya territories". It has been suggested by some scholars that Babur never visited Ayodhya for conducting the affairs of the state. Professor Grover stated that "This is a completely misconceived notion as according to Babur's own statement, he camped at a place just 4 to 6 miles from Awadh (Ayodhya) proper for settling the affairs of Awadh" and he met Mir Baqi. Mir Baqi was appointed as *hakim, i.e.,* the commander-cum-administrator of Awadh on March 28, 1528 and he remained in office at least till June 20,

1529. It was during Mir Baqi's tenure as *hakim* that the Vaishnava Hindu Temple of Janmasthan at Ayodhya was demolished and a 'mosque' was built on the same site which was completed in the year 935 A.H./15th September 1528 to 5th September 1529. According to the indigenous and traditional Hindu sources also, Mir Baqi overpowered the Hindus of the region and took possession of the entire fort-like (Kot) premises of *Janmasthan,* wrote Professor Grover.

Professor Grover also questioned the amended *khasra* records of the Nazul Department of the District Faizabad (U.P.), prepared in 1931 A.D. wherein the disputed area is shown as a graveyard and assigned in *waqf.* According to him, "The map maintained by the Nazul Department is not authenticated, nor prepared under any law, nor is it according to any ascertainable scale. In fact, the map and the survey made by the Nazul Department at the instance of the plaintiffs (Central Board of Waqfs, U.P. and others) in a Suit No. 12 in 1961, was rejected by the Lucknow Bench of the Allahabad High Court in 1990 which ordered a new survey on the basis of revenue records in order to ascertain the exact situation of the land involved in the Suit." Professor Grover's thorough study of the revenue documents from 1858-61 to 1991 A.D. showed that there was no *waqf* land associated with the 'Baburi Masjid' situated at the *Janmasthan* site and the *Janmasthan* complex.

A significant document cited by Professor Grover (Shah Jahan's *Farman,* 3rd July 1648) proves as invalid the theory of All India Baburi Masjid Action Committee that a Muslim masjid once dedicated to Allah cannot be surendered as temple of another religious community. According to Professor Grover, "The *Farman* refers to two significant matters, which otherwise are not known from any other source." Firstly, the *Farman* refers to the fact that Prince Aurangzeb had in the place of a Jain temple built by Shanti Das, constructed some *mihrabs* and given it the name of a masjid. The *Farman* ordered a complete restitution of this property (temple) to Shanti Das and ordered the removal of the arch constructed thereupon." Secondly, most significantly, the *Farman* refers to a representation made by Mullah Abdul Hakim to "His Majesty that this building, by reason of its being the property of another person, could not be considered a 'masjid' according to the inviolable Islamic Law..." Professor Grover personally visited the descendents of the family of Shanti Das at Ahmedabad and examined the *Farman* and other documents with the family and found the translation of the *Farman* from Persian to English to be correct and reliable. (He also compared the photo plate provided by Commissariat in his book with the original *Farman* and found it completely authentic). This throws a significant light on the present controversy whether a temple can be re-built on the site of the masjid. Based on this documentary evidence, Professor Grover said, "The assertion on the part of the All India Baburi Masjid Action Committee that in accordance with the Hanifa Law applicable in India, a Muslim masjid once dedicated to Allah cannot be surrendered as temple of another religious community is not tenable." He, therefore, concluded that "As such, any 'masjid' constructed on the premises of a temple can be restored to the original owner/religious community to which it belonged. So according to the Islamic Law, as applicable in India during the Mughal age, reconversion of the structure of a 'masjid' having been built or declared as such forcibly on the sacred premises/temple back to a temple of original religious community is absolutely valid".

Another significant point clarified by Professor Grover is the claim by some that the 19th century works of English and Muslim writers on the history of Awadh were biased and based upon the British 'Divide-and-Rule' policy. According to Professor Grover, such an approach brought about a "serious crisis in the Indian historiography posing a great challenge to objective and scientific historians..." Upon an examination of the literary works of the British as well as Muslim writers who wrote detailed accounts of the regional history of Awadh based on the past authentic contemporary sources, Professor Grover rejected the claim that the controversy over *Janmasthan* by the Hindus versus 'Baburi Masjid' was a creation of the British 'Divide-and-Rule' policy. He wrote: "...it is clear that the existence of the *Janmasthan* temple, its demolition during Babur's reign and the construction of a mosque is not a

Introduction

The "Ayodhya controversy" revolves not only around the issue of whether any Hindu temple existed prior to the construction of the so-called Ramjanmabhoomi-'Baburi-Masjid' in the area on which the structure stood but also revolves around the issues of the validity of the geographical location of Ayodhya as well as the tradition of birth of Lord Rama there. In view of these issues, a brief documented history is provided in the Introduction of the said subject to dispel some of the fallacious assumption in this regard.

The Wikipedia Encyclopedia and the Encyclopedia Britannica refer to Ayodhya as one of the very ancient cities most sacred to Hinduism. According to Wikipedia Encyclopedia, "Ayodhya was the capital of the kingdom of Kosala (7th century B.C.). Long associated with the Hindu legend of Rama and his father Dashratha, the town is a center of pilgrimage and is one of the seven sites sacred to Hindus". The Encyclopedia Britannica descrbes Ayodhya as "Lying on the banks of the Ghaghara River just east of Faizabad, of which it is now a suburb, Ayodhya in ancient times was one of India's greatest cities; today, it is one of the seven holy cities of Hinduism".

Ayodhya, in fact, has always been a very sacred city and a leading centre of religious pilgrimage for not only the Hindus but also Buddhists and Jains as their literature also maintain the same. Ancient Indian Sanskrit texts like the *Vedas, Ramayana, Mahabharata, Puranas,* etc. as well as the Buddhist and Jaina sacred literature shed a flood of light on Ayodhya's origin, development and historical authenticity. The earliest reference to Ayodhya is believed to be in the Atharvaveda where the word is used as an epithet of the city (*pur*) of the gods, as prosperous as the paradise itself: *"Aăcakră navadvără devānām devānām pūrayodhyă" (Atharvaveda,* 10.2.31), although various other interpretations have also been offered on this verse. In the *Purāṇas,* which constitute the most comprehensive foundation of our knowledge for the geography of ancient and medieval India, Ayodhya is listed as first among seven cities of ancient India that are considered sacred and lead to salvation: *Ayodhyā Mathurā Māyā Kasi Kānci Avantikā Puri Dvārāvati caiva saptaitā mokṣ adāyikāḥ.*

The word 'Ayodhya' has been also used in the *Taittiriyaranyaka* and the *Skanda Purana* has explained the term in a mythological manner, stating that "it represents the combined form of Brahmā, Viṣṇu and Śiva – 'A' for Brahmā, 'Ya' for Viṣṇu and 'Dha' for Rudra: "*Akāro brahma ca proktam yakaro viṣṇurucyate, dhakāro rudarūpaśca ayodhyā nama rājate" (Skanda Purāṇa, Vaisnava, Ayodhya, 60).* Further explanation given in the *Skanda Purāṇa* is thus: "...this great city was situated on the wheel of Viṣṇu named *Sudarśana...(Ibid.).* In the *Mahabharata,* the city of Ayodhya is given the epithet of *'puṇyalakshaṇā'* i.e., endowed with auspicious signs. Hence, Ayodhya has existed as a splendid city since at least the later Vedic period.

Ayodhya is recognized as an ancient sacred place according to the traditions of Jainism and Buddhism as well. According to the Jainism accounts, Ayodhya was the birth-place of the first and fourth pathfinders of Jainism and five *Tīrthaṅkaras* out of the twenty-four hailed from Ayodhya. Also, it is believed that Lord Adinath attained enlightenment on the Astavata mountain near Ayodhya. According to the Buddhist tradition, Lord Buddha is said to have visited Ayodhya several times and he lived on the banks of the Sarayu river.

Moreover, numerous references are found about Ayodhya in the ancient Sanskrit texts and inscriptions relating to the period between Lord Buddha and Guptas. For example, the mention of Ayodhya in *Kathāsaritsāgara* testifies to the existence of Ayodhya during the fourth century B.C. The city is mentioned in *Yoginitantra* and the name 'Saketa' (the name was used to mean 'Ayodhaya' – see discussion on the said subject later in the Introduction) appears frequently in the well-known text of the

Yugapurāṇa. An inscription found during the Sunga period (2nd century B.C.) in the kingdom of Pusyamitra Sunga mentions that King Pusyamitra performed two horse sacrifices in Ayodhya during his reign (*Epigraphia Indica,* XX, p. 57). According to a Gaya plate, Ayodhya was the seat of a Gupta *jayaskandhavara* or 'Camp of Victory' as early as the time of Samudra Gupta. All these references in the epics and Sanskrit texts as well as the inscriptions thus testify to the existence of Ayodhya from ancient times. Archaeologically also, it was proven by the eminent archaeologist and former director of Archaeological Survey of India, Professor B.B. Lal, during different excavations at 14 different spots in the '70s, including the *Janmabhoomi* at Ayodhya, that the town existed at least as early as the sixth century B.C. and that the modern Ayodhya is the same as the epic city (See B.B. Lal, "Was Ayodhya a Mythical City?" *Puratattva,* No. 10, 1978-79, pp. 45-49).

Regarding the location of Ayodhya, in the *Skanda Purāṇa,* it was described thus: "It was in extent one *yojana* from the Sahasradhara in the east, one *yojana* from the Sarayū in the south, one *yojana* from the Sama in the west and one *yojana* from Tamasa in the north" (*Skanda Purāṇa & Vaisnava, Ayo.,* 4/6. I/64-65). Sanskrit dramas as well as Pali texts also locate Ayodhya on the river Sarayū. Moreover, it is also evident from the Gaya Copper Plate inscription of Samudragupta that Ayodhya was situated on the book of Sarayū (See, Alexander Cunningham, *Ancient Geography,* 1963, p. 325). The location is thus given by all as situated on the bank of the river Sarayū, which is where the present city of Ayodhya is situated—on the right bank of the river Sarayū. The region around Ayodhya is generally identified with the term *'Kosala janapada',* i.e., the country of the Kosalas. According to historian B.C. Law, who studied the geographical position of Ayodhya before the partition of India, "Ayodhya is described in the *Ramayana* as being situated on the banks of the river Sarayu in the land of Kosala which was a big *janapada* or country and the well-known town of Ayodhya was included in it". (B.C. Law, "Ayodhya in Ancient India," *Journal of the Ganga Nath Jha Research Institute,* Vol. I, 1943, p. 425). The first detailed description of Ayodhya was found to be that of Maharisi Valmiki: "The famous city of Ayodhya was founded by Manu himself—that foremost of men. The city was twelve *yojanas* long with a breadth of three *yojanas*. It was a magnificent city, full of wealth and paddy..." (*Ramayana,* Bala K., 5.5-8, 10, 12, 13). According to the Jain account, Ayodhay was "twelve *yojanas* long and nine *yojanas* broad" (*Vividhatirthakalpa,* Ch. 24). This fits in with the description given by Valmiki noted above.

In the Jain sources, Ayodhya has been at times called Saketa, Vinita, Ramapuri, Sukosala or Iksvakubhumi, among others (See *Adipurāṇa,* Vol. I, pp. 1277-78). In the Buddhist literature also, the names of Saketa and Ayodhya are found, although sometimes separate references were made to Ayodhya and Saketa. Some controversy has arisen over whether Saketa and Ayodhya were identical or whether these were two distinct places. According to historian Rhys Davids, Ayodhya and Saketa were like two parts of one city and adjoined like London and Westminister (*Buddhist India,* p. 34). Another theory is that Ayodhya could be the earlier capital and Saketa the next. Thus, most of the historical evidences point towards the direction of oneness of Saketa and Ayodhya. This fact is borne out by other sources of history as well. According to Brahmanical and Jain literature, Saketa was identical with Ayodhya. Several earlier writers and pilgrims made no distinction between Saketa and Ayodhya. For example, Kalidasa, the famous Sanskrit poet of the first century B.C. or according to some scholars of the 5th century A.D., referred to Ayodhya in his Mahākāvya *Raghuvaṁśam* numerous times and used the names interchangeably. Hence, Saketa and Ayodhya were used for one and the same place. According to historian Alexander Cunningham, Saketa and Ayodhya are identical (*Ancient Geography of India,* p. 464). According to Hans Bakker, the eminent historian who wrote a masterly treatise on Ayodhya, Ayodhya is the name of the town in its earliest phase, and the name Saketa is used during the period of Buddha (6th centuy B.C.) and thereafter (*Ayodhaya,* p. 4). Bakker also stated that Skandagupta (455-467 A.D.) had the royal court installed in Ayodhya and the royal court had probably moved from Patalipura to Saketa/ Ayodhya during the reign of Kumaragupta, as the first inscription featuring the name Ayodhya dated from the reign of this king (*Ayodhya,* pp. 27-30). In the late 5th century A.D., Saketa was clearly identified as Ayodhya when the royal court of the late Guptas was installed there. Ptolemy, the famous Greek scholar of 1st century A.D., mentioned Saketa as Sogeda (*Ptolemy's Geography,* 2:25). Hence, there is considerable evidence that Saketa and Ayodhya are one and the same. Moreover, the fact that the name did not disappear in the historical records right from the Vedic times and that the location of present-day Ayodhya being situated on the right bank of the river Sarayū is consistent with that of the description of earlier times, reinforces the theory that Ayodhya is not a fictional city and that the present-day Ayodhya is the same as the Ayodhya of the epic times. Hence, the ancient Indian tradition as well as historical and archaeological evidence leads us to believe that the present day Ayodhya has been in existence since the Vedic times.

Similarly, there is sufficient evidence to indicate that Lord Rama's association with Ayodhya as his birth-place as well as his identity with god Vishnu-Narayana is not fictional either. Ayodhya derives its historical as well as religious importance due to its association with the solar dynasty, Ṛṣi Vasistha and particularly as the birth-place of Lord Rama. The *Ayodhya Māhātmya* upholds the divinity of Ayodhya and its sacredness, being the birth place of Rama: "*Tasmatsthanata aisane ramajana pravarttate, Janmasthanamidam proktam moksadiphalasadhanam" (Skanda Purana, Vaisnava, Ayo,* 10/18). The ancient city of Ayodhya is thus glorified in the *Ayodhya Māhātmya* of the *Skanda Purāṇa.* Maharishi Valmiki, in the great epic of Ramayan, has justified the importance and authenticity of Ayodhya's name by associating it with not only Rama, son of Dasaratha, but also his ancestors of the Ikvaku dynasty (Iksvaku, son of Manu, is believed to be the founder of the solar dynasty, which ruled the country from the capital city of Ayodhya). And so did the poet-laureate Kalidas in his, *'Raghuvaṁśam'* according to which Ayodhya played an important part in the story of the Ramayana, as Lord Rama, the king of Ayodhya, was born in the *'Treta Yuga'* (second aeon), thousands of years before Christ, as the eldest son of Dasaratha, the fifty-sixth monarch of the Solar line in descent from Raja Manu, the first king of the Solar dynasty.

A vivid description about Rama's birth in Ayodhya is found in Tulsidas's *Ramayana (Rāmacharitamānasa).* In the epic, Rama himself thus speaks of his birth-place in Ayodhya:

> Hearken, Monkey King, Angad and king of Lankā; this is a holy city and this land a land of beauty. Though all have praised Vaikuntha, renowned in the Vedas and Purāṇas and known to all the world, yet it is not so dear to me as this city of Avadh; and few are they who comprehend this mystery. This lovely city is the place where I was born (*Janmabhoomi*), and to the north there flows the purifying Sarayū, and all who bathe therein win effortless a home near me. Very dear to me are those who dwell therein; this city is the city of perfect bliss, granting its citizens a home with me hereafter (*Ramacharitamanasa,* I, 35, also cited in Bakker, op. cit., p. 37).

Tulsidas (1540-1623) further states that he started composing the sacred story at Ayodhya itself and thus glorifies the sanctity of the place:

> The very sight and touch of the Sarayū, a dip in its waters or a draught from it cleanses one's sins...The beautiful town of Ayodhya grants an abode in Rama's heaven; it is celebrated as the most holy place in all the worlds...Whoever dies in Avadhapuri is never born again. Knowing the town to be charming in every way, a bestower of all forms of success and a storehouse of blessings, I commenced writing this sacred story there (*Rāmacharitamānaṣa,* I. 35, 1-3).

Moreover, according to *Ramacharitamanas,* devotees made pilgrimage to Rama's birth-place to celebrate his birthday every year on the occasion of *"Ramanavami"* (9th day of *Chaitra*):

> All the 'holy places' (*tirtha*) gathered together in Avadhapuri; demons and serpents, birds, men, sages and gods went there and did reverence to Raghunayaka; and wise men celebrated the birthday festival and sang the high renown of Rama. Great companies of devotees bathed in the Sarayu's purifying stream; they meditated on Rama's beautiful dark body and repeated his name (*Rāmacharitamānasa,* I. 34).

The *Ayodhyamahatmya* of the *Skanda Purāṇa* also associated birth-place with the ritual of *Ramanavami* according to which the performing of ablution and charity at the site on *navami,* one is liberated from the cycle of rebirths (*Skanda Purāṇa,* II. 8, 10. 20-21). In the history books, one of the earlist references to this festivity is in the *Ain-i-Akbari* by Abul Fazl (1598 A.D.) wherein a detailed description is given about *Ramanavami* festival that is celebrated in Ayodhya. Abul Fazl wrote that "a great religious festival was held" in Ayodhya in Chaitra at the time of the Mughal Emperor Akbar (1556-1605 A.D.) (*Ain-i-Akbari,* Vol. III, tr. H. J. Jarrett, Asiatic Society of Bengal, 1949, p. 305).

Rama came to be recognized as an incarnation of god Vishnu, according to the epigraphic and numismatic data, around second century A.D. An inscription on a stone-slab from the well-known antiquarian site of Kausambi (modern Kosam, Allahabad district, Uttar Pradesh), which has been discovered recently, provides the most important evidence on Rama's supreme deity. It is stated in Bulletin of the Indian Archaeological Society (*Puratattva,* No. 23, 1992-93, p. 35): "The inscription is very fragmentary, and much of its important portion is lost due to the damage to the stone, including the date...Although the date is lost irretrievably, the paleographic features, the mode of dating and the employment of *Prakriti* clearly show that the inscription belongs to about the middle of the second century A.D." Furthermore, Bhasa, the well-known Sanskrit dramatist, associated Rama with divinity in his *Pratimanataka* and the famous Sanskrit poet, Kalidasa, cited Bhasa with reverence. It can be thus assumed that Rama's distinctiveness with god Vishnu came into being much before the start of the Christian era.

Regarding the existence of Vaishnava temples in Ayodhya from at least the second century B.C., evidence is found in the works of Valmiki, Kalidasa and Bhasa. For example, according to the *Ayodhyakanda* of Valmiki, there were high temples in Ayodhya resembling the Himalayan peaks. According to the *Ramayana* of Valmiki, at least one temple in Ayodhya was dedicated to Lord Narayana Vishnu: "Rama of subdued mind together with the large-eyed Sita bathed (in the Sarayu) and went to the (shrine) of Lord

Narayana. They offered oblations into the sacred fire and meditated on the God there. Observing silence with purified minds, Rama and Sita slept in the temple dedicated to Vishnu" (Ramayana, II. 6.1-4). The *Ayodhyamāhatmya* of the *Skandpūrana,* dating from about the 13th century A.D., according to Hans Bakker, also refers to an idol called "Chandrahari" in the Vasudeva temple at the Svargadvara ghat in Ayodhya which was believed to have been installed by the Gahadavala King Chandradeva who had come on a pilgrimage to worship Vishnu. Bakker, in fact, has repeatedly stated in his study that an old Vaishnava temple was situated on the holy spot where Rama was born. He wrote: "From the data given...we tentatively conclude that there existed an ancient Visnu temple at the Gopratara ghat (possibly erected before A.D. 1000) named Harismrti. The idol of the temple came to be known as Guptahari" (Bakker, *op. cit.,* p. 45). Moreover, the discovery of a seal bearing *chakra* in Gupta characters also supports the theory of the presence of Vaishnava shrines at Ayodhya in Gupta times also (See K. K. Thapalyal, *Studies in Ancient Indian Seals,* p. 160). Hence, several evidences exist that a magnificent Vaishnava temple was built at the birth site of Lord Rama in the 11th-12th centuries about which the references were made repeatedly in the subsequent writings. In researching the Persian and Urdu literature on the existence of temples in Ayodhya, Professor B.R. Grover also concluded that it is this Vaishnava temple which was later on described as "Sita Rasoi".

The fact that Vaishnava Hindu Temple of Janmasthan at Ayodhya was demolished on the orders of the first Mughal monarch, Zahiruddin Muhammad Babur and replaced by a 'mosque' on the same site in 1528 A.D. has been corroborated by authentic literary and historical evidences, Persian, Urdu and Hindi included, found by Professor Grover. (For all the evidences, see the text).

The archaeological evidence found from the *'Ramjanambhoomi-*Baburi mosque's site in 1992 is equally important and cannot be ignored. During July 1992, when the ground of the disputed structure acquired by the UP government was being leveled up, Professor Grover personally examined the area and discovered large floor areas, in the pre-Islamic levels, which were carefully paved with burnt bricks. The reports of his findings to the press eventually prompted the Historians' Forum to send the archaeologists to examine the reported discoveries. A team of eight eminent archaeologists went there in July 1992 to examine the findings and concluded that the inner boundary of the disputed structure rests, at least on one side, on an earlier existing structure, which may have belonged to an earlier temple. The team's leader, Dr. S.P. Gupta, said that "the team found that the objects were datable to the period ranging from the 10th through the 12th century A.D., i.e., the period of the late Prathiharas and early Gahadvals....There was other evidence – of cornices, pillar capitals, mouldings, door jambs with floral patterns and others – leaving little doubt regarding the existence of a 10th-12th century temple complex at the site of Ayodhya" (cited in Wikipedia Encyclopedia). Finally, the recovery of a large rectangular stone-slab bearing a twenty-line inscription in Sanskrit during the excavations upon the demolition of the mosque in December 1992 cannot be overlooked either. According to the inscription, the temple was dedicated to "Vishnu, slayer of Bali and the ten-headed one". According to Professor Ajaya Mitra Shastri, an eminent epigraphist, whose article was published in the Bulletin of the Indian Archaeological Society, *Puratattva,* no. 23, pp. 35-39, Line 15 of the Sanskrit inscription, for example, clearly states that a beautiful temple of Vishnu-Hari, built with heaps of stone...and beautified with a golden spire...unparalleled by any other temple built by earlier kings...was constructed. This wonderful temple...was built in the temple-city (vibudhalayan) of Ayodhya situated in the Saketamandala (district-line 17) showing that Ayodhya and Saketa were closely connected, Saketa being the district of which Ayodhya was a part.

In the debris of the disputed structure were also found some intact and broken stone images. One marble image of the 19th century, in all probalility, depicts Rama as holding bow-and-arrow by posture and that affirms that Rama worship continued at this place even after the demolition of the original Hindu temple during Baluer's time. According to Tiffenthaler, the Jesuit missionary, also, who visited Ayodhya in 1766-67 A.D., 'there was a *vedi* (platform) erected in the court of the mosque which was three times circumambulated by the pilgrims who then made a prostration'. (I, 181). Based on documentary evidence, Professor Grover also concluded that "the land comprising the outer courtyard and covering Ram Chabutra/platform, 'Sita-ki-Rasoi/Kaushilya Rasoi with *Pacca Chula, Chakla* and Belan as well as footprints of Ram, Lakhan, Bharat and Shatrughan—has never been disputed and has always remained in the ownership and possession of the Hindu *Mahants*" and the Hindus have worshipped there all through the ages. (See references to this at several places in the present text). Moreover, Professor Grover stated that 'Sita Rasoi' should not be jeered at as a part of functional history. It is a part and parcel of Indian history. He pointed out at the Indian History Congress Session in 1995 that "the framers of the Indian Constitution emphasized the cultural heritage of India especially through a list of illustrations as contained in the Constitution and engraved in the Chapters 1 to 22. Amongst the various other historical figures/phrases which find a mention in the above mentioned illustrations of the Constitution are Shri Ram and Sita in a scene from the Ramayan depicting conquest of Lanka and recovery of Sita by Rama". (See Indian History Congress Session 1995: A Critique, *Itihas Darpan,* Vol. 3, No. 1, p. 48). Professor Grover further stated: "By depicting these portraits, the Indian Constitution recognises these personages as historical and a part and parcel of Indian history. Here in the portraits, Shri Ram and Sita are as much a real part of authentic Indian history and culture as later on Lord Buddha or Akbar, or Mahatma Gandhi's Dandi March 1931". (*Ibid*). As a matter of fact, an eight anna silver coin issued by Akbar and displayed in the Museum of Bharat Kala Bhavan, BHU, Varanasi, portrayed Rama with bow and arrow followed by Sita with a flower in hand; the coin bears the legend 'Ram-Siya', in Devanagari script.

Since the birth place of Lord Rama has been an entity of profound devotion for Hindus throughout the centuries, it is no wonder then that anything revovling around Ayodhya has become such a sensitive and controversial issue. Although books on the subject have been proliferating, Ayodhya remains the subject of controversy, study and concern. We hope that the readers will have the experience of seeing this issue in a different light and in its proper perspective since the material presented in this book is based on critical historical analysis and a scientific study of the land rights of *Janmasthan* versus 'Baburi Masjid'.

This comprehensive book, divided into fourteen chapters, is based on a study of original Persian, Urdu, Punjabi and English documents. It throws a new light on the subject and provides a significant insight into the various issues involved with the '*Ramjambhoomi*/Baburi Masjid' controversy to dispel several earlier erroneous assumptions on the said subject. The matter has been dealt with by Professor Grover in a scientific and objective manner without any religious or political bias.

We hope that this book will be valuable to the history scholars as well as the general public and contribute significantly towards establishing communal harmony.

Chapter 1 gives the historical background starting from the intermittent Turkish (Muslim) campaigns during the 11th and 12th centuries, to Muslim and Hindu Kingdoms in North India during the second half of the 12th century, to the position of Ayodhya vis-a-vis Manhaich during the Sultanate period (1193-1398 A.D.), to the position of Ayodhya in 1528-29 A.D. vis-a-vis Jaunpur in the Mughal administrative territorial set-up during the reign of Babur (1526-30 A.D.), and leading up to a brief note on Babur's Memoirs.

Chapter 2 is about *Ramjanmabhoomi* as depicted in the Land Revenue Records (1856-1993 A.D.). (The land revenue records in English, Persian and Urdu were personally dug up by Professor Grover in the dusty files of District and Tehsil offices at Faizabad and various libraries and archives.

Chapter 3 presents the evidence from the Revenue Record—Record of Rights Relating to Janmasthan (*Ramjanmabhoomi*) from 1856-1861 A.D. to 1992 A.D. The evidence is provided from the revenue records, settlement reports and maps, including the settlement maps, boundary demarcation maps and revenue maps of the village Ramkot.

Chapter 4 deals with the Shilanyas Controversy regarding the title to the plot.

Chapter 5 pertains to the Ayodhya dispute and its reference to the Supreme Court under Article 138 (2).

Chapter 6 is concerning the Election Commission of India's election of the references to the Ram temple at Ayodhya and the role of the Pakistan's Inter Service Intelligence in promoting violence in India.

Chapter 7 analyses the revenue documents from a historical perspective relating to *Ramjanmabhoomi* versus 'Baburi Masjid' at Kot Ram Chandra, Ayodhya.

Chapter 8 gives literary sources from the early 18th century to the 20th century regarding the existence/demolition of the *Janmasthan* temple at Ayodhya.

Chapter 9 stipulates that as recorded in the 1st regular Settlement Report of 1861 A.D., there is no plot/sub-plot in the *Janmasthan* complex which has been put as a *waqf* attached to 'Baburi Masjid'.

Chapter 10 talks about Prince Aurangzeb's conversion of a Jain temple at Ahmadabad into a mosque and its reconversion as temple under orders of Shahjahan, the Mughal emperor in the years 1645-1648 A.D.

Chapter 11 deals with the literary, revenue and judicial records as well as archaeological evidence pertaining to the *Ramjanmbhoomi* vs. 'Baburi Masjid' controversy.

Chapter 12 is a comprehensive paper presented at the World Archaeological Congress, Inter-Congress on Destruction and Conservation of Cultural Property in Croatia in 1998 by Prof. Grover and Ms. Amrita Grover on "The Rama Temple at Awadh (Ayodhaya) and the Historical Records of its Destruction Based on the Testimony of the Muslim Scholars and Western Sources".

Chapter 13 pertains to the judgments of the Lucknow Bench of Allahabad High Court on the Ayodhya issue with special reference to *Ramjanmabhoomi* versus 'Baburi Masjid' during the 19th and 20th centuries.

Chapter 14 is a note on omissions in the Government of India's White Paper on Ayodhaya, dated February, 1993.

Ms. Amrita Grover
Dr. Anju Grover Chaudhary

1
Historical Background

Historical Background Note: 1
Intermittent Turkish (Muslim) Campaigns into the Indo-Gangetic plains from the North-West during the 11th and 12th Centuries

(i) Most of the Indian campaigns of Mahmud of Ghazni (from 1000 A.D. to 1027 A.D.) remained confined to Baluchistan, upper Sindhu, Multan, Punjab, Mathura, Saharanpur and some portions of Western Uttar Pradesh. However, it was only in 1018-1019 A.D. that he conquered Kanauj after repulsing the Pratiharas. He plundered the town and destroyed idols. In 1021-22, Mahmud led another expedition against the Chandellas of Vidyadhara, and 'enroute' also conquered the forts of Gwalior and Kalanjara. In 1024, he invaded and destroyed the temple at Somnath in Kathiawar. His last Indian campaign in 1027 A.D. remained confined to the Jat territories of Sindhu and Multan. He destroyed temples and images but it is doubtful if he reached Benares or Awadh (Ayodhya) territories. However, according to the *Ain-i-Akbari*, Mahmud marched to Benares in 410 AH/1018-1019 A.D. and effected disruption of the old faith: (Hinduism). Mahmud of Ghazni died in 1030 A.D.

(ii) Saiyyed Salar Masud Ghazi (son of Salar Sahu of Ajmer) was nephew (sister's son) of Sultan Mahmud of Ghazni. Even during the latter's life time, he led military expedition for the propagation of Islam (*Tabligh wa Jihad*). Having conquered Multan, Uch (Sindh), Ajodhan (Pakpattan), Delhi, Meerut, Gharh Mukteshwar, Sambhal, Kanauj, Kara Manakpur and Bilgram, he, along with his sardar and lieutenant named Malik Fazl Alvi,

Historical Background Note: 2

Muslim and Hindu Kingdoms in North India during the second half of the 12th century

During the second half of the 12th century, India was divided into various kingdoms and chieftainships.

I

Muslim Kingdoms

(i) North India, in the South-western region, Lower Sind with capital at Debal, which had been earlier conquered by the Arabs in the early 8th century, was governed by a local Muslim Sumra tribe. The greater part of Upper Sind and Multan were under the Muslim *Qaramitah* (Shai sect) rulers.

(ii) The whole of Punjab stretching from Peshawar in the North-West to regions approximately bordering Hansi, Bhatinda and Sirhind etc. in the East was under the Ghaznavid rulers of the Yamini dynasty.

Hindu Kingdoms

(i) Kashmir was ruled by the Second Lohara Dynasty (Hindu rulers) and the local Muslim rule in Kashmir was established only in the 14th century (1318 A.D.).

(ii) From around the middle of the 12th century, the territories of Delhi ruled hitherto by the Tomaras were conquered by Visalaraja, the Ghahamana ruler of Ajmer. However, the Tomara chief of Delhi continued to be a feudatory of the Ghahamana rulers of Ajmer. In fact, even after the raids of Mahmud of Ghazni which had resulted in the annexation of Punjab to the Ghaznavid Sultanate, all through the 11th and 12th centuries, the Ghaznavid Governors of Punjab made intermittent raids into the Indo-Gangetic plains (Doab region) for the purpose of pillage, destruction of the Hindu temples and exaction of tribute. However, on the decline of Chalukyas, the Paramaras of Malwa, the Chamanas of Ajmer—also known as the Chauhans—established a mighty kingdom extending from Ajmer to Delhi and its region. Visalraja (also known as Visaladeva/Vigraharaja IV) conquered not only Delhi from the Tomaras but even Hansi from the Ghaznavid rulers of Punjab.

Henceforth, the Chahamanas (Chauhans) occupying the bordering regions with the Ghazanvids of Punjab acted as the guardians of the frontiers of remaining Hindu kingdoms of Hindustan. Prithviraja III (1177/1192 A.D.), the famous Rai Pithora of Muslim writers, confronted Muizzuddin Shahabuddin Ghauri, who by 1186 A.D. had already conquered Uch, Multan, and Punjab from the local chieftains and Ghaznavid rulers. Prithviraja even won the first battle of Tarain (1191 A.D.) against Shahabuddin Muhammad Ghauri but was defeated by the latter at the second battle of Tarain in 1192 A.D.

(iii) Another powerful state in North India—a neighbour of the Chahamanas—was that of the Gahadavalas who during the reign of Jayachandra always showed animosity towards the former as well as towards the eastern neighbourly states.

(iv) The other eastern independent rulers were Chandellas of Kalinjar, the Kalachuris of Chedi, the Palas of District Bihar, the Senas of Bengal, the Chiefs of Brahmaputra Valley and Kamrup etc. Rajasthan was, of course, ruled by many independent chiefs. In Western India, apart from numerous chieftains, the Chalukyas of Gujrat were the most powerful.

Throughout the 11th and 12th centuries, whenever confronted with a Turkish inroad, each one of the affected states in North India barring the Gahadavalas, with rare exception, fought against the invaders. However, as explained further, the role of Chandradeva, the founder of the Gahadavala dynasty as well as that of Jayachandra fundamentally altered the fate and map of Hindustan.

The Gahadavalas

The earliest known chief of the Gahadavala family was Yasovigraha who was succeeded by his son Mahichandra, also known as Mahitala/Mahiyala, who ruled in some part of Uttar Pradesh. He was succeeded by his son Chandradeva. In fact, the real founder of the Gahadavala dynasty was Chandradeva whose kingdom covered the territories of Kanauj, Kasi (Benaras), Kausika (Allahabad region), Kosala (Awadh comprising Ayodhya) and Indrasthana/Indrapura (modern Indore in District Bulandshahar). He conquered most of these territories and made Kanauj as his capital and Kasi as the second capital. During his period, Prince Mahmud (son of Sultan Ibrahim of the Yamini dynasty), the Governor of Punjab (1075-1099) made inroads into the *Doab* region (sometimes between 1086 and 1090) for plundering Kanauj, Kalanjara and thereafter Ujjain. Exploiting this opportunity, Chandradeva joined hands with Mahmud and with his help seized the throne of Kanauj from Gopala, the Rashtrakuta ruler. In fact, Chandradeva, (Chand Rai as put by the Muslim Persian Chronicles) entered into an agreement with Mahmud, looked after the latter's elephant forces, and as an ally gave him armed support against the still powerful Parmara and Kalachuri kingdoms. (For details, "Indian Culture", Hyderabad-Deccan, 1942, p. 422; Majumdar and Pusalkar, *History and Culture of the Indian People*, Vol. V, *The Struggle for Empire*, Bombay, 1957, pp. 51-55, 94-95). He also imposed a tax called *Turushkadanda* upon the people for the payment of annual tribute to the Sultans of Ghazni. In view of the circumstances in which this tax was imposed by Chandradev, it was not a levy for the defence of the kingdom as considered by some historians. (vide *The Struggle for Empire*, *Ibid*).

II

At the second battle of Tarain (1192 A.D.), Prithviraja got support from his Tomara vassal Govindraja of Delhi as well as about one hundred and fifty Rajas and Chiefs from Hindustan. They all fought with determination against foreign aggression. But the Gahadavala ruler Jayachandra, who was on inimical terms with Prithviraja, did not help the latter. Even though the Persian chronicles (from the 13th century onwards) are silent about the attitude and role of Jayachandra at this juncture, the Hindu accounts categorically state that at the second battle of Tarain, the latter formed an unpatriotic alliance with Muizz-ud-din Shahabuddin Muhammad Ghauri against Prithviraja and actually participated in the war against him which ultimately resulted in the Turkish victory and the fall of the Hindu Kingdom of the Chahamanas (vide Wolseley Haig, *The Cambridge History of India, Vol. III—Turks and Afghans*, S. Chand & Co., 1965, Page 42). It is rather significant to note that such an action on Jayachandra's part was not unprecedented in regards to the Gahadavala dynasty. Even earlier at the time of the campaign of Mahmud, the Ghaznavid Governor of Punjab (1086-1090),

Chandradeva (Chand Rai as put by the Muslim Persian Chronicles), the Prince of Kanauj, *i.e.,* the founder of the Gahadavala dynasty entered into agreement with Mahmud and as his ally gave him armed support against the Rashtrakuta, Paramara and Kalachuri Kingdoms and annexed Kanauj to his kingdom.

The connection of the landed intermediaries in the Western part of the Gahadavala dominions with the Turks during the operations of Shahbuddin Muhammad Ghauri and Qutub-ud-din Aibak in 1193 A.D. is further confirmed by the fact that Muizzuddin Mohammad bin Sam, *i.e.,* Shahbuddin Muhammad Ghauri made a land grant to Ajaipal Lanba, Chaudhary of Baran (Bulandshahar) in upper Doab and a relation of the Dhor Chief Chandrasena, a feudatory of Jayachandra for having helped Shahbuddin Muhammad Ghauri in the process of conquest of Hindustan. This was undeniably a case of treachery on the part of Ajaipal. When all these facts for the years 1192-93 A.D. are collated, the role of Jayachandra having been an ally of Shahbuddin Muhammad Ghauri at the second battle of Tarain (1192) is well confirmed as narrated by the Hindu accounts of the medieval age.

As narrated above, Jayachandra had political enmity with Prithviraja and inspired by personal ambition did not realize the gravity of the situation upon which the fate of Hindustan rested. The story narrated by *Prithviraj Raso* by Chand Bardai — a work of a late period — to the effect that Samyogita, the daughter of Jayachandra, being in secret love and correspondence with Prithviraja and the latter having abducted her at the time of *swaimber* ceremony, is merely a figment of poetical imagination and has absolutely no historical truth. Jayachandra's role during the fatal battle of Tarain (1192) and his initial relationship with Shahbuddin Muhammad Ghauri can be analyzed only in the traits of his personal character, family inheritance of opportunism for betraying the Indian cause since the time of Chandradeva, the founder of the Gahadavala dynasty who joined hands with Mahmud, the Ghaznavid Governor against the other Indian chieftains who fought both for their motherland and Hindu religion.

Ironically and contrary to the expectation of Jayachandra, within a year, with Aibak's planning, in 1193 A.D., Muiza-ud-din Shahbuddin Muhammad Ghauri again marched into India with a large army and having eventually defeated Jayachandra in the vicinity of Chandwar on the Jamuna (between Kanauj and Etah) subordinated the Gahadavala dominion to his newly established Sultanate in India. Temples and other Hindu shrines were razed to the ground and relieved of their fabulous treasures. Nearly one thousand temples are said to have been destroyed at Benaras alone, and mosques were constructed at most of these places. As the territories of Awadh (comprising Ayodhya) formed a part of the Gahadavala kingdom, they were annexed to the Sultanate of Delhi and in due course of time were placed under the administration of a Governor (*muqti*). Many Hindu, Buddhist and Jain shrines were demolished in Ayodhya as well, which in due course of time became equally a Muslim cultural center with numerous mosques and *Khankahs* therein.

Such is the irony of history that Jayachandra, according to the Hindu accounts, when confronted with Muizzuddin Shahbuddin Muhammad Ghauri's determination for the annexation of other parts of Northern India (1193 A.D.) involving the overthrow of his own dynasty, is said to have repented his earlier 'unholy' alliance with him during 1192 A.D. at the battle of Tarain. In fact, due to his personal ambition and political rivalry with Prithviraja, he had miserably failed to read the real designs of Shahabuddin Muhammad Ghauri. He probably thought that like Mahmud of Ghazni or even later Ghaznavid Turkish marauders, Shahabuddin would withdraw after pillage and plunder leaving a political vacuum and that like his great-great grand father Chandradeva, he would be a political beneficiary at the expense of the other Indian neighbourly chieftains. This was a shortsighted and foolish diplomacy which not only belied him in the future but also sealed the fate of Hindustan.

Jayachandra was succeeded by his son Harish Chandra to the *Gadi*. In fact, during the latter's period or a little thereafter, the Gahadavala kingdom ceased to exist as an independent state and was reduced to the status of a feudatory chieftainship under the sovereign Turkish rule of Delhi Sultanate. Like many other suppressed rulers, the Gahadavala chiefs, even though confirmed as Rajas by the sovereign Turkish State, were reckoned as Chief Zamindars as collectors of the revenues on behalf of the State and were granted some jagirs (*iqtas*) within their own erstwhile state, of course, with limited autonomy. Broadly speaking, such a position continued all through the medieval and even the Mughal age right till the establishment of the British power in India. However, during the British Raj, the Gahadavala Chiefs of Manda (with erstwhile *Zamindari/jagir*) confirmed as Rajas were incorporated, like other Indian large or small native states, within the British pattern of Paramountcy which lapsed with the Indian Independence in 1947 A.D.

III

It is clear from the geneaological list of the erstwhile ruling family (*raj-vanash*) of the Manda Chieftainship that the *Vanshavali* was apparently prepared during the 19th and 20th centuries. However, when examined in the light of the available past archival and epigraphic records of the medieval age, the *Vanshavali* is defective and incomplete in some respects. Some of the names of the earlier rulers based upon the Persian and Urdu Chronicles have been spelt inaptly. They have not been correctly recorded as known from the still available Sanskrit accounts and epigraphic sources. Moreover, the genealogical list mentions Vijyachand as the founder of the "Ghaharwal" dynasty followed by Jai Chand in the line of succession. The list omits the first two rulers as according to the Sanskrit and epigraphic accounts. The founder of the Gahadavala ruling dynasty was Chandradeva (Chand Rai of Persian Chronicles) followed by Govindachandra, Vijayachandra and Jayachandra (Jai Chand of Persian Chronicles). As such, according to the medieval Sanskrit accounts and the epigraphic sources, Jayachandra (Jai Chand) was the fourth ruler in the line of succession rather than the second as erroneously recorded in the Manda genealogical list of *raj vansh*.

During the later medieval age, Kanwar Chattarsal Singh, son of Raja Prithvipal (the 31st Gahadavala ruler in the line of succession of the Mand *raj* — not 29th as put by the *Vanshavali*), branched off from the main family and established his own independent chieftainship at Dhaiya with the title of Raja. Since then this family also continued to exist both during the late Mughal age and the British *raj* as a small native chieftainship. The present incumbent is Raja Vikram Singh, son of late Raja Chandershekhar Prasad Singh (10th in line of succession of the Dhaiya family) and the grandson of Raja Bhagwati Prasad Singh (9th in line of succession).

Asni at Manhaich as well. Udaipal (son of Jayachandra) having been defeated fled away to the jungle. Later, Shahabuddin Muhammad Ghauri himself visited Manhaich and held his *darbar* at *Kot* Asni, where the neighbouring Hindu Chiefs acknowledged his suzerainty. After the flight of Udaipal, his *diwan,* Jeet Singh, was declared as the ruler of Manhaich. One of his successors, Saket Singh revolted against the Delhi Sultanate but he was suppressed by Zafer Khan, son of Sultan Ghiasuddin Tughlaq in 1324 A.D. In fact, Saket Singh was the last ruler of Manhaich which was annexed directly by the Delhi Sultanate (1324 A.D.). Saket Singh and his successors continued to avail of only some assignment as *Jagir* in this territory all through the Sultanate and the Mughal periods. However, after its annexation by Ghiasuddin Tughluq in 1321 A.D., the town of Manhaich was named as Zafarabad (the place of victory).

(iv) After the establishment of the Turkish rule of Delhi, most of the Hindu chiefs who had been defeated in the course of war accepted its suzerainty subject to the payment of the stipulated amount of the revenue in *Kharaj* as well as *Jizya.* As such, they had become vassals of the Delhi Sultanate. Some of the Hindu chiefs accepted the allegiance and vassalage of the Delhi Sultans of their own, just out of fear and even without waging a war. But the Hindu chiefs, even when reduced as vassals and landed intermediaries (Zamindars) continued to maintain their own armies/militia in accordance with their resources. At the same time, many of them, unless completely subjugated and suppressed, intermittently remained in revolt and evaded the payment of the revenues. As such, Harichandra, son of Jayachandra, the Gahadavala ruler of Kanauj who had been killed in action in war against Shahabuddin Ghauri, regained the possession of Kanauj, Manhaich territories (Jaunpur) and Mirzapur District in 1197 A.D. He was succeeded by Adakkamalla. However, the Gahadavala rulers of Kanauj also accepted the suzerainty of the Delhi Sultanate and ultimately were reduced to the status of petty chiefs/zamindars with entitlement of assignation of revenues (as *jagir*) even though they retained the title of Raja.

(v) The Chiefs of Ayodhya were the scions of the Rashtrakuta dynasty of Kanauj whose rule had been overthrown by the Gahadavalas of Kanauj during the later half of the 11th century A.D. Thereafter, the Chiefs of Ayodhya became the vassals of the Gahadavala rulers of Kanauj. It has already been stated in part No. 1 that around mid-12th century A.D., Nayachandra, the re-builder of the *Janmasthan* (Ramjanmabhoomi) temple at Ayodhya in Saket *Mandalam*, was feudatory/vassal of Govindchandra of the Gahadavala kingdom. The relationship of the vassalage of the Ayodhya chiefs with the Gahadavala kingdom of Kanauj continued right till the end of the 12th century A.D. or formally even for a few more decades in the early 13th century when the Gahadavala chiefs themselves had, in fact, become the vassals of the Delhi Sultanate.

It is known from the Persian chronicles that during the reign of Sultan Iltutimish (1210-36 A.D.), a Raja named Bartu was the ruler of Awadh (Ayodhya) who was also feudatory of Adakkamalla, the Gahadavala ruler of, more or less, defunct kingdom of Kanauj. The Ayodhya chief, Bartu, had fought against Iltutimish and is said to have killed thousands of Turkish soldiers. Ultimately, he was overthrown and killed by Malik Nasir-ud-din Muhammad Shah, the eldest son of Iltutimish. Bartu of the Persian chronicles has been identified with Mahasamanta Bharahadeva, a scion of the Rashtrakuta dynasty and successor to Lakhanapala.

In due course of time, with the reduction of the Gahadavala ruling family as mere landed intermediary with *zamindari* cum *jagirs* as the Raja of Manda, the chieftain of Awadh (Ayodhya), an erstwhile feudatory of the Gahadavala kingdom, assumed direct vassalage of the Delhi Sultanate. Even though from the 14th century onwards, the Persian chronicles seldom mention the names of the Awadh (Ayodhya) chiefs, they describe them as powerful chieftains with large number of contingent forces. For the Tughlaq period, both Ziauddin Barani, the author of *Tarikh-i-Firoz Shahi* and the anonymous author of *Sirat-i-Firoz Shahi* bear out the fact that when Firoz Shah Tughlaq ascended the throne in 1351 A.D., exploiting the weakness of the Sultanate under Muhammad bin Tughlaq, the powerful chieftain of Awadh (Ayodhya), like other chiefs of Kangra, Gorakhpur and Tirhut had long ceased to pay *kharaj* (tribute) to the state.

(vi) This statement (vide para no. v), on the part of the contemporary writer Barani, confirms the fact that alongwith the chiefs of Kangra and Tirhut, the chieftains of Awadh (Ayodhya) and Gorakhpur were considered powerful Hindu chiefs to have confronted the Sultanate through the evasion of the payment of the revenues (*kharaj* and *jizya*).

However, it seems that very soon, the chieftains of Awadh (Ayodhya) and Gorakhpur were pacified by Firuz Tughluq through the policy of reconciliation. This was necessitated by the fact that the ruler of Bengal, Shams-ud-din Haji, Ilay Shah had raided the territories of Sultanate of Delhi, *i.e.,* Benaras, Gorakhpur and Bahraich and had, in fact, taken possession of Tirhut and Bihar and had challenged the supremacy of the Sultan of Delhi. In order to checkmate the aggressive designs of the Bengal ruler, Firoz Tughluq started march towards Lakhnauti on 8th November 1353 A.D. As he crossed river Saryu near Ayodhya, the chief of Awadh (Ayodhya) also joined him along with his forces. At the same time, Rai Udai Singh of Gorakhpur, after having cleared the arrears of twenty lakh *tankas*, made submission to the Sultan by presenting two elephants and also joined the campaign along with the other Awadh chiefs. Similarly, the Rai Kanwar, the chief of Kharosa (in the *iqta* of Bahraich), cleared the arrears of tribute (*kharaj*) and after having made submission, joined the army of the Sultan along with his own armed forces.

(vii) The statement made in the preceeding para No. vi shows the economic as well as political-cum-military power of the Awadh (Ayodhya) as well as that of the other chieftains in this region. Incensed by any political or strong religious factor, an open revolt through the evasion of the payment of the revenues (*kharaj* and *jizya* etc.) was always a powerful weapon in the hands of the Hindu chiefs. This would always hit at the financial and military stability of the Sultanate which, ordinarily, the state could ill afford. Apart from this, despite all mutual political rivalries, the sense of unity on the part of the Hindu chiefs in the territories of Awadh and neighbouring regions for the protection of the *Janmasthan* temple at Ayodhya was quite marked in these regions even though it was not possible for the local chiefs to have met the challenge of the powerful military machinery, especially the artillery firing-power of the Mughals which had emerged on the political scene of North India during the early 16th century. This accounts for the fact that the *Janmasthan* (Ramjanmabhoomi) temple of Ayodhya, reconstructed in the mid-12th century, remained undesecrated all through the Sultanate period until it was razed to the ground in the early 16th century (1528-29 A.D.) by Mir Tashkindi (Mir Baqi), the *hakim* of Awadh (Ayodhya) appointed by Babur.

(viii) The viewpoint that the *Janmasthan* (Ramjanmabhoomi) temple at Ayodhya had already been demolished and replaced by a 'mosque' on the same site by either Sultan Ibrahim Sharqi of Jaunpur or Sikandar Lodhi (Sikander *but shikan*—the iconoclast) and that Mir Baqi simply carried out repairs and renovation under the order of Babur is not at all correct. Such a version is contradictory to the text of the inscriptions installed on the 'disputed structure' which clearly put the date of construction/completion in the year 1528-29 A.D. Moreover, if the theory of the destruction of the temple and construction of the 'mosque' thereupon prior to Babur's reign were to be true, there would have been no inscription slab (*Shila lekh*) embedded in the disputed structure demolished on 6th December, 1992.

(ix) There is a common cultural trait between Manhaich (named later on Zafarabad/Jaunpur) and Ayodhya. As they formed part of the Gahadavala kingdom, the Gahadavala rulers built sacred Hindu temples at both the places. A feudatory of Govindchandra built the *Janmasthan* temple at Ayodhya whereas Vijayachandra and Jayachandra built Hindu temples at Manhaich. The Deval Atal (*Atal Devi ka Mandir*) and two other temples, which fell under the direct administration of the Jaunpur State, were converted into mosques by Sultan Ibrahim Sharaqi (1402-1436) of Jaunpur State. The Ayodhya *Janmasthan* temple was, however, destined to meet the same fate during the reign of Babur, the first Mughal ruler of India.

B

The Sharqi Rule in the Jaunpur State (1399-1479 A.D.)

(x) The city of Junapur/Jaunpur was founded on the northern side of river Gomti, in the vicinity of Manhaich, *Kot* Asni/Zafarabad by Sultan Firuz Shah Tughlaq after the name of his cousin Muhammad bin Tughlaq alias Juna Shah. (According to *Ain-i-Akbari*, Firuz Shah named it after his cousin Fakhruddin Jaunsh). As such, Jaunpur became the headquarters of the eastern (Sharqi) regions of the Delhi Sultanate.

(xi) Firuz Shah appointed his eunuch Malik Sarwar with the title of *Sultan us Sharq* as the Governor of Jaunpur territories in 1394 A.D. His son, named Mubarak Qaranful, exploiting the weakness of the Delhi Sultanate, set up an independent state of Jaunpur in 1399 by reading *Khutbah* and striking coin in his own name. This came to be known as Sharqi dynasty which lasted till 1479 A.D. when it was overthrown by the Delhi Sultan, Bahlol Lodhi, who incorporated the Jaunpur State into the Lodhi kingdom.

(xii) The Arabic/Persian chronicles of the medieval age corrupted the word Ayodhya (meaning invincible) into Awadh. As such, Awadh (Oude as later on spelt by the English writers) was a corruption of the original word Ayodhya.

(The province of Awadh in the British period lay between 25° 34' and 28° 42' N, and 79° 41' and 83° 08' E. That 'the name Awadh is a corruption of the ancient city of Ajodhiya' is also supported by the *Imperial Gazatteer of India*, Vol. XIX, p. 277). Ever since the conquest of North India by Shahabuddin Muhammad Ghauri and Qutubuddin Aaibak and the establishment of the Turkish (Muslim) rule of the Delhi Sultanate, Ayodhya/Awadh, even though a neighbouring territory of Jaunpur, had always been a distinct separate administrative unit (*iqta*) from the latter. In fact, both Ayodhya/Awadh and Jaunpur, earlier Manhaich (*Kot* Asni/Zafarabad), had been separate distinct administrative divisions (*iqtas*). As such, till at least the establishment of the Sharqi kingdom of Jaunpur (1399), Ayodhya/Awadh was never a part of the neighbouring administrative territorial division of Jaunpur.

(xiii) The Sharqi Sultans of the independent state of Jaunpur pursued the policy of territorial expansion at the cost of the Delhi Sultanate.

(xiv) Finding the Delhi Sultanate as weak, many chiefs and *Rais* (inclusive of Gwalior) evaded the payment of tribute to the state. In such circumstances, by 1436 A.D., Sultan Ibrahim Sharqi of Jaunpur (1402-36) took possession of certain neighbouring divisions of the Delhi Sultanate. Later on, in 1452 A.D. (856 AH), Sultan Mahmud Sharqi (1436-58) due to party intrigues at the Delhi Court invaded and even gained possession of Delhi. But he soon retired to Jaunpur. Next year (1453 A.D.), he again occupied many territories of the Delhi state from Jaunpur to Itawa. His son, Muhammad Shah and grandson, Hussain Shah (1458-79) also pursued aggressive policy. Hussain Shah even marched to Delhi. But he was checkmated and defeated by Sultan Bahlol Lodhi with the help of the Afghan forces. In 1478 A.D., Sultan Bahlol Lodhi invaded and occupied Jaunpur and left his son Barbak as governor. In 1479 A.D., Sultan Bahlol Lodhi annexed the Jaunpur territories to the Delhi Sultanate. This ended the Sharqi dynasty of Jaunpur.

(xv) Apparently, from the period of Sultan Ibrahim Sharqi (1402-36) to the end of the Sharqi rule in Jaunpur in 1479 A.D., the chiefs of Ayodhya/Awadh territories accepted the suzerainty of the Jaunpur Sharqi rule and paid tribute to the latter.

The Sharqi domination also affected the local architecture of the Awadh territories. This equally accounts for the fact that like the *Atala Masjid* (1408), *Masjid Khalid Mukhlis* (1417-19) and *Janjari Masjid*, all the three mosques built by Sultan Ibrahim Sharqi on the sites of the demolished Hindu temples, the 'mosque' built by Mir Baqi (1528) in Babur's reign at the site of the erstwhile *Janmasthan* temple at Ayodhya, did not have any minarets attached to it. Otherwise, too, parallel architectural features in respect of main gates, ceilings and *mehrabs, delans* and re-used temple materials could be traced in the above mentioned 'mosques'.

(xvi) There is no denying the fact that during the early 19th century, Francis Hamilton Buchannan in his "*Survey of Gorakhpur District*" (1813-14) recorded another Arabic inscription prevalent on the walls of the 'mosque' which later on was smashed in the communal riots either in 1855 A.D. or 1934 A.D. Having misconstrued the text of this inscription, some scholars consider that this 'mosque' was, in fact, constructed by the Sharqi ruler, Hussain Shah in 1467-68 A.D. (872 A.H/2 August, 1467-21 July, 1468) and that Mir Baqi merely renovated it on the basis of Babur's orders. This is a mistaken view as Francis Hamilton Buchanan has also confirmed that there was the Persian inscription on the wall which clearly stated that the structure was constructed by Mir Baqi in 1528-29 (935 AH) on the basis of Babur's orders. There could not be two inscriptions, one in Arabic and another in Persian, installed simultaneously on the same structure with two different chronograms. Whereas one of the verses of the Persian inscription specifically mentioned the year of construction (*sal-i-banaish*) coverable in the chronogram "Bavad Khair Baqi" which comes to 935 AH/1528-29 A.D., the Arabic inscription has been misinterpreted as it does not cover any authentic chronogram. Moreover, if any 'resting place of the angles' had been constructed on this site supposed to have been an open plot unoccupied by any earlier structure on it, there could not have been any Sanskrit inscription of Hindu deities buried in the walls of the disputed structure demolished on 6th December, 1992 A.D.

As already stated in para No. ii, the text of the Sanskrit inscription discovered in the rubble in the aftermath of the demolition of the disputed structure clearly states that the inscription was intended to be a foundation-stone giving details about the sanctity of the Vaishnava temple as well as the builder of the temple around mid-12th century.

C

The Lodhi (Afghan) Rule in Jaunpur and Ayodhya/Awadh (1479-1526 A.D.)

(xvii) After the overthrow of the Sharqi dynasty by Sultan Bahlol Lodhi (1479), the territories of the erstwhile Jaunpur state as well as Ayodhya/Awadh were annexed and incorporated in the Lodhi kingdom of Delhi. This position continued under Sultan Sikander Lodhi and Sultan Ibrahim Lodhi who was defeated by Babur in the battle of Panipat (1526). This meant the end of the Lodhi/Afghan rule and establishment of the Mughal rule at Delhi.

(xviii) During the Lodhi/Afghan rule, for the purpose of administration and assignment of its revenues, the territories of Awadh constituted a full-fledged division, *i.e., iqta/sarkar* under an administrator (*muqti*) and was absolutely distinct from the Jaunpur *iqta/sarkar*. Bahlol Lodhi gave the whole of *sarkar* of Awadh and other *parganas* in assignment (*jagjr*) to his nephew (sister's son) Mian Muhammad Kalaphar Farmuli. During the reigns of the three Lodhi Sultans, namely Bahlol, Sikander and Ibrahim, the Awadh *jagirs* remained with the same family. Sultan Ibrahim bestowed most of the *parganas* (smaller administrative units) in *sarkar* Awadh on Shaikh Mustafa (grandson, *i.e.,* son of daughter of Mian Muhammad Kalapahar and latter's successor) and some Awadh *parganas* on Mian Niama, an adopted son of the Mian Muhammad Kalapahar who was otherwise son of his slave couple. After his death, Shaikh Mustafa was succeeded by his younger brother, Shaikh Bayazid Farmuli as the *muqti*, *i.e.,* administrator cum *jagirdar* of Awadh. Shaikh Bayazid Farmuli was in position at the time of the conquest of India by Babur.

Summary/Conclusion of Note No. III

(i) For the sake of clarity, the period from the 12th century to early 16th century (pre-Mughal) may be divided into four distinct phases viz. the Gahadavalas, Delhi Sultanate, Sharqi Kingdom and the Lodhi Kingdom.

(ii) Under the Gahadavala rule, the chiefs of both the territories viz. Manhaich (future Jaunpur) and Ayodhya owed allegiance to the Gahadavala rulers of Kanauj and were their vassals. Both Manhaich and Ayodhya, though distinct and separate from each other, were important divisions of administration. It was during this phase that around mid-12th century, as per Sanskrit inscription discovered on 6th December, 1992 A.D., Nayachandra, the feudatory of Govind Chandra, the ruler of Kanauj, built the *Janmasthan* temple at Ayodhya.

(iii) With the establishment of the Turkish rule in North India in the late 12th and early 13th centuries, the Gahadavala rule of Kanauj declined and the Rajas of Awadh territories (Ayodhya) became direct vassals of the Delhi Sultans.

(iv) It is known from the contemporary Persian sources that during the Sultanate period, the Rajas of Awadh (Ayodhya) like the Rajas of Kangra (Punjab Hills), Tirhut (Bihar) and Gorakhpur were powerful chiefs and even defied the Delhi Sultans many a time by evading payment of the revenues (*kharaj, jizya*—tribute) to the state. The chiefs of Awadh (Ayodhya), Gonda, Bahrarich and Gorakhpur weilded considerable economic, political cum military power which accounts for the fact that all through the centuries till the establishment of the Mughal rule, the *Janmasthan* temple at Ayodhya remained undesecrated.

(v) Jaunpur was founded on the northern side of river Gomti by Firuz Tughluq, which covered the territories of erstwhile Manhaich. The governors of Jaunpur became quite powerful and exploiting the weakness of the Delhi rulers, Sultan Mubarak Qaranful established an independent kingdom named Sharqi (*i.e.,* eastern kingdom in 1399 A.D. The rulers of the Sharqi kingdom) also pursued expansionist policy and extended their suzerainty even over the Awadh territories. However, the Sharqi rule in Jaunpur and the Awadh territories, etc. was ended by Sultan Bahlol Lodhi, the Sultan of Delhi in 1479 A.D.)

(vi) It was during the Sharqi rule in Jaunpur state that the Hindu temples at Jaunpur like *Atal Devi ka Mandir* with the others, earlier constructed by the Gahadavalas were converted into mosques by Sultan Ibrahim Sharqi (1402-1436). The viewpoint that the *Janmasthan* (Ramjanmabhoomi) temple at Ayodhya was demolished and converted into a 'mosque' by Sultan Ibrahim Sharqi or by Sultan Sikander Lodhi at a later stage is not correct. Nor is the view that the 'mosque' at the old site of *Janmasthan* at Ayodhya was built by the Sharqi ruler, Sultan Hussain Shah in 1467-68 A.D. on an open plot unoccupied by any previous structure has any valid justification. The latest Sanskrit inscription discovered on 6th December, 1992 confirms the fallacious character of the above theories.

(vii) The Lodhi rule in Jaunpur and Awadh (Ayodhya) lasted from 1479 to 1526 A.D. Under the Lodhi rule, both Jaunpur and Awadh were separate administrative units (*sarkars* etc.) and were governed by separate governors (*muqtis*). Sultan Bahlol Lodhi entrusted the administration and *jagir* of Awadh territories (Ayodhya) to Mian Muhammad Farmuli whose successors continued with this position till the establishment of the Mughal rule (1526 A.D.). In 1526 A.D., when Babur conquered North India, Shaikh Bayazid Farmuli was the governor of Awadh (Ayodhya). However, even during the last few years of the Lodhi rule, the governor Shaikh Bayazid Farmuli along with the governor of Jaunpur and other Afghan chiefs was in revolt against the Lodhi Sultans. It is at this stage that Babur became the monarch of India in 1526 A.D.

Historical Background Note: 4

The position of Awadh (Ayodhya) in 1528-29 A.D. vis-a-vis Jaunpur in the Mughal Administrative Territorial Set-up During the Reign of Babur (1526-30 A.D.) Demolition of the Ayodhya Janmasthan Temple (Ramjanmabhoomi) and Construction of the 'Mosque' Thereupon.

(Based upon Persian—Turkish Historical Sources as well as Epigraphic Sources—Both Sanskrit and Persian)

(i) After Babur won the battle of Panipat (1526) and *Khutbah* was read in his name, he became the king (*padshah*) of all the territories of the Lodhi kingdom (from Behra in North West to Bihar in the East). As such, the territorial division of both the *sarkars*, *i.e.,* Jaunpur and Awadh *ipso facto* became an integral part of the Mughal kingdom. In his Memoirs, Babur puts the revenues of *sarkar* of Jaunpur at four krore, eighty eight thousand, three hundred and thirty three *tankas* whereas for the *sarkar* of Awadh combined with Bahraich, the revenues are recorded as one krore, seventeen lakhs, one thousand three hundred and sixty-nine *tankas* respectively.

(ii) Initially, based on expediency, Babur adopted the policy of reconciliation and accorded recognition to the Afghan *iqtadars*, *i.e., jagirdars* and *muqtis i.e.,* governors of the eastern regions of the Sultanate appointed during the Lodhi regime, provided they accepted his sovereignty and undertook to be loyal to him. As such, Babur granted 1 krore, forty lakhs and fifty thousand *tankas* to Firuz Khan from Jaunpur as *wajh* (*jagir*), to Sheikh Bayazid Farmuli from Awadh, and 90 lakhs and 35 *tankas* to Mohammad Khan as *wajh* (*jagir*), and 20 lakhs *tankas* to Qazi Zia from Gazipur. In fact, from the administrative aspect, the *sarkars* of Jaunpur, Awadh and Gazipur, constituting the eastern territories of the Lodhi kingdom, were distinctly separate territorial divisions for the collection and assignment of the revenues of *iqtas* (*jagirs*). This position continued during the early Mughal period as well till the reign of Akbar when with the introduction of the *subah* system, the *sarkar* of Jaunpur and Ghazipur were incorporated in the *subah* of Allahabad while Awadh was declared as a separate *subah* wherein the *sarkar* of Awadh was one of the *sarkars* of the entire *subah* with the headquarters at Ayodhya, also called Awadh. As a matter of fact, Ayodhya/Awadh was the capital of the entire *subah* of Awadh during the Mughal age.

It may be re-emphasised that during the reign of Babur, as inherited from the Lodhi regime, the territories/*sarkar* of Awadh with headquarters at Ayodhya/Awadh was not at all a part of the Jaunpur territorial division as both were separate *sarkars* with their respective revenues. Of course, both of them were governed by separate Afghan *muqtis* (governors).

(iii) Even during the last few years of Ibrahim Lodhi's reign, the Afghan chiefs who held Kanauj and other eastern districts viz. Awadh, Jaunpur and Ghazipur etc., revolted against the Lodhi kingdom and raised son of the Afghan chief Bihar Khan to the throne with the title of Sultan Muhammad who claimed his empire up to Bihar. They were still in a state of revolt when Babur conquered Delhi-Agra (April-May, 1526). Babur detailed Mughal forces to suppress the Afghans. It was at this stage that Sheikh Bayazid Farmuli, the governor (*muqti*) of Awadh and Firuz Khan, the governor (*muqti*) of Jaunpur tendered submission and were granted *wajh, i.e., jagirs* as stated in para No. ii.

(iv) The submission on the part of the Afghans of the eastern districts, inclusive of Awadh and Jaunpur, was short-lived. This time, the Mughal forces were sent under the command of Prince Humayun who drove away the Afghan recalcitrant chiefs, *i.e.,* Sheikh Bayazid Farmuli and Firuz Khan from Awadh and Jaunpur and captured Jaunpur (August-September, 1526) from Sultan Muhammad Nuhani. He also took Bihar from Nasir Khan Luhani and cleared Kanauj from the rebel Afghan Chief, Maruf Farmuli. Before returning to Agra (January, 1527), Humayun appointed Mir Shah Hasan and Jaunaid Barlas as joint governors (*hakims*) of Jaunpur and he ordered the *wajhdar, i.e., jagirdar* Firuz Khan Sarang Khani and others to protect the eastern frontiers from the Afghan depredations.

(v) In the meantime, Rana Sanga of Mewar and Hasan Khan Mewati raised to throne one of the sons of Sultan Sikander

Lodhi, Sultan Muhammad, with the title of *Padshah* (king). The latter marched into the Mughal territories up to Fatehpur Sikri and later on joined hands with Rana Sanga at the battle of Kanwa (March 29, 1527 A.D.) where both were defeated by Babur.

(vi) After his disaster at Kanwa, Sultan Muhammad Lodhi fled to Bihar which now became the real center of rebel Afghans. The latter were also joined by Nusrat Shah, the Sultan of Bengal.

(vii) This time, Babur detailed his other son Hindal to march against the Afghans. Hindal defeated the Afghans and recovered Jaunpur. Mian Biban, the Afghan chief and Sheikh Bayazid Farmuli, the *hakim*/administrator of Awadh (Ayodhya) were also defeated and ousted. Awadh was restored to the Mughal territories.

(viii) After having won the battle of Kanwa (March, 1527) against Rana Sanga and suppressed the chief of Chanderi (December, 1527), Babur himself started marching towards the eastern districts to finish the hostility of the Afghans. News had already reached Babur about the 'misconduct' and 'the hostile intentions' of Sheikh Bayazid Farmuli whom Babur himself had earlier conferred *wajh, i.e., jagjr* in Awadh. Babur sent an advance party under the command of Muhammad Ali *Jang-Jang* to 'move against the hostile Afghans and to drive off Sheikh Bayazid Farmuli (of Awadh) if the latter did not join him to fight against the other Afghans.

(ix) The advance forces sent by Babur (as stated in para viii) were beaten by the Afghans and having been forced to abandon Lucknow (in Awadh) retired towards Kanauj.

(x) Babur continued his march towards Kanauj via Sikri, Chandwar, Chambal, Kalpi, Kachwa, Chanderi, Burhanpur, Kanar and built a bridge over the river Ganges to confront the Afghan forces positioned across the Ganges.

(xi) After a pitched battle, the Afghan rebels having been defeated fled away. Babur dispatched contingent under the command of Sultan Chintimur, Baqi of Tashkint and others to follow up the enemy.

(xii) Babur of his own, along with the Mughal forces, moved towards Awadh. After having covered and occupied the lake area belonging to Bangarmawu (16th March, 1528), Lucknow (21st March, 1528), he continued his march and after having crossed the river Saryu, camped at the junction of the rivers Gagar (Gogra) and Saryu (28th March, 1528/7th *Rajab* 834 AN), a place just 2 or 3 *kuroha* (4 to 6 miles) from Awadh/Ayodhya proper, the capital of larger division (*sarkar*) also named Awadh. In the meantime, the Afghan rebel, Sheikh Bayzid Farmuli, the former *wajhadar/jagirdar* cum *hakim* of Awadh, fled away across the river Saryu. Not being trusted by Sultan Mahmud Lodhi either and being further pressed by the Mughal forces dispatched by Babur from the Awadh (Ayodhya) camp, the Afghans were further routed and Sheikh Bayzid and his family and relations all fled away to the jungles.

(xiii) The Afghan menace having been completely purged from the Awadh territories, Babur established a peaceful administration at Awadh (Ayodhya). Babur himself comments in his Memoirs that, "We stayed a few days on that ground (near Aud) in order to settle the affairs of Aud." As such, Babur entrusted the administration of Awadh as *hakim* to one of his commanders, Baqi Tashkindi. This is very well confirmed by the fact that when after over a year, Babur again came to the territories across the river Ganges in further pursuit of the Afghan rebels, Biban and Sheikh Bayzid, he camped on the bank of Ganges having crossed Dalmud (Dalmau) on 13th June, 1529 A.D./7th *Shawwal* 935 AH. Babur records in his Memoirs that, "Today Baqi Tashkindi came in with the army of Aud (Ayodhya) and waited on me."

(xiv) The recorded stay of Babur at Awadh (Ayodhya) camp in 1528 A.D. is at least for six days, *i.e.,* 28th March to 2nd April 1528 A.D. (7th to 12th *Rajab,* 934 AH). Thereafter, there is a gap in Babur's Memoirs w.e.f. 3rd April to 17th September, 1528 A.D. (13th *Rajab* 934 AH to 2nd *Muharram* 935 AH). Babur stated in his Memoirs that while staying at Awadh (Ayodhya) on April 2nd 1528, he rode out intending to hunt. After this, there is a break in the narration till 17th September 1528. So, it is difficult to say about the total duration of Babur's stay at the Awadh (Ayodhya) camp after having returned from hunting.

(xv) It has been suggested by some scholars that Babur never visited Awadh (Ayodhya) proper for conducting the affairs of the state. This is a completely misconceived notion as according to Babur's own statement, he camped at a place just 4 to 6 miles (2 or 3 *kurohs*) from Awadh (Ayodhya) proper for settling the affairs of Awadh. Even though Awadh (Ayodhya) was the headquarters of the *sarkar* (larger territorial division) of Awadh, there was no big fort in the premises of Awadh (Ayodhya) town where Babur could have possibly stayed along with his army. Moreover, during this visit, Babur's main purpose was to camp at a place near Awadh from where he could easily follow a route for ultimately fighting the fleeing Afghan rebels. At the same time, being very fond of natural environments and hunting the games, Babur preferred to camp over there from where he could easily conduct the administrative affairs of Awadh. Later on, even when the Mughal Empire was well established, some of the Mughal monarchs visiting the *subah* (provincial) capitals preferred to camp outside the main city, at a little distance. For example, when Emperor Jahangir visited Lahore, the capital of *subah* Lahore (Punjab), he camped at Shalimar Gardens laid out 5 to 6 miles in the east from the proper city of Lahore even though a magnificent fort earlier constructed by the Emperor Akbar existed on the north-western side of the city of Lahore, on the eastern bank of river Ravi. Like Babur, Jahangir also preferred natural environment for encampment at a little distance from the capital provincial city and conducted the affairs of the state.

(xvi) As stated in para No. xii, Baqi Tashkindi was appointed by Babur as *hakim, i.e.,* the commander-cum-administrator of Awadh on March 28, 1528/7th *Rajab,* 934 AH and he remained in office at least till June 20, 1529/14th *Rajab*, 935 AH when after having paid obeisance to Babur, he was granted leave by the latter to return to his headquarters at Awadh/Ayodhya. In fact, Baqi Tashkindi had remained in attendance on Babur for nearly a week as he had also continued to march along with Babur for about five days, w.e.f 13th June, 1529 till 17th June, 1529 when Babur camped for a few days on an island on the bank of river Jun (Jamuna). Significantly, Babur uses the name

Mir Baqi rather than Baqi Tashkindi as he comments: "…. leave was given to Baqi and the army of Aud/Ayodhya." Apparently, Baqi Tashkindi remained posted at Awadh/Ayodhya for even more period. It was during this tenure as *hakim, i.e.,* commander cum administrator of Awadh that Baqi Tashkindi (Mir Baqi) demolished the Vaishnava Hindu temple of *Janmasthan* (Ramjanmabhoomi) at Ayodhya/Awadh, earlier built by Nayachandra (chief of saket *Mandalam* and a feudatory of the Gahadavala ruler of Kanauj, (1114-1154 A.D.) around mid-12th century and built 'resting place of the angles' on the same site which was completed in the year 935 AH/15th September 1528 to 5th September 1529.

(xvii) According to the inscriptions installed on the disputed structure of *Ramjanmabhoomi*—'Baburi Masjid' demolished on 6th December 1992, the 'resting place of the angles' was built/completed by Mir Baqi/Mir Baqi entitled *Asif saani* (Asif, the second) in the year 935 AH (15th September, 1528-6th September, 1529 A.D.) on the basis of Babur's order. As a matter of fact, the word "Mir" is the title affixed out of courtesy by the scribe of the inscription. In another inscription, the scribe in his poetical verses has compared Mir Baqi to Asif who was known for his faithfulness and justice in the Islamic history and as such by way of praise calls him *Asif saani, i.e.,* Asif the second. In fact, the name of the *hakim, i.e.,* the commander cum governor of Awadh/Ayodhya as used by Babur in his Memoirs is Baqi Tashkindi or Baqi and not Mir Baqi or Mir Baqi, *Asif saani*. Babur could not have used the epithet of *Asif saani* for his subordinate *hakim, i.e.,* governor of Awadh/Ayodhya territories. However, Babur is fond of using the names of his *begs*/commanders/subordinates in brief, at times in varying manners. An examination of the text of Babur's Memoirs and the afore-mentioned inscriptions shows that Baqi Tashkindi/Baqi of the text of the Memoirs and Mir Baqi/Mir Baqi, *Asif saani* as stated in the inscription is the same person who as *hakim, i.e.,* commander cum governor of Awadh/Ayodhya in 1528-29 A.D. demolished the Hindu *Janmasthan* temple and constructed 'mosque' on the same site, even with some of the re-used materials.

Note

It seems that Baqi was a very common name in Central Asia. In his memoirs, Babur mentions six different persons whose name was Baqi, though with different surnames/designations. In his early days when Babur fought against the Uzbegs at Farghana (908 AH/ 1500-1501 A.D.), one of his adversaries named Khwaja Baqi was killed. Another person named Baqi Khiz, also belonging to the enemy's group, was chopped off during the same period. The third person named Baqi Tarkhan had been one of the loyal *begs* of Babur who had helped the latter in the conquest of the provinces between Samarqand and Bokhara towards the river Amu (906 AH/ July, 1501 A.D.). The fourth person named Baqi Chaghaniahi had served Babur as an important *beg*, even as *darogha* of Kabul, Panjhir and Hazara, etc. (911 AH/1505-1506 A.D.) but owing to serious differences with Babur, was exiled towards Hindustan, when *enroute,* he joined a caravan of a fifth Baqi named Baqi Gagiani. But after having crossed Nilab (Indus), Baqi Chaghaniani was killed by Yar-i-Hussain, a supporter of Babur. The sixth Baqi, who as one of the *begs*, named Baqi Tashkindi, had faithfully served Babur in India in many a campaign from 1526 to 1530 A.D., more especially, against the rebellious Afghans in the eastern districts across the Ganges covering the territories of Awadh/Ayodhya and Jaunpur etc. It is this Baqi Tashkindi who has been twice specifically mentioned by Babur for the years 934-935 AH/1528-1529 A.D. commanding the army of Awadh/Ayodhya. In fact, it is Baqi Tashkindi who as *hakim* had been entrusted with the administration of Awadh/Ayodhya during the days when Babur had camped near Awadh/Ayodhya on 28th March-2nd April, 1528 and even for a little longer period. It is only after this that Babur refers to Baqi Tashkindi essentially as the commander of Aud/Ayodhya army. However, it is significant to note that at times Babur is very fond of using varying titles for the same person. At times, he calls Baqi Tashkindi as Baqi *Mingbashi, i.e.,* Baqi, the head of a thousand troops. Still at another place, he calls the same person as Baqi *Shagawal*, the designation of *Shagawal* being used for a high official, who is supreme over all *qazis* and *mullas*. At times, Babur calls the same person merely as Baqi. All the same, a minute reading of the text of the *Babur Nama* for the years 1526 to 1530 A.D. would show that Baqi

Tashkindi, Baqi *Shagawal,* Baqi *Mingbashi* and sheer Baqi is the same person operating on different occasions. However, in his Memoirs, Babur never calls him as Mir Baqi or Mir Baqi, *Asif saani*. It is equally significant to note that many a scholar has misread Mir Baqi, *Asif saani*, as recorded in the inscription installed on one of the walls of the demolished disputed structure as Mir Baqi Isfahani. For example, Saiyyed Shihabuddin Abdur Rehman, in his well-known book on 'Babri Masjid' (published) by Darul Musanfin, (National Academy, Azamgarh, 3rd edition, 1987, pp. 1-3) has misread/deciphered the word *'Asif saani'* as Isfahani, which is, in fact, completely wrong. Such an erroneous version of Mir Baqi as 'Isfahani' has already found currency in many other popular books on *Ramjanmabhoomi*/'Baburi Masjid'. Apparently, 'Baqi Tashkindi', as recorded in Babur's Memoirs, could not be 'Mir Baqi Isfahani' as Tashkind/Tashkand is in Central Asia whereas Isfahan is in Iran. An absolutely correct reading and decipherment of the word *Asif saani* has already been recorded by late Maulavi Ashraf Hussain in "Archeological Survey of India" volume, titled "*Biographica Indica-Arabic and Persian*" (Supplement, 1965, pp. 50-51).

(xvii)(a) It is evident from the description in the foregoing paras No. xii-xiii that by the time the administration of Awadh/Ayodhya was entrusted to Baqi Tashkindi (Mir Baqi) on 28th April, 1528 A.D. or so, the Afghan menace had been stamped out from the Awadh territories. It is also known from the *Babur Nama* that for nearly a year and a quarter (1528-29 A.D.), Baqi Tashkindi (Mir Baqi) was the *hakim, i.e.,* the commander cum governor of the Awadh territories which he governed with complete support of the army under his command. It is also on record that during this period, Baqi Tashkindi (Mir Baqi) did not have to face any threat of war within the Awadh territories from the Afghan rebels or the local chiefs/zamindars. There was no recalcitrance on the part of the local chiefs either within Awadh, *i.e.,* Ayodhya proper. At any rate, the Hindu *Janmasthan* temple at Awadh/Ayodhya was not demolished in the course of any war or any battle. There is no authentic evidence to show that any battle was fought between the Mughal forces and the local Raja of Ayodhya. As a matter of fact, the *sarkar* of Awadh/Ayodhya as headquarters had already been a regular part of the Lodhi administration which continued as such under the Mughal administration as well. No battle was fought between the Mughal army and the local chief for the occupation of Awadh, *i.e.,* Ayodhya proper. As such, the demolition of the Hindu *Janmasthan* temple at Ayodhya and construction of the "mosque" on the same site by Mir Baqi (Baqi Tashkindi), the governor *hakim* of Awadh/Ayodhya was a sheer act of vindictiveness and vindication of the supremacy of Islam over "heathenism (*kufr*)," a spirit so dear to the ruling Mughal monarch, Zahiruddin Babur. It was an act of Mir Baqi (Baqi Tashkindi) accomplished after Babur had left Awadh/Ayodhya on 2nd April, 1528 or a little later in pursuit of the revolting Afghans in the east.

(xviii) According to the indigenous and traditional Hindu sources, when Baqi Tashkindi (Mir Baqi), the governor (*hakim*) attacked the *Janmasthan* (Ramjanmabhoomi/temple) of Ayodhya, Shyamanand, the chief Brahamin, priest of the temple, along with numerous other Hindus of the region defended the sanctuary by offering stiff resistance for about seventeen days. But ultimately, Baqi Tashkindi (Mir Baqi), backed by the armed forces, overpowered and took possession of the entire fortlike (*Kot*) premises of *Janmasthan*. The priest, Shyamanand, along with his family members, was killed by Mir Baqi. However, before his death, realizing the futility of any further resistance and in order to save the sacred deity, he threw the latter in the river Saryu flowing at the back of the temple complex. Most surprisingly and luckily, during the early 20th century, some *mahants* of the Kalai Ram Temple, Ayodhya, while taking morning bath at one of the main *ghats,* claimed to have found the same deity which they have installed in their own temple. According to the temple archives, the mahants reported the matter to the District and higher government authorities to the effect that it was the same deity which had been thrown in the river by the *Janmasthan* priest more than three centuries back. In the Kalai Ram temple, Ayodhya, apart from installing the deity after puja and performance of sacred ceremonies, a marble slab was erected on which the entire story of the holy deity, having originally belonged to the *Janmasthan* temple, being thrown in the river when the temple was attacked by Mir Baqi and its chance rediscovery from the low waters of one of the main *ghats* has been narrated. An examination of the temple documents shows that on the discovery of the deity in the early 20th century, the temple priests also got the *dhat* of the sacred deity scrutinised before having accepted it as genuine old deity.

(xix) According to the inscriptions installed on the walls (as stated in paras No. xii-xiv) of the erstwhile disputed structure demolished on 6th December, 1992, the 'mosque' was constructed/completed by Mir Baqi in 1528-1529 A.D. (935 AH) on the basis of Babur's order. The inscriptions do not give any indication, whatsoever, that the 'mosque' was constructed on the same site of *Janmasthan* (Ramjanmabhoomi) after the latter's demolition. Nor does Babur in his Memoirs makes any statement either about the demolition of the *Janmasthan* temple at Ayodhya or even about the construction of the masjid over there in accordance with his order. As already stated in paras No. xii-xiv, during his six days stay at a place near Aud/Ayodhya (28th March, 1528—2nd April, 1528, (934 AH), Babur settled the administrative affairs of Aud/Ayodhya. Here he does not even mention that he entrusted the charge of administration of Aud/Ayodhya to Baqi Tashkindi (Mir Baqi). It is only later on when Babur visited the eastern territories next year (1529 A.D.), as already stated in paras No. xiii, he clarifies that Baqi Tashkindi, the commander cum governor of Awadh/Ayodhya came to meet him for paying obeisance and stayed at his camp for nearly a week.

(xx) There is no denying the fact that there is an abrupt break in Babur's Memoirs w.e.f. 3rd April, 1528 to 17th September, 1528. So it is difficult to say as to whether Babur instructed at all Baqi Tashkindi (Mir Baqi) for the destruction of the *Janmasthan* temple or the construction of the 'mosque' at Awadh/Ayodhya. However, it is not certain that if there were no sudden break in Babur's Memoirs, especially when he was camping at Awadh (Ayodhya) itself (from 28th March to 2nd April, 1528) and the gap too being quite prolonged (from 3rd April to 17th September,

1528), Babur would have essentially mentioned about any instruction/order issued to Baqi Tashkindi (Mir Baqi), the *hakim, i.e.,* the commander cum governor of Awadh (Ayodhya) for the demolition of the *Janmasthan* temple and the construction of 'mosque' thereupon. In any case, as already stated in paras No. xiii and xvi, Babur visited the eastern territories after more than a year in 1529 A.D. but there is no break or gap for this period in Babur's Memoirs. In fact, Baqi Tashkindi (Mir Baqi) specially came to pay respects and obeisance to Babur at Dalmud (Dalmau) on the eve of the latter's march for going back to Agra. Even though during this second visit to the eastern regions in 1529 A.D., Babur does refer to some of his activities for the events of 1528 A.D., for which there is a gap in his Memoirs, there is no reference to either the demolition of the *Janmasthan* temple or construction of any 'mosque' in Ayodhya.

(xxi) Babur calls his own Memoirs as truthful History. While writing retrospectively in 1528-29 A.D. (934 AH) about some of the past events (of the year 916 AH-1511 A.D.), especially with regard to his concern and consideration for his relations and subordinates, Babur comments, "...I have written the plain truth... In this History, I have held firmly to it that the truth should be reached in every matter, and that every act should be reached in every matter, and that every act should be recorded as it occurred. From this it follows of necessity that I have set down of good and bad whatever is known...." Whether in his own History, Babur has followed this dictum of plain and truthful narration of the past political events, especially in India, is a moot point. For example, Babur's statement on the eve of the battle of Kanwa (1527 A.D.) against Rana Sanga of Mewar that while he was still in Kabul, he had received message from Rana Sanga that in case of attack by him (Babur) against Ibrahim Lodhi, the Sultan of Delhi, from north-western side, Rana Sanga would also move against the latter from the south-eastern side but Rana Sanga did not fulfill his commitment at that time, *i.e.,* at the battle of Panipat (1526), has been well refuted by many an Indian historian (especially Rajasthani scholars) based on the indigenous Rajasthani sources.

(xxii) In the field of historiography, deliberate omission of certain inconvenient facts is equally tantamount to falsification and distortion of history. It has been noted that even for the periods when there are no gaps in Babur's Memoirs. Babur preferred to remain silent on certain significant events which are otherwise well confirmed by other contemporary or near contemporary sources. A few instances can be cited for both the periods, relating to the earlier phase (1511-14) of his conflict with the Uzbegs for the establishment of supremacy over Samarqand as well as his post-1526 activities in the North Indian territories conquered by him as the Mughal king (*padshah*). In 1511 A.D., when Babur's kingdom was confined to more or less Kabul (*i.e.,* Afghanistan) territories, Babur captured Samarqand from the Uzbegs with the conditional military help received from Shah Ismail Safvi, the king of Iran. According to this understanding, Babur was to substitute Shah's name for his own in the *Khutba* as well as to strike coins in his name and above all to propagate Shia doctrines in his dominions. As such, Babur read the *Khutba* and struck the coins bearing names of twelve Imams. This clearly implied that Babur had accepted the vassalage of the Shah of Iran. In his Memoirs, even though there is no gap or break in the narration, Babur is completely silent about the above mentioned facts, which are well covered by the contemporary Iranian sources. Of the Mughal sources, excepting Mirza Haider Doghlat's *Tarikh i-Rashidi*, all other accounts have blacked out these facts. Later on, even the great Mughal historian, Abul Fazl, the author of *Akbar Nama,* remains completely silent in this regard. However, in 1514 A.D., Samarqand was again lost to the Uzbegs and with this Babur also forgot the inconvenient fact that he had once accepted the Shia faith as well as the suzerainty of the Shah of Iran.

(xxiii) For the last four years of his life spent in India (1526-30) as the Mughal monarch, Babur in his Memoirs is completely silent about the destruction of the two Hindu temples, *i.e.,* Hari Mandir at Sambhal (December 1526 A.D.) and *Janamasthan* (Ramjanmabhoomi) at Ayodhya—Awadh (1528-29) and construction of the 'mosques' thereupon by his generals, Hindu

Beg and Baqi Tashkindi (Mir Baqi) respectively. The inscriptions installed on the walls of both the 'mosques' stated that the 'mosques' were constructed on the basis of Babur's orders. The inscriptions installed on the Ayodhya 'mosque' are no more after 6th December, 1992 A.D. but the inscription on the Sambhal masjid *prevalent* till date confirms the fact that the masjid was constructed on the basis of the '*Farman of Shahanshah* of the World' Muhammad Babur, '*Shah Jam Jah'* in the year December, 1526 A.D. (*Rabi* I, 935 AH). However, in his Memoirs, Babur has not mentioned about the construction of the masjid by Hindu Beg or any order issued by him to demolish the Hindu temple and construct a masjid over it. This is despite the fact that for this period, there is no break in Babur's Memoirs. Later on, Babur visited Sambhal in September-October, 1527 A.D. and stayed there for three days but he does not say a word about the earlier fanatical activities of Hindu Beg resulting in the destruction of a Hindu Hari temple and construction of a masjid thereupon. Even till today, it is discernable that like the Ayodhya *Janmasthan* temple, here too, the material of the erstwhile Hari temple was used in the construction of the masjid. Even though the Hindu temple's materials have been used to conceal the ornamentation, the two rosettes on the stone slabs of the steps leading from the eastern gateway to the quadrangle still speak eloquently about the earlier existence of the temple over there. As such, the archaeological evidence at Sambhal or as already stated in para No. xvi, the recently discovered inscription at Ayodhya in the aftermath of the demolition of the disputed structure on 6th December 1992 fills the gaps in Babur's Memoirs or make up for his deliberate silence about the existence of the Hindu temples at the site of these 'mosques'.

(xxiv) During his own rule (1526-1530 A.D.), Babur had completely emancipated the *sarkars* of Awadh (Ayodhya) and Jaunpur from the earlier Afghan menace as well as of the apprehended danger from the erstwhile administrator/*muqti/jagirdar, i.e.,* Sheikh Bayazid Farmuli, Mian Biban and other Afghan chiefs. The administration of Awadh (Ayodhya) had been put under the charge of Baqi Tashkindi (Mir Baqi) as *hakim* whereas the administrative charge of Jaunpur had been entrusted to Sultan Junaid Barlas and then to Muhammad Zaman Mirza as joint *hakims*. Babur had also broken the bone of the Afghan resistance in Bihar as well. He had also ultimately made peace with Sultan Nusrat Shah, the ruler of Bengal. In fact, after the battle of Ghagra (May 1529) till his death (December, 1530 A.D.), the Afghans had ceased to be a challenge to the Mughal state, more especially in the territories of Awadh (Ayodhya) and Jaunpur.

(xxv) It is only after the death of Babur (on 26th December, 1530 A.D.) that the hopes of the Afghan resurgence brightened and the Afghan chiefs inclusive of Sultan Mahmud Lodhi, claimant to the Delhi throne, who had earlier fled away after defeat at the hands of the Mughals, re-gathered and captured Bihar. By this time, Sher Khan (future Sher Shah Suri), who had earlier made submission to Babur and accepted *Jagir* in Bihar, also joined hands with the revolting Afghans. He arrived at an understanding with Sultan Mahmud Lodhi that in case of conquest of the eastern regions, he would retain Bihar while Sultan Mahmud Lodhi would be given Jaunpur for the establishment of their respective kingdoms. Accordingly, during few months of 1531 A.D., the Afghans under the leadership of Sultan Mahmud Lodhi recaptured Jaunpur from the Mughals and having made Jaunpur as the headquarters, occupied the territories of *sarkar* Awadh as well upto Manikpur in the west and Lucknow in the north. However, during this campaign despite earlier understanding, Sher Khan had not joined Sultan Mahmud Lodhi. Humayun *padshah* advanced against the Afghans and in October, 1531 A.D. inflicted crushing defeat upon them in the battle of Daurah (*i.e.,* Do-rah, mid-way between Jaunpur and Lucknow, near the junction of Kunda Nala with the river Gomti). Sultan Mahmud fled away towards Orissa side and Sheikh Bayazid Farmuli, one of his chief supporters and earlier administrator of Awadh (Ayodhya) under the Afghan and early phase of Babur's rule was doomed to death. Humayun appointed his own *hakims* in Awadh (Ayodhya) and Jaunpur. Mir Hindu Beg was appointed the new *hakim* of Jaunpur. (Some late 16th century sources and modern writers have put all these events of Sultan Mahmud's occupation of Jaunpur and the battle of Durah etc. in the year July 1537 A.D. (944 AH) which does not seem to be a correct version). But the rise of Sher Khan as a vital force in Bihar and the eastern regions hit at the Mughal rule in India. By 1538 A.D. (945 AH), Sher Khan accomplished complete hold over the regions from Kanauj to Bahraich and from Sambhal to Monghyr. As such, the territories of both Jaunpur and Awadh (Ayodhya) came under the Afghan domination of Sher Khan. By 1539, after the decisive battle of Chausa, Humayun was forced to flee from India and Sher Khan formally crowned himself as Sultan Sher Shah Suri at Agra on 10th June, 1539. The Afghan rule of the Suris lasted till 1554 when Humayun returned from Persia and having defeated the weak ruler in the lineage of Sher Shah Suri reoccupied the Mughal throne for the second phase of his rule (1554-55 A.D.). But the virtual occupation of the Afghans in Jaunpur lasted till 1558-59 A.D. (4th Regnal year of Akbar) when the Mughals took possession of Jaunpur through Ali Quli Khan which was incorporated in the Mughal dominions. The territories of Awadh (Ayodhya) had already been reoccupied by Humayun during the second phase of his rule (1554-55 A.D.).

Summary/Conclusion of Historical Background Note No. IV

(i) After Babur won the battle of Panipat (1526) against Ibrahim Lodhi and *Khutbah* was read in his name, he became the king (*padshah*) of North India comprising all the territories of the Lodhi kingdom (from Behra in the North-west to Bihar in the East). As such, the territorial divisions of both the *sarkars, i.e.,* Awadh (Ayodhya) and Jaunpur *ipso facto* became an integral part of the Mughal kingdom.

(ii) During the reign of Babur, as inherited from the Lodhi regime for the purpose of administration, Awadh (Ayodhya) and Jaunpur were separate territorial divisions (*i.e., sarkars*) with their respective revenues and were governed by separate *jagirdars* cum governors. As is, often, wrongly considered, Awadh (Ayodhya) was not at all a part of the Jaunpur territorial division.

(iii) Initially, based on expediency, Babur adopted the policy of reconciliation and accorded recognition to the Afghan chiefs appointed as *jagirdars*/governors of the eastern regions during the Lodhi regime provided they accepted his sovereignty. As such, both Sheikh Bayazid Farmuli, the *jagirdar* cum governor of Awadh and Firuz Khan, the *jagirdar*/governor of Jaunpur made submission to Babur and were granted *jagirs* in their respective territories. But the submission on their part and that of the other Afghan chiefs of the eastern districts was short lived. As they had done during the last few years of the Lodhi rule, this time, they again revolted against the Mughal state and evaded the payment of the revenues. Babur sent his son Prince Humayun to suppress the Afghans. Humayun captured Awadh (Ayodhya) and Jaunpur (August-September, 1526) and ousted the local governors, *i.e.,* Bayazid Farmuli of Awadh (Ayodhya) and Firuz Khan of Jaunpur. But in the meantime, the Afghans found another leader in Sultan Mahmud, son of late Sultan Sikander Lodhi and declared him the *padshah.* The Afghans again captured their lost territories. This time, Babur sent his second son Hindal to fight against the Afghans. Hindal defeated the Afghans and restored the territories of Awadh and Jaunpur to the Mughal State.

(iv) After having won the battle of Kanwa (March, 1527) against Rana Sanga of Mewar and suppressed the chief of Chanderi (December 1527), Babur himself started march towards the eastern districts to give a final blow to the recalcitrant Afghans. He crossed the Ganges and moved towards Awadh. After having stayed at Lucknow (21st March 1528), he continued his march and camped at the junction of rivers Gagra and Saryu, about 4 to 6 miles from Awadh (Ayodhya) proper and settled the administrative affairs of Awadh (Ayodhya). He camped here at least for six days or so. In fact, this was Babur's official stay at Awadh (Ayodhya). Even later on, many a time, the Mughal monarchs camped outside the provincial capitals. The Afghan menace having been completely purged from the Awadh territories, Babur established peaceful administration in Awadh. It is at this time that Babur appointed Baqi Tashkindi (Mir Baqi) as the governor (*hakim*) of Awadh (Ayodhya). Thereafter,

the tents and the damage done to the manuscript which was dried up, Babur does not mention anything about the ultimate loss or disappearance of the folios of the manuscript. If some folios/pages were missing or completely damaged due to drenchness, he would have mentioned it.

5(f) There is another prolonged gap for about five years and ten months, *i.e.*, w.e.f. 24th January, 1520 A.D. to 18th October, 1525 A.D. (926 to 932 AH) in Babur's Memoirs. It was during this period that Babur led three campaigns against Hindustan, occupied most of the territories of the Punjab and indulged in bloodshed, pillage and plunder of the towns inclusive of Lahore. His army was equally responsible for barbarous acts of rape and dishonouring the womenfolk. During these campaigns, Babur destroyed numerous sacred Hindu temples. At times, in general devastation and burning of the houses of the people, adjacent mosques were not spared either.

5(g) Another significant illustration can be afforded from Babur's rule in Hindustan. As already stated (in paras No. xii-xiv, xvii in Historical Background Note IV on the position of Awadh (Ayodhya) in 1528-29 etc.), Babur visited Awadh (Ayodhya) on 28th March, 1528 and stayed there for at least six days, if not more and that there is a sudden break in Babur's Memoirs w.e.f. 3rd April 1528 to 17th September, 1528. Babur states that during his stay near Awadh (28th March-2nd April, 1528), he settled the affairs of Awadh but he does not spell out the details of the affairs thus settled. However, the inscriptions installed on the disputed structure of *Ramjanmabhoomi*—'Baburi Masjid' demolished on 6th December, 1992 stated that the 'mosque' was built/completed by Babur's commander cum administrator (*hakim*) Mir Baqi posted at Awadh (Ayodhya) in 1528-29 A.D. on the basis of Babur's order. In fact, Mir Baqi demolished the Hindu *Janmasthan* temple and constructed 'mosque' on the same site, even with some of the re-used material. This is well confirmed by the latest inscriptional evidence discovered in the aftermath of the demolition of the disputed structure on 6th December, 1992 at Ayodhya which bears out the fact that around mid-12th century, Nayachandra, the chief of the Saket *Mandlam* with headquarters at Ayodhya, who was the feudatory of Govindchandra (1114-1154 A.D.), the ruler of the Gahadavala kingdom built the Vaishnava temple at this site. It was this temple which was demolished by Mir Baqi for the construction of a 'mosque' at the same place. There is no denying the fact that w.e.f. 3rd April, 1528, for nearly four and a half months, *i.e.*, till 17th September, 1528, there is an abrupt break in Babur's Memoirs but when Babur again visited the eastern districts, *i.e.,* Jaunpur territory etc. next year in May-June, 1529 and at that time, Mir Baqi also came to pay obeisance to him on 13th-17th June, 1529 A.D. even at that time, Babur does not mention about the construction of a 'mosque' at Awadh (Ayodhya) on the basis of his earlier orders and least of all to the construction of a 'mosque' on the site of a demolished Hindu temple. Even when it is conceded, as argued by Mrs. Beveridge, the translator of *Babur-Nama*, that the gaps/breaks in Babur's Memoirs were not intentional but rather accidental, it cannot be denied that Babur deliberately observes complete silence about the destruction of the Hindu Vaishnava temple at Awadh (Ayodhya) and construction of a 'mosque' thereupon during his campaigns in the eastern districts of Jaunpur etc. in 1529 A.D., the period for which there is no break in his Memoirs. This is notwithstanding the fact that during his second visit (1529 A.D.) to the eastern territories, Babur does refer to some other matters of the previous year, which otherwise fall in the gap period of his Memoirs. But Babur does not make any retrospective reflection on the demolished Ayodhya Hindu temple and construction of a 'mosque' thereupon by Mir Baqi.

5 (h) Babur's deliberate silence in such matters is further confirmed by the instance of the destruction of the Hari temple of the Hindus at Sambhal in December, 1526 A.D. and construction of a masjid on the same site out of the debris of the demolished temple by Babur's general Hindu Beg. In fact, initially Sambhal (at present in Uttar Pradesh) had been assigned by Babur to Qasim Sambhali. But later on, it was bestowed on Humayun, in addition to his guardianship of Hisar-Firoza and Hindu Beg was attached in his service. It was during the latter's tenure that the Hindu Hari temple was demolished and a masjid was

constructed thereupon (situated in *mohalla Kot*). That the masjid was constructed out of the re-used material and debris of the Hindu temple is evident from the two rosettes on the stone slabs of the steps leading from the eastern gateway to the quadrangle and the concealed ornamentation. All this is visible even till date. The chain for hanging the temple-bell and a passage at the back for the performance of *parikarma* by the worshippers are still in existence. The construction of a masjid at Sambhal by Hindu Beg on the basis of Babur's order to the former is borne out by the inscription on the 'mosque' constructed on 6th December, 1526 A.D. Even though for this period covering November-December, 1526 A.D., there is no break in Babur's Memoirs, there is not a word about the construction of a 'mosque' at Sambhal by Hindu Beg in compliance of his orders in this regard. Nor does Babur mention that he gave any orders to Hindu Beg to demolish the Hindu temple and construct a masjid over it. At the same time, there is no break in his Memoirs for September-October, 1527 A.D., when according to his own statement, Babur visited Sambhal and stayed there for three days (2nd-4th October, 1527), there is no reference to any 'mosque' earlier constructed by Hindu Beg on the basis of his orders. This event had been quite significant as Hindu Beg, only after a brief stay had been forced to flee Sambhal on account of opposition by the Hindu *riaya* after the destruction of the Hari temple. Babur does not say that Hindu Beg was summoned or transferred by him in December, 1526 A.D. Nor does he say anything about the reason for the sudden arrival of Hindu Beg at Agra. Apparently, the hostile Hindu population at Sambhal did not permit Hindu Beg to stay there any longer. Nor did Babur send him back to Sambhal. The fact that on September, 1527, Humayun left Darwish (-i-ali) and Yusuf Ali in Sambhal shows that Hindu Beg had left Humayun's service long ago and was no longer with him at this time. Nor does Babur mention about him when he visited Sambhal in October, 1527 A.D.

6. Babur calls his Memoirs as his History comprising all his military, political and personal activities, both as a man and monarch from June, 1494 to 1529-30 A.D. (899-930 AH). For the

narration of his History, Babur has moved in a chronological order, *i.e.,* date/day/month/year wise. Despite numerous gaps, as already stated in paras No. 4-5(d), Babur recorded the past events connected with his life based mostly on memory. As all through his life, he had been involved in hectic military and political activities, it was well nigh impossible to keep up daily diary narrating the activities of the day being recorded every night or even every week or month of a year. Babur himself throws considerable light on this issue. While tracing his own five expeditions into Hindustan, Babur states that "From the date 910 (1505 A.D.) at which the country of Kabul was conquered, down to now (932 AH/1525-1526 A.D.) (my) desire for Hindustan had been constant... .From then till now we labouriously held tight to God the most High, by his own mercy and favour, made such a foe as Sultan Ibrahim (Lodhi) the vanquished and loser, such a realm as Hindustan our conquest and possession." Apparently, this portion of the Memoirs was written after the battle of Panipat (April, 1526) and victory over Sultan Ibrahim Lodhi. Here, Babur mentions about his previous expeditions into Hindustan. Even earlier, while narrating his conquest of Kabul in 1505 A.D. (910 AH), he had described the roads from Hindustan to Kabul and had also commented that last time he crossed the river Nilab (Indus) for leading an expedition to Hindustan was in 1525 A.D. (932 AH) when later on he defeated Ibrahim Lodhi and conquered the country. It is evident that the portion regarding the conquest of Kabul in 1505 A.D. (910 AH) was written after the conquest of Hindustan in April, 1526 A.D. As regards having written about his activities even for the earlier years during the period of his rule in India after April, 1526 A.D., another illustration may be quoted from his Memoirs.

6(a) While at Kabul during the years, May 24th, 1506 to May 13th, 1507 A.D. (912 AH) regarding the treatment of his blood relations and members of the Chaghtai dynasty, Babur gives an example of his patronage of Sultan Said whom he gave the title of Khan in 1511 A.D. (916 AH). Babur gives further examples of his benevolent attitude towards his other blood relations till the day of his writing of his Memoirs in 1527-28

A.D. (934 AH). Babur records, "...Again, down to the present time (circa 934 AH), I have not looked upon any member of that family who has come to me, in any other light than a blood-relation." It is at this stage that Babur asserts that he had recorded the events of his History in a truthful manner. Thus, it is very clear that Babur wrote his Memoirs intermittently and that even the major portions of his life and activities were recorded when Babur had settled in Hindustan as monarch after April, 1526 A.D. This is even acknowledged by Mrs. Beveridge, the translator of *Babur-Nama* that "from several references made in the *Babur-Nama* and from a passage in Gulbadan's *Humayun Nama* (f. 15), it is inferrible that Babur was composing the annals of 914 AH (1508 A.D.) not long before his last illness and death."

6 (b) It is difficult to say whether Babur had been keeping rough notes about his daily activities right from the earlier days without which it would not have been possible to mention the exact dates for the occurrence of different events. However, it is also evident that for the past events, Babur was mostly relying on memory. To what extent, any person relying on memory, even though aided by brief notes taken from time to time, if any, could record the past events years after the actual occurrences in a completely reliable manner is a questionable hypothesis. Moreover, any person writing his autobiography at a later stage when further events have also moulded his life career, is likely to be more prone to subjective and selective description of the events, which may entail either deliberate omission or distortion of facts.

6(c) Despite Babur's assertion about the truthfulness of his statements, his bias as well as deliberate omissions of certain facts, especially those rather inconvenient to him for his public image of the posterity, are marked features of his Memoirs. This can be further well illustrated by citing the well-known event of the battle of Kanwa (27th March, 1527) fought by Babur against Rana Sangram Singh (Rana Sanga) of Mewar. Babur makes a categorical statement in his Memoirs that while he was still in Kabul, Rana Sanga had sent an envoy to testify to his good wishes along with a proposed plan that in case

Babur (*padshah*) reached near Delhi from that side (*i.e.,* North-West), Rana Sanga would move on Agra (against Ibrahim Lodhi). Babur further states that even though he had defeated Ibrahim Lodhi, and taken Delhi and Agra, there was no sign of any movement on the part of that Pagan (Rana Sanga) who on the other hand was extending his kingdom and had laid siege to Kandar fort (in Rajasthan) and taken its possession from *Makaan* Hasan. Babur's statement about the receipt of the above mentioned proposal from Rana Sanga while he was still at Kabul is not borne out by the Rajasthani sources. Moreover, Babur does not clarify as to how he responded to the good will message and the proposal of Rana Sanga. The way Babur is showing grudge against Rana Sanga for breach of faith indicates as if Babur had accepted the proposal and arrived at some formal understanding to that effect for which there is no clear-cut statement in the Memoirs. Whether Babur, as explained further, who later on while having waged war against Rana Sanga, proclaims himself as the champion of Islam as against a pagan (*kafir*) could have made any formal understanding with Rana Sanga is another aspect for consideration. If on the other hand, Babur had not positively responded to Rana Sanga's proposal, then it remained only one-sided offer, if ever made. As a matter of fact, Babur wrote about all this after he had won the battle of Kanwa (March, 1527) against Rana Sanga and offered belaboured justification for war against the latter. The eminent writer, Kavi Raj Shyamal Dass, who compiled all Rajasthan documents of the Mewar state in his monumental work titled *Vir Vinod* (1877-78), has equally brushed aside the afore-mentioned statement on the part of Babur as fallacious in character.

6(d) Babur himself concedes that apart from Ibrahim Lodhi, Rana Sanga was one of the five powerful rulers of Hindustan. As some of the hostile nobles of Ibrahim Lodhi posted in the Punjab had already been in touch or connivance with Babur for waging war against Ibrahim Lodhi and Babur during the course of four campaigns between 1519 A.D. and 1525 A.D. had already occupied many portions of the Punjab from Behra towards the east and put these territories inclusive of Lahore to pillage and plunder, it is hard to imagine, as done by some scholars, that Rana Sanga had extended the joint plan of movement against Ibrahim Lodhi being under the illusion that like many of the past invaders, Babur would go away after plunder and amassing the wealth leaving the throne of Delhi for him. No doubt, Rana Sanga had territorial ambition for expansion in Rajasthan or could cherish further designs against the kingdoms of Gujrat or Malwa but there is no evidence to show that he had any covetous eyes on the Delhi throne during the Afghan regime. However, after Babur defeated Ibrahim Lodhi and became *padshah* of Delhi-Agra, the political rivalry and conflict between him and Rana Sanga became inevitable. Rana Sanga gave full protection to Sultan Mahmud Lodhi (son of Late Afghan Sultan Sikander Lodhi), the claimant to the Delhi-Agra throne as well as Hasan Khan Mewati and other Muslim chiefs who considered Babur as an alien usurper and made common cause against the latter. For further expansion, both Babur and Rana Sanga had eyes on Bayana, Jahan Nagar, Gwalior and Dholpur. The Mughal forces took the initiative, attacked and occupied Bayana held by Nizam Khan. But shortly after, Rana Sanga's Rajput army compelled the Mughal garrison to evacuate and captured Bayana (16th February, 1527 A.D.). In his Memoirs, Babur does not mention about it clearly. However, later on both Babur and Rana Sanga moved towards Kanwa for decisive battle (27th March, 1527 A.D.) which was lost by Rana Sanga and his Afghan allies.

6(e) In his war against Rana Sanga, Babur comes out in his true colours as the champion of Islam. All through the description about the battle of Kanwa, Babur calls his own army as the 'army of Islam' and the war waged as crusade (*jihad*) against Rana Sanga, the pagan (*kafir*). After the victory, he quotes letter of victory composed by his courtier Sheikh Zain which addresses Babur as the "Exalter of the pillars of Islam... overthrower of the pedestals of idols...Exterminator to the uttermost of the followers of darkness!" Sheikh Zain puts the victory of Babur as 'Victory of the Faith of Islam' (*Fath-i-padshah-i-Islam*) as the chronogram of the victory. Babur himself describes his own victory "as manifest of the victory of the strivers and of the up-roaring of the standards of Islam..." as against the infidels/pagans (*Kafir*) and absurd (*batil*) Hindus. Hereafter, Babur assumed the title of *Ghazi* (Victory in a holy war). All this explains the real motives of war waged by Babur against Rana Sanga.

List of Gaps in Babur's Memoirs

(i) Gap of 10 years & 8 months — *i.e.*, 3rd May, 1508 to 2nd January, 1519 A.D./914-25 AH.

(ii) Gap of 5 years & 10 months — *i.e.*, 24th January, 1520 to 8th October, 1525 A.D./926-32 AH.

(iii) Gap of 5 months & 17 days — *i.e.*, 2nd April, 1528 to 18th September, 1528 A.D.

(iv) Gap of 6 days — *i.e.*, 6th October, 1528 to 11th October, 1528 A.D.

(v) Gap of 3 days—*i.e.*, 20th October, 1528 to 21st October, 1528 and 23rd October, 1528 A.D.

(vi) Gap of 11 days — *i.e.*, 25th October, 1528 to 3rd November, 1528 A.D.

(vii) Gap of 9 days — *i.e.*, 12th November, 1528 to 20th November, 1528 A.D.

(viii) Gap of 5 days — *i.e.*, 27th November, 1528 to 1st December, 1528 A.D.

(ix) Gap of 6 days — *i.e.*, 6th December, 1528 to 11th December, 1528 A.D.

(x) Gap of 3 days — *i.e.*, 25th December, 1528 to 27th December, 1528 A.D.

(xi) Gap of 1 day — *i.e.*, 29th December, 1528 A.D.

(xii) Gap of 4 days—*i.e.*, 16th January, 1529 to 19th January, 1529 A.D.

(xiii) Gap of 7 days — *i.e.*, 11th July, 1529 to 17th July, 1529 A.D.

(xiv) Gap of 16 days — *i.e.*, 29th July, 1529 to 10th August, 1529; 13th August to 15th August, 1529 A.D.

(xv) Gap of 1 year, 3 months & 24 days — *i.e.*, 7th September, 1529 to 26th December, 1530 A.D.

2

Janmasthan (Rama Janamabhoomi) as depicted in the Land Revenue Records (1856 to 1993 A.D.)

JANMASTHAN, situated on the ancient fortress called *Ram Kot* in Ayodhya, considered by the Hindus as the birth-place of Shri Ram Chandra, has been one of the holiest places of pilgrimage since the ancient times. There is mass of literary, historical and archaeological evidence which establishes the fact that the disputed structure situated at *Ramkot*, named as the "Baburi *Masjid*" from the second half of the nineteenth century onwards, was constructed in the early sixteenth century (1528 A.D.) by replacing the earlier Hindu temple, built afresh on the ancient sacred site during the early medieval age in the 11th-12th centuries A.D. However, the land revenue documents right from the inception of the British rule in Awadh in 1856 A.D. till date add a very significant dimension to the entire issue as none of the revenue maps mentions the disputed structure as a "mosque" or any land in *Ramkot* attached to it as '*waqf*'. In fact, all through the revenue operations, the documents mention only the *Janmasthan* and the land of the *Janmasthan* complex has always been vested in the ownership of the Hindu *mahants*.

Ever since the Mughal age, *Kot* Ram Chandra had been one of the villages of the suburban *Pargana* of the *sarkar* and *subah* Awadh and as per revenue records was quite distinct from the city of Ayodhya. The identity of *mauza Kot* Ram Chandra as a distinct separate revenue village was maintained right from the inception of the British Raj (1856) till 1947 and, in fact, continued to be so even till date. In the Awadh territories, the British Government assumed all the proprietary right in the soil which completely altered the earlier position. As distinct from the *taaluqdari* and *zamindari* estates, there were villages which were declared as *nazul* property wherein the Government claimed absolute right in the ownership of land. The pre-British landed intermediaries like the *mahaldars* of the villages were declared as quasi proprietors and the landowners, inclusive of the *mahants* of the temples, were declared *malikan-i-matahit*, *i.e.,* subordinate owners. In the first regular settlement (1861) and its aftermath for revenue operations lasting till 1878, all land of *Kot* Ram Chandra was declared as *nazul* in toto. Its subordinate land-owners, inclusive of the holy shrines too, unless totally or partially exempted, were required to pay rent which was duly recorded in the *khewat* and *khata khatauni* of the village records. *Janmasthan* land was exempted from the payment of *lagan.*

The revenue records relating to village *Ramkot*, *Haveli* Awadh, district Faizabad, are extremely significant and clarify the factual proprietary position of *Janmasthan* versus 'Baburi Masjid'. As per land revenue procedure, they offer details of the numbered plots (*khasras*) of the entire village *Ramkot* in respect of nature of land rights. In fact, the records comprise various categories of revenue documents, *i.e.,* survey, *bandobust* (settlement), *khasra kishtwar* denoting plots originally earmarked for cultivable fields, *khasra abadi*, *i.e.,* habitation plots, *misl hadbast*, *i.e.,* file relating to earmarked boundaries, *khewat* of the *mahals* and *khewat* of the under-proprietors, *khasra khatauni* comprising list of numbers belonging to each *mahal*, and maps, etc. right from the 1861 A.D. till 1993-94 A.D. All these records are available at the District Records Office, Tehsil Office and Nazul Office, Faizabad (U.P.). Of course, all these have to be supplemented by the records of the Civil Judge, Faizabad, Waqf Boards, Lucknow and above all the Uttar Pradesh State Archives, Lucknow.

The first Regular Settlement Report (1861) of *Kot* Ram Chandra, appended by two maps, is the most comprehensive document relating to the *Janmasthan* complex. It equally reflects the earlier position and was prepared taking into consideration the past records of the *Nawabi* period. The *khasra kishtwar* record puts its total area at five bighas and four *biswas* divided into nine sub-plots. It covered both the core area of *Ramjanmabhoomi*-erstwhile 'Baburi Masjid' as well as the present day misnomered *Janmasthan*. The latter structure built during the early 18th century, to the north of *Ramjanmabhoomi*, comprising a couple of sub-plots, constituted an integral part of the *Janmasthan* complex. A comparative study of the Settlement maps of 1861 and 1893-95 shows that the road dividing the two structures, *i.e., Ramjanmabhoomi*-'Baburi-Masjid' and the present day *Janmasthan*, also known as Sita *Rasoi* was built during the intervening period. As distinct from the *khasra kishtwar*, the *khasra abadi* vide parts of Nos. 431-456, complex Nos. 92-93, covering *Janmasthan* show *abadi* in this area. None of these Nos. does mention the existence of any 'mosque' though in the *kafiyat*, *i.e.,* general remarks, they do mention the existence of *pacca* graveyard, a few trees and houses on the campus. The *khasra hadbast* of 1861 Settlement vide No. 152 also mentions only *makaan Janmasthan*, *i.e.,* structure and houses of *Janmasthan*.

Quite significantly, the *hadbast* map appended to the Settlement Report (1861) as well as the *abadi* map of *Kot* Ram Chandra (1866) show only the *Janmasthan* in the *abadi Janmasthan* complex plot No. 163. They do not indicate any mosque therein. Even though the physical existence of an extraneous structure believed to be 'mosque' built by the Mughal emperor Babur at the *Janmasthan* site was alleged, and most significantly, the Revenue Settlement maps of 1861, 1893 and 1936-37 A.D. do not bear any indication of a 'mosque' at the *Janmasthan* site and indicate only the *Janmasthan* temple at the site. The detailed lists provided in the 1893 Settlement Records, in respect of mosques, *waqf*, graveyard and mutations etc., do not put any of the sub-plot of the *Janmasthan* complex *i.e.,* 163/1 to 163/5 with any of these categories.

During the course of the inspection of the revenue documents in January 1990, the present writer found that the *khasra kishtwar* folios of the original records pertaining to the 1861 Settlement Reports preserved at the District Record Office and the Tehsil Office, Faizabad, have been tampered with and certain interpolations have been carried out during the past few decades. In the settlement report of the District Record Office in the *khasra* No. 163 folios, under column No. 2, along with *abadi Janmasthan* in bold letters, 'Jamai masjid' have been added in thin letters. Similarly, a few minor additions have been made in the columns 3 and 4 but in the parallel Tehsil copy of the 1861 Settlement, only the words 'Jamai Masjid' have been added under column 2 but no other alteration has been made under any other column. In the second Settlement Report of 1893-94, in *khasra kishtwar* No. 163, under column No. 2, only the name of *abadi Janmasthan* occurs and no additions have been made in any of the columns as done earlier in the 1861 Settlement Report in the District and Tehsil copies. As such, tampering is very clear from the additions to the original entries, difference in the ink, the handwriting, space and style of writing of the added letters. These interpolations were confirmed by the Uttar Pradesh Government in 1992 after having got the original documents examined in the laboratory and by the handwriting experts.

As per *khasra bandobast* and *khatauni* documents of the 1893 settlement, the core area of the *Janmasthan* complex *i.e.,* the proper *Ramjanmabhoomi*-'Baburi Masjid' which in the recent years has become disputed land was under *mahal nazul sarkar* comprising two *khasra* Nos. 163/1 and 163/2 with an area of 2 *bighas*, 14 *biswas* and 2 *biswansies* respectively. These were shown as *abadi i.e.,* habitation and were vested in the subordinate ownership and occupation of the Hindu *mahants* Raghubar Das, Gopal Das and Thakurdwara Sita Ram.

The existence of *chabutra* (cradel of baby Ram) within the precincts of *Ramjanmabhoomi*- 'Baburi Masjid' during the Mughal age is well borne out by historical evidence. The map dated 6.12.85 appended to the report of the Amin's commission filed in the suit for the construction of a temple over the *chabutra* provides significant details. Apart from the disputed structure, *chabutra*, Sita *Rasoi* and *chappars* for the residence of the *chela* of the *Mahant* within the core area of *Janmasthan*, the map also indicates an ancient *khai parikrama* on all the four sides beyond the boundary walled courtyard and just adjacent to it.

The Government of India's White Paper on Ayodhya, February 1993, New Delhi, vide para 2.12 concedes the fact that the Ram-*Chabutra* and Kaushalya *Rasoi* continued as places of worship during periods of Muslim and British rule. The judgement of the Hon'ble Supreme Court dated 24.10.94 on the issues of Special Reference No. 1/93 under Article 143(1) of the Constitution and I.A. No. 1/94 in TC(C) No. 44/93, pages 7-8 having accepted the White Paper's version as correct, comments that a structure called the Ram-*chabutra* stood on the disputed site within the courtyard of the disputed structure, and that "worship of Hindu devotees at Ram-*chabutra* by Hindu devotees in general, it appears, had been performed for a considerable period of time without any objection by the Muslims to its worship at that place, prior to the shifting of the idols from the Ram-*chabutra* to the disputed structure in December 1949." While the Hon'ble Supreme Court has conceded the fact that the Ram-*chabutra* being a Hindu place of worship since the Muslim period had existed side by side with the disputed structure known as *Ramjanmabhoomi*- 'Baburi-Masjid', it has not examined the circumstances as to how it happened. Why did not the Muslims object to a Hindu place of worship within the courtyard of the disputed structure claimed to be the 'Baburi Masjid' and which was hardly at a distance of about 4-5 feet of the eastern wall and entrance gate of the latter structure? Was it due to compassion and fellow-feeling for the Hindus and belief in coexistence and communal harmony all through the ages since the early 16th century or else it was due to the historic fact that the Muslims themselves were trespassers and had taken adverse possession of the *Janmasthan* land under dispute?

(Continued in Part II, p. 59)

refrained from calling the commissioner's report as "motivated", described it as "absurd". It refused to keep this report on record in the pending case and directed the survey to be done with reference to Settlement maps of 1861 and 1937 A.D. as already ordered.

The 1936-37 Settlement Report set the record straight. As per procedure of the revenue settlement, the *khasra* Nos. of the plots underwent a change. The core area of the *Janmasthan* complex on which the disputed structure of *Ramjanmabhoomi*-'Baburi-Masjid' stood has been recorded in *khasras kishwar* No. 159 of the disputed structure, with an area of 13 *biswas*, and is declared *banjar* land under Nazul. While the superior ownership rests with the Nazul, the subordinate ownership is vested with 'Shri Dhanush Dhari Ji Bhagwan Virajman, Mandir Bara Asthan, Mohalla *Ramkot*, Shahar Ayodhya,' through the basarbkari of Mahant Raghubar Prasad, disciple of Ram Manohar Das, Bairagi, resident of the above temple. The remaining portion of *khasra* No. 160 covers the area of *Janmasthan* to the east of the structure, vested with other Hindu Mahants. The *khasra* and *khewat* records put the *Janmasthan* named Sita *Rasoi* to the north of the disputed structure, under *khasra* Nos. 146 and 147 R with an area of 1-6-7, *bighas*. Here too, the superior ownership is with Nazul and the subordinate ownership is vested with Har Har Das and Ram Saran Das, the residents of *Janmasthan*. The *khasra* No. 158 denotes the road dividing the disputed structure from the northern portions of *Janmasthan*/Sita *Rasoi*. The *khatauni* records reiterated the above stated position. In the *khasra* Nos. connected with the *Janmasthan*, there is no area in any of the plots or sub-plots, which is shown as graveyard or in *waqf*.

Since 1936-37 A.D., no further settlement has been effected in *Kot* Ram Chandra. As such, *khasra* plot Nos. of the *Janmasthan* complex along with their respective areas have remained the same. However, as per *khata khewat* revenue records for all these years till 1993-94 A.D., the core area of *Janmasthan* relating to disputed *Ramjanmabhoomi*-'Baburi Masjid' under plot No. 159 remains vested with the superior ownership of Nazul and subordinate ownership of Shri Dharam Dhariji Bhagwan Bara Asthan, Ayodhya, whereas plot No. 160 M has been recorded in the ownership of Sarkar Nazul. There is no *muafi* or *waqf* associated with the so-called 'Baburi Masjid'.

As regards the issue of *waqf* relating to the so-called 'Baburi Masjid' on the *Janmasthan* area, the earliest reference in this regard is traceable in the documents dating back to 25th September, 1878 A.D., when Muhammad Akbar, *darogha* of Nazul lands, recorded at the back of a duplicate copy of *khasra kishtwar* map of *Kot* Ramchandra, to the effect that for the so-called 'Baburi Masjid' situated on *Janmasthan*, there was no Nazul land or house or garden in *Kot* Ram Chandra under *waqf*, which had been entrusted to Mir Muhammad Asghar, the landlord in village Shahnawa, who claimed himself to be the *khatib* and *muazzan* of the above structure. The latter, of course, had been granted land and garden in the villages of Baharanpur and Sholapur worth rupees three hundred and two only, from which he incurred some expenditure for the 'mosque'. In fact, Muhammad Asgar had been granted the afore-mentioned revenue free land by the British Government in 1870, along with *malkiyat, i.e.,* proprietary rights subject to the rendering of the police and military service.

Later on, serious controversy on the *waqf* issue arose in 1938 when after the Waqf Act of 1936, the Waqf Commissioner, District Faizabad, wanted to put the lands owned by Pir Mir Taqi, the descendant of Asghar Ali, in the villages of Baharanpur and Sholapur as a *waqf* property for the maintenance of the 'masjid' *Janmasthan*. Despite all protests, the Commissioner gave a ruling to the effect that the land grant to Mohammad Zaki must be regarded as *waqf* for "the maintenance of religious building known as Baburi *Masjid*". Thereafter, Mohammad Zaki and Malik Hussain etc., the *muzzans* and *khatibs*, who were Shias continued to clarify their position and in their application submitted to the Sunni Central Board of Waqf, U.P., Lucknow, took a clear stand that there was no *mutawalli* of the said 'mosque' and that there was no *waqf* for their properties in the villages of Bahoranpur and Sholapur, which had been recorded in the revenue records only as *nankar muafi*, *i.e.,* revenue free land for their maintenance.

In the Shia-Sunni legal tussle that followed, the Sunni Central Board of *Waqf* claimed that the disputed structure was published as a Sunni 'Mosque' in the *U.P. Gazette* dated 26.2.1944, even though in reality, the particulars of the 'Baburi Masjid' of the *qabristan* (graveyard) attached to it, do not find any place in the list of waqfs published in the *Government Gazette* dated 26.2.1944. As the Shia Board claimed it to be Shia *Waqf*, it filed a suit to get over the effect of the Waqf Commissioner's report on the assumption that the 'Baburi Masjid' had been notified to be a Sunni *Waqf* in the above mentioned *Gazette* notification dated 26.4.1944 under section 5(1) of the U.P. Muslim Waqfs Act, 1936. In this suit No. 29 of 1946 between the Shia and the Sunni Central Boards of Waqfs of U.P., in his judgement dated 30.3.1946, Shri Akhtar Ahsan Naqvi, civil judge, Faizabad, based on historical evidence, while admitting the fact that the 'mosque' was built by Babur after destroying the Hindu temple, held the property in suit for the Sunni *Waqf* as the Mughal Emperor, Babur was Sunni and the Friday prayers had been offered in it both by the Shias and the Sunnis. In the continued litigation between the above two parties, the Court of the civil judge, Faizabad, which tried the case as a preliminary issue, vide judgement dated 21.4.1966 held that "no valid notification under Section 5(1) or U.P. Muslim Waqf Act No. XIII of 1936 was ever made" relating to the specific disputed property. As such, the judge made it clear that the alleged notification of 26.2.1944 did not specify the property in suit as *waqf* property and that it was of no legal effect. This finding became final between the two parties. Later on, in the case of Gulam Abbad V State of U.P. (vide AIR 1981 SC 2196, P. 2217-18, paragraph 17), in the case between the Shia and the Sunni Muslims, the Hon'ble Supreme Court of India also found the above mentioned notification of the U.P. Government dated 26.2.1944 to be "of doubtful validity and probative value" and held it to be of no legal effect. As such, in view of the judgement of the Supreme Court, the said notification dated 26.2.1944 was invalid and that the suit No. 29 of 1946 could not have been filed under Section 5(2) of the Waqf Act, with the result that the judgement in that case dated 30.3.1946 in that suit is without jurisdiction and the findings recorded therein are of no legal effect. In fact, the judgement of the above mentioned Supreme Court has foreclosed the matter forever.

The Hon'ble Supreme Court in its judgement on 24.10.94 regarding the acquisition of the land in Ayodhya on 7.1.93 did not take up the issue on merit as to whether the core area on which the disputed structure of *Ramjanmabhoomi*—'Baburi Masjid' stood was in *waqf* property as claimed by the Sunni Waqf Board. However, it is clarified that even when considered as a 'mosque', the State as a sovereign power could acquire it for "undoubted national purpose, if the masjid happens to be located in the property acquired as an ordinary place of worship without any particular significance attached to it for the practice of Islam as a religion." As such, it clearly implies that the so-called 'Baburi Masjid' had never been of any particular significance for the Islamic religion in India. Most significantly, it categorically rejected the view that "once a consecrated masjid, it remains always a place of worship as a masjid" as it was not against the Mohomedan Law of India as approved by the Indian Courts." To the various judgement cases quoted by the Hon'ble Court for the period since the enforcement of the present Indian Constitution (1950), an instance could as well be cited for the Mughal age when the well-known Jain temple of Chintamani-Parshavanath, built by the great jeweller Shantidas was desecrated by Prince Aurangzeb, the governor of the Province of Gujrat and converted into a masjid in 1645 A.D. was re-converted into a temple on the basis of the *farman* issued by the Mughal Emperor, Shah Jahan, on July 3, 1648 A.D.

As against the majority judgement of the Hon'ble Supreme Court, the minority judgement delivered by Hon'ble Justice (now Chief Justice) A.M. Ahmadi and Hon'ble Justice S.P. Bharucha held that the acquisition of Ayodhya land by the Government of India in 1933 had deprived "the Sunni Waqf Board and the Muslim community of the right to plead and establish adverse possession as aforesaid and restrict the redress of their grievance in respect of the disputed site to answer the limited question posed by the reference and to negotiations subsequent thereto.." and that it offended "the principle of secularism, which is a part of the basic structure of the Constitution, being slanted in favour of one religious community as against another." In fact, as already stated in the historical analysis of the *waqf* problem, ever since the establishment of the British rule in Awadh (1856), no *waqf* property had ever been attached to the so-called 'Baburi Masjid' and that the claim of the Sunni Waqf Board in this regard had been legally contested by the Shia community. Moreover, as per the judgement of the Hon'ble Supreme Court itself, the various suits relating to the title to the core area of the disputed structure and other issues involved in the suits pending before the Lucknow Bench of the Allahabad High Court till 6.1.93 have been revived for adjudication. Until the final judgement in this regard is pronounced, it cannot be maintained that the acquisition of the disputed core area of *Ramjanmabhoomi*- 'Baburi Masjid' by the Government of India has denied the Sunni Waqf Board and the Muslim community in general of any right, more especially when at the disputed structure considered by the Muslim community, as an erstwhile 'mosque', no *namaz* had been offered in it, at least admittedly since December, 1949.

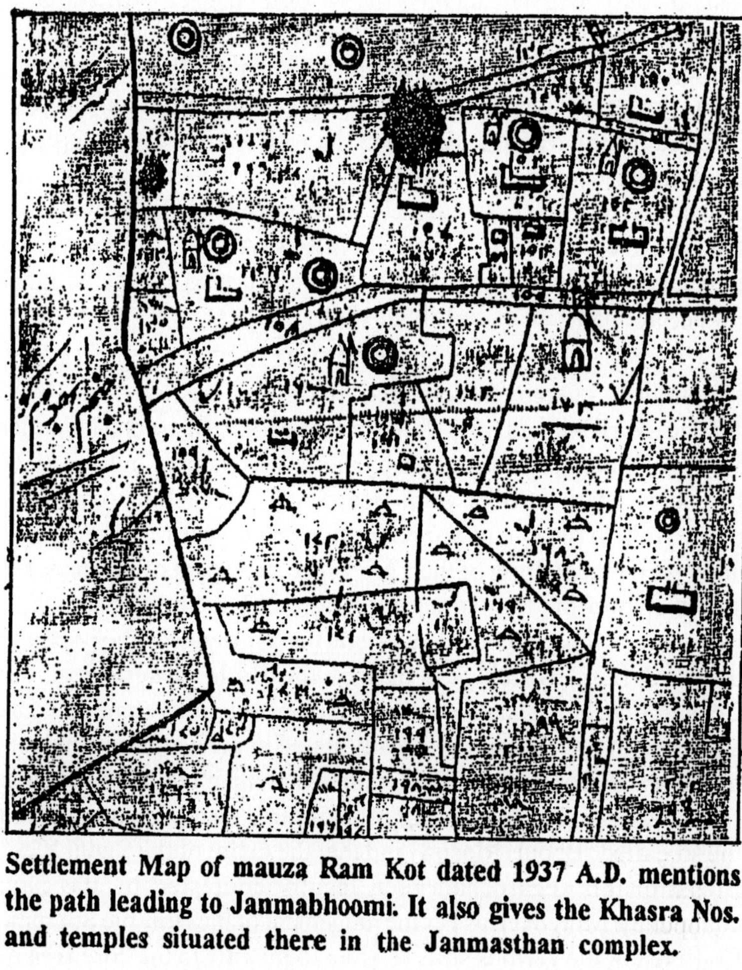

Settlement Map of mauza Ram Kot dated 1937 A.D. mentions the path leading to Janmabhoomi. It also gives the Khasra Nos. and temples situated there in the Janmasthan complex.

3

Evidence from the Revenue Record—

Record of Rights Relating to Janmasthan (Rama Janamabhoomi) from 1856-1861 A.D. (1277F) to 1992 A.D. (1399F)

(1) After the annexation of the territories of Awadh by the English East India Company in 1856 A.D., summary settlement of the revenues was started during the same year (1856) and the revenue operations continued till 1857-58 A.D. Notwithstanding all changes effected during the *Nawabi* period and the early British phase, the pattern of revenue administration in Awadh had direct linkage with the Mughal agrarian system. Ever since the Mughal age, *Kot* Ram Chandra had been one of the villages (*mauzas*) of the suburban *mahal/pargana* of Awadh and as per revenue records was quite distinct from the city (*shahar*) of Ayodhya. Also known as *Ramkot*, it adjoined Awadh (proper city of Ayodhya) on the east and formed the greater part of the high plateau of the suburban *mahal* of Awadh containing as well "the birth-place of Rama and other temples" (vide J.W. Hose's Note on Nazul and Government estates in the Faizabad District, dated 1 April, 1905, p. 21, para 49; Annexure No. 1). It was also surrounded by the villages of Barhata in the south, Jalwanpur in the south-west and *Haveli* Awadh Khas (Ayodhya proper) in east and north-west. This identity of *mauza Kot* Ram Chandra as a district separate revenue village was maintained right from the inception of the British Raj (1856) till 1947 A.D. and, in fact, continues to be so even till date.

(2) As such, after the British occupation, during the course of the summary settlement (1856) and the following revenue operations (1857-58), like the other *mauzas*, viz., Faizabad,

Barhata, Jalwanpur, Bagh Bijesi and Awadh (Ayodhya), etc., *Kot* Ram Chandra was settled separately. During the Mughal age, the land revenue comprised of two main categories, *i.e., mal-o-jihat* (proper land revenue) and *sair-o-jihat* (cesses/ dues/*abwab*, etc.). During the *Nawabi* period, *Kot* Ram Chandra was farmed out and constituted as a part of the *Sair* income. The same position was maintained by the early British administration during the summary settlement period. However, after the first regular settlement (1277F/1861 A.D.), *Kot* Ram Chandra was decreed to the Government in 1869, and ordered to be assessed (as a Nazul property) to revenue in 1872. As such, complete record of rights along with maps of *Kot* Ram Chandra were prepared. Mr. Hose remarks that in case of *Ramkot*, the proprietary rights were accurately recorded and no difficulties arose in this regard as compared to the *mauzas* of Faizabad and Awadh (Ayodhya) (vide Hose's Note, *Ibid.*; Annexure No. I, p. 21, paras 46-49).

(3) In the first regular settlement (1277F/1861 A.D.) and its aftermath for revenue operations lasting till 1878, all the land of *Kot* Ram Chandra was declared as Nazul to be administered by a separate department under the Deputy Commissioner, District Faizabad (vide Hose's Note, *Ibid.*; pp. 1, 6, paras 1 & 9). Even though the concept of separate management of the Nazul lands was a continuation of the *Nawabi* regime, two distinct changes occurred during the British administration. Firstly, in the Awadh territories, the British Government assumed all the proprietary right in the soil that completely altered the position of the erstwhile *taaluqdars*, zamindars and land-holding *riaya*. Apart from the *taaluqdari* estates wherein the rights of land ownership were transferred by the British Government to the *taaluqdars* and the *zamindari* estates settled by the Government with the zamindars, there were villages which were declared as Nazul property wherein the Government claimed absolute right in the ownership of land. The erstwhile landed intermediaries like the *mahaldars* were declared as quasi proprietors and the land owners as subordinate owners (*malikan-i-matahit*). The *mahaldars* as quasi-proprietors were only entitled to a share/percentage in the collected

revenues/rent realised from the subordinate owners and could not claim any title to the properties of the latter. At the same time, the subordinate owners could claim only ownership of the houses/structure built on land, which they could inherit, mortgage or sell after paying dues to the Government but they could not sell the land as the Government would not seal a deed purporting to sell a house with land. However, in practice, as before, the subordinate owners always continued to consider themselves as owners of the land. There was, of course, Government property other than the Nazul land but during the course of the settlement operations, the revenue department recorded it as Nazul property (vide Hose's Note, pp. 9-14, paras 13-19).

(4) The second fundamental change was the application of the theory of rent in Awadh, which the British administration had already enforced in other portions of North India. According to this concept, the term 'revenue' was understood to mean the amount paid by the superior land owners (zamindars etc.) to the State while 'rent' was the amount payable to the superior land owners by those who held under him whether they were the actual occupants or intermediate holders. The landlord or the rent receiver was the owner of the land and the rent payer, even when he was in occupancy, paid for the use and occupation only of the land (vide Annexure No. II—B.R. Grover, "Elements of Continuity and Change in Land Ownership and Rights from the Mughal Age to the Early British Administration in India," Presidential Address, Indian History Congress, Calicut, December, 1976, pp. 23-29). This implied a complete change from the Mughal or the *Nawabi* period's concept of property and agrarian relations. However, the British Government claimed that in many a region, even during the *Nawabi* regime of Nawab Saadat Ali Khan (1798-1814 A.D.), in the lands declared Nazul by the latter, the occupant owners could sell materials only of their houses but not the land. As such at the annexation, the British Government succeeded to these rights. But this assertion was invariably resisted by the people at the time of preparation of records of rights. In this regard, there was considerable litigation in the Civil Courts

(vide Hose's Note pp. 9-12, paras 13-19) and in 1880 for the first time a decision was given that land belonged to the Government only when it became waste. In 1885, sales of land by people who did not own it were recognized by the Nazul department and in 1888, the courts were suffered to give a decree for land only when the house had been purchased. These legal verdicts had taken place because from 1884 to 1890, the Government simply asserted its claim of general ownership of land and insisted on the doctrine of lapse of abandoned sites. However, later on from 1894 to 1900, there was reassertion of the concept of absolute ownership of land on the part of the Government based on historicity, *i.e.,* Lord Canning's Proclamation (1858) as well as the fresh inquiry conducted (1900) into the history of proprietary right in Faizabad/Awadh during the *Nawabi* regime and detailing the rights of old owners of houses. Henceforth, there was revision to the record of rights as incorporated in the 1st regular Settlement Report (1861), even though in practice certain compromise was made in 1903 by accepting the *sakini* (perpetual residence) rights of the houseowners/land occupants which conceded the rights of the landowners not paying Nazul grant through the introduction of paper of assignment for long tenure leases, though with no right to transfer the land. More so, the small plots of land for building were nor saleable and could only be let on lease.

(5) As the *mauza* of *Kot* Ram Chandra in toto fell under the Nazul category, the subordinate land owners (*malikan-i-matahit*) were required to pay rent (*lagaan*) in lieu of their holdings, both for the houses/structure as well as the open/cultivable land along with the wells (*pacca/kachcha*) and fruit bearing trees, if any. The entire cultivable land of the village was reckoned *parti* (brought under cultivation intermittently), tobacco being the most favoured crop, even though wheat and barley were also grown. The assessable trees were mostly the *imli* (tamarind), *musli* (taproot) and *neem* (Azadirachta Indica). The assessment of the rent of a plot/sub-plot of land was done taking into consideration the above mentioned factors and the valuation of the structure under occupation. However,

the subordinate land owners of the plot/sub-plot with a holy shrine situated on it may pay the rent in full or may be partially or totally exempted from it, which was duly recorded in the *khewat/khata khatauni* of the village records.

(6) After the I[st] settlement (1861), another marked feature of the *mauza Kot* Ram Chandra was that apart from being a Nazul land, it was declared intra-municipal in character. This was a typical British innovation, which did not exist in the *Nawabi* period. Even though the rent *abnitio* fixed by the settlement department on the Nazul land was realizable by the Nazul office and actual dealings with Nazul property were to be carried on by the Nazul officials under the Deputy Commissioner, the entrustment of the Nazul work in the hands of 'local fund committee/municipal committee' was tantamount to dual management, which ultimately was bound to result in laxity, corruption, interpolation, inaccuracy and improper maintenance of the village records (vide Hose's Note pp. 5-7, paras 9-11). More than *Ramkot*, the worst affected intra-municipal villages in this regard were Awadh (Ayodhya) and Faizabad which led to number of general inquiries and remedial proposals by the Government of India. In this regard, the report of the Nazul officer, Munshi Vindeshwari Prasad (1894) tracing the historical genesis of the property rights and expressing difficulty in preparing proper Nazul register, as required by the Board of Revenue, due to encroachments, willful wrong entries and changes of all kinds from the original *khasras* effected in 1873-75, 1878 and 1894 is most revealing (vide Hose's Note, pp. 7-8, paras 11-12).

(7) Based on experience, it was considered that the most effective remedy was the correction of the records at the next regular settlement which was effected in *Ramkot*, Awadh (Ayodhya) and other villages of District Faizabad in 1893-94 A.D. (vide Hose's Note, pp. 7-8, paras 11-12). Taking the Settlement Report (1893-94) into cognizance, general Nazul rules were framed in 1899 and fresh survey of the Nazul property and *khasra abadi* was undertaken in January, 1901 with Chaudhuri Maharaj Singh, assistant settlement officer as the record officer who completed his report by March-April, 1905. All the above

mentioned enquiries and reports fully bear out the fact that fresh entires/additions in the Nazul property records made during the interregnum of the two regular settlement operations could be inaccurate and misleading, more especially in the intra-municipal Nazul villages/*mahals*, unless supported by the next Settlement Report incorporating not only the *khasra kishtwar/ khasra abadi* but also the *khewat* and *khata khataunis* of the village. Hitherto, it has been much less realised that the Nazul office, district revenue administration, the municipal committee and the settlement office were distinctly separate departments. The regular revenue administration was under the direct charge of the Deputy Commissioner as Collector of the District. The Nazul office and the municipal committees also fell under the charge of the Deputy Commissioner for general supervision and implementation of guidelines of the Government. However, the settlement office was set up only periodically after about thirty to forty years during the course of the settlement operation lasting over a few years. The settlement officer enjoying at least equal status, though invariably senior to that of the district Deputy Commissioner, was head of his own revenue staff and even though working in co-ordination with the latter, was directly responsible to the Commissioner of the Faizabad region and the Board of Revenues. Even after the assessment of the rent and preparation of record of rights, he decided all disputes in this regard in his own court. As such, the settlement records, unless contested by any party in a civil suit, were/are always considered most authentic and take precedence over the records of any of the other above mentioned departments of the Government.

(8) The first report of Settlement of the Land Revenue of Faizabad District by A.F. Millett, C.S., Officiating Settlement Officer (published by N.W.P. and Oudh Government Press, Allahabad, 1880) vide paragraphs 618-619; 666-669, while tracing the past history of *Janmasthan*/'Baburi Masjid' in *Kot* Ram Chandra/ Ayodhya, confirms the fact that Babur came to Ayodhya in 1528 A.D. and halted here for a week during which he destroyed the *Janmasthan* Temple and on its site built a masjid

using largely the materials of the old structure. This must have occurred about the time of Babur's expedition to Bihar. The author of the Settlement Report further adds that according to Scyder's Memoirs of Babur, the emperor encamped about two or three kos east (5 or 6 miles) from Ayodhya and stayed for a week settling the surrounding country, though it was remarkable that his doings at Ayodhya from April 2, 1528 onwards were wanting in his Memoirs (*Babar-nama*).

(9) As a matter of fact, for his Settlement Report, A.F. Millett has completely relied upon or rather virtually reproduced from the earlier historical sketch given by P. Carnegy, Settlement Officer and Officiating Commissioner (vide Historical Sketch of Tehsil, Zilla Fyzabad, with the Old Capitals Ajudhia and Fyzabad, Lucknow, 1870, pp. 5-7, 19-21). The latter has provided details about the ancient history of Ayodhya, the various monastic orders/religious sects settled therein during the medieval age as well as the *Janmasthan* and other temples. He is also emphatic on the aspect that in 1528 A.D., the Emperor Babur built the *mosque* on the very site of *Janmasthan*—a fine temple—and many of its *Kasauti* columns carved with different devices, still in existence, were re-used in the construction of the Baburi mosque. Most significantly, according to Carnegy, till 1855 A.D., when the Hindu-Muslim rupture took place over the alleged demolition of a "mosque" in Hanuman Garhi and the possession of the *Janmasthan* premises, the possession of both the places, *i.e.,* the supposed site of the non-existent "mosque" at Hanuman Garhi as well as the site of the 'mosque-temple structure in the *Janmasthan* premises rested with the Hindus. However, during the course of 1855 riots, whereas the Hindus completely occupied the Hanuman Garhi, the Muslims took possession of the *Janmasthan*. It is only after the third attempt that the Hindus were successful in taking possession of the *Janmasthan* after having killed about 75 Mohammedans who were buried in "Martyrs' Grave" *('Ganj-Shahid'/Ganj-i-Shahidan)*.

(10) Later on, it was only during the British rule (w.e.f. 1856 A.D.), in order to prevent disputes, a railing was put up in the courtyard dividing the "mosque" structure and the other courtyard

whereupon the Hindus raised a platform for making their offerings. Apparently, according to P. Carnegy, the first Settlement Officer of District Faizabad, who had firsthand knowledge about the events of his official tenure or a couple of years preceding him, the division of the courtyard of the *Janmasthan* site unto inner one for the "mosque" structure and the outer position comprising a platform as a Hindu place of worship was effected by the British Government and that hitherto (1855-56), the possession of the entire premises of *Janmasthan* had rested only with the Hindus. In fact, in 1873 A.D., in order to give a separate suit on fair days to visitors to the *Janmasthan*, a doorway was opened in the wall which in front was divided from the "mosque" by a railing. Even though the Mohammedans could have no interest in the opening of the second door, merely to annoy the Hindus by making them dependent for opening or closing the second door, Mohammed Asghar, "incharge of the Janam Asthan at Ajodya" appealed against the decision of J. Pereins, the Deputy Commissioner, Faizabad, for opening the second door, but the Commissioner, Faizabad Division, vide his order dated 13.12.77 rejected the appeal in the case of Misc. Appeal No. 56 in re. Mohd. Asghar VS Khem Das.

(11) The fact that after the establishment of the British rule in Awadh (February 1856 onwards), the Settlement Officer of the first regular settlement (1861) clarifies that till 1855-56 A.D., the possession of the entire premises of *Janmasthan* comprising both the inner portion with structure of the alleged 'mosque' thereupon and the outer portion with Ram Chabutra, etc., rested with the Hindus is of vital importance. This is notwithstanding the fact that during the 1855 riots in Ayodhya *Kot* Ram Chandra, the Muslims had temporarily forcibly occupied the premises of the 'mosque'/Ram Chabutra for some time from which they were evicted by the Hindus after an armed conflict. Apart from this, all through the centuries, the Hindu *mahants* had always claimed and owned absolute ownership of the land of the entire *Janmasthan* complex. As explained in the succeeding paras, only this can account for the fact even after the establishment of the British rule in Awadh, even though, as a

matter of land policy, enforced in Awadh after 1857-58, the superior ownership of land of the *Janmasthan* complex was vested in the Nazul (Government), all through the revenue settlements (1861, 1893-94 and 1936-37) and the annual operations for the determination of record of land rights, the Hindu *mahants* had continued to be recorded as subordinate owners (*malikan-i-matahit*) till date in all the relevant revenue documents comprising *khasra kishtwar, khata khatauni* and *khewat* relating to the *Janmasthan* complex.

(12) The assertions made by P. Carnegy, as stated in paras 2, 3 and 4, are reiterated and confirmed by the Gazetteer of the Province of Oudh, Vol. I, 1877, pp. 6-7. Later on, H.R. Neville, the editor of Barabanki District Gazetteer (Lucknow, 1902, pp. 168-169) as well as that of Faizabad District Gazetteer (Lucknow, 1905, pp. 172-177) stresses the fact of the destruction of the *Janmasthan* Temple in 1528 by Babur and construction of the '*mosque*' on the same site with the structural material of the erstwhile *Janmasthan* Temple, the building of a little '*Chabutra*' of Sri Ram Chandra in the outside courtyard for worship, the continual and intermittent tussle between the Hindus and the Muslims over the site of the disputed structure (*i.e., Ramjanmabhoomi*/Baburi *Masjid*) culminating in a communal riot in 1855 A.D. He equally mentions the hitherto possession of the disputed site with the Hindus from which the latter were temporarily ousted during the course of conflict but soon reoccupied by them after a severe pitched battle and signal victory over the Muslims.

(13) As the Settlement Report as a book of reference is admissible under the law, *i.e*, under the Evidence Act, its validity is undeniable, in the Regular Suit No. 29 of 1945 over the *Waqf* issue between the Shia Board of Waqf, U.P. verses Sunni Central Board of *Waqf,* U.P., in his Judgement dated 30.3.1946, Akhtar Ahsan Naqvi, Civil Judge, Faizabad, maintained that the Gazetteer of the District or the Settlement Report as books of reference were admissible under Section 57 of the Evidence Act.

(14) The revenue records relating to village *Ramkot*, *Haveli* Awadh, District Faizabad are extremely significant and clarify the

factual proprietary position of *Janmasthan* versus 'Baburi-Masjid'. As per land revenue procedure, they offer details of the numbered plots (*khasras*) of the entire village *Ramkot* in respect of nature of land rights, their topographical position, the nature of the soil along with the area of each plot with complete further details, whether inhabited with *abadi* (population) or a graveyard or arable land growing particular crops along with fruit-bearing trees, if any, and paying land rent or treated as *muafi* (exempted from rent payment), the wells, tanks, gardens, paths (roads), *Shivaalayas*/Mandirs (temples), graveyards and mosques, etc. In fact, the records comprise various categories of revenue documents, *i.e., survey, bandobast* (Settlement), *khasra kishtwar, khasra abadi, misl hadbast, khewats, khasra khataunis* and maps, etc., right from 1861 A.D. till date (1995-96). All these records are available at the District Record Office (*Mahafaz Khana*/ Tehsil Office), Faizabad.

(15) In the 1861 settlement, the plots of land traditionally associated with *Janmasthan* complex are shown mostly as settled with *abadi* (population) and constructions thereupon. *Janmasthan*, as a populated area, is the most important landmark of the village *Kot* Ram Chandra. This is well confirmed by the fact that of the plots recorded in the *khasra kishtwar*, a few plots, viz., *khasra* Nos. 51, 55 and 56 which fell on the pathway towards *Janmasthan,* have been described as the *khasra* plots on the way to *Janmasthan* (*Janmasthan* ke Raah) or preceding *Janmasthan* (*Janmasthan* ke Urai). The plot Nos. 55 & 56, being in *Muafi* and situated in *Mahal* Azhar Hussain, have been put under the subordinate ownership of Dinna Murari, son of Gopal, resident of the village. This shows that in 1861 A.D., the road running from Hanuman Garhi in the east towards *Janmasthan* in the north-west was popularly known as *Janmasthan Path*. In fact, the *khasra* plot No. 272 of the *khasra abadi* record of 1861 settlement in its *Kaifiyat* Column (general statement) mentions the path as *Shah Rah Janmasthan, i.e.,* the main path of *Janmasthan*.

(16) The first Regular Settlement Report (1861) of *Kot* Ram Chandra, appended by two maps, is the most comprehensive

document relating to the *Janmasthan* complex. It equally reflects the earlier position and was prepared taking into consideration the past records of the *Nawabi* period. The entire complex of *Janmasthan* is covered under *khasra* No. 163 with 9 sub-plots (*goshas*, from *alf* to *ain i.e.*, 'a' to 'I') with total area of 5 *bighas* and 4 *biswas*. However, under column No. 16 of *Kaifiyat*, it is stated that in the area of *Janmasthan* there is one *pacca* well, trees whose number is recorded in *khasra abadi* and some graveyard (*qabristan*).

(17) For each of the 9 sub-plots, the area has been reported. Of the total 5 *bighas*, 4 *biswas* are of *Janmasthan* (vide *khasra* No. 163) complex, 4 *bighas*, 13 *biswas* are owned by the Nazul Department (*Sarkar Bahadur* Nazul) as superior *malik* and Hindu *Mahants* as subordinate proprietors (*malikan-i-matahit*), whereas 11 *biswas* (0-11-0) owned by Hindu *mahants* are put under the *mahal* of Azhar Hussain, & c., (the lambardars). Unlike the detailed description of the sub-plots of the other *khasra* numbers, the 1861 settlement does not show any specific sub-plot under *mahal* Azhar Hussain and *muafi* (exempted from payment of the revenue). The words Azhar Hussain and *muafi* have been put only at the top in the relevant columns along with Sarkar Nazul, which is misleading and apparently an interpolation effected at a later stage. However, the position is partly clarified by *khatauni* No. 1 (attested by Muhammad Akbar, *darogha* Nazul, dated 25th September, 1878) which under the heading of column 2 (name of *thok patti*) puts *khasra* No. 163 M in *muafi* (*taraf haqiqat muafi*) with habitated (*abadi*) area of 11 *biswas* (0-11-0) under the jurisdiction of Azhar Hussain, &c., the superior owner (*malik* or *haqdar* vide column 4). Here too, the specific No./Nos. of the sub-plots of *khasra* No. 163 are not mentioned. But later on, the position is absolutely clarified in the 1301 F/1893 A.D. settlement when the same sub-plot is shown under *khasra* No. 163/3 in the *mahal* jurisdiction (*thok patti*) and superior ownership of Nazar Hussain and Tahir Hussain (descendants of Azahr Hussain as *maliks*) along with Mehta Balram Das as subordinate owner (*malik matahit*). All the same, the 1301 F/ 1893 A.D. settlement does not put this sub-plot (No. 163/3)

under the category of *muafi* and merely shows it being a non-Nazul land under the *mahal* of Nazar Hussain, & c. Most significantly, the map of 1893 settlement dated 1894-95 shows *khasra* No. 163/3 to the east and outside the boundary wall of the *Ramjanmabhoomi*/'Baburi Masjid' area which is covered by *khasra* plots Nos. 163/1 and 163/2. As such, clearly, the sub-plot No. 163 M recorded in the *khatauni* No. 1 dated 1878 A.D. as *muafi* in *mahal* Azhar Hussain has nothing to do with the land associated with *Ramjanmabhoomi*/*Chabutra*/ 'Baburi Masjid', which are separately shown under Nazul and subordinate ownership of the Hindu *mahants*.

(18) To the north of the present *Ramjanmabhoomi*-erstwhile 'Baburi Masjid' and the walled compound (*ahata*), lay the inhibited (*abadi*) area covered by a structure still known as *Janmasthan*. In fact, all through the centuries, right till the late 19th century, the latter structure comprised only a couple of sub-plots of *Janmasthan* and formed a part and parcel of the entire *Janmasthan* complex and the road dividing the two structures, *i.e., Ramjanmabhoomi* erstwhile 'Baburi Masjid' and the present day structure also named *Sita Rasoi/ Janmasthan* was constructed in the late 19th century during the British rule. This is well established by the revenue records. A careful study and comparison of the 1861 settlement *khasra kishtwar* map of *mauza* (village) Ram Chandra with the 1893 settlement *khasra kishtwar* map dated 1894-95 of the said village fully bears out this fact. Whereas, in the 1861 settlement map, the sub-plots of the northern portion of the *Janmasthan* complex (denoted by the present day structure, also named *Sita Rasoi/Janmasthan*) are contiguous to the southern plots comprising the *Ramjanmabhoomi*/erstwhile '*mosque*' structure alongwith the walled boundary, in the 1893 settlement map dated 1894-95, the former northern portion of *Janmasthan* (vide *khasra* No. 163/5, also named *abadi Sita Rasoi*) is distinctly separated from the latter portion of *Ramjanmabhoomi* erstwhile '*mosque*' structure & c. (vide *khasra* Nos. 163/1 and 163/2) by a regular road (vide *khasra* Nos. 109 M and 162 M) which runs from the border of the Ayodhya city and Hanuman Garhi temple in the east of the

village towards the *Janmasthan* and after dividing the latter complex proceeds towards the Jalanpur village in the west. As this has become a permanent topographical feature, this is equally reflected in the 1936-37 settlement map, operative till date, wherein the road comprising *khasra* No. 158 divides the *Ramjanmabhoomi*/erstwhle 'Baburi Masjid' (vide *khasra* Nos. 159 and 160 M) from the present day structure, also named *Sita Rasoi/Janmasthan* (vide *khasra* No. 146). As a matter of fact, the *khasra kishtwar* date of the 1861 settlement gives specific area as well as digical geographical directions for each sub-plot in the *Janmasthan* complex which comprised the areas of both the portions, *i.e.,* the *Ramjanmabhoomi*/erstwhile 'Baburi Masjid' and the present day structure, also named *Sita Rasoi/Janmasthan*.

(19) As stated later (vide paras No. 42-47), in the course of the proceedings of the regular suit No. 12 of 1961 and other CS No. 2 of 89 and 4 of 89 Sunni Central Board of *Waqf* VS. Gopal Singh Visharad and other Miscellaneous Application, the first report submitted by Survey Commissioner on 25th July, 1990, for the location of the disputed plots with reference to the documentary evidence on record "was rejected by the Hon'ble High Court of Judicature, Allahabad at Lucknow Bench, which in its further order, dated 18th September, 1990, directed the Survey Commissioner to submit a supplementary report after carrying out survey on the settlement maps of 1861 and 1937," and "to indicate the numbers which cover the property in dispute according to 1861 maps as well as according to 1937 map". In his supplementary report submitted to the Hon'ble Court in 08.01.91, Shri J.P. Srivastava, the learned Survey Commissioner, has committed numerous factual errors and he completely failed to understand the settlement operation procedure. He contends that the original maps of 1861 and 1937 settlements deposited in the Board of Revenue, Lucknow, were washed away by the floods of Gomti River in the sixties and that "the settlement map of village *Ramkot* for the settlement conducted during 1861-70 available in the District Record Room was actually prepared on 17th October, 1873, many years after the settlement was over" and that as it does not bear the

signature of the Settlement Officer, "it cannot be said with certainty that it is the original map for it could also be a trace." As a matter of fact, the settlement operations in a district usually covered a number of years and the name of the year of the Settlement Report goes by the *Fasli* year of the starting of the actual operation. The settlement is done village-wise or revenue circle-wise in a Tehsil but all the Tehsils in a district are not taken up simultaneously for the purpose of settlement. After the actual field survey operation and preparation of records, the disputed ownership cases are decided by the Settlement Officer vested with judicial powers in this regard. As such, in case of the village Ramkot, the entire process of settlement operation involving survey, preparation of revenue records of various categories, the decisions on the disputed cases by the Settlement Officer/Nazul Officer and the finalisation of the records thereafter was accomplished in 1878. This is well borne out by the details of the revenue documents listed in the Settlement Report (1861). The judicial decisions of 31 disputed land cases of *Kot* Ram Chandra were taken by the Settlement Officer in 1870, 1871 and 1872. Whereas the *robkars* (orders/ proceedings) listed in the Settlement Register were finally verified in 1877, the list of documents comprising the Settlement Reports, initiated in 1861 were finally signed by the Settlement Officer on October 07, 1878. The *khatauni* documents No. 1/ 43 comprising a part of 1861 Settlement were attested and finalised by Muhammad Akbar, *darogha* Nazul, on September 25, 1878 and December 07, 1878. The *hadbast* documents No. 571, initiated on February 06, 1861, were finally decided and signed by the British Settlement Officer on December 12, 1878. All documents relating to census, record of right of the owners of the orchards, trees or the *asamis* for the cultivation of the arable land and miscellaneous matters were finalised by Muhammad Akbar, the *darogha* (of Nazul) on December 25, 1878 after due attestation by Gopal Sahai, the *mukhtar* and Ganga Prasad as witness. For all such revenue matters, the aforementioned *khasra kishtwar* map and other *hadbast* and *khasra abadi* maps were taken into consideration. Most significantly, all the *bandobast* (settlement) documents comprising measurement, *hadbast, kishtwar* boundaries, the assessment and the annual *jama* (total assessed revenues) with effect from 1277 *Fasli* (1861) to 1306 *Fasli* (1898) were attested by J.M. Millet, the Assistant Settlement Officer of District Faizabad.

(20) It is well borne out by the contents of the original 1861 Settlement Report (in Urdu) available at the District/Tehsil Record Offices, that the survey and demarcation (*nishan dehi mutabiq dhaulbandi sarhad* and boundary demarcation (*Hadbast*) of the village (*mauza*) *Kot* Ram Chandra, *Pargana Haveli* Awadh, Tehsil and District Faizabad was accomplished in 1861. It is presumptuous on the part of the Survey Commissioner to have remarked that "the boundary of village *Ramkot* was not correctly traversed during the Settlement of 1861" and that the 1861 settlement map had not made a correct delineation of the boundary of the village *Ramkot*. As a matter of fact, the 1861 Settlement provides a detailed Report, dated February 15, 1861, submitted by Bhagwan Dass, the *amin hadbast* to Muhammad Jafar, the zamindar and *malguzar* of the village. After having determined the boundaries in all the four directions (east, west, north and south), some adjustment was made with the neighbouring village of Awadh (Ayodhya) with the consent of the zamindars and as such, some portion of Awadh and three orchards, after due measurement, were incorporated in the Nazul land of the village *Ramkot*. In fact, the 1861 Settlement Report equally spells out details about the procedural declarations made by Muhammad Jafar, the *malguzar*, Shiv Nath, *darogha* Nazul of *shahar* Awadh about the demarcation of the boundaries and the preparation of the *dhaulbandi sarhad* document, which was implemented by Bhagwan Das, the *amin*. The documents dated February 12, 1861 were signed by Saiyed Muhammad Jafar, the *malguzar*, Bhagwan Das, the *amin* and duly witnessed by the Patwari (named Talku) of the Nazul land, village Awadh, the patwari (named Shiva) of the village of *Kot* Ram Chandra as well as Ali Beg, the Chowkidar of the village. As these documents of 1861 settlement are dated and bear the signatures of different subordinate officials of both the villages, viz., *Ramkot* and

Awadh (Ayodhya), the afore-mentioned viewpoint of the Survey Commissioner (vide para No. 19) about the boundary demarcation of the villages of *Ramkot* and Awadh (Ayodhya) is absolutely incorrect and unreliable.

(21) The viewpoint of the Survey Commissioner that the *khasra kishtwar* map of 1861 settlement, as available today, is rendered unreliable as it was prepared in 1873, "many years after the settlement was over" is basically incorrect. As already stated in para No. 19, the 1861 settlement being the first settlement of District Faizabad after the establishment of the British rule in Awadh, lasted from 1861 to 1878. This is well confirmed by the fact that the list of documents comprising the 1861 Settlement Report was signed by the Settlement Officers both on March 01, 1861 and October 07, 1878. Moreover, this very map was attested by Muhammad Akbar, *darogha* of Nazul lands on September 25, 1878, who also made certain notings on the reverse side of the map. Above all, as stated (in the para), the settlement officers and Nazul officers relied on this very map for the settlement of various cases and finalisation of revenue records of various categories.

(22) As distinct from the *khasra kishtwar*, the *khasra abadi* (1861) vide Nos. 431-456, *makaan* (complex) nos. 92-93 (as recorded corresponding to No. 163 of the former) show *abadi* (population) in this area. The *khasra hadbast* of 1861 settlement (No. 152) incorporated in the Report (available at the District Record Office, Faizabad) also mentions only *makaan Janmasthan* (mansion of *Janmasthan*). In the *hadbast* map of *mauza Ramkot*, *Pargana*, *Haveli* Awadh, Tehsil and *Zilla* Faizabad appended to the 1861 Settlement Report (*Bandobast* vide No. 132) available at the Tehsil Office, District Faizabad, there is a lay out sketch plan given at the bottom of the map (but distinct from it) which mentions "*Asthan* Ram Chandra"-'104'. The site of the plan Numbered as 91, 92 and 230 is the same which corresponds to the premises of the *Janmasthan* as recorded in the 1861 settlement. This clearly establishes that at the time of the preparation of the 1861 Settlement Report, the site was identified only as "*Asthan* Ram Chandra" (*Ramjanmabhoomi*). Apart from it, the *khasra*

abadi document of the 1861 settlement shows that the inhabitants of *Janmasthan* (*sakna Janmasthan*) also owned other plots/sub-plots (vide *khasras* Nos. 203, 206, 214) or owned *musli* (taproot) and *imli* (tamarind) trees in the other plots of the village. This shows that the *Janmasthan* complex was fairly inhabited and that the *mahants/bairagis* of *Janmasthan*, with a network of land ownership in the village, had a sound financial and social status. None of the *khasra abadi* numbers, as mentioned above, parallel to the *abadi Janmasthan* of *khasra kishtwar* No. 163, does mention the existence of any "mosque" though in *kaifiyat*, these *khasra abadi* numbers do mention the prevalence of *pacca* graveyard (*qabargah pukhta*), a few *imli* (tamarind), *musli* (taproot) trees and *makaans* (houses) etc., on the campus. Even *khasra abadi* No. 444 conjectured and identified by the so-called amended *khasra* Nazul Record of 1931 as an equivalent to a sub-plot of *khasra kishtwar* No. 163 M of 1861 settlement comprising the *Janmasthan* in its *kaifiyat* describes only *ahata pukhta* (*pacca* campus) and two trees (neem and ghauz) in possession of a Thakur of the village. The *khasra abadi* record under its column No. 8, *i.e., kaifiyat* (general statement) specifically mentions *pacca* mosques (*masjid pukhta* against *ahata* plot Nos. 13, 47, 124 and 160, but it does not mention the existence of any mosque against any of the *ahata* plot numbers (*i.e.,* 431-456) associated with the *Janmasthan* complex, of the specific plots Nos. 443-447 which can be well established as the site of the present day *Ramjanmabhoomi* premises which formed a part of the larger complex of *Janmasthan*.

(23) According to the land revenue system, as inherited by the early British administration from the Mughal/*Nawabi* periods, the settlement of the village in respect of boundaries of the village and their landmarks, land-holdings, the proprietary/land rights of various categories of the *riaya*, the *abadi* comprising *ahatas/makaans* (houses), religious places, temples, *shivalas/ akharas/chabutras* and *masjids* etc.) the *waqf, muafi* lands, the wells (*kaccha/pacca*), pasture land (*chaaraagaah*), if any, the regular and the intersecting *paths* (roads) was done

only after due attestation by the village Zamindar/*malguzar* (revenue payer after customary deductions), *amin* (assessor), the local patwari (*lekhpal*) and even the chowkidar. After the preparation of the record of rights, the original records were maintained at the District Record Office (*Muhafaz Khana*) whereas the copies of the same were also kept by the Tehsil office, Municipal Committee, if any, and the local patwari (*lekhpal*). This would equally obviate the chances of later interpolation or any wrongful entry in the records. As such, as per settlement procedure, the *hadbast*, and *dhaulbandi sarhad* documents (February/March, 1861) relating to the demarcation of the village boundaries spelling out the parts of the fields/gardens of Ayodhya village incorporated in the Nazul lands of the village *Ramkot* have been duly attested by Muhammad Zafar, the Zamindar *malguzar* of the village and Bhagwan Das, *amin* witnessed by both the Nazul patwaris of Ayodhya and *Ramkot* as well as the chowkidar. Similarly, the *khasra kishtwar, khasra abadi* giving the details of the owners (*maliks*) and other related documents have been verified by them before being finalised by the *darogha* Nazul and Settlement Officer of the district.

(24) Quite significantly, both the *hadbast* (boundary demarcation) map titles *Naksha Hadbast Mauza Kot Ram Chandra, Pargana Haveli Awadh, Tehsil and Zilla Faizabad Babat 1861 A.D.* and the *abadi* map titled *Naksha abadi Mazua Ramkot, Pargana Haveli Awadh* appended to the Settlement Report (1861) show only the landmark of *Janmasthan*. They do not indicate any symbol or description of the "mosque" therein.

(25) The *hadbast* map (boundary demarcation map) (1861), based on defined scale of *jarib* for measurement recorded on it, is shown with boundary lines, numbered with scale units, which separate the village Ramkot from the villages of Barhatta in the south, Jalwanpur in south-west and the city of Awadh (*shahar* Awadh) in the east and north-west. The boundaries on the three sides are attested by the subordinate revenue officials, viz., *darogha* Nazul (Muhammad Akbar), and

Plan of the City of Ayodhya: Ramkot Awadh "Khas"

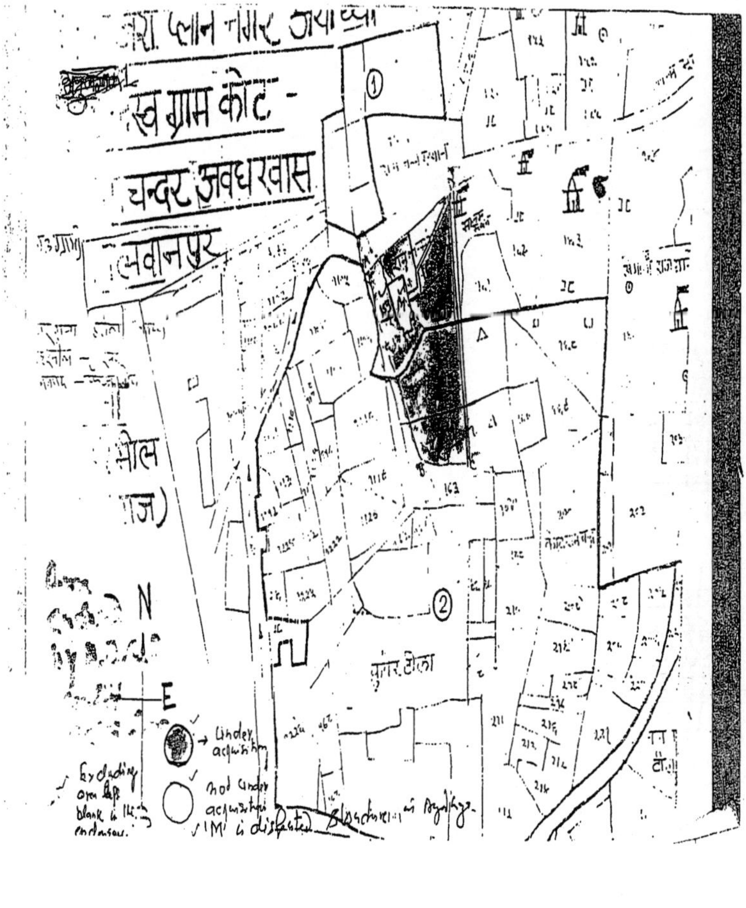

Map of acquired area (67 acres) surrounding Ram Janambhoomi, Ayodhya

under Acquisition of Certain Area Act no. 33 of 1993

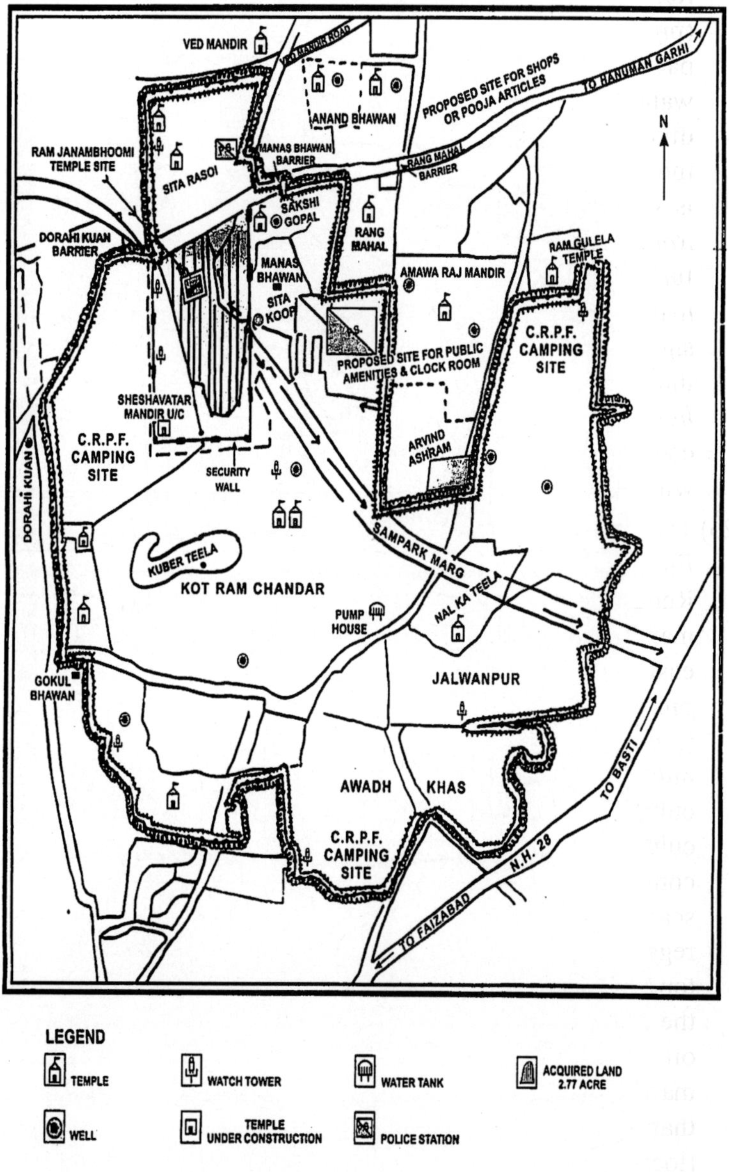

Saligram. A large complex in rectangular shape with symbols of some structure on it has been put as *Janmasthan* in bold letters in Urdu. In fact, there are two parts of the complex in rectangular shape, a larger one on the southern side (present *Ramjanmabhoomi*) and smaller one on the northern side (present day *Sita Rasoi/Janmasthan*). Even though a small path divides the two areas, both are shown in one large four-walled premises. In fact, the path constitutes as an internal dividing line and is not shown as a regular road running from the east to the western boundary of the village and beyond as is shown later in the 1893 settlement and 1894-95 map of *Ramkot*. That the 1861 *hadbast* map is absolutely authentic is further confirmed by the fact that the middle portion of the map, to the north-east of *Janmasthan*, bears the attestation signatures by Muhammad Zafar, the zamindar (in Urdu), Shiva, the patwari (in Hindi) and Pandit Bhagwan Das, the *amin* of *hadbast* (in Urdu). Above all, the map has also been countersigned by a British officer (in English-illegible) connected with the settlement.

(26) The *khasra abadi* map titled *Naksha Abadi Mauza Ramkot, Pargana Haveli, Awadh*, appended to the 1861 Settlement Report, seems to have been prepared in a most scientific manner. Apart from the landmark of Hanuman Garhi in the east, it has provided symbols for *pacca* houses (*makaan pukhta*), *kachcha* houses (*makaan kham*), graveyards (*qabargahs*), *shivalas*, mosques (*masjid*), *pacca* wells (*chaha pukhta*), deserted (*wiran*) land, ponds (*talao*), roads (*sarak*), cultivable land *(parti)*, deserted houses (*makaan wiran*), cultivated (*mazrua*) plots, *pacca* staircases (*siri pukhta*) and complexes with structures (*ahatas*). The scale of the map and scale units of the boundaries have also been provided. As regards its authentic character, there is an official seal on the top and after proper verification, it was finalised and signed by the Revenue Officer (name illegible—Muhammad Asikan?) on October 17, 1873. All the 467 *khasra* plots have been marked on the map. The distinguished feature of this map is that it has clubbed the *khasra* plots of the different *abadis* (localities) with enclosed boundary lines against which the plot

numbers of the *khasra kishtwar* (1861) have also been recorded. The co-relationship between the *khasra abadi* and *khasra kishtwar* plots has been indicated. As such, the *khasra abadi* plots No. 431-456, along with the relevant symbols and boundary lines, have been shown as parallel to the *abadi* of the *khasra kishtwar* plot No. 163 of the *Janmasthan* complex of *Ramkot*. Like the *khasra abadi* record in the 1861 Settlement (vide para 22) the afore-mentioned *abadi* map does not show any symbol of a mosque in any of the *khasra abadi* plots which formed part of the *Janmasthan* complex.

(27) For the proper evaluation of the 1861 settlement, it is essential to coordinate and cross check all the available maps, viz., *hadbast*, *abadi* and *khasra kishtwar*. As stated in the paras No. 25 and 26, the *hadbast* and *khasra abadi* maps appended to the 1861 Settlement Report were prepared on scientific basis. Moreover, the *khasra kishtwar* document comprise not only the areas of the 167 *khasra* Numbers; it has also provided digical topographical figures in respect of each plot. This procedure well confirms the authentic nature of the 1861 Settlement and completely belies the erroneous conclusions of the Survey Commission.

(28) Later on, at the back of a duplicate of *khasra kishtwar* map, Muhammad Akbar, *darogha* of Nazul lands, dealing with the issue of rights of the land owners (*malikan*) vis-a-vis tenants (*muzarin*) of the village and also the question whether there was Nazul *Waqf* attached to the *pacca* "mosque" built by Emperor Babur and situated on *Janmasthan*, recorded on 25th September, 1878 A.D. categorically states that (in the village *Ramkot*) there was no Nazul land/house/garden assigned to Mir Muhammad Asghar (*khattib/muazaan*) for an expenditure on the said mosque. However, he further records that the latter (Muhammad Asghar) had been granted some cultivable land/garden worth Rupees three-hundred and two only (Rs. 302/-) in the villages of Baharanpur and Sholapur. Apparently, this noting was done by the *darogha* Nazul in 1878 A.D. as Muhammad Asghar, etc., had already been given conditional land grant by the British Government in 1870, along with *malkiyat* (proprietary) rights in land, subject to the rendering

of the police and military services as well as for looking after some of the essential needs of the "resting place of the angles".

(29) It may be observed that the recording of a "mosque" at the back of a duplicate settlement map of *khasra kishtwar*, as late as 1878 A.D., by a *darogha* of the Nazul lands is of peripheral nature, especially when the map itself does not comprise any indication of a "mosque" thereupon. Even though the physical existence of an extraneous structure believed to be "mosque" built by the Mughal Emperor Babur at the *Janmasthan* site was alleged, most significantly, the revenue settlement maps of 1861, 1893 and 1936-37 A.D. do not bear any indication of a "mosque" at the *Janmasthan* site and indicate only the *Janmasthan* at the site.

(30) In the original document of the Settlement Report of 1861 A.D. available at the District Record Office (*muhafaz khana*)/Tehsil Office, Faizabad, interpolations/additions have been effected in certain columns of the *khasra kishtwar* folios. In the District Record Office document, under column No. 2, to the original reading of *abadi Janmasthan*, the words 'and juma masjid' have been added so as to read '*abadi Janmasthan* and juma masjid' Under column No. 3, to the words 'taraf Nazul', the words 'and muafi' have been added and under column No. 4, the words Sarkar Bahadur, 'and Azhar Hussain' have been added.

(31) The above alterations/additions are confirmed by the fact that in the Tehsil Office copy of 1861 settlement, though under column No. 2, the words 'and *juma masjid*' have been added to the original words '*abadi Janmasthan*' in a very crude manner. The Tehsil copy does not carry any interpolation of 'and *muafi*'/Azhar Hussain under column No. 3 & 4 respectively as done in the case of the District Record Office copy. Moreover, the second settlement report of *Ramkot* dated 1301 F/1893-94, even though for *Janmasthan*, carries the same *khasra kishtwar* No. 163 and due to clubbing of the sub-plots is divided into five sub-plots instead of nine as noted earlier in the case of 1861 settlement. It does not record the name of '*jama masjid*' nor does it put '*muafi*' under the relevant column

numbers, which have been shown only under Sarkar Bahadur Nazul. However, in sub-plot No. 163/3 with an area of 11 *biswas* (0-11-0), Azhar Hussain and Tahir Hussain have been put as *mahaldars* whereas Mahant Balram Das has been recorded as subordinate owner (*malik matahit*). All the same, the word '*muafi*' does not occur even in this column number.

(32) In the 1301 F/1893 A.D. settlement, the *khasra* number of *Janmasthan* complex, *i.e.,* No. 163 remains the same as earlier in the 1861 settlement, though due to clubbing of some areas of the sub-plots, the number of the sub-plots is reduced from 9 to 5. In the *khasra kishtwar* (vide *Basta* No. 132), further endorsed by the *khatauni* (vide form 15), the area of each sub-plot is recorded. As earlier recorded in the 1861 settlement, the total area of the *Janmasthan* complex is 5 *bighas* and 4 *biswas* (5-4-0), of which 4 *bighas* and 13 *biswas* (4-13-0) is under Nazul whereas 11 *biswas* (0-11-0) (vide No. 163-3) are shown in the *mahal* of Nazar Hussain and Tahir Hussain (the lambardars). But unlike the 1878 *khatauni,* as already stated in para No. 31, the 1893 Settlement Records do not show it in *muafi*. As per *khasra bandobast* and *khatauni* documents, the portion of the *Janmasthan* complex, *i.e.,* the proper *Ramjanmabhoomi*/"Baburi *Masjid*" land inclusive of courtyards, being under *mahal* Nazul Sarkar,, comprises two *khasra* sub-plots No., *i.e.,* 163/1 and 163/2, with an area of 2 *bighas*, 14 *biswas*, (2-14-0) and 2 *biswas* (0-2-0) respectively. These are shown under habitation (*abadi*) and are vested in the subordinate ownership and occupation of the Hindu *mahants* Raghubar Das, Gopal Das and Thakurdwara Sita Ram. *khasra* sub-plot No. 163/3 located on the east and outside the *Ramjanmabhoomi*/"Baburi *Masjid*" courtyard and boundary wall covers an area of 11 *biswas* (0-11-0). This position is well confirmed by the *kishtwar* map of 1894-95 as spelled out in paras No. 17 and 33-34. As per 1893-94 Settlement, as already noted in para No. 17, it is shown in the *mahal* of Nazar Hussain and Tahir Hussain as non-Nazul area, but under the subordinate ownership of Mahant Balram Das as *malik matahit*. *khasra* sub-plot No. 163/4 with an area of 7 *biswas* (0-7-0) covers the road which separates the *khasra* sub-plots No. 163/1-2,

(*i.e., Ramjanmabhoomi*/"Baburi *Masjid*" land) of the *Janmasthan* area from the northern portion of the complex with *khasra* sub-plot No. 163/5, named as *abadi Sita Rasoi*. The latter portion with an area of 1 *bigha* 10 *biswas* (1-10-0), also being under Nazul is vested in the subordinate ownership of *Mahant* Kalyan Das. Three trees inclusive of an *imli* tree have been shown in the possession of Kalyan Das. The detailed lists provided in the 1893 settlement records in respect of mosques, *waqf*, graveyards (*qabristan*) and mutations, etc., do not put any of the sub-plots, *i.e.,* No. 163/1 to No. 163/5 of the *Janmasthan* complex with either of these categories.

(33) The amended *kishtwar* map of *Kot* Ram Chandra, *Pargana*, *Haveli* Awadh, Tehsil & District Faizabad, dated 1894-95 (*Naksha Kishtwar Tarmim Shuda Mauza Kot Ram Chandra Pargana Haveli Awadh, Tehsil Wa Zilla Faizabad, Mutabiq* (1894-95) prepared after the 1893 settlement slightly varies in respect of the division of the *Janmasthan khasra* plot No. 163. It shows all the sub-plots No. 163/1-5 under habitation (*abadi*). The boundary lines of the four sub-plots, *i.e.,* 163/1-4 have been marked in a consecutive manner on the southern side of the road which separates them from sub-plot No. 163/5 in the north of the road. The road running from the east towards the western boundary of the village, which divides the afore-mentioned *khasra* sub-plots No. 163/1-4 of *Janmasthan* from the northern wing with *khasra* sub-plot No. 163/5 (*abadi Sita Rasoi*) has been put under *khasra* numbers 109 M, 54 and 162 M. The *khasra* sub-plot No. 163/4, earlier shown as road in the 1893 settlement, has been put as a sub-plot with habitation (*abadi*) to the east and in continuation with the boundary line of *khasra* sub-plot No. 163/3. Apparently, this amended redistribution of the numbers of the sub-plots of the main *Janmasthan khasra* plot No. 163 was effected in the aftermath of the 1893 settlement.

(34) The above map dated 1894-95 (vide para No. 33) is significant in many a respect. In its list of depicted symbols, it does not cover the symbol of a *shiwala* (temple) or a mosque. But it does denote the symbols of *abadi*, road, graveyard (*qabristan*), *pacca* well, nature of land (*i.e., parti/qadim*) and non-payment

of *lagaan*, etc. As such, it shows *khasra* sub-plot No. 163/1 (*i.e.,* the site of *Ramjanmabhoomi*/"Baburi *Masjid*") with habitation (*abadi*) and a *pacca* well in the north-eastern direction. The small sub-plot No. 163/2 to the north-east of the sub-plot No. 163/1 with no symbol of its own, has been put as part of *abadi* as indicated in the latter larger sub-plot. The sub-plot No. 163/3 has been shown only with symbol of *abadi*. The sub-plot No. 163/4 has been shown with symbols of *abadi*, orchard (*bagh*) without the payment of grant (*lagaan*). The sub-plot No. 163/5 (*abadi Sita Rasoi*) to the north of the dividing road (as described in para No. 33) comprises the symbols of *abadi* along with three *pacca* wells and a portion of self-cultivated land (*khud kasht*).

(35) Above all, most significantly, there is no symbol of a graveyard (*qabristan*) in any of the sub-plots of *khasra* No. 163 of the *Janmasthan* complex, though, there are symbols of graveyard in the neighbouring plots, *i.e., khasra* Nos. 161, 158, 56-57 etc. Even though earlier in the *khasra kishtwar* No. 163 of the 1861 settlement relating to *Janmasthan*, the column (No. 16) of the general remarks (*kaifiyat*) as well as the *khasra abadi* No. 444 and 452 of the same settlement do mention about the existence of graveyard (*qabargah*) in the complex of *Janmasthan*, it is well confirmed by the above mentioned map that by 1894-95 A.D., there was no graveyard in any of the sub-plots of *Janmasthan* complex. Later on, this position is reiterated by the 1344 F/1936-37 A.D. Settlement Report and the map appended on it.

(36) As distinct from the above mentioned Revenue Records, the Nazul Department of the District Faizabad (U.P.) also prepared its own amended *khasra* records of the *abadi* settlements (*tarmimi khasra abadi*) in 1931 A.D. In these so-called revised *khasras* of village *Ramkot*, both '*masjid*' and *chabutra* indicating the temple at *Janmasthan* have been recorded in *khasra* plot No. 583 with an area of 9 *biswas*, 15 *biswansis* and 4 *kachwansis* (0-9-15-4). The 'mosque' has been shown in *waqf* under column 'Name of the present possessor' (*Nam Hal Qabiz*). At the same time, *Mahant* Charan Das in 1931 and thereafter *Mahant* Raghunath Das (1941) have been

declared under-proprietors (*Malik matahit*) of the entire plot. Moreover, in these *khasra* records, *arazi, i.e., khasra* plot No. 586 with an area of 11 *biswas*, 16 *biswansis* and 16 *kachwansis* (0-11-16-16) being in *abadi* is shown as graveyard (a *pacca qabristan* known as *Ganj-i-Shahidan*) and assigned in *waqf* since the *Shahi* (*i.e.,* Mughal) era (*waqf ahad Shahi*).

(37) A note of caution is necessary with regard to the alleged *khasra abadi* record and map maintained by the Nazul Department in the Faizabad Collectorate which is relied upon by the plaintiffs of Suit No. 12 of 1961 (now O.O.S. 4 of 1989 before the Lucknow Bench of the Allahabad High Court), *Sunni Central Board of Waqf and others VS. Gopal Singh Visharad and others*. The map maintained by the Nazul Department is not authenticated, nor prepared under any law, nor is it according to any ascertainable scale. The survey made on the basis of the *khasra abadi* and that map of the Nazul department at the instance of the Plaintiffs in that Suit has been rejected by the Hon'ble High Court's Full Bench. It is noticeable that the plot numbers given in the Plaint of that Suit are based on the said *khasra abadi* of the Nazul department. There is no *Fard Mutabiqat* comparative table between the plot numbers given in the *khasra abadi* of the Nazul department and the *khasra abadi* maintained by the Revenue Department of the Government.

(38) The very title '*tarmimi khasra abadi*' of the 1931 Nazul document suggests that apparently it represents the amended *khasra abadi* numbers of the village *Kot* Ram Chandra as compared to the previous *khasra abadi* (1861) prepared during the course of the First Regular Settlement (1861). This is evident from the fact that the 1931 Nazul *khasra* numbers in column No. 3 under the heading *arazi* (*i.e.,* area) provide not only the respective areas of the numbered *khasra* plots but also mention the *khasra* numbers of the past *khasra abadi* (1861-1866) of the village. However, the table of contents of the Nazul *khasra* numbers being quite comprehensive, covers the name of the *muhalla* (street), serial number, both present and past; area, name of the superior owner (*malik ala*), name of the subordinate owner (*matahitdar*), if any, name of the present

possessor (*qabiz hal*), nature of land (*qism*), its area; whether the *lagaan* (assessed revenue) or without *lagaan* as per conditions of *muafi* or under the Government possession; encroachments (*kanhdal* and *dast andazi*); name of file (*misl*) with date; area (of encroachment), *lagaan* (assessed revenue), statement of *Shamlati* number and general remarks (*kaifiyat*) about the *khasra* plot. As against this, the table of contents of the earlier *khasra abadi Ramkot* (Revenue Form No. 230) dated 1861 covered only 8 main headings, viz., number of premises (*ahata*); number of the house (*makaan*); name of the owner of the house (*malik makaan*); head of the family (*sardar khandan*); profession of the owner of the house of head of the family; caste (*zat*) of the owner of the house of head of the family; total number of males and females, both major and minors; total number of ploughs (*hal*) and finally, the general settlement (*kaifiyat*) indicating the nature of the land, building, temple, mosque, graves and trees, etc., if any. In the 1861 settlement *khasra abadi* records, excepting column No. 1 (No. *ahata*) and general statement (*kaifiyat*) relating to a *khasra* number, most of the columns are invariably left blank. The total number of *khasra* plots is put at 467 but later on, the 1931 Nazul *khasra abadi* puts the total number at 671. Significantly, the plot numbers of the *khasra abadi* (1861) do not show the areas of the plots which are later on indicated in the 1931 Nazul *khasras*. As a matter of fact, the earlier *khasra abadi* was considered as an integral part of the Regular Settlement (1861) which had provided details about the areas of the plots/sub-plots in the *khasra kishtwar*. All this is well confirmed by the fact that for many *khasra* plots numbers, the details of the *khasra abadi* (1861) corelate its serial plot numbers with those of the *khasra kishtwar* numbers. As such, the serial plot numbers from 431 to 456 of *khasra abadi* have been put parallel to *khasra kishtwar* No. 163 relating to *Janmasthan*. As the general statements/remarks (*kaifiyats*) relating to temples/mosques/graveyards/trees etc., have been provided in both the *khasra kishtwar* and *khasra abadi*, the *kaifiyat* columns of some of the *khasra kishtwars*, notably No. 163 relating to *Janmasthan* refer for details to the *kaifiyat* as given in the *khasra abadi*. Similarly, the *khasra abadi* map has also mentioned and demarcated some of the plots of *abadi* in relation to the *khasra kishtwar* numbers. As such, the boundaries of the relevant plots of *abadi* have been demarcated under the *khasra kishtwar* No. 163 relating to *Janmasthan*.

(39) In contrast to the above mentioned *khasra abadi* of the 1861 settlement, the 1931 Nazul *khasra* are unrelated to any of the settlements, past or future. Not only the 1931 Nazul document does not provide any *Farad Mutabiqat* to the *khasra kishtwar* numbers of 1893-94 or 1861 settlements, by itself it finds no reference in the 1936-37 settlement. As such, it is absolutely irrelevant to the 1936-37 settlement which in its *khasra kishtwar, khata khatauni* and *khewat* details gives factual description about the superior or the subordinate owners of the land, their respective titles to the plots or parts thereof (*minjumla*), category of the plots whether with or without *lagaan* in *muafi* or *waqf*, if any, *abadi* with *ahatas*, temples, mosques, roads, graveyards, wells and fruit-bearing trees, etc. A comparative evaluation of the 1931 Nazul document with just 5 to 6 years later, 1936-37 settlement renders the Nazul *khasra* numbers as redundant and of absolutely unauthentic nature. As a matter of fact, these alleged Nazul *khasra abadi* plot numbers have no existence in law or in fact, as they have not been prepared under any law, at the most, they constitute serial numbers of properties in the unfinished Nazul list so as to identify the encroachments on the Nazul land of the Government. But such a list of properties cannot be a substitute for record of settlement or survey as required under order VII Rule 3 C.P.C. for identification by the plaintiff in land dispute. Moreover, the use of the term '*waqf ahad-Shahi*' (*waqf* since the *Shahi* regime) meant to denote '*waqf az ahad-i-Mughalia*' (*waqf* since the Mughal age) is rather unprecedented in the official records. Here the word 'Shahi' has been used in contrast to the 'Nawabi', but such a terminology is not traceable in any of the official Mughal records or the period of the Nawabs in Awadh. As such, it is extremely doubtful if such entries against the plot numbers were based on any past record.

(40) The 1931 Nazul register maintained at the Nazul Office, Faizabad, while recording the amended *khasra abadi* (*tarmimi khasra abadi*) mentions the name of the village as *Kot* Ram Chandra and under column No. I for the name of the *mohalla* (street), it mentions Ram*kot* for most of the *khasra* plots of the village. However, under this column, for *khasra* No. 583, it puts '*Masjid* Babar *Shahi*'. This plot has been shown as parallel to *khasra abadi* plot No. 444 of the earlier (*sabiqa*) record (*i.e.,* of 1861 Settlement) and its present area (*raqba jadid*) is put at 9 *biswas*, 15 *biswansis* and 4 *kachwansis* (0-9-15-4) as compared to the former numbers (number *sabiq*, *i.e.,* 444) area which is shown as 7 *biswas*, 11 *biswansis* and 14 *kachwansis* (0-7-11-14). Under column 6, *i.e.,* the name of the present possessor (*naam qabiz hal*), 'mosque under *waqf*) since the Shahi' *i.e.,* the Mughal age (*masjid waqf ahad-i-Shahi*) and under column 7 (*i.e., qism*/nature) *masjid* has been recorded. At the same time, under columns 12 to 15, it is recorded that Ram Charan Das was the *Mahant* of the site, who was later on, vide file no. 427-6/47, Rai Ganj, dated 26th February 1941, succeeded by *Mahant* Ram Charan Das. This was further duly attested on June 14, 1941. The general statement (*kaifiyat*) notes that there was a *pacca masjid* since the Shahi, *i.e.,* Mughal times named after the deceased Shah Babur, a *pacca chabutra,* some thatched *chhappar* and tinned structures inside the courtyard along with a few trees such as *golar, neem* and *peepal*. Similarly, *khasra abadi* plot No. 586, supposed to be the site of *Shilanyas* laid in November 1989, with an area of 11 *biswas*, 16 *biswansis* and 16 *kachwansis* (0-11-16-16) is shown as *pacca qabristan* known as *Ganj-i-Shahidan*, which is also under '*waqf*' since the Shahi, *i.e.,* Mughal times.

(41) Apart from the above mentioned (vide para No. 38 to 40) 1931 Nazul document available at the Nazul Office, Faizabad, there is another version of the same document which has been widely in circulation and included in the Report of the Delegation of the Members of the Standing Committee of the National Integration Council and Members of the Parliament to Ayodhya under the Chairmanship of Shri S.R. Bommai-1992 A.D. This

document puts the title as *khasra mauza Ramkot* Ayodhya, *pargana haveli* Awadh, tehsil and *zilla* Faizabad as compared to the supposed official document available at the Nazul Office, which, as stated in para No. 38, puts the title as *tarmimi khasra abadi, mauza Kot* Ram Chandra, *pargana haveli* Awadh, tehsil Faizabad, *Zilla* Faizabad. The afore-mentioned *khasra* document included in the S.R. Bommai Report also puts the title of the *mohalla* under column I as Ram*kot*, but unlike the Nazul Office document, it does not put the words '*Masjid Babur Shahi'* against *khasra* plot No. 583. Also realizing the fact that when the 1931 Nazul *khasra* plots number had been put exactly parallel to *khasra* plots number of *khasra abadi* (1861) relating to *Janmasthan*, the areas of these two *khasra* plots had to be identical rather than at variance with each other as recorded in the so-called official 1931 Nazul document. The Nazul *khasra abadi* document (1931) included in the S.R. Bommai Report does not mention the respective areas of the 1861 *khasra abadi* plots and omits the specific sub-column meant for this purpose as provided in the above mentioned official Nazul office document. As such, it does not provide the area of the 1861 *khasra abadi* plot No. 444. All the same, under the column *raqba* (area) of the Nazul plot No. 583, *i.e.,* 9 *biswas,* 15 *biswansis* and 4 *kachwansis* (0-9-15-4), it also mentions the *khasra* plot No. 444 of the *khasra abadi* of 1861 settlement right under the given area. This deliberate summary method of recording is rather misleading so as to give an impression that the area of the *khasra* plot No. 444 of the 1861 settlement *khasra abadi* is also the same. In fact, under a separate column No. 8 meant for *raqba* (area) the area of the Nazul *khasra* plot No. 583 is mentioned again. However, in other respects, the document included in the Bommai Committee Report is similar to the Nazul Office Record. All the same, it is rather inexplicable that when the official *khasra abadi* records (1861-66) do not provide area for any of the *khasra* plots, now could the 1931 Nazul documents, after having presumed *khasra* plot No. 583 being parallel to *khasra* plot No. 444 of the *khasra abadi* (1861), show the latter's recorded area as well. When the recorded areas of the two comparable *khasra* plot numbers were found to be at variance with each other, taking it to be just an 'error', another corrected version of the 1931 Nazul document was prepared which has also been included in the Bommai Committee Report as well. All this casts serious doubt on the authenticity of the so-called 1931 official Nazul document. Moreover, the revenue documents of the later 1936-37 settlement show *khasra* plot No. 159 where upon the disputed structure of *Ramjanmabhoomi*/'Baburi Masjid' stood, with an area of 13 *biswas* (0-13-0-0) only, which, of course, did not take any cognisance of the 1931 Nazul document. There are a number of other Nazul *khasra* plots which have been associated with *waqf* (*waqf ahad-i-Shahi*) or graveyards (*qabristan*). But in many a case, this fact is not borne out by the 1937 settlement *khasra kishtwar*_plots which have been considered to be parallel in full or part to the Nazul numbers by the Survey Commissioner or the Sunni Central Board of *waqf*. The revenue records of the 1937 settlement do not support the contention of the Nazul document with regard to '*waqf*' or *qabristan* for the supposed parallel *khasra* plots. If the Nazul *khasra* plot No. 583 comprising the disputed structure of *Ramjanmabhoomi*/'Baburi Masjid' had been under *waqf* since the Mughal age (*waqf ahad-i-Shahi*), this would have definitely found such description in the revenue records of the 1861, 1893-94 and 1937 settlements in the respective *khasra kishtwar/khata khatauni/khewat* plot considered parallel to the afore-mentioned Nazul number. In fact, in the Nazul document, to have put the words *waqf* (*waqf ahad-i-Shahi*) under column No. 4, *i.e.,* name of the present possessor (*naam qabiz hal*) is contradictory in nature. If it were *waqf* since the Mughal age, how could it be put under the column of current possession? It could have been shown under the column Nos. 4 & 5 relating to ownership or column No. 9 regarding the payment or exemption from *lagaan.*

(42) In fact, the purpose of the Nazul (Municipal) survey and the map prepared in 1931 A.D. was to identify the encroachment made on the Nazul property. Such a survey map cannot take precedence over the regularly conducted revenue settlement

operations and the maps prepared thereupon, especially when the title to land is involved. In its order dated 10.1.1990, the Lucknow Bench of the Allahabad High Court directed the Board of Revenue, U.P. State, to survey the site and submit Report accordingly with the assistance of the Municipal Records and such other records which it considered to be useful and its further order dated 23.5.1990, directed it to execute the commission and locate the plots with reference to documents on record only. The Commissioner, Shri J.P. Srivastava, appointed by the Board of Revenue for the purpose, submitted his report on 25.7.1990 wherein he had located the disputed property with reference to the Nazul map of 1931, even though he conceded that the Nazul map and the Settlement maps were on different scales and that it was not possible to juxtapose the two maps and prepare *Fard Mutabiqat* and correspond the Nazul *khasra* numbers with the settlement *khasra* numbers. All the same, the Commissioner, instead of surveying the land of his own, had just accepted the fresh map supplied by the plaintiff, which in matters of details offered a completely inaccurate position in respect of *Janmasthan*/"Baburi *Mosque*", graveyards, the *Shilanyas* site and various other plots. Such an act on the part of the Commissioner, for having accepted the Plaintiff's map and adopting it as his own official map for submission to the court, was characterised by the latter as "wholly unwarranted". Thereupon, the Hon'ble Court passed another Order on 18th September, 1990 to obtain identification of the disputed property on the spot from the plaintiff, to prepare a plan of the property as indicated by the plaintiffs on the spot and to carry out a survey on the basis of settlement maps of 1861 and 1937 so as to indicate the disputed numbers which cover the property according to the settlement maps of 1861 and 1937.

(43) Contrary to the order of the Lucknow Bench of the Hon'ble Allahabad High Court, the map obtained by the Survey Commissioner from the plaintiff just indicating the boundary of the disputed property by A,B,C,D,E,F,G,H covering 23 plots with Nazul numbers divided into 10 blocks did not identify or locate this property separately as it had not been demarcated

by meats and bounds or fixed wooden pegs along with it. All the same, the Survey Commissioner accepted this map without identification of the property on the spot mainly on the plea that the block comprising the 'mosque'/temple complex, the 'Shilanyas site' and the adjacent block of vacant land was heavily barricaded by multiple rows of iron posts, railings packed with barbed wires and many other type of obstructions and that it was neither possible to go across it or reach any particular location through it or within it. The Survey Commissioner conceded the fact that in the absence of the original 1931 Nazul map in the District Record Room, the measurement and references undertaken by him were based on trace map which was highly defective in respect of demarcation of boundaries of many a plot cited by him, and further that where there was no clear demarcation in the map, it was measured and plotted on the basis of location pointed out by the plaintiffs, which, he considered, indicated the location of the disputed property "with sufficient clarity". Such was the erroneous concept and exercise undertaken by the Survey Commissioner which resulted more in confusion rather than clarity.

(44) As a matter of fact, for the location and indiction of the numbers of the disputed plots, as ordered by the Hon'ble Court, in reference to the 1861 and 1937 settlement maps, the entire procedure adopted by the Survey Commissioner was perverse in character. He thought that all the three maps, *i.e.,* the 1861 and 1937 settlement maps and the 1931 Nazul map, had been prepared on scale of Shahjahani chain of 27.5 yards, even though in fact the settlement maps had been prepared on the double chain, *i.e.,* 55 yards being equivalent to one inch, the Nazul map had been prepared on the half chain whereby full chain comprising 27.5 yards stood for two inches. As such, considering the fact that the Nazul map was four times bigger in size to the settlement maps, he made the former as the base and imposed the settlement maps upon it for the determination of the numbers of the plots/sub-plots in terms of identity and equivalence to each other. In such an unscientific exercise, where he experienced difficulties and found gaps in the parallel identification of the Nazul and settlement plot numbers, he

insisted on the reliance of the trace Nazul map while challenging the authenticity and accuracy of the settlement maps.

(45) As the very procedure of interaction of arcs for the identification of the settlement *khasra* numbers by imposing the settlement map over Nazul map is of doubtful validity, the carving out of the settlement plots overlapping the disputed Nazul *khasra* numbers could never be a correct process. The Survey Commissioner conceded the fact that none of the Nazul plots and settlement plots were similarly bounded and yet when confronted with the difficulty for identical alignment, he opted to regard a *minjumla* (a part of the whole) plot as a plot partitioned theoretically but not physically. All this resulted in inaccurate mapping of the identical Nazul/settlement plots and the Survey Commissioner himself admitted that the spot position was not in conformity with the settlement map. As such, an ill conceived exercise would put both the "most disputed mosque/ temple complex", and the 'Shilanyas site' on the road sites, the Survey Commissioner concluded that the contradiction between the site and the map was "basically on account of inaccuracy in the two settlement maps". He not only challenged the accuracy of the traversed boundaries of the village *Ramkot* in respect of both the settlement maps, he found that "metalled road along the northern boundary of temple/'mosque' complex had been shown on the western boundary of the village before the bend making it consistent with the spot". In fact, the learned Survey Commissioner failed to understand that unlike the 1937 settlement map, in the 1861 settlement map, there is no regular "metalled road" along the northern boundary of the "temple/ mosque complex" which separated the latter on the western boundary of the village from the northern portion covered by the building, also today known as *Janmasthan/Sita Rasoi.*

As such, as already stated in paras Nos. 11, 16 to 18, in the 1861 settlement, the entire complex was named *Janmasthan* and there was no separate "temple/mosque complex" as distinct from the latter. Apart from these fallacies, the worst mistake committed by the Survey Commissioner in his plan for identification of Nazul/settlement plot numbers was that he considered that as parallel to the Nazul map. In the 1937 settlement map, the entire "temple/mosque complex" should have been shown in *khasra* plot No. 160 which itself was wrongly plotted in the 1937 settlement map. Only if the learned Survey Commissioner had proper understanding for co-relating the map plot numbers with the other revenue records of 1937 settlement, viz., *khasra kishtwar, khata khatauni* and *khewat*, he would have realised that the *Ramjanmabhoomi/* 'Baburi *Masjid*' complex falls in *khasra* No. 159 and 160 (a) which have been shown absolutely correctly in the 1937 settlement map.

(46) In fact, for the cadestral survey of the village *Ramkot* and determination of the disputed property, the Survey Commissioner should have based his survey operation upon the 1861 *khasra kishtwar* map in co-ordination with the *hadbast* (1861) and *khasra abadi* (1861-1866) maps as well as the later 1937 *khasra kishtwar* map and thereafter tried to co-relate the plot numbers. For this purpose, it is equally essential to keep in mind the changed numbers and areas of the plots since the 1861 settlement which can well be discerned from the *Fard Mutabiqats*, revenue records comprising *khasra kishtwar, khewat* and *khata khatauni* affixed to the settlement reports or recorded in the intervening period based upon the annual revenue operations. As the Nazul *khasras* (1931) relate only to *abadi* plot Numbers providing an area of each plot and their total number is much larger than the 1861 or 1937 settlement *kishtwar* numbers whose areas are provided separately in the *khasra kishtwar, khata khatauni* and *khewat* records, it is feasible to examine the co-relationship of the settlement plot numbers with the Nazul plot numbers. As the area of each settlement *khasra* plot number is comparatively much larger than the Nazul *abadi khasra* numbers, the latter numbers have to be clubbed in full or parts thereof for determining the identical location with the former. This procedure would clearly bring out the inaccuracies and the unauthentic character of the Nazul (1931) documents.

(47) Having gone through the pros and cons of the entire case, the Hon'ble Court in its judgement on 08.08.1991, even though it refrained from calling the Commissioner's report as 'motivated',

described it as "absurd". It refused to accept the Commissioner's view that correct map and report about *Kot* Ram Chandra were possible only in reference to Nazul map and that the settlement maps were not correctly prepared. In its judgement, it refused to keep the report of the Commissioner on record in the pending case.

(48) As per procedure of the revenue settlement, the *khasra* numbers in respect of *kishtwar, khewat* and *khata khataunis* often undergo a change due to alteration, addition and clubbing for adjustment with the neighbouring plots from one revenue settlement to the other. At times, a change in numbers is effected even during the interregnum of the two settlement operations. However, they are all duly recorded in the Comparative Tables of the *khasra* numbers (*Fard Mutabiqat*) appended in the ensuing settlement report as well as in the relevant *khewat* and *khata khatauni* numbers. As such, since the first Regular Settlement of village *Ram Kot*, *Pargana* Awadh, District Faizabad effected in 1861 A.D. to the 1344 F/ 1936-37 A.D. settlement, the *khasra* numbers had changed three times. The maps of the villages in respect of plots are always prepared in accordance with the *khasra kishtwar* numbers. The *khasra kishtwar, khewat* and *khata khataunis* adopted in the 1344 F/1936-37 A.D. continue to be in vogue in the latest revenue operations 1995-96 A.D. However, the mutations effected during the interregnum have been recorded in the relevant revenue documents.

(49) According to the 1344 F/1936-37 A.D. settlement, the plots of the *Janmasthan* complex have been recorded in the *Saaf khasra* (fair/final *khasra*) documents of village *Kot* Ram Chandra, *Tappa* and *Pargana Haveli* Awadh, Zilla Faizabad. These records provide details in respect of each plot/sub-plot of the village regarding its area, name of *mahal* as per *khata khewat* as to whether under *mahal* Nazul or *mahal* Azhar Hussain (name of the Zamindar); number of the *khata khewat* of the subordinate owners (*malikan-i-matahit*); number of *khata khatauni*, nature of land, *i.e.,* whether *banjar* or under *abadi* or road etc. The *Saaf khasra* documents are also endorsed by the separately maintained *khewat* and *khata*

khatauni records, which apart from the data available from the afore-mentioned *Saaf khasra* document also provide details about the names of the subordinate owners (*malikan-i-matahit*) of the plots/sub-plots, their respective shares, with or without *lagaan*, amount of *lagaan*, if any, nature of land, roads, with or without garden or water resources etc.

As per *Saaf khasra* record, the *Janmasthan* complex comprises *khasra kishtwar* plots No. 159, some portions of No. 160, 158 (road) and 146. The major portion of the *Janmasthan* complex falls under *khasra* plots Nos. 159, 160 [159 and 160 (a)] constituting the site of *Ramjanmabhoomi*-'Baburi Masjid' inclusive of the outer and inner courtyards, 146 (*abadi Sita Rasoi*) and 158. The *khasra* plot No. 158 is recorded as a road which divides the *khasra* plots No. 159 and 160 in the south from the *khasra* plots No. 146 and 147 (R) in the north respectively.

(50) As per *Saaf khasra* (final *khasra/kishtwar*), *khewat* and *khata khatauni* records, *khasra* plots No. 159 and 160 (a) (which constituted the erstwhile disputed structure of *Ramjanmabhoomi*-'Baburi Masjid' inclusive of the premises of the inner and outer courtyard) have been detailed separately. The *khasras* plot No. 159 is declared *banjar* land with an area of 13 *biswas* (0-13-0) and falls under *mahal* Nazul vide *khata* No. I, *khewat matahitdaran* (subordinate owners) No. (5a) 20 and *khata khatauni* No. 58/2. While the superior ownership rests with the Nazul, the subordinate ownership (as *malik matahitdar*) is with Shri Dhanushdhariji Bhagwan Virajman Mandir *Bara Asthan*, Mohalla *Ramkot*, *Shahar* Ayodhya through the *sarwarahkari* of Mahant Raghubar Das, disciple of Ram Manohar Das *Bairagi*, resident of the above temple. In fact, under *khewat* No. 20, the plot No. 159 with an area of 13 *biswas* (0-13-0) is clubbed with eight other plots/ sub-plots No. 55a, 60a, 62, 63a, 199, 202 and 210 with their respective areas without any *lagaan*, all in the subordinate ownership of the afore-mentioned Shri Dhanushdhariji Bhagwan... through *sarwarahkari* of Mahant Raghubar Das. In the *khatauni* record vide *khata* No. I, *khata khatauni* No. 58/2, it has been shown *banjar* (No. 3) and with 13 *biswas*

and has been clubbed with the other *banjar* plots, *i.e.,* 55 and 199 with their respective areas.

The *khasra* sub-plot No. 160a as per afore-mentioned *Saaf khasra, khewat* and *khata khatauni* records, with an area of 3 *biswas*, 13 *biswansis* (0-3-13) is put under *mahal* Nazul vide *khata* No. I, *khewat matahitdaran* No. 21 and *khata khatauni* No. 59/1. In the *khatauni* record vide *khata* No. 1, *khata khatauni* No. 59/1, it has been shown in *abadi* with an area of 3 *biswas,* 13 *biswansis* (0-3-13) as uncultivable land (*gair mumkin*) without (irrigation) water and exempted from the payment of any *lagaan*. The subordinate ownership of the sub-plot as *malik matahit* under the superior ownership of Nazul has been vested in Sita Ram (minor), s/o Kewal Ram, resident of the village and Lachhman Prasad, s/o Sita Ram, caste Kurmi, resident of the village, with one-half (1/2) share each. The details about the other sub-plots of *khasra* plot No. 160, both in the *Janmasthan* complex and non-*Janmasthan* areas have been further stated in para No. 53.

(51) As already stated in paras No. 18, 25-26, 32-34 and 49, the plot along with structure popularly known as *abadi Sita Rasoi*, that lay to the north of *Ramjanmabhoomi*-'Baburi Masjid' across the dividing road (vide *khasra kishtwar* No. 158) had always formed an integral part of the *Janmasthan* complex. Earlier in the 1301 F/1893-94 A.D. settlement, as per *khasra kishtwar* and *khatauni* records, *abadi Sita Rasoi* had been shown in the *mahal* Nazul vide *khasra* sub-plot No. 163/5 with an area of 1 *bigha,* 10 *biswas* (0-10-0) under the subordinate ownership of *Mahant* Kalyan Das. However, the available *khewat* records relating to the subordinate and superior (*ala*) owners (*matahitdaran wa ala*) of the village *Kot* Ram Chandra Ji, No. 132, Form No. p. 18, dated 1342 F/ 1934-35 A.D., *khasra* No. 129, *khewat* No. 1/11 put it in *mahal* Nazul under the subordinate ownership of *Mahant* Ram Kishore Das, disciple (*chela*) Kalyan Das *Bairagi*, resident of *Janmasthan* with an area of 1 *bigha*, 6 *biswas* and 7 *biswansis* (1-6-7). These documents had been signed by the patwari of the village, Ayodhya Prasad, and were later on attested by the *qanungo* of *Pargana Haveli,* Awadh on

9.7.1937. This clearly shows that even though since the 2nd regular settlement of 1301 F/1893-94, there was no regular settlement till 1344 F/1936-37, as per revenue procedure explained in para No. 48, the *khasra* numbers and their areas, etc., had undergone change during the interregnum. This is equally confirmed by the *Fard Mutabiqat* appended to the 1344 F/1936-37 Settlement Report. However, in the latter settlement, for the *abadi Sita Rasoi* plot, the *khasra kishtwar* number is 146 in *mahal* Nazul with the same area, *i.e.,* 1 *bigha*, 7 *biswas*, and 6 *biswansis* (1-7-6) as recorded in the pre-settlement *khasra* plot No. 129. All the same, there has been no change either in the number of this *khasra* plot or in its area since 1936-37 settlement which continued to be the same till date in the annual revenue records.

(52) The *khasra* plot No. 146 situated across the road (vide *khasra* No. 158), to the north of *khasra* plots No. 159 and 160a comprising the monument popularly called *abadi Sita Rasoi*, formed a significant portion of the *Janmasthan* complex. In the 1936-37 settlement, as per revenue records, the *khasra* plot No. 146 vide Nazul *khata* No. 1, *khewat khata* No. (5a) 32, *khata khatauni* No. 70/1 has been shown as a part of *mahal* Nazul with an area of 1 *bigha*, 6 *biswas*, and 7 *biswansis* (1-6-7) under habitation (*abadi*). In the *khewat matahitdaran*, under No. 32, this plot has been clubbed with another *khasra* plot No. 147a and both these *khasra* plots with their respective areas in *mahal* Nazul have been vested in the subordinate ownership of Hari Har Das, disciple of Ram Sharan Das *Bairagi*, resident of *Mandir Janmasthan*, *Ramkot*, *Shahar* Ayodhya.

Apart from this, of the *Janmasthan* complex, *khasra kishtwar* plot No. 158 vide *Saaf khasra* record *khata* No. 2 of *mahal* Azhar Hussain, *khewat* No. 2 and *khata khatauni* No. 155/2 comprising an area of 4 *biswas* (0-4-0-0) has been shown as *pacca* road (*Sarak Pukhta*) which divides *khasra* plots Nos. 159 and 160a in the south from the afore-mentioned *khasra* plot No. 146 in the north. To this path (*rasta*), 3 *biswas* and 9 *biswansis* (0-3-9) have added from the non-*Janmasthan* area from *khasra kishtwar* plot No. 155/2 vide *khata* No. 1, *khata khatauni* No. 4 making the total area of the Path as 7 *biswas* and 9 *biswansis* (0-7-9-0). However, the entire path comprising both the afore-mentioned *Janmasthan* and non-*Janmasthan* areas has been put under *mahal* Azhar Hussain. All the same, mostly significantly, the afore-mentioned path shown in the *khasra kishtwar* map of 1344 F/1936-37 settlement, clearly mentions 'leading to *Janmabhoomi*'. As these words have been written right below the northern boundary line of the *khasra kishtwar* plots Nos. 159 and 160a, this confirms the fact that even till 1937-38 A.D. in the revenue documents, the structure and its premises (comprising both the inner and the outer courtyards) covered by the *khasra kishtwar* plots Nos. 159 and 160a was named as *Janmabhoomi* (*i.e., Janmasthan*) and not as 'Baburi *Masjid*'.

(53) In the 1936-37 settlement, the *khasra kishtwar* plot No. 160 being quite large with five sub-plots covers both the *Janmasthan* and non-*Janmasthan* areas and falls under both *mahal* Nazul and *mahal* Azhar Hussain. As already stated in para No. 50, the sub-plot No. 160a comprising an area of 3 *biswas* and 13 *biswansis* (0-3-13) under *mahal* Nazul and the subordinate ownership of Sita Ram and Lachhman Prasad constituted a part of the core area of the disputed structure of *Ramjanmabhoomi*-'Baburi *Masjid*'. The *khasra* sub-plot No. 160b with an area of 3 *bighas* and 12 *biswas* (3-12-0) has been put under *mahal* Nazul and *abadi* vide Nazul *khata* No. 1 and *khata khatauni* No. 35. As distinct from the Nazul sub-plots, *i.e., khasras* Nos. 160a and 160b, the other sub-plots bearing *khasras* Nos. 160c, 160d and 160e, as stated further, have been put under *mahal* Azhar Hussain. In fact, some portions of the *Janmasthan* complex under *abadi* and exempted from payment of rent (*lagaan*) also fall in these sub-plots. The *khasra* sub-plot Nos. 160c under *mahal* Azhar Hussain vide *khata khewat* No. 2, *khata khatauni* No. 19/1, *khewat* No. 10 with an area of 7 *biswas* and 3 *biswansis* (0-7-3-0) under habitation (*abadi*) and without payment of any rent (*lagaan*) is in the subordinate ownership (as *malik matahit*) of Rameshwar Das, disciple Gopal Das *Bairagi*,

resident of *Mandir Ramkot*, *Shahar* Ayodhya. The *khasra* sub-plot No. 160e, under *mahal* Azhar Hussain vide *khata khewat* No. 1 *khata khewat matahitdaran* No. 4, *khata khatauni* No. 7/1 with an area of 3 *biswas* and 17 *biswansis* (0-3-17-0) under *abadi* and without payment of any rent (*lagaan*) has been recorded in the subordinate ownership (as *malik matahit*) of Raghubar Das. The *khasra* sub-plot No. 160e being under *mahal* Azhar Hussain vide *khata* No. 2 and *khata khatauni* No. 14 has an area of 1 *bigha,* 6 *biswas,* and 7 *biswansis* (1-6-7-0) (as per *kacha* village *bigha*).

(54) In the 1344 F/1936-37 A.D. Settlement Report of the *khasra* plot numbers of *kishtwar, khewat khatauni* associated with the *Janmasthan* complex in the *mahals* of Nazul and Azhar Hussain as detailed above, there is no area in any of the plots/ sub-plots which has been shown as graveyard (*qabristan*) or in *waqf.* The settlement report has also provided a separate detailed list of the *khasra* plots along with their respective areas which are declared graveyards (*qabristan*) under *waqf* but there is no *khasra* plot/sub-plot of the *Janmasthan* complex which fall in this category.

(55) The map of *khasra kishtwar* of the village *Ramkot,* dated 1344 F/1937 A.D. of the settlement, depicts the territorial boundaries of the *khasra* plots of the village along with symbols of various categories, viz., *banjar, abadi,* roads, temple (*Mandir*), graveyards (*qabristan*) and *pacca* wells, etc. Of the *khasra* plot numbers of the *Janmasthan* complex No. 159 with a symbol of *banjar* land; No. 160 with symbols of *abadi* and a temple in the north-east of the plot (*Shakshi Gopal* Temple) along with a well to its east; No. 158, a *pacca* road; No. 146 (*abadi Sita Rasoi*), *abadi* along with a temple in the north-west and two wells. In none of the plots/sub-plots of the *Janmasthan* complex, there is any symbol of a graveyard (*qabristan*), even though symbols of graveyards have been shown in the other and neighbourly *khasra* plot number, *i.e.,* 172, 173, 168 and 169 etc.

(56) The learned Survey Commissioner's self-conceited remarks in his Supplementary Report (1991) about the 1344 F/1936-37

settlement map are not only completely fallacious but self-contradictory as well. He maintains that during the "regular settlement of 1937 meticulous field survey was not conducted by the officials" as the latter just adopted the field boundaries of 1861 map. He further comments that for village *Ramkot*, the district revenue officials from *lekhpal* upwards did not perform their statutory duties, many field boundaries were just imaginary for they did not correspond to the spot and the mistake of earlier 1861 settlement was continued. He further contends that the district administration as well was not aware of the serious mistakes in the village map. At the same time, the afore-mentioned Survey Report concedes that consequent on the construction of new roads since 1861, changes in *abadi* plots were made, the *zamindari mahals* were well identified and that in contrast to 1861 settlement, the 1937 settlement has also incorporated the *khewat* records in respect of proprietary rights. As a matter of fact, apart from *khasra kishtwar* map, as already stated in para No. 49-53, the 1344 F/1936-37 settlement has also incorporated complete *khasra kishtwar, khewat* and *khatauni* records comprising both Nazul *mahals* and *zamindari mahals*. As these records provide complete data about the areas and numbers of the plots/sub-plots, any reading/delineation of the field boundaries provided in the *khasra kishtwar* map has to be essentially done in co-ordination with the latter categories of the revenue records. As such, the learned Survey Commissioner's remarks about the 1936-37 settlement as well as the 1861 settlement betrays complete ignorance about the operation of the settlement work.

(57) In view of the position as available from the above mentioned original records of the 1344 F/1936-37 settlement of the village *Ram Kot*, the Nazul records of 1931 A.D., which have altogether different *khasra* number of the plots unaccompanied by any table of equivalent *khasra* numbers (*Fard Mutabiqat*) are absolutely unauthentic with regard to *waqf* land vide *khasra* plot No. 583 and *qabristan* land vide *khasra* plot No. 586 and other *khasra* plot numbers which have been considered to be a part of the *Janmasthan* complex. As already noted, even the second revised Report of the Survey Commissioner, based

on the above mentioned Nazul document comprising so-called amended *khasra* numbers (1931) was rejected by the Lucknow Bench of the Hon'ble High Court of Allahabad on 08.08.1991. It is not without justification that in the Ordinance issued by the President of India on January 07, 1993, titled "The Acquisition of Certain Area at Ayodhya Ordinance, 1993 No. 8 of 1993" vide Registration No. DL-33004/92, the areas acquired in village *Kot* Ram Chandra in Ayodhya and in the adjacent villages of Awadh Khas and Jalwanpur in *Pargana, Haveli* Awadh, Tehsil Faizabad Sadar, District Faizabad, State of Uttar Pradesh, describe the areas based upon the *khasra kishtwar* numbers of the 1936-37 settlement continued till date rather than the unauthentic Nazul (1931) *khasra* numbers adopted by the Sunni Central Board of *Waqf* in its 1961 suit against Gopal Singh Visharad and others (vide para No. 28 of the Plaint) which is at present pending before the Lucknow Bench of the Hon'ble Allahabad High Court. The description of the area in the schedule of the Ordinance [Section 2 (a)] provides data about the area of the entire *Janmasthan* complex covered by *khasra kishtwar* plots Nos. 146, 158, 159 and 160. The area of the proper *Ramjanmabhoomi*-'Baburi *Masjid*' (including the premises of inner and outer courtyards of such structure) is recorded under *khasra* plot No. 159 with 13 *biswas* (0-13-0) and a part of *khasra* plot No. 160, *i.e.,* 160 M whereas the total area of *khasra* plot No. 160 is put at 3 *bighas*, 11 *biswas*, 4 *biswansis* and 6 *kachwansis* (3-11-4-6). However, later on under the Act of Parliament (Act No. 33 of 1993), the measurement is reckoned in accordance with the standard *bigha* of the district of Faizabad, U.P., made up of 3025 sq. yards which resulted in slight increase in the areas of *khasra* plots Nos. 159 and 160 relating to *Ramjanmabhoomi*-'Baburi *Masjid*'. As such, the area of *khasra* plot No. 159 is put as 13 *biswas*, 8 *biswansis* (0-13-8) whereas the total area of *khasra* plot No. 160 acquired amounts to 5 *bighas*, 13 *biswas* (5-13-0) resulting in an increase of 2 *bighas*, 1 *biswa*, 15 *biswansis* and 4 *kachwanis* (2-1-15-4). Of course, as stated, the *Rama janamabhoomi*-'Baburi *Masjid*' area is denoted fully by *khasra* plots Nos.

159 and 160 (M)/160 (a), *i.e.,* only a part of *khasra* plot No. 160.

(58) Since the 1344 *Fasli* (F) /1936-37 A.D. settlement, the annual revenue records of the village *Ramkot* pertaining to *khewat* and *jamabandi, i.e., khata khatauni* have been maintained in the Tehsil office/District Record Office, Collectorate, District Faizabad for all the years till date. For all the *khasra* plots of the *Janmasthan* complex, their serial numbers, along with their respective areas as well as the position regarding the ownership whether under *mahal* Nazul or under the *mahal* of a particular zamindar, are the same as in the last settlement (1936-37), excepting that the entries of the names of the succeeding subordinate owners (*malikan-i-matahit*) *mahants*/ other persons or the succeeding Zamindars of the *mahal* have been made in the relevant revenue documents. In fact, the present record of rights and the *khasra* plots number, etc., were recorded in 1344 F/1936-37 and since then no further settlement (*bandobast*) has been done in village *Kot* Ram Chandra, *Pargana Haveli* Awadh, Tehsil and District Faziabad (U.P.). As such, the same *bandobast* (1936-37 Settlement) has continued to be in vogue till date. As a matter of fact, even though ever since 1861 settlement, the revenue records as well as the *hadbast/abadi/khasra kishtwar* maps continued to specifically refer to the relevant plots as associated with *Janmasthan/Janmabhoomi* or the road leading to *Janmasthan/Janmabhoomi* right till 1936-37 settlement. Thereafter in the annual revenue records, no specific entry has been made in the name of either 'Baburi *Masjid'* or Janma Bhoomi. All the same, the 1397 F/1989-90 A.D. revenue records of *Graam Kot* Ram Chandra do refer to the fact that *Janma Bhoomi*/'Baburi *Masjid*' falls in the *khasra* plot Nos. 159 and a portion of *khasra* plot No. 160 (*i.e.,* 160 M, 160a) wherein entries have been made in the name of Sri Dhanushdhari Bhagwan Bara Asthan Ayodhya and Sita Ram Sharan respectively.

(59) The available revenue records for the years 1393-1394 F/1985-87 A.D. as well as the documents covering the years 1397 F/1989-90 continued till 1398 F/1991-92 A.D. clarify the position

of the disputed structure, *i.e., Ramjanmabhoomi*/'Baburi Masjid' (including the premises of the inner and outer courtyards) as it stood on 06.12.1992 A.D. when it was demolished. The nature of land rights relating to the *khasra kishtwar* plots No. 159 and 160 M (*i.e.,* 160/160a) which covered the site of the above mentioned disputed structure as it stood on 06.12.1992 is rather the same as it stood in the 1936-37 settlement. From the years 1393 F/1985-86 A.D. to 1397 F/1989-90 A.D. in the *khewat* records *khasra kishtwar* plot No. 159 vide *khata khewat* No. 22 has been shown with an area of 13 *biswas* (0-13-0) as *banjar* land. The superior ownership is with the Nazul *Ala* whereas the subordinate ownership (*malik matahit*) rests with Sri Dhanushdhari Bhagwan Bara Asthan Ayodhya, *sarwarahkar Mahant* Vaish Nath Prasada Char disciple (*chela*), Ram Kripal Prasada Char. For this plot, the same position is reiterated in the revenue records for the years 1397 F/1989-90 A.D. to 1399 F/1991-92 A.D. As regards *khasra kishtwar* sub-plot No. 160 M (*i.e.,* 160/160a), in the year 1393-94 F/1985-87 A.D. as per *khata khewat* No. 23, it has been shown under *mahal* Nazul with an area of 3 *biswas*, 13 *biswansis*, (0-3-13) under *abadi* (habitation). The subordinate owners (*malikan-i-matahit*) of this sub-plot are Sita Ram Sharan, s/o. Kewal Ram and Lachhman Prasad, s/o. Sita Ram (each with one half share). For this plot, same position is reiterated in the revenue records of the years 1397-99 F/1989-92 A.D. as well. In *khasra khewat* No. 23 and *khatauni* No. 54/1, it has again been put under Nazul *Ala* with an area of 3 *biswas* and 13 *biswansis* (0-3-13) under *abadi* (habitation) vide column 19 of the *khasra* and is vested in the subordinate ownership (*malik-i-matahit*) of Sita Ram Sharan, s/o. Kewal Ram and Lachhman Prasad, s/o. Sita Ram.

As such, the disputed structure, *i.e., Ramjanmabhoomi*-'Baburi *Masjid*' (including the premises of both the inner and outer courtyards) covered by *khasra kishtwar* plot Nos. 159 and 160 M (160 a) with total area of 16 *biswas*, 13 *biswansis* (0-16-13) has been, ever since the 1936-37 settlement and the subsequent available revenue records till 1397-1399 F/1989-

92 A.D., under *mahal* Nazul vested in the superior ownership of Nazul *Ala* and the subordinate ownership (*malikan-i-matahit*) of Sri Dhanushdhariji Bhagwan Bara Asthan, Ayodhya through the *sarwarkari* of the Hindu *mahants* and other afore-mentioned Hindu *mahants* as subordinate owners. As per revenue records, no part of *khasra kishtwar* plots No. 159 and 160 M (160 a) comprising the disputed structure, *i.e., Ramjanmabhoomi*-'Baburi *Masjid*' (including the premises of both the inner and outer courtyards) has been shown in *waqf* or *muafi* or associated with any *qabristan* (graveyard).

(60) For the years 1397-99 F/1989-92 A.D., apart from the disputed structure, *i.e., Ramjanmabhoomi*/'Baburi *Masjid*' (including the premises of both the *inner* and *outer courtyards*) *covered* by *khasra kishtwar* plots Nos. 159 and 160 M (160a) as already stated in para No. 59, the remaining portions of the *Janmasthan* complex fall under *khasra kishtwar* plots Nos. 160 and 158 and 146. In fact, the position is the same as it stood in the 1344 F/1936-37 settlement which has been stated in the paras No. 49-56. The detailed position in respect of *khasra kishtwar* plot No. 160 is explained further in para No. 61. However, for *khasra kishtwar* plot No. 146 comprising *abadi Sita Rasoi* across the road to the north of the disputed structure of *Ramjanmabhoomi*—'Baburi *Masjid'*, the 1989-92 revenue records just reiterate the 1937-38 settlement position and vide *khasra khewat* No. 35 put it under *mahal* Nazul with an area of 1 *bigha*, 6 *biswas*, and 7 *dhur* (1-6-7) in the subordinate ownership (as *malik matahit*) of Hari Har Das, disciple Ram Saran Das, resident *Janmasthan*, Ayodhya.

(61) In the 1393-97 F/1985-86 to 1397 F/1989-90 revenue records, the position of the *khasra kishtwar* plot No. 160 remains the same as earlier in the 1344 F/1936-37 settlement stated in para No. 53. In fact, *khasra* No. 160 being a large plot measuring 5 *bighas* and 13 *biswas* (5-13-0), covers both *Janmasthan* and non-*Janmasthan* areas and falls both under *mahal* Nazul and *mahal* Azhar Hussain. Three *bighas* and 12 *biswas* (3-12-0) vide *khatauni* No. 28 are declared Nazul *Ala* and vide column No. 19 of the *khasra* plots. All numbers under Nazul

have been entered under *abadi*. In this *mahal* Nazul *Sarkar*, as already stated in para No. 59, three *biswas* and 13 *biswansis* (0-3-13-0) vide *khasra* plot No. 160a, *khatauni* No. 54/1 and *khewat* No. 23 under *abadi* have been entered in the name of (Sita Ram Saran, s/o. Kewal Ram, and Lachhman Prasad, s/o. Sita Ram) as subordinate owners (*malikan-i-matahit*). In the *khasra* plot No. 160, as distinct from the *mahal* Nazul, the details about the entries of the areas in the names of respective subordinate owners (*malikan-i-matahit*) under *mahal* Azhar Hussain have also been provided. In *mahal* Azhar Hussain, as per *khatauni* records, there are three entries, viz., 3 *biswas* and 17 *biswansis* (0-3-17-0) vide *khatauni* No. 5 in the name of Awadh Behari, 1 *bigha*, 6 *biswas* and 7 *biswansis* (1-6-7-0) vide *khatauni* No. 9/2 in the name of Ishtiaq Ahmed, etc., and 7 *biswas* and 3 *biswansis* (0-7-3-0) vide *khata khatauni* No. 13/1 in the name of Awadh Behari (2nd entry in his name). In the *khatauni* records, all these entries have been put under *abadi*. However, the *khewat* records from 1393-97 F/1985-86 to 1989-90 follow the 1344 F/1936-37 settlement pattern and mention the numbers of the sub-plots of *khasra* plot No. 160 as well which can be well identified on a map. As such, the sub-plots, *i.e.,* 160c vide *khata khatauni* No. 11, 160d vide *khata khewat* No. 4 as well as 160e vide *khata khewat* No. 9 have been shown in the subordinate ownerships (as *malik matahits*) of Awadh Behari Das, disciple (*chela*), Rameshwar Das, *Ramkot*, Ayodhya with total area of 11 *biswas* (0-11-0-0) (both for sub-plots 160c and 160d) and Ishtiaq Ahmed, s/o. Sarfaraz Ahmed etc., for sub-plot No. 160e with an area of 1 *bigha*, 6 *biswas* and 7 *biswansis* (1-6-7-0) respectively. Significantly, all the above mentioned sub-plots of *khasra kishtwar* plot No. 160 as per revenue records, have been recorded under *abadi* and no area of any of the sub-plots has been shown as graveyard (*qabristan*) or under (*waqf*).

(62) As per revenue records, the *Shilanyas* site on which the foundation of the proposed construction of *Ramjanmabhoomi* Mandir was laid by Sri *Ramjanmabhoomi* Nyas in November, 1989 with the consent of the Government of India and *karseva* was performed on 30th October, 1990 and in June-July, 1992,

falls in *khasra* plot No. 160 M. In the ongoing and pending suit (now O.O.S. 4 of 1989) between the Sunni Central Board of *Waqf* and other Vs. Gopal Singh Visharad and others before the Lucknow Bench of the Allahabad High Court, the contention of the Plaintiff that the *Shilanyas* site identifiable with the plot No. 586 of Nazul *khasra abadi* (1931), had been a graveyard (*qabristan*) called *Ganj-i-Shahidan* and had as well been under *waqf* since the *Shahi* (Mughal) period, is not tenable. Based on the unauthentic character of the so-called amended *abadi khasra* record (1931) of the Nazul Department, similar assertions made by the Personal Law Board Working Committee, All Indian Baburi *Masjid* Action Committee and various other political organizations for holding the *Shilanyas* site as a part of the graveyard and *waqf* land, are equally fallacious. The character and deficiency of the 1931 Nazul amended *abadi khasra* plots has already been stated in detail in paras No. 36-41. At the same time, as also stated in paras No. 42-47, the Lucknow Bench of the Hon'ble Allahabad High Court has twice (23-5-1995 and 08.08.1991) rejected and refused to keep on record the report of the Survey Commissioner regarding the identification of the 1931 Nazul *khasra* plots number in relation to the 1861/1893 settlements *khasra kishtwar* plots of village *Kot* Ram Chandra mainly on the ground that the report was defective and not prepared according to law. It has also been stated in paras No. 49-61 that in the 1344 F/1936-37 settlement and the subsequent annual revenue records till 1397 F/1989-90 A.D. of all the five sub-plots, *i.e.,* 160a and 160e of the *khasra kishtwar* plot No. 160, there is not a single sub-plot which has been associated with graveyard (*qabristan*) or *waqf* land. All these sub-plots have been shown under *abadi*. In fact, for all issues relating to land rights, only the settlement reports and the annual revenue records are the proper records. A perusal of the records in respect of holdings in the village *Kot* Ram Chandra since 1301 *Fasli*/1893 A.D. settlement, even the Nazul Department's the so-called revised *khasra* (1931 A.D.) and the 3rd Regular Settlement of 1344 *Fasli*/1936-37 shows that there have been numerous mutations, even in respect of the desolate graveyards (*qabristan*) areas. All these amendments have to be discerned carefully as reflected in the relevant columns of the varying categories of the revenue records. Since the 1936-37 settlement, all amendments/mutations have been recorded in the yearly *khata khataunis* and *khewats*. The *Shilanyas* site falls under *khasra* No. 160 M under *abadi* and in July-December, 1981 A.D., the entries in the revenue documents stood in the name of *Mahant* Abhiram Das. After the death of Abhiram Das as per latter's will, the revenue entry was made in the name of his disciple *Mahant* Dharam Das, who further bequeathed all his legal rights of the plot to Sri Ramanandacharya Shivaramacharya of Sri *Ramjanmabhoomi* Nyas under registered deed, dated 29th April, 1986 as *Ramjanmabhoomi* Sthal for the proposed construction of the temple. All this is clear from the revenue documents/registered deed in the sub-Registrar's court as well.

(63) The concept of division of the courtyard of the disputed structure (Sri *Ramjanmabhoomi*-'Baburi *Masjid*') as underlined in the Government of India's White Paper on Ayodhya (Febuary-1993), the Acquisition of Certain Area at Ayodhya Act, 1993 (No. 33 of 1993), dated 3rd April, 1993 and Reference made by the President of India to the Supreme Court under Article 143 of the Constitution of India, unto inner and outer courtyards of the disputed structure, is not at all supported by the revenue records or the records of rights stated therein. However, as explained later, these terms have been used just for the convenience of describing the premises of the disputed structure with two parts, *i.e.,* the site of the proper structure and its courtyard.

(64) As already stated in para 10, the division of the *Janmasthan* site into inner one for the site of the disputed structure and the outer portion comprising Ram *Chabutra* and other places of Hindu worship was effected by the British Government for the purpose of law and order and that according to the then British Reports (as stated in paras No. 9, 11-12) the possession of the entire premises of *Janmasthan* prior to the establishment of the British rule in Awadh (1856 A.D.) had rested with the Hindu *mahants*. However, apart from the proper site of the

disputed structure (Sri *Ramjanmabhoomi*-'Baburi Masjid') there was only one courtyard known as courtyard of the disputed structure stretching on three sides, viz., east (front), north and west whereas the southern site comprised the back side slope of the disputed structure.

(65) There are three Commission Reports along with plans/maps attached to the judicial records which spell out the details of the outer courtyard. These pertain to the Suit of *Mahant* Raghubar Das (Plaintiff) Vs. Secretary of State and Saiyyad Asghar (Defendants) dated 6th December, 1885; the Regular Suit No. 95 of 1941 by *Mahant* Ram Charan Das (Plaintiff) Vs. *Mahant* Dass and others-Defendants, dated 18.4.1941 and finally, the Regular suit No. 2 of 1950 by Gopal Singh Visharad-Plaintiff Vs. Zahur Ahmed and others-Defendants, dated 25.5.1950. Of these, the last report dated 1950 by Shiv Shankar Lal, Pleader/Commissioner is the most comprehensive which has provided details about the eastern and northern gates named "Hanumant Dwar" and "Singh Dwar" respectively, the Arch on the two *kasauti* stone pillars containing images of 'Jai' and 'Vijay' engraved thereon; at the eastern gate, a fixed stone slab on the ground of the gate containing the inscription with "Sri Janma Bhoomi Nitya Yatra" and a big coloured picture of Hanumanji, the top image of Garud on the "Singh Dwar" gate and with flooring on the northern and eastern sides marked by letters 'CHJKDCO' a *Bhandara* (kitchen/store room) to the south, further south Ram *Chabutra* (7'x21'x4') having idols of Ram and Jaanaki and at the southern eastern corner, a joint *neem* and *peepal* tree surrounded by a semi-circular *pacca* platform on which marble idols of Panch Mukh Mahadev, Parvati, Ganesh and Nandi were placed. Most significantly, on the eastern floor of the 'Singh Dwar', there was a *pacca* platform (8'x 9') called "*Sita Rasoi*" (mentioned as *Kaushalya Rasoi* by the Government of India's White Paper on Ayodhya) with a *pacca chulha* along with *chakla* and *belan* and to its east, four pairs of marble foot-prints of Ram, Lakshman, Bharat and Shatrughna. The entire structure was surrounded by *Parikrama* (circumambulation), about 20' below on the eastern side and 10' below on the *pacca* road on the northern side.

(66) As per afore-mentioned Commissioner's Report, dated 25.5.1950, the *pacca* courtyard in front of the inner (main) building, *i.e.,* the disputed structure (*Ramjanmabhoomi*-'Baburi *Masjid*') was enclosed by iron bars and at the end of this courtyard, the 14 stairs led to the roof of the building. There were three arched gates of the building whereas the central gate had a *chhajjaa* projected roof over the arch comprising a slab (with images of Hindi deities on the reverse side) taken from the erstwhile Hindu temple demolished by Mir Baqi in 1528 A.D. The three arches rested on 12 black *kasauti* stone pillars, some pillars with *Kamal* (lotus) flowers thereon, other with images of Shankar Bhagwan in Tandav Nritya, Hanumanji and Lord Krishna engraved therein.

(67) The Government of India's White Paper on Ayodhya, Febuary-1993, (paras No. 2.7, 2.12, 2.13, Chapter II) refers to Hindu structure in the outer courtyard of the *Ramjanmabhoomi*-'Baburi *Masjid'*, especially Ram *Chabutra* and *Kaushalya Rasoi* (i.e, *Sita Rasoi*), which had existed as places of worship "during the periods of Muslim and British rule". The White Paper makes a categorical statement that some survey records of 1807-14 mention the disputed site marked as '*Yanmasthan*', *i.e., Janmasthan*. Based on the White Paper's description as well as that of the Government of India's Ordinance (1993) (later on Act of Parliament) for the Acquisition of Certain Area at Ayodhya (vide Registration No. DL-33004/92, No. 8 of 1993) relating to the inner and outer courtyards of the disputed structure of *Ramjanmabhoomi*-'Baburi *Masjid'*, the President of India in the Reference to the Supreme Court under Article 143(1) of the Constitution also posed a similar question. The reference ran as, "Whereas a dispute has arisen whether a Hindu temple or any Hindu religious structure existed prior to the construction of the structure (including the premises of the inner and outer yards of such structure), commonly known as the *Ramjanmabhoomi*-'Baburi *Masjid'*, in the area in which the structure stood in a village *Kot* Ram Chandra in Ayodhya..........").

(68) Even though the Hon'ble Supreme Court of India declined to answer the afore-mentioned Reference made by the President

of India under Article 143(1) and did not take up the case on merit, in its judgement dated October 24, 1994, it accepted the viewpoint of the Government's White Paper on Ayodhya (vide Background Chapter) that the Hindu places of worship like the Ram *Chabutra* and *Kaushalya Rasoi* (*Sita Rasoi*), etc., had existed in the premises of the outer courtyard all through the 'Muslim' and British periods. The Hon'ble court observed that "A structure called the Ram *Chabutra* stood on the disputed site within the courtyard of the disputed structure" and further remarked that the "the worship of the idols installed at the Ram *Chabutra* by Hindu devotees in general, had been performed for a considerable time without any objection by the Muslims to its worship at this place and this was beyond controversy."

(69) Notwithstanding the afore-mentioned judgement of the Supreme Court being on record, the Sunni Central Board of *Waqf* in its amended Plaint vide Misc. plaint/suit No. 4/1987 of 1955 in (O.O.S. No. 4 of 1989) in the suit of Sunni Central Board of *Waqf* Vs. Gopal Singh Visharad and other pending in the High Court of Judicature at Allahabad, Lucknow Bench, Lucknow, the plaintiff has sought for an addition of clause (bb) to the original Plaint whereby "the defendants 23 and 24 (*i.e.,* Gopal Singh Visharad and others) be commanded to hand over the property in dispute including the land of the inner and outer courtyard of the masjid and the graveyard land appurtenant thereto and described in the Schedule 'A' of the Plaint by removing the unauthorised structures erected thereon in violation of the orders of this Hon'ble Court and the Hon'ble Supreme Court". Here in the amended Plaint, the words "the land of the inner and outer courtyard of the mosque" have not only been left undefined but being extremely vague and indefinite leave lot of scope for further manipulation for the identification of the property. The Plaint while describing the property in dispute (vide para 2) states: "in the sketch map attached, wherein main construction of the said mosque is shown by letters A,B,C,D and land adjoining....shown in the sketch its ancient graveyard covered by the graves of the Muslims who lost their lives in the battle between Emperor

Babur and the previous ruler of Ajudhya. They are situated in Mohalla *Kot* Ram Chandra, also known as Ram*kot*." Such a statement is absurd as there is no historical evidence on record to show that any battle was fought over there between Emperor Babur and the then ruler of Ayodhya resulting in the graveyard of the Muslims killed in the battle in *Kot* Ram Chandra. It has already been clarified in paras Nos. 34-35, 54-55, 59 and 61-62 that as per revenue records, at least since the settlement of 1301 F/1893, there are no graveyards situate in the *Janmasthan* area. The very statement that the graveyards "are situated in Mohalla *Kot* Ram Chandra, also known as Ram*kot*", is extremely vague as Ram*kot* denotes the entire revenue village of *Pargana* Awadh and *Mohalla Kot* Ram Chandra, named after the village, denotes the main road stretching from Hanuman Garhi in the east to the *Janmasthan* in the north-west. As already stated in paras No. 35 and 55, there were, of course, graveyards in the other *khasra kishtwar* plot numbers which have nothing to do with the *Janmasthan* complex. Even the *Ganj-i-Shahidan* graveyard which came into being in the wake of the Hindu-Muslim pitched battle in 1855 A.D. is outside the area of the *Janmasthan* complex. Above all, even the revised Plaint is based upon the 1931 Nazul plot numbers, which, as already stated in paras No. 36-47 are absolutely unauthentic in character. As such, any determination and identification of "the land of the inner and outer courtyard of the mosque" is bound to be completely fallacious. As already stated vide paras Nos. 15, 22, 24-26, 28-29, 35 and 52, ever since the 1861 settlement, the revenue records inclusive of the maps do not mention or indicate any 'mosque' on the disputed land and insist on calling the disputed structure as only *Janmasthan/Janma Bhoomi*. All the same, in view of the latest judgement of the Hon'ble Supreme Court cited in para No. 68, any claim of the plaintiff in the revised Plaint, at least, on the 'outer courtyard' of the disputed structure becomes redundant and infructuous.

(70) As a matter of fact, according to the revenue records, the area supposed to be comprising the premises of the inner and outer courtyards of the disputed structure (*Ramjanmabhoomi-*

'Baburi Masjid'), as spelt out in paras Nos. 50, 57-59 and 63-64, fall under the *khasra kishtwar* plots Nos. 159 and 160 (M) which do not take any cognisance of the division of the courtyard, of the disputed structure into inner and outer courtyards. As already stated in paras Nos. 17, 22, 31-33, 49-51 and 59-60, ever since the 1861 settlement, the revenue records mention the ownership of the entire *Janmasthan* complex in the name of the Hindu *mahants*. Also, as spelt out in the afore-mentioned paras, as per 1936-37 settlement and the subsequent annual revenue records till 1397 F-1399 F/1989-90 and 1991-92 A.D., *khasra* plots No. 159 and 160 (M), claimed in the suit by the Sunni Central Board of *Waqf* as disputed property show the superior ownership with the Nazul and as *malikan-i-matahit*, the subordinate ownership lies with Sri Dhanushdhariji Bhagwan, Virajman, Mandir Bara Asthan, *Mohalla* Ram *Kot*, *Shahar* Ayodhya and the Hindu *mahants/ bairagis, i.e.,* Sita Ram Sharan, s/o Kewal Ram as well as Lachhman Prasad, s/o Sita Ram respectively.

(71) ***Unauthorised Interpolations in Revenue Records:***— In the settlement report of 1861 A.D., interpolations/additions have been effected in certain columns of the *khasra kishtwar* folios. In village Ram*kot*, the total number of the *khasra kishtwar* plots is 167 and as per proforma, there are 16 columns for each *khasra* plot. The first four columns record (i) the serial number, (ii) name of the field (*abadi* etc.), (iii) name of *thok/ patti* (nature of subordinate agency for revenue collection), (iv) name, lineage and caste of the owner (*naam wa waldiyat zaat malik*) respectively. The serial number of *Janmasthan* is plot no. 163 with specific description under the columns followed by 9 sub-plots with required description under each column. In the copy of the 1861 settlement report, available at the District Record Office (*Muhhafaz Khana*) Faizabad under column No. 2, to the original recording of *abadi Janmasthan*, 'and *juma masjid*') have been added. Under column No. 3 to the words *taraf nazul*, 'and *muafi*' have been added and under column No. 4 to the words *Sarkar Bahadur* 'and Azhar Hussain' have been added.

Further Evidence for Interpolations may be submitted as under:

(i) Under column 2, the words *abadi Janmasthan* are in thick hand-writing. As there was no space below this for writing in a similar way, a small 'wa' denoting 'and' has been put to the right of *Janmasthan* and '*juma masjid*' has been put above towards the left of *abadi*. The very crude construction of the sentence shows the later insertions of the above words of 'wa' and '*juma masjid*'. If these words had been written abnitio, the correct version of the sentence should have read as '*abadi Janmasthan wa Juma Masjid*', and the thickness/thinness of the words written by the same reed pen should have been uniform.

(ii) In the 1861 settlement copy of the Tehsil Office under column No. 2 *abadi Janmasthan* had been written in thick bold hand and as no space was available for further addition in the manner done in the District record, the words 'and *juma masjid*' have been inserted below it. But for want of space these words have been put in thinner manner so as to disturb the entire symmetry of the entries made therein.

(iii) The Tehsil Office copy of 1861 settlement does not carry any incorporation of the words 'and *muafi*' 'and Azhar Hussain' under column No. 3 & 4 respectively as in the case of the District Record Office copy.

(iv) The second settlement of 1301 *Fasli*/1893-94 A.D. in the *khasra kishtwar* record, though carrying the same *khasra* No. 163, due to clubbing, is divided into 5 sub-plots instead of 9 sub-plots as earlier in the 1861 settlement report. But it does not record the name of '*jama masjid*' nor does it put '*muafi*' under the relevant columns, which have been shown only under Sarkar Bahadur Nazul. However, in sub-plot No. 163/3 with an area of 11 *biswas* (0-11-0-0) Azhar Hussain and Tahir Hussain have been put as *mahaldars* whereas Mahant Balram Das has been accorded as subordinate owner (*malik matahit*).

(v) In many a other *khasra kishtwar* plot numbers of the 1861 settlement record of the District Record Office, e.g., 16, 21, 25, 29, 32 and 167, there are clear instances of tampering, rubbing of the original entries and over-writing and even striking off of the original words and substituting them with others. Ordinarily, such changes are never made in the official revenue records and even when any change has to be effected for the correction of an error, the original words are distinctly struck off so as to be substituted by other words above it. But rubbing off is never done.

(vi) Another evidence for determining the fact as to whether it is a correction of an error by the scribe himself or a later interpolation/alteration is the ink whether thick or medium or thin, as well as the variation in the handwriting of the letters/ words, if any. In the 1861 settlement document of the District Record Office, for *khasra kishtwar* plot No. 163, for all the columns, quite thick black ink has been used and the handwriting is also uniform with the use of the same *qalm* (reed pen). The thickness of the ink, words and style of writing is uniform. But for the words 'and Azhar Hussain' put below the words the words of '*Sarkar Bahadur*' in column No. 4 are absolutely dim in ink. Thereafter, the description about all the other sub-plots (*goshas*) is again written in thick black ink. At the same time, for all the folios/*khasra* plot numbers following *khasra* plot No. 163 are written in equally black thick ink and uniform handwriting excepting *khasra* plot No. 167 wherein again under column No. 3, the words *taraf* nazul are in thick ink and broad handwriting whereas the additional words *wa muafi*, *i.e.,* 'and *muafi*' are written in rather thin and dim ink. Similarly, under column No. 4, the original words '*Sarkar Bahadur*' are written in thick black ink but the words '*wa Azhar Hussain*' have been added in dim ink. It is very clear that the words '*wa muafi*' and '*wa Azhar Hussain*' under column No. 3 and 4 of both the *khasra* plots Nos. 163 and 167 are later additions. All the same, the handwriting of the scribe who made these additions in both the numbers is the same, even though it is apparently quite different from that of the original writing.

1. Arch of the Temple Top (Aamlak)

2. Broken Idol of Shiva and Parvati

3. Broken Pillar of Black Stone

4. Entrance of the Gate (Every Idol is Broken)

5. Half-Lotus Like Sun

6. Vishnu and other Deities

7. Inscription on a plate found in the Debris

4

The Shilanyas Site Controversy—*Rama Janamabhoomi*-Baburi *Masjid*

Ever since *shilanyas* for the proposed construction of *Ramjanmabhoomi* temple was performed in November 1989 at a site near the present *Ramjanmabhoomi*/Baburi *Masjid* in *Kot* Ram Chandra (Ayodhya), there has been a lot of controversy regarding the title to the plot. The situation has aggravated since the BJP President L.K. Advani undertook his *Rathyatra* to perform *karseva* at the *shilanyas* site on 30th October, 1990, followed by Vishwa Hindu Parishad's programme for the same purpose. At present, *Satyagraha* has been undertaken by the latter organisation at the same site for the realisation of the programme for the construction of the *Ramjanmabhoomi* temple. In the meantime, the Muslim Personal Law Board Working Committee has issued statements (dated 6th and 8th December, 1990) to the effect that the *shilanyas* site proposed for the performance of *karseva* by VHP is the property of the U.P. Waqf Board and that 'the *shilanyas* on the disputed land surrounding the *Mosque* (Baburi) was illegal as the dispute is pending in the court and that the court has ordered the maintenance of status quo until the decision." Shri E.M.S. Namboodiripad, General Secretary, Communist Party of India (Marxist), has taken the same view. However, Sardar Buta Singh, the former Minister for Home Affairs (Congress-I) has reiterated his previous stand that the *shilanyas* during the tenure of office was not performed on a disputed site, and "that the site where *shilanyas* was performed last year was clearly outside the specifications given in the stay order on November 14, 1989, by the full bench of the Allahabad High Court. Subsequently, that stay order was taken up by the U.P. Government with the Court for certain clarifications...The Court had left no doubt whatsoever about the application of its stay order with the help of a map submitted to it by the Sunni *Waqf* Board..." and further "that the *shilanyas* site was out of operation of the stay order at that time and continues to be even now." (dated December 6, 1990, New Delhi).

An examination of the matter based on the official revenue records shows that the viewpoint of the Muslim Personal Law Board Working Committee that the *shilanyas* site is a 'disputed' one and that the performance of the *shilanyas* on it last year and the performance of *karseva* by V.H.P. on the same site this year was in violation of the orders of the High Court is not tenable. This stand is contrary to the factual position as seen from the revenue records and the relevant maps. For a proper understanding of the issue, the procedure for the preparation of the Revenue Settlement may be briefly stated. It is important to note that as per the procedure of Revenue Settlement, the *khasra* numbers (*kishtwar*) often undergo a change due to alteration, addition and clubbing for adjustment with the neighbouring plots from one Revenue Settlement (*Bandobast*) to another. As such, since the I[st] Regular Settlement of *Pargana* Awadh, District Faizabad, effected in 1861 A.D., the *khasra* numbers have undergone change three times. However, the previous numbers are always reflected in the new Settlement Report. At the same time, the numbers of the plots recorded in the *khataunis* and *khata khewats* are always different from those of the *khasras. The* maps of the villages in respect of the plots are always prepared in accordance with the *khasra* numbers. Equally significant is the factor of mutations effected from time to time in respect of particular plots of land, in full or in part, from one owner to another. These are also always recorded in the relevant categories of the *khasra/khewat* and *khata khatauni* records. An analysis of the records in respect of the holdings in the village *Kot* Ram Chandra since the 1301 *Fasli*/1893 A.D., the Nazul Department's revised *khasras* (1931 A.D.) and the Regular Settlement of 1344 *Fasli*/1936-37 A.D., shows that there have been numerous mutations, even in respect of the desolate graveyards (*qabristan*) areas/graveyard plots mentioned as *waqf* hitherto. All these amendments have to be discerned carefully as reflected in the relevant columns of the varying categories of the revenue records.

After the revised *khasra abadi* (*tarmimi khasra abadi*) Report of 1931 A.D. prepared by the Nazul Department, District Faizabad, the next Regular Revenue Settlement (*bandobast*) covering ownership of the holdings along with details of areas and *abadi* etc. in the revenue units (*mahals*) of the village *Kot* Ram Chandra along with new *khasra, khatauni* and *khata khewat* numbers was effected in the year 1344 *Fasli*/1936-37 A.D. According to the *khewat* record of this settlement, the afore-mentioned *shilanyas* site falls in *khasra* No. 160A with an area of 3 *biswas* and 13 *biswansis* in the ownership of Sita Ram Saran s/o Kewal Ram and Lakshman Prasad s/o Sita Ram with half share each. The latter are the subordinate proprietors (*matahitadars*) and the holding being in *mahal* Nazul, the superior proprietor (*malik-i-ala*) is Sarkar Nazul (Government). Thereafter, the records comprising *jamabandi* (*khatauni*) and *khewat* of village *Kot* Ram Chandra have been maintained at the District Record Office (*Muhafaz Khana*), Faizabad, for all the years till date. In these *khatauni* records, for the last fifty three years, the subordinate proprietorship of the *shilanyas* site has been shown in the name of Sita Ram Saran and Kewal Ram. In the records for the years 1393-94 *Fasli*/1985-86, this area has been shown under *khewat* No. 63 of 160A in the ownership of Sita Ram Saran s/o Kewal Ram and Lakshman Prasad s/o Sita Ram. The latest Settlement has been made in 1397 *Fasli*/1989-90 A.D. after a period of fifty three years. In this Settlement Report, the *shilanyas* site has been covered in *khasra* No. 160 and the ownership entry along with an area of 3 *biswas* and 13 *biswansis* has been made in the name of Sita Ram Saran. At the same time, this Settlement has incorporated the *khata khatauni* of the *Fasli* years 1393-94/1985-86 A.D. and the same position has been maintained for the 1397 *Fasli* year/1989-90 A.D. In 1989, when the V.H.P. announced its determination to lay the foundation of the proposed construction of the *Ramjanmabhoomi* temple in the *Janmasthan* premises, the Sunni *Waqf* Board took the matter to the Allahabad High Court, Lucknow Bench, before which five suits registered since 1950, 1959, 1961 and 1989 but transferred in 1989 A.D. involving many parties had been pending for decision. The Special Bench of the Court comprising Hon'ble judges K.C. Agarwal, U.C. Srivastava and S.H.A. Raza passed an injunction Order dated 14.8.1989 that the parties to the above suits "shall maintain 'status quo' and shall not change the nature of the property in question." It may be observed that the V.H.P. is not a direct party to any of the suits as the parties involved are the *Mahants* Vs. Sunni *Waqf* Board, U.P. and a few *Mahants* themselves against each other. However, the V.H.P. has been supporting a couple of *Mahants* from outside.

As the V.H.P. was bent upon the fulfillment of its programme for the performance of *shilanyas* on the above mentioned site, the Baburi *Masjid* Action Committee claimed that it was a part of the erstwhile *khasra* No. 586 and that it was a disputed property in the suits pending in the High Court. In order to avoid any breach of law, the U.P. Government sought clarification and definition of the disputed property from the Lucknow Bench of the Allahabad High Court. The Special Bench of the Court held on 7th November, 1989 that the order was effective in all the 23 plots mentioned in the suit of the SCWB, (Sunni Central Board of *Waqfs* U.P.). It further clarified "that the order dated August 14, 1989 was in respect of the entire property mentioned in the suit including Plot No. 586 (.) In-so-far included within the boundary described by the letter EFGH (Reference possible to the sketch map of the original suit in the Sunni *Waqf* Board case (.)"

According to the Nazul Department's Revised *khasra* (1931 A.D.) of the village *Kot* Ram Chandra, the *arazi* No. 586 with an area of 11 *biswas*, 16 *biswansis* and 16 *kachwansis* (11-16-16) being in the *abadi* was a graveyard (a *pacca qabristan* known as *Ganj-Shahid*) and assigned in *waqf* (*waqf ahad shahi*). Thereafter, the *khasra* Nos. of the village were changed in the next regular Settlement Report (1344 *Fasli*/1936-37 A.D.) after taking into account alteration, branching off, adjustment and clubbing of the plots of the village as per established procedure for revenue settlements. At the same time, a number of mutations had been done in respect of many parts of the plots even covering graveyards and some of the latter's parts erstwhile declared as *waqf*. Similar is the position with the latest Settlement of 1393-94 *Fasli*/1989-90.

In view of the above mentioned facts, it is reasonable to hold that when the entire controversy about the performance of *shilanyas* involving the V.H.P., the Baburi *Masjid* Action

Committee, the then U.P. Government and the Government of India, arose in 1989, the 1344 *Fasli*/1936-37 Settlement Report should have been utilised for the determination of the *khasra* No. 160 and other related revenue numbers. The latest Settlement operations were already on and now are being finalised in the 1397 *Fasli*/ 1989-90 Report. In this Report, *khasra* No. 160 (wherein the site of *shilanyas* is located) has a total area of 5 *bighas* and 13 *biswas*. Under this *khasra* number and related *khata khatauni* and *khata khewat*, there are four owners of the plots, *i.e.,* Nazul Ala (Government), Awadh Bihari, Ishtiaq Ahmad and Sita Ram Saran owning 3 *bighas* and 13 *biswas*; 11 *biswas*; 1 *bigha*, 6 *biswas* and 7 *biswansis* and 13 *biswas* and 13 *biswansis* respectively. Of course, *khata khatauni* and *khata khewat* have different numbers for each plot associated with either of the fiscal units (*mahals*), *i.e.,* Azhar Hussain and Nazul. Significantly, the plot of Ishtiaq Hussain vide *khasra* No. 160 R and *khata khatauni* No. 9 under *mahal* Azhar Hussain, like other ownership under *khasra* No. 160, has been clearly shown under proprietorship and not as *waqf*. The plot of Sita Ram Saran (vide *khasra* No. 160 A, *khatauni* No. 54/ 1 and *khata khewat* No. 23) where *shilanyas* was performed falls under *mahal* Nazul.

As a matter of fact, the major portion of the *Janmasthan* complex comprising *Ramjanmabhoomi*/Baburi *Masjid* as well as misnomered *Janmasthan* to the north of *Ramjanmabhoomi*/Baburi *Masjid* falls under *khasras* Nos. 159, 146 (vide *khata khewat* No. 35) and 147 R wherein the names of the *Mahants* along with the areas in their ownership have been recorded. Only a small portion of the complex falls under *khasra* No. 160, which too, is shown under *mahal* Nazul Sarkar. This is supported by the maps of the concerned plots. The erstwhile *khasra* No. 586 (of 1931 A.D.) which has been claimed by the Muslim Personal Law Board Working Committee as the alleged site of *shilanyas* and property of the U.P. *Waqf* Board falls under *khasra* No. 160 and is mostly a part of the *mahal* Nazul *Sarkar Ala* (Government).

During the course of the proceedings (on 18.09.90) of the suit between Sunni Central *Waqf* Board U.P. and others Vs. Gopal Singh Visharad and others, relating to the proprietary titles to the various plots connected with *Ramjanmabhoomi*-Baburi *Masjid*, it was contended on behalf of the defendants that the Commissioner appointed for the survey had committed mistake in not indentifying the property in dispute with reference to Settlement maps of 1861 and 1937 and instead locating it with reference to the Nazul map of 1931. It was also contended by them that the Commissioner did not proceed correctly in as much as he proceeded to prepare the map without requiring the plaintiffs to identify the property in dispute at the spot. The Special Bench of the High Court, Allahabad/Lucknow comprising of Hon'ble Judges S.C. Mathur, B. Kumar and S.H.A. Raza, directed the learned Commissioner "to submit supplementary report after carrying out survey on the basis of settlement maps and *khasras* of 1861 and 1937. The learned Commissioner, before proceeding with the survey, shall obtain from the plaintiffs identification of the property in dispute at the spot. Therefore, he shall indicate the numbers which cover the property in dispute according to 1861 map as well as according to 1937 map. The supplementary report shall be submitted by 15th October, 1990." The order has indeed given right direction to the case as the Ist Regular Settlement Report (1861 A.D.) of *Kot* Ram Chandra, *Haveli* Awadh, Tehsil and District, Faizabad (vide Registrar No. 132, District Record Office/Tehsil Office, Faizabad) is the most comprehensive document relating to the *Janmasthan* complex comprising *Ramjanmabhoomi*/Baburi *Masjid.* It is also appended with two survey maps in respect of the plots, *abadi* and religious monuments, etc. In fact, the Report reflects the position as inherited from the *Nawabi* period and also forms the basis of the future Settlement Reports. Similarly, the Settlement Report of the 1344 *Fasli* year/1936-37 A.D. serves as a guideline to the latest 1397 *Fasli*/1989-90 settlement operation. It is learnt that the survey of the property in dispute by the Commissioner, which was earlier postponed to 14-20 December, 1990, has since been further postponed.

5

The Ayodhya Dispute and its Reference to the Supreme Court Under Article 138 (2)

I. The recent announcement by the newly constituted United Front Government in its common minimum programme to refer the long-standing disputed Ayodhya issue to the Supreme Court of India under Article 138 (2) needs careful consideration. The Article 138 (2) of the Constitution of India reads as:

"The Supreme Court shall have such further jurisdiction and powers with respect to any matter as the Government of India and the Government of any State may by Special agreement confer, if Parliament by Law provides for the exercise of such jurisdiction and powers by the Supreme Court." It may be recalled that earlier (7th January, 1993), the President of India had referred a specific issue relating to the Ayodhya dispute, as Special Reference, to the Supreme Court of India for consideration and opinion under clause (1) of article 143 which reads as: "If at any time it appears to the President that a question of law or fact has arisen, or it is likely to arise, which is of such a nature and of such public importance that it is expedient to obtain the opinion of the Supreme Court upon it, he may refer the question to that court for consideration and the Court may, after such hearing as it thinks fit, report to the President its opinion thereupon."

The Reference relating to the Ayodhya dispute under Article 143 (1) of the Constitution made by the President of India reads as: "Whereas a dispute has arisen whether a Hindu temple or any religious structure existed prior to the construction (including the premises of the inner and the outer courtyard of such structure), commonly known as *Ramjanmabhoomi*-Baburi *Masjid*, in the area in which the structure stood in village of *Kot* Ram Chandra in

Ayodhya, in *Pargana Haveli* Awadh, in Tehsil Faizabad Sadar, in the district of Faizabad of the State of Uttar Pradesh..." As such, the exact question referred by the President of India to the Supreme Court was: "Whether a Hindu Temple or any Hindu religious structure existed prior to the construction of the *Ramjanmabhoomi*-Baburi *Masjid* (including the premises of the inner and outer courtyard of such structure) in the area on which the structure stood?"

II. For proper evaluation of the entire issue, the following significant and relevant background aspects may be taken into consideration:

(i) Ever since the *Janmasthan* temple was demolished by Mir Baqi, the Commander of Babur, the first Mughal monarch in 1528 A.D. and the mosque was constructed on the very site of birth-place of Shri Ram (*Janmasthan*), there has been a long standing dispute and continual tussle, at times even armed conflict over its possession, which is rather unprecedented in the history of India.

(ii) Right from the Mughal age to the mid-20th century (*i.e.,* pre-1947 era), there are numerous contemporary archival, literary as well as judicial records which confirm the fact that the disputed structure situated at *Janmasthan*, named *Ramjanmabhoomi*-'Baburi *Masjid'* was built after the demolition of the *Janmasthan* temple in 1528 A.D., which accounts for continual conflict and judicial litigation between the Hindu and the Muslim communities over the physical possession of the premises.

(iii) It is well borne out by the documentary evidence since the Mughal age that of the large *Janmasthan* complex, excepting the small area (about 13 *biswas*) upon which the disputed structure stood, the rest of land comprising the outer courtyard and covering Ram *Chabutra*/platform called *'Sita Rasoi'*/ '*Kaushilya Rasoi'* with *Pacca Chula, Chakla* and *Belen* as well as footprints of Ram, Lakhan, Bharat and Shatrughan as well as the *Bhandara* etc. (measuring 4 *bighas*, 11 *biswas*) has never been disputed and has always remained in the ownership and possession of the Hindu *Mahants* The Hindus have been worshipping over there all through the ages. This fact is well conceded both by the Government of India's White Paper on Ayodhya (February, 1993) as well as the Hon'ble Supreme Court of India in its Judgement dated 24th October, 1994 on the Special Reference as mentioned in para I under Article 143 (1) of the Constitution.

(iv) It is also on record that before the British occupation of Awadh (1856), for most of the period since its very construction (1528), the disputed structure comprising the so-called *masjid* was regarded as *masjid-i-zarar* wherein prayers could not be offered by the Muslim community as it was built on the very site of the place of worship of another community and was rather deserted. At the same time, it is also well borne out by the contemporary evidence that since the 1855 A.D. Hindu Muslim riots in Ayodhya and at the time of British occupation of Awadh (1856), its possession lay with the Hindu *Bairagis*. It is only during the British Raj that the disputed structure came to be known as 'Baburi *Masjid'*.

(v) The revenue records of the late *Nawabi* period, and more especially from 1861 A.D. onwards till date (1995-96), show the superior ownership of the *Janmasthan* Complex inclusive of the sub-plot on which the disputed structure of *Ramjanmabhoomi*-'Baburi *Masjid'* stood in the name of *Sarkar* Nazul (Government) and the Hindu *Mahants/Bairagis* have been put as the under-proprietors (owners). The revenue records/maps do not mention the existence of any '*mosque*' or any *waqf* land attached to it.

(vi) Even though the Shia-Sunni tussle over the possession of the disputed structure considered as 'mosque' is on record from 1938 to 1947, there is no evidence that after the 1934 Hindu-Muslim riots in Ayodhya over the possession of disputed structure, any prayers (*namaz*) were offered by the Muslim community therein.

(vii) With the installation of the idol of Bhagwan Sri Rama Lala under the central dome of the disputed structure on 23/12/1949, a new phase of Hindu-Muslim continuous litigation started which has continued till date. On 23/12/1949, the idol and deities were transferred from the Ram *Chabutra* in front of the disputed structure to inside the structure which has been claimed by the Sunni, Central Board of *waqf* as 'Baburi *Masjid'*. The disputed structure was attached by the City Magistrate in 1950 A.D. which was followed by civil suits, both by the Hindus and the Muslims. On 18.12.1961, a few days in advance of the twelve years possession of the disputed structure by the Hindus, suit was instituted in the Court of Civil Judge, Faizabad, by the Sunni Central Board of *waqfs* U.P. and some Sunni Muslims for a declaration that the disputed structure was a mosque and for the removal of the idols from it and its delivery to them. Another landmark was the judgement of the District Judge, Faizabad on 1.2.1986 which directed the opening of locks on the gates for the entry of the pilgrims for offering *puja*. In order to expedite the judicial decision, all five main suits relating to various property matters in respect of *Ramjanmabhoomi*-'Baburi *Masjid'* were withdrawn by the Allahabad High Court to be disposed of by the High Court itself. On 10/10/1991, Notification Under Section 6 of the Land Acquisition Act, acquiring a part of Shri *Ramjanmabhoomi Sthal* (including the disputed structure) for public purpose of development of tourism and providing amenities to the pilgrims at Ayodhya was passed by the U.P. State. This was challenged which further complicated the legal tussle. On 6th December, 1992, the disputed structure was pulled down as a sentiment of protest against inaction in the progress of the judicial suits pending before the High Court since the early 1950's.

(viii) The archaeological evidence shows that the material of the demolished Hindu temple was also used for the construction of a mosque on the same site. In the erstwhile disputed structure of *Ramjanmabhoomi*-'Baburi *Masjid*', there were 14 *kasauti* pillars carved with several Hindu sacred motifs and Gods and Goddesses which served as an integral part of the structure. During June-July, 1992, at the time of the ground levelling operation around the *Shilanyas* site, apart from the discovery of the *pacca* bricked-wall and flooring of the ancient temple, a number of artifacts and architectural pieces of the 12th century demolished temple were unearthed. In the wake of the demolition of the disputed structure on 6th December, 1992, the archaeological remains at the site have revealed, apart from numerous architectural pieces, three dedicatory inscriptions in Sanskrit written in Devanagri script. Of these three, one Hari-Vishnu 12th century inscription narrates that the temple was built in the temple city of Ayodhya situated at Saket *mandala*. The Vishnu-Hari inscription associates the construction of the temple with Govind Chandra, a ruler (A.D.1114-1154) of the Ghadaval dynasty. This is an eloquent proof of the fact that at the very site of *Ramjanmabhoomi* at Ayodhya, there stood a Vishnu temple from at least early 12th century which was destroyed by Mir Baqi in Babur's reign for building a mosque in 1528-29. Both Hon'ble Justice H.N. Tilhari at the Allahabad High Court in his judgement, dated 1st January, 1992 and the Hon'ble Supreme Court of India vide its order on 21.9.1993 have directed to preserve and protect the material and articles of historical/ archaeological importance which were taken out or found on the spot in the debris of demolished structure or the nearby area. On the basis of the Supreme Court's Order, the estampage of the above mentioned 12th century inscription has already been taken by the Archaeological Survey of India. However, its official decipherment should end the age long controversy for ever.

(ix) During the tenure of Shri Chandra Shekhar as Prime Minister of India, the process of mutual negotiations between the Vishva Hindu Parishad and the All India Baburi *Masjid* Action Committee were conducted (December, 1990 and 24th January, 1991), to sort out the Ayodhya problem. During the course of the proceedings, it emerged that the main issue was whether there was a Hindu temple at Ayodhya which was replaced by a mosque (1528). Both the sides were required to submit relevant historical documents comprising literary, revenue, judicial and archaeological aspects in support of their contentions and were to be assisted by expert-historians/ lawyers, whereas V.H.P. not only submitted documentary evidence as well as rejoinder to the evidence submitted by A.I.B.M.A.C., the latter could not submit statement of the case or any rejoinder material. When the meeting of the nominated experts took place on 24th January, 1991, the

A.I.B.M.A.C. experts expressed their inability to discuss the issue on the plea that they needed another six weeks to study the V.H.P. material for reply. In fact, they could not gather any counter evidence for rebuttal of the V.H.P.'s viewpoint. They deliberately absented themselves from the meeting on 25th January, 1991 without any prior intimation. However, mutual negotiations were resumed in October-November, 1992 during the Prime Ministership of Shri P.V. Narasimha Rao. In a meeting held on 8th November, 1992, being presided over by the Co-ordinator, Shri P.R. Kumaramangalam, it was argued by the V.H.P. delegation's expert-historian (Prof. B.R. Grover) that some Hindu architectural pieces and deities were well discernable on the walls and projections of the disputed structure and that the Archaeological Survey of India might be asked to remove the white washing and scrape the walls without any damage to them but this proposal was rejected by the Co-ordinator. If only this suggestion had been accepted, it would have brought out fresh archaeological evidence which should have helped in the amicable settlement of the issue. However, the mutual negotiations which had been going well were suddenly sabotaged by the A.I.B.M.A.C.—Government of India representative/Co-ordinator on the pretension that the V.H.P. had announced further *karseva* work in the *Ramjanmabhoomi*-Baburi *Masjid* Complex. The sudden abandonment of the mutual dialogue was a severe setback to finding an amicable solution and ultimately resulted in the great tragedy of 6th December, 1992.

(x) It is rather ironical that in all personal conversations, many of the Muslim intellectuals and A.I.B.M.A.C. members do concede the fact that the erstwhile disputed structure of *Ramjanmabhoomi*—'Baburi *Masjid*' was indeed constructed on the site of a Hindu temple after the latter's demolition, but they are not willing to admit this fact publicly because they think that it would re-open a 'pandora's' box as there is ample irrefutable contemporary evidence regarding Mathura and Banares Hindu temples having been replaced by mosques by Aurangzeb, the Mughal monarch.

III. Of course, the best solution of the Ayodhya issue is either through the resumption of mutual dialogue between the Hindu and the Muslim communities or through legislation by an Act of the Parliament. This is because, of late, the Ayodhya problem has assumed much more political dimension than ever before. In case, it is considered expedient to resume the negotiations, the hard facts of the events which have moulded the character of history since November, 1992, when the earlier negotiations were dropped, have to be taken into consideration. In this regard, the discovery of the dedicatory inscription (1114-1154) from the remains of the demolished structure on 6th December, 1992, as already mentioned in para viii deserves special attention which should go a long way to convince the Muslims or expert historians/archaeologists on their behalf about the existence of the Hindu temple prior to the construction of the mosque on the same site after its demolition. The Muslim leaders may as well be reminded to fulfil their commitment to shift the site of the erstwhile so-called 'Baburi *Masjid'* to another place if it were found that the mosque named 'Baburi *Masjid'* was constructed after the demolition of the Hindu temple.

In case the proposal of solving the Ayodhya issue through dialogue or legislation is not acceptable to the United Front Government and the latter is bent upon referring the issue to the Supreme Court, under Article 138(2) after having secured outside support of the Congress (I) and then the approval of the Parliament as per Constitutional requirements, it is worthwhile to consider the exact question/contents of the matter which might be the subject of Reference to the Supreme Court.

In this regard, all the Civil suits pending before the Lucknow Bench of the Hon'ble Allahabad High Court might abate but they cannot possibly be enblock transferred to the Supreme Court with the original Jurisdiction created for the purpose of the Reference. Practically all the suits relate to various aspects of land-ownership or other property matters of the erstwhile disputed structure, *i.e., Ramjanmabhoomi*/'Baburi *Masjid*' and the premises of the inner or the outer courtyards attached to it. Such is the dilatory procedure for the adjudication of the Civil suits that it will take considerably long time for the Supreme Court to give final judgement after having completed all the legal procedural requirements. As such, the very purpose of the Reference to the Supreme Court for an expeditious trial of the suits will be defeated. In fact, such suits involving mostly land ownership or proprietary rights can be better settled in the High Court than in the Supreme Court.

In view of the above position as well as the fact that the most relevant and the real issue of the entire Ayodhya tangle is the determination of the historical fact as to whether in the past the *Ramjanmabhoomi*-'Baburi *Masjid*' structure was raised after the destruction of a Hindu temple/religious place, any reference would, in fact, be reiteration of the same question with exactly the same language as earlier posed by the Presidential Reference on 7th January, 1993 under Article 143 (1). As such, even under Article 138 (2), the Reference should be, whether a Hindu temple or any Hindu religious place existed prior to the construction of *Ramjanmabhoomi*/'Babri Masjid' (including the premises of the inner and outer courtyards of such structure) in the area on which the structure stood?".

It goes without saying that under Article 138 (2) of the Constitution, the judgement of the Supreme Court will be of a mandatory and binding character whereas earlier under Article 143(1), the final opinion of the Supreme Court to the President/ Government of India would have been merely of an advisory character. It may as well be recalled that in the latter Reference which the Supreme Court had declined to answer, one of the reasons "for not answering the Reference was that the Central Government did not propose to settle the dispute in terms of the Court" which could be either pro-temple or pro-mosque. All the same, the minority judgement of the Supreme Court maintained that this did not imply that the court of law was not competent to decide about such a case. It could be done if expert evidence of archaeological and historians was led and was tested in cross-examination. But at the time, the principal protagonists of the two stands (*i.e., Ramjanma bhoomi Nyas* and A.I.B.M.A.C.) were not appearing in the Reference. They would neither lead evidence nor cross-examine. However, at that time Sri *Ramjanmabhoomi Nyas* had responded on the merits of the factual question referred for decision by the Supreme Court of India and submitted its material/evidence on April 10, 1993 but it would have become party only if the Supreme Court had agreed to answer the Reference. But the A.I.B.M.A.C. neither responded for submission of material on the merits of the Factual Question nor participated in the proceedings of the Reference to the Court. It was, of course, represented by some other individuals/institutions by proxy, who during the course of the proceedings of the case opposed the Reference made by the President of India. However, the present position in case of Reference under Article 138(2) would be different than in the past in case of 143(1), as in the present case, both the Union Government, and the State Government would give their consent and if the litigants involved in the suits at present pending at the Lucknow Bench of the Allahabad High Court are required to plead their respective cases in respect of the Reference to be made under Article 138(2) at the Supreme Court, the requirement of law for leading the evidence and its cross-examination could as well be fulfilled. This would definitely be an expeditious process for adjudication of the afore-mentioned basic issue to be referred to the Supreme Court.

the respective mosques for casting votes in favour of the "Congress Party even though they would not forgive Prime Minister Narasimha Rao for the demolition of Baburi *Masjid*" and holding the "B.J.P. and the Shiv Sena as definitely fascist and communal parties" and finally the appeal made by the All India Baburi *Masjid* Action Committee to the Muslims in favour of the Congress, do or do not violate the judgement of the Hon'ble Supreme Court and the secular concept of the Indian Constitution?

When the assurance on the part of B.J.P. to facilitate the construction of Shri Ram Mandir at *Janmasthan* in Ayodhya dedicated to *Bharat Mata*, after having come to power, is a part of the B.J.P. election manifesto, then how does Kalyan Singh's promise for the construction of Ram temple at Ayodhya in an election broadcast tantamount to making an appeal on religious grounds, more especially when he had in December, 1992, resigned from the office of the Chief Ministership of Uttar Pradesh in the aftermath of the demolition of the disputed structure by the mob? When as a result of the regrettable demolition of the disputed structure on December 6, 1992, the archaeological remains at the site have brought out a clinching evidence of a Hari-Vishnu 12th century Inscription written in Sanskrit in Nagari script narrating the construction of the temple on this site by Govind Chandra (1114-1154 A.D.) of Ghadaval dynasty, which apparently was later destroyed by Mir Baqi, the Commander of Babur, for the construction of a mosque thereupon and this Inscription is being preserved under the orders of the Hon'ble Supreme Court (21.9.1993), what more evidence is needed to convince the All India Baburi *Masjid* Action Committee and other Muslim leaders to fulfill their commitment for the construction of the temple on the same site? Moreover, when there is already a make-shift Ram temple on the disputed site at Ayodhya, which is legally fortified by the judgements of the Allahabad High Court (1.1.1993) as well as the Act of the Parliament to maintain status-quo as on 7.1.1993 with reduced right of worship by the Hindus in this area, already held valid by the Judgements of the Hon'ble Supreme Court (24.10.1994 & 11.12.1995), being neither with a slant in favour of Hindu Community nor anti-secular, then how any further reference for the construction of a regular temple with normal mode of worship is against the code of conduct? Ironically, all the facts about the above mentioned 12th century Inscription from the archaeological remains of the demolished disputed structure as well as further judicial judgements regarding their importance for preservation, referred to above, are well known to the All India Baburi *Masjid* Action Committee which has been crying hoarse during the election period, for the reconstruction of the mosque on the same site. In this regard, the Imams as well as a few political parties have been out to exploit the religious feelings of the Muslim minority community for their own political ends and to all this the Election Commission has been a mute witness and has turned a blind eye.

If B.J.P.'s manifesto about the construction of the *Janmasthan* temple at Ayodhya cannot be referred to by any speaker under the model code of conduct and law, how can the Congress manifesto promise for the reservation of the Dalit Christians and the concessions to be given to the religious minorities be referred to in the speeches by the Congress leaders for gathering votes be considered valid under the same model code of conduct? The Congress party's approach to the Election Commission to derecognise the B.J.P. for having promised to build Ram temple at Ayodhya is obviously a cover up for its own pronouncements for the appeasement of the religious susceptibilities of the minority communities.

Apart from the above, the objection of the Election Commission to the use of the greeting slogan of 'Jai Sri Ram' considered as an appeal to the religious sentiments of the electorate is uncalled for. This mode of greeting on the part of the dominant sections of the Hindus, as a part of the cultural heritage of India, can be traced back to ancient times and has persisted all through. This is similar to the words of greetings like *Ram Ram/Pranam/Namaskar/Jai Mata Di/Jai-Hind* or any other sectarian or regional shiboleth like 'Radha Swami' adopted by many a section of the Hindus. As a parallel to this, as a cultural heritage, the Muslims in India, for offering greetings have been using the words *Adab/Selam/Adabarz/Selam elakam* etc., whereas the Sikhs have been greeting with the words of *Sat Sri Akal/Wahi Guru Ji Ka Khalsa, Wahi Guru Ji Ki Fateh.* As a matter fact, all such words of greetings on the part of the Hindus or Muslims or Sikhs underlining submission to God, His

Truth, peace with each other, humility, salute to the Motherland are equally intended to show affinity and oneness of the speaker with the addressed people regardless of their caste or religion. One has to simply to go through the historical literature to see how all these epithets have been used in the past even during the colonial struggle against the British imperialism. Even till date, the words of greetings of 'Ram Ram', 'Salam' and 'Sat Sri Akal' are in vogue in many a unit of the Indian Armed Forces, which as per the Constitution, are completely secular in character. Similarly, one fails to understand the rationale behind the objection made by the Election Commission to the use of the words 'vande mataram' by the B.J.P. leader Ram Das Agarwal. This expression is simply a salutation to 'Bharat Mata', the land we belong to and protect as Indian nationals. To attribute or to associate the use of such words of greetings with merely the religious feelings of the respective communities is complete denial of the cultural heritage of India.

Above all, an incorporation of the programme on the foreign policy, especially the security measures to be adopted by any country, in the respective manifesto of the political parties has been an accepted principle in all democracies. In view of this, the reference by Kalyan Singh in his proposed broadcast script to I.S.I.'s role in India cannot, by any stretch of imagination, be construed as violation of the model code of conduct on the pretext that it affects India's relations with a neighbouring country. If such issues can be taken up by the political parties in the Parliament or in the print media by the Fourth Estate, or can form a part of the manifestos of the political parties, how come it cannot be referred to in a speech. As the taking up of the issues of national security and the relations with the neighbouring countries is an important and a normal feature during the election days, it, by no means, can be treated as violative of any model code of conduct. This stand taken by the Election Commission is not at all rational. In fact, the Election Commission should have viewed Kalyan Singh's and B.J.P.'s programme for Ayodhya and foreign policy of the country in a more dispassionate manner. Singling out B.J.P. definitely smacks of partisan attitude which is least expected from an august body like the Election Commission of India— a Constitutional Authority in the country.

7

An Analysis of the Revenue Documents Relating to *Janmasthan* *(Rama Janamabhoomi)* Versus 'Baburi *Masjid'* at *Kot* Ram Chandra, Awadh (Ayodhya) in Historical Perspective*

During the course of the last few years stormy controversy over the title to the *Ramjanmabhoomi* versus 'Baburi *Masjid'*, copious literature comprising monographs and newspaper articles in English, Hindi and regional languages has been produced on an unprecedented scale. Based upon ancient, medieval and modern literary sources, archaeological evidence and 19th-20th centuries judicial records, the writers have dealt with various aspects ranging from the identification of historic Ayodhya, its association with Lord Ram, the God incarnate of the Ramayana, the Ram cult and the fact whether a Vaishnav Ram temple existed on the very site whereupon, after the demolition of the latter, the superstructure of a 'mosque' (named as 'Baburi Masjid' during the second half of the 19th century) was raised in 1528 A.D. by Baqi Tashkandi (*i.e.,* Mir Baqi), the local commander of Zahiruddin Muhammad Babur, the first Mughal ruler in India or it was built by the latter out of his pious wish on a vacant plot of land for the 'angels to descend on earth'. Further controversy has been raised about the itinerary of Babur in the territories of Awadh and as to whether the demolition of the Ram temple took place on the basis of his personal order or by Mir Baqi's own initiative at the behest of some local Muslim *faqir*. Even though the entire issue has been, unfortunately, sufficiently communalised, a dispassionate appraisal on scientific lines based on historicity and facts is rather imperative.

After the communal riot at Ayodhya in 1855 A.D., during the 19th century, numerous independent and judicious writers, both Muslims and Hindus, specialised in the past history of Awadh dealing with many of the above mentioned issues relating to *Janmasthan* and Baburi Masjid'[1]. Some of them claimed to have utilised the authentic 16th-18th centuries works enumerated by them in support of their narrations. They were all of the unanimous view that on the basis of Babur's order, the *Janmasthan* of Shri Ram Chandra at *Kot* Ram Chandra, *Pargana Haveli* Awadh comprising residential palace *(mahal sarai)* of King Dashrath and Shri Ram along with a temple and a kitchen—the latter portions popularly known as *Sita ki Rasoi*—were all demolished and a 'mosque' constructed thereupon in 1528 A.D. under the guidance of Baqi Tashkandi (Mir Baqi), the local commander/administrator of Awadh and Syed Musa Ashikan, a Muslim *faqir*. This version has continued to prevail uncontested in all works on the regional history of Awadh, even by the most eminent scholars, all through in the 20th century inclusive of the post-1947 era of independent India till the early 1980's when due to sudden change in the concept of Indian historiography and for political reasons, the above mentioned views about the demolition of the *Janmasthan* temple and construction of the 'mosque' thereupon have been expunged in the revised editions of the earlier 19th-20th centuries published works[2]. A mushroom growth of historians has come up who call such a version about *Janmasthan*/ 'Baburi masjid' a myth based on tradition, local belief, the British 'Divide and Rule' policy and its legacy in Free India rather than a historical fact.

Notwithstanding the fact, a vast number of the original official records of the *Nawabi* rule in Awadh during the 18th-19th centuries (till 1846 A.D.) have vanished, a few documents still extant touch upon Hindu-Muslim tussle not only over Hanuman Garhi/*Mosque* but also *Janmasthan*/'*Masjid*'[3]. Quite significantly, they refer to the old judicial/revenue documents which are not available today. At the time of the 1855 Hindu-Muslim riot in Ayodhya, an official letter *(Purcha)*[4] from Nawab Wajid Ali Shah, the king of Oudh to Major James Outram, the British resident, dated 12th August, 1855, appended by five original documents received by the king of Oudh from Hafeezullah, the *Darogha* of Faizabad and Maulvee

Mehamed Nchaloodeen and others refer to the Hindu-Muslim conflict not only with regard to Hanuman *Garhi*/'*mosque*' but to *Janmasthan*/'Masjid' as well. One of the appended documents traces a similar riot in the first half of the 18th century during the period of Boorhonool moolk (Burhan ul Mulk), the *Subedar* (Governor) of Oude[5]. (The title of Burhan ul Mulk was held by two *Subadars* of Awadh during the reign of Muhammad Shah, the Mughal Emperor. Firstly, by Nawab Saadat Khan who died in 1739 A.D. and secondly, by his son Nawab Safdar Jang, 1739-1744 A.D. The latter had also acted as governor of Awadh in 1738 during the absence of his father, Saadat Khan. As known from the contemporary sources, during this year, there was considerable violence and lawlessness in the *Subah.* Earlier too, during Saadat Khan's tenure of governorship, there has been much turbulance, apparently in Ayodhya as well, which is fully confirmed by the inclusion of the *kazi's* report mentioned hereafter). Another significant document comprises a copy of paper sealed with the seal of *Kazee (Qazi)* of Faizabad, dated 1735 A.D.[6] These referred to documents fully bear out the fact that the Hindu-Muslim conflict over the territorial jurisdictions of the above mentioned temples/ mosques was a long drawn battle even during the Mughal rule in Awadh in the early 18th century. Still another significant note covering the opinion of Hafizullah, the *darogha* of Faizabad, submitted to the Awadh Royal Court (19th century) clearly states that "the mosque constructed by Babur was situated at the birth-place of Ram, son of Raja Dashrath, and adjacent to the kitchen of Sita, wife of Ram (*i.e., Sita-ki-rasoi)*". Apparently, in the official brief submitted to the Royal Court, Hafizullah relied upon the past records supported by the revenue documents. In fact, in all matters relating to property disputes, there is an integrated relationship between the judicial records and the revenue records for as per procedure of the Mughal/*Nawabi* judicial system, the relevant attested copies or at times even in original were always appended for the perusal of the court before the judgement was given. It is apparent from the available judicial records of the British administration in Awadh that in the case of *Janmasthan* versus 'Baburi *Masjid*, the same procedure was followed. Similar is the position even today in the same case pending before the Lucknow Bench of the Allahabad High Court.

For matters relating to land rights during the medieval or modern periods, the importance of the original revenue documents, for whichsoever region available in series or in fragments, cannot be underestimated. They command primacy over the literary sources or archaeological theories. Of course, the latter sources can be well utilised, if correctly interpreted, to support the evidence deduced from the revenue documents. For the issue of *Janmasthan*/'Baburi Masjid', as at present, the earliest revenue documentary evidence is traceable to the early 18th century. A Map of Ayodhya, painted on white cotton fabric (with a size: 213x178cm) forms a part of the *Kapad-Dwara* Collection (Private collection of the rulers of Amer/ Jaipur state) preserved at the City Palace Museum, Jaipur (Rajasthan).[7] This map depicts *Janmasthan* along with various other religious places of Ayodhya and the river Saryu. It shows the structure of the *Janmasthan*/'Masjid' on the western corner of the fort *(i.e., Kot* Ram Chandra) along with the crenellated *parkota* (rampart). The complex has a rectangular plan with an arched entrance in the middle of the eastern side, a vast open court on the one side of which is a *chabutra* (raised platform) marked as *Janmasthan.* Figures representing the visiting pilgrims are shown circumembulating and worshipping the *Janmasthan/chabutra.* By its Western side, with some gap, stands the main structure (claimed as main *Janmasthan/'Masjid'*) divided into three bays, each containing a *chowki* with *masnad,* the central one marked as chhathi. Unlike the present superstructure, the map depicts the latter composed of three *shikaras* (curvilinear like temple spiers), the central one of these being larger and higher. It seems in the context that the present day domes and their finials of the structure were built in the later period of the 18th century, which replaced the earlier *shikaras,* probably with corbelled ceilings.

Even though the above mentioned map of Ayodhya is undated, it may be taken up with the other early 18th century revenue documents relating to Ayodhya, which equally form a part of the *Kapad-Dwara* Collection. A *chaknama* (a document detailing the measured land along with land marks and boundaries in all the four geographical directions, duly attested by the local revenue officials) dated 2 *Rajab,* AH 1129/1st June, 1717 A.D. (reign of Farrukh Siyar, the Mughal Emperor) records the assignment of land (983 acres in present day measurement unit) to Swai Jai Singh (Amer Chief, the Mughal *mansabdar)* for a garden and a *pura* (smalltownship/settlement) at Ayodhya[8]. It is well known that Swai Jai Singh, the Amer Chief *(zammidar-i-umda)* occupied high status as the Mughal *mansabdar* and was assigned vast *jagirs* in lieu thereof. He also remained posted as the *subadar* (governor) in various *subahs*. The Mughal archives record number of *Jaisinghpuras* inhabited by him in the *subahs* of Malwa (Ujjain), Patna, Agra (Mathura, Vrindaban), Awadh (Ayodhya, Benaras), Delhi, Lahore, Multan, Kabul and in the Deccan at Burhanpur, Aurangabad, Elichpur and other places. The settlement of the *puras* essentially required the preparation of various revenue documents and a map for the purpose. So it is evident in the context that the map of Ayodhya was prepared for the pilgrims as well during the same period when Swai Jai Singh inhabited a *pura* and the *chaknama* dated 1st June, 1717 A.D. was prepared by the local revenue officials for this purpose. In fact, similar maps for the towns in other *subahs*, where Swai Jai Singh established *puras*, are also available in the *Kapad-Dwara* collection, Jaipur (Rajasthan).

Most significantly, about half a century later, the visual depiction of the above map is well confirmed by the European traveller, Joseph Tieffenthaler, a Jesuist Austrian, who travelled the Awadh region around 1766-71 A.D.[9] While briefly narrating the past facts about the demolition of the birth-place temple of Ram and utilisation of its pillars for the construction of the '*mosque*' by Babur, Tieffenthaler states that despite the prohibitive efforts of the Mughals, the Hindus continued to visit the place for worship and consequently they had constructed the *Ram Chabutra* in the main courtyard of the *Janmasthan*/'*Mosque*' complex, which they used to parabulate thrice, then prostrate on the ground. The Hindus used to practice their devotion at the *chabutra* as well as in the main structure of *Janmasthan*/'Mosque'. That the Hindus had been not only worshipping at the *chabutra* for hundreds of years but the *Bairagis* would even enter the premises of the '*Mosque*' structure and write the words "Ram, Ram" with characoal on the inner walls of the main structure is further confirmed by Muhammad Asghar, the *khatib* and *muazzan* of the 'Baburi *Masjid'* in his representation dated 30.11.1858 to the British Government for alleged interference

1861 A.D. to 1990 A.D., distinctly cover the nature of land rights of the *Mahants* in the entire *Janmasthan* complex. The first Regular Settlement Report (1861 A.D.) of *Kot* Ram Chandra, appended by two maps, is the most comprehensive document relating to the *Janmasthan* complex comprising Ram Janmabhoomi.[22] The Report reflects the position as inherited from the *Nawabi* period. In the revenue documents, the superior ownership of the land has been declared in the name of *Sarkar Bahadur Nazul* and the *Mahants* have been declared as the under proprietors *(malikan-i-matahit)* in the entire *Janmasthan* complex. The Settlement Report of 1893 A.D. distinctly mentions the sub-plot on which *Masjid* is situated as *Sita Ki Rasoi.*[23] The subsequent Settlement Reports of 1936-37 and 1989-90 maintain the same position.

For proper scientific study of the land rights of *Janmasthan*/ 'Baburi *Masjid'*, it is rather essential to refer to the revenue maps, either appended to the past Settlement Reports or otherwise officially prepared by the District Administration, Faizabad, Uttar Pradesh. These have been listed below:—

(i) The *Hadbast* map appended to Settlement Report (1861) vide Basta No. 132 of 1861, *mauza Ramkot*, *pargana haveli* and *zilla* Faizabad. This map shows only the temple at *Janmasthan* in a significant manner and the 'Baburi *Masjid'* is not even indicated.

(ii) The latest official map of the Revenue village 'Ramkot' for the years 1344-45 *Fasli* corresponding to the year 1937 A.D.

(iii) The map of the 'Ram Katha Park' superimposed on the *Shajra* plan of Ayodhya town consisting of Revenue villages named '*Kot* Ram Chandra', 'Awadh Khas' and 'Jalwanpur'. Ram Janmabhoomi along with the mark of a temple is shown on plot No. 160.

(iv) The map of the disputed site prepared by the Ayodhya Special Area Development Authority. It is headed as '*Ramjanmabhoomi Sthal*' at Ayodhya. The original of it is signed by the District Magistrate, Faizabad, Chairman of the said authority and other concerned officers.

(v) The official map of the towns of Ayodhya and Faizabad. It shows Ram Janmabhoomi but does not show any 'Baburi *Masjid*'.

The entire Revenue Records dating from the First Settlement (1861 A.D.) have been examined. There is no record of any of 'Baburi *Masjid*' anywhere in the documents maintained by the Revenue Department of the Government of U. P. at the Collectorate and the Tehsil at Faizabad, that were made available during the course of long search extending to a period of over two months during 1990.

As distinct from the above mentioned Revenue Records, the Nazul Department of the District Faizabad, (U.P.) also prepared its own amended *khasra* records of the *abadi* settlements *(tarmimi khasra abadi)* in 1931 A.D.[24] In these revised *khasras* of village *Ram Kot*, both 'masjid' and *'chabutra'* indicating the temple at *Janmasthan* have been recorded in *khasra* No. 583. The '*mosque*' has been shown in *waqf* under column 'Name of the present possessor' *(Nam Hal Qabiz)*. At the same time, *Mahant* Charan Das in 1931 and thereafter *Mahant* Raghu Nath Das in 1941 have been declared under-proprietors (*malik matahit*) of the entire plot. Moreover, in these *khasra* records, *arazi* No. 586 with an area of 11 *biswas,* 16 *biswanis* and 16 *kachwanis* (11-16-16) being in *abadi* is shown as graveyard (a *pacca qabristan* known as *Ganj-i-Shahidan*) and assigned in *waqf (waqf ahad Shahi).*

A note of caution is necessary with regard to the alleged *khasra* and map maintained by the Nazul department in the Faizabad Collectorate which is relied upon by the plaintiffs of Suit No. 12 of 1961 (now O.O.S. 4 of 1989 before the Lucknow Bench of the Allahabad High Court), *Sunni Central Board of Waqf and others Vs. Gopal Singh Visharad and others.* The map maintained by the Nazul department is not authenticated, nor prepared under any law, nor is it according to any ascertainable scale. The survey made on the basis of the *khasra abadi* and that map of the Nazul department at the instance of the plaintiffs in that Suit has been rejected by the High Court's Full Bench which is trying the case and a fresh survey has been ordered on the basis of revenue records in order to ascertain the exact situation of the land involved in that Suit. It is noticeable that the plot numbers given in the plaint of that Suit are based on the said *khasra abadi* of the Nazul department. There is no *Fard Mutabiqat* comparative table between the plot numbers given in the *khasra abadi* of the Nazul department and the *khasra abadi* maintained by the Revenue Department of the Government.

In fact, the purpose of the Nazul (Municipal) survey and the map prepared in 1931 A.D. was to identify the encroachments made on the Nazul property. Such a survey map cannot take precedence over the regularly conducted revenue settlement operations and the maps prepared thereupon, especially when the title to land is involved. In its order dated 10.1.1990, the High Court directed the Board of Revenue, U.P. State, to survey the site and make report with the assistance of the Municipal records and such other records which it considered to be useful and in its further order dated 23.5.1990 directed it to execute the commission and locate the plots with reference to documents on record only[25]. The commissioner, Shri J.P. Srivastava, appointed by the Board of Revenue for the purpose, submitted his report on 25.7.1990 wherein he had located the disputed property with reference to the Nazul map of 1931, even though he conceded that the Nazul map and the settlement maps were on different scales and that it was not possible to juxtapose the two maps and prepare *Fard Mutabiqat* and correspond the Nazul *khasra* numbers with the settlement *khasra* numbers[26]. Thereupon, the Hon'ble court passed another order directing the commissioner to submit supplementary report surveying and locating the property with reference to settlement maps of 1861 and 1937 A.D. The commissioner submitted his supplementary report, dated 8.2.1991, appended by 14 Annexures, to which serious objections were made by the Defendants to the effect that in gross violation of the directions of the court, the land had been surveyed primarily on the basis of Nazul map and not settlement maps, consultation of the records not on file in the case, non location and checking of proper fixed point and faulty measurement of land which was not done even according to the improperly fixed point[27]. In fact, the commissioner instead of surveying the land on his own had just accepted the fresh map supplied by the Plaintiff, which in matters of details offered a completely inaccurate position in respect of *Janmasthan*/'Baburi *Mosque*', graveyards, the *shilanyas* site and various other plots. Such an act on the part of the commissioner for having accepted the Plaintiff's map and adopting it as his own official map for submission to the court was characterised by the latter as "wholly unwarranted"[28]. The commissioner's plea that he could not undertake full survey of the disputed land of his own because of the iron barricades erected by the Government for security purpose was not accepted by the court. More than this, the commissioner in his report had found various faults with the settlement map of 1861 which according to him had not made correct delineation of the boundary of village *Ramkot* and that the second settlement of 1937 had adopted the earlier map of 1861 without meticulous field survey and spot verification. He also stated that the original map of the village *Ramkot* of the 1861-70 settlement operation had been washed away by the floods of river Gomti and that the map appended to the settlement was prepared on 17th October, 1873 and was not attested by the Settlement Officer. As such, according to the commissioner, the settlement maps of 1861 and 1937 tally with each other but they do not tally with Nazul map of 1937 and that the latter map is correct and the settlement maps are wrong. Having gone through the pros and cons of the entire case, the Hon'ble court in its judgement on 8.8.1991, even though it refrained from calling the commissioner's report as 'motivated', described it as "absurd"[29]. It refused to accept the commissioner's view that correct map and report about *Kot* Ram Chandra were possible only in reference to Nazul map and that the settlement maps were not correctly prepared. In its judgement, it refused to keep the report of the commissioner on record in the pending case.

A thorough examination of the 1861 Settlement Report would show that it is not only the most comprehensive document but meticulously prepared after an on-the-spot survey and measurement of the *khasras* relating to *kishtwar* and *abadi* but also in accordance with the erstwhile *Nawabi* and Mughal practice duly attested in every respect by the local zamindars/*pattidars* of various *mahal* units, the local revenue officials and witnesses etc[30]. The 1861 Settlement Report, also based upon the earlier 1858-60 summary settlements, depicts the exact position about *Janmasthan*/'Baburi Masjid' and the neighbouring plots as inherited from the pre-British rule in Awadh. The commissioner's observations in respect of the survey and measurement of the village *Kot* Ram Chandra adopted in the 1861 Settlement Report are completely untenable.

As per revenue records, the *Shilanyas* site on which the foundation of the proposed construction of the *Ramjanmabhoomi* Mandir was laid by Sri *Ramjanmabhoomi Nyas* in November, 1989 with the consent of the then Government of India and *karseva* was performed on 30th October, 1990 does not fall in the disputed areas around *Janmasthan*/'Baburi *Mosque*' declared as such by the Injunction Order of the Allahabad High Court, Lucknow Bench on 14.8.1989 and subsequent order, dated 7 November, 1989 for the maintenance of "status quo" and not changing the "nature of property in question" by the parties to the suit. The parties in suit are Sunni *Waqf* Board versus various *Mahants* in five suits registered since 1950, 1959, 1961 and 1989 but transferred in 1989 at present pending for decision before the High Court. The *Vishva Hindu Parishad* is not a direct party to any of the above suits as the parties involved are the Mahants vs. Sunni Waqf Board, U.P. and a few *Mahants* against each Other. However, the V.H.P. has been supporting a couple of *Mahants* from outside. All the same, the Muslim Personal Law Board Working Committee made statements to the effect (dated 6 and 8 December, 1990) that the *shilanyas* and *karseva* site chosen by Sri *Ramjanmabhoomi Nyas* was the property of the U.P. *Waqf* Board and that "the *shilanyas* on the dispute land surrounding the *Mosque* (Baburi) was illegal as the dispute is pending before the court and that the court has ordered the maintenance *of status quo* until the decision".

An examination of the official revenue records shows that the viewpoint of the Muslim Personal Law Board Working Committee and the U.P. *Waqf* Board that the *shilanyas* site claimed to be a part of the Nazul *khasra* No. 586 (stated in *waqf)* is a disputed one and that the performance of the *shilanyas/karseva* by Sri *Ramjanmabhoomi Nyas* in November, 1989/October, 1990 was in violation of the orders of the court is not tenable. A perusal of the records in respect of holdings in the village *Kot* Ram Chandra since the 1301 *Fasli* (1893 A.D.), even the Nazul Department's revised *khasras* (1931) and the third Regular Settlement of 1344 *Fasli* (1936-37) shows that there have been numerous mutations, even in respect of the desolate graveyards *(qabristan)* areas[31]. All these amendments have to be discerned carefully as reflected in the relevant columns of the varying categories of the revenue records.

It has already been stated that the High Court in its order dated 23.5.1990 that the commissioner's survey report based upon the Nazul records was defective and not according to law. In fact, for property issues, only the revenue records based upon the Settlement Reports are the proper records. Since the 1936-37 settlement, all amendments/mutations have been recorded in the yearly *khata khataunis* and *khewats*. The *shilanyas* site falls under *khasra* No. 865 and in July-December, 1981, the entries in the revenue documents stand in the name of *Mahant* Abi Ram Das[32]. After the death of Abi Ram Das, as per the latter's Will, the revenue entry was made in the name of his disciple, *Mahant* Dharam Das, who further bequeathed all his legal rights of the plot to Acharya Ram Nand of *Ramjanmabhoomi Nyas* under registered deed dated 29 April, 1986 as *Ramjanmabhoomi sthal* for the proposed construction of the temple[33]. All this is clear from the revenue documents/registered deed in the sub-Registrar's court as well.

A thorough study of the revenue documents from 1858-61 to 1991 A.D. shows that there was no *waqf* land associated with the 'Baburi Masjid' situated at the *Janmasthan* site and the *Janmasthan* complex. Nor was there any *mutawalli* for it. However, a serious controversy about the nature of the land grant in the village of Bhuraipur and Sholapur earlier given by the British Government to the assignees *(khattib/muazzans)* which was also in a way connected with the 'Baburi *Mosque*' at *Kot* Ram Chandra, Ayodhya, arose in 1938 A.D[34]. The District *Waqf* Commissioner, Faizabad (Eligible-S.M. Omais) vide his decision dated 16.9.1938 while interpreting the *sanad* earlier given by the British Government to the assigness *(khattib/muazzan)* maintained that even though the grant was conditional on the performance of duties of land holders in the matter of Police, Military or Political Service, etc., the object for which the grant was made was the maintenance of the 'mosque'[35]. Muhammad Zaki, the *khattib/muazzan* raised serious objections to the decision of the Commissioner, Waqf Board. He maintained that the particular grant of land in Sholapur and Bhuraipur had been made by the British Government which was a non-Muslim body and hence the grant could not be taken as a Muslim *waqf.* Moreover, as per *sanad,* it was a conditional grant subject to the performance of military, police and other duties, etc., and in case of non-fulfilment of the latter services, the grant was resumable and in view of these conditions, the grant could not be regarded as a Muslim *waqf*[36]. He contended that after the annexation of Awadh, the British Government in lieu of cash *nankar* and *madad-i-maash* (as inherited from the *Nawabi* period) granted land to Muhammad Asghar and Muhammad Afzal and in the First Regular Settlement (1861), it was entered in the latter's *malkiyat* (ownership)[37]. Thereafter, on February 03, 1870 A.D., Muhammad Asghar and Muhammad Afzal got a decree in their favour whereby they were entered in the revenue records as superior proprietors and possessors in possession of the property *(malik-i-ala qabiz wa mutsarif jadaid)* and since then, their descendants have continued with the same status. As such, the property falling in the category of superior proprietorship *(malkiyat-i-ala)* did not fall in the definition of the Muslim *waqf*. He further contended the descendants of Muhammad Asghar, etc., had been bearing the expenses for the essential items of expenditure for the maintenance of the 'Baburi *Masjid*', the family property was outside the jurisdiction of the Muslim *waqf* Act. No. 12, 1936 as the major amount of the income had been spent by them on their own subsistence as *madad-i-maash,* etc. This had always been recorded in the *khewat* records as such.

Apart from the above valid arguments, Muhammad Zaki always maintained that Sayed Abdul Baqi, the first *muazzan/khattib* of the '*mosque*' appointed by Babur was a Shia and his descendants all through the ages, till date, belonged to the Shia sect and could not be coerced to accept the spurious contention that the 'Baburi *Mosque*' might be put under the control of the Sunni *Waqf* Board. This position was taken by the *muazzan/khattib* family before the District *Waqf* Commissioner, Faizabad (1944). Muhammad Zaki and Malik Hussain, etc., the *muazzans/khattibs* vide their Application dated 26th September, 1943 A.D., serial No. 26, submitted to the Sunni Central Board of *Waqf*, U.P., Lucknow, took a clear stand that there was no *waqf* for their properties in the villages of Buharanpur and Sholapur with total annual income of Rs. 528/14 as (Rupees Five hundred and Annas Fourteen only), *i.e.,* Rupees Three-hundred fifty one and annas six (Rs. 351/6 as) from the village of Bahoranpur and Rs. 177/8 as (Rupees One-hundred, seventy-seven and annas eight) from Sholepur[38]. They further maintained that the *khewatdars* (*i.e.,* the revenue authorities/records) did not recognise this as *waqf* and that it had been recorded in the revenue records only as *nankar muafi.* Of course, in the past they had been looking after the white washing, lighting arrangements of the '*mosque*' and as well making payment of the salaries of the *muazzans/imams*, etc. Notwithstanding all this, the legal tussle continued and in 1945 A.D., it was considered that the *muazzan/khattib* family (at this time Kalab Hussain, the brother of the deceased Muhammad Zaki) had been all through Shias, even though the prayers in the past had been offered both by the Shias and the Sunnis. However, the legal battle has continued till 1981 A.D.[39] and in fact, till date.

It is equally important to note that during the 30s of the 20th century, as per statement of Muhammad Zaki, the *muazzan/khattib* even though he was looking after some of the essential items of the maintenance of the 'mosque' (*i.e.,* whitewashing, lighting and flooring, etc.), from the income of the *nankar/muafi* grant held as *malkiyat* in perpetuity, he did not spend any money on the repairs of the 'mosque' in the aftermath of the riot in Ayodhya in 1934 A.D[40]. The Collectorate and the P.W.D. records of the District Faizabad bear out the fact that the entire expenditure for the repairs of the 'mosque' was met by the District administration/P.W.D. At the same time, a thorough scrutiny of the records, especially as per various witnesses examined in the Shia versus Sunni *Waqf* Boards case, (1945), the last collective prayers said in the 'Baburi *Mosque*' were in 1932 and 1936 A.D. and never thereafter till 1947-49 A.D. or even till date. According to all the available information including that available in the court records of the Suits pending before the Lucknow Bench of Allahabad High Court, there is no other registration of any *Waqf* having the remotest connection with the 'Baburi *Masjid*' in the records of the Sunni Central *Waqf* Board.

References

1. For details, see B.R. Grover, '*Janmasthan Versus 'Baburi Masjid*', published by Bar Council of India, New Delhi/Allahabad, 1991.
2. *Ibid.,* also Evidence for the *Ram Janmabhoomi Mandir,* Vishva Hindu Parishad, New Delhi, 1991, p. 18.
3. National Archives of India, *Foreign, Political*, 28th December, 1855, No. 355, Para No. 5, *Purcha* from Nawab Wajid Ali Shah, the king of Oudh to Major James Outram, the British Resident in own, dated 12th August 55.
4. *Ibid.*
5. *Ibid.*
6. *Ibid.*
7. G.N. Bahura and C. Singh, *Catalogue of Historical Documents in Kapad-Dwara Jaipur,* Part II (Maps and Plans), His Highness's Secretariat, Jaipur, p. 36. Serial No. 179; also *Kapad-Dwara Documents,* Private Collection Series, N.A.I., New Delhi.
8. *Ibid.,* also G.C. Verma, 'Jai Singh puras' Proceedings of the Rajasthan History Congress, Vol. XI, 1978, pp. 74-83.
9. Joseph Tieffenthaler, *History and Geography of India,* published in French by Bernoulli, Description *Historique et Geographique de* a Province D'Oude, pp. 253-254.
10. Also Saiyyed Sabbaud Din Abdur Rehman, *Baburi Masjid,* Azamgarh, 1986, 3rd edition, 1987, pp. 29-31.
11. Abul Fazl, *Ain-i-Akbari* (Persian text) vol. II, Nawal Kishore Press, Lucknow, 1881, p. 78.
12. District Record Office, *(Muhafazkhana),* Faizabad (U.P.), B*asta* No. 132 of 1861 pertaining to *khasra kishtwar, mauza Ram Kot*, *Pargana Haveli* and Zilla Faizabad); Hose's Note dated 1st April, 1905. No. 37, Nazul Office, Faizabad.
13. District Record Office, Faizabad, *khasra abadi,* 1861.
14. *Ibid., Bandobast;* 1301 *Fasli*/1893 A.D.
15. *Ibid., Bandobast;* 1344/45 *Fasli*/1936-37 A.D.
16. *Op. Cit., No.* 12.
17. Tehsil Record Office, District Faizabad,. *Basta* No. 132 of 1861 relating to *khasra kishtwar, mauza Ram Kot*, *Pargana Haveli* and Zilla Faizabad.
18. *Op. Cit., No.* 14.
19. *Tehsil Record Office*, Faizabad, District Faizabad.
20. *Op. Cit.,* No. 9.
21. Map appended to *Bandobast,* 1861, *op. Cit.,* No. 12.
22. *Op. Cit.,* No. 12.
23. *Op. Cit.,* No. 14.

24. Nazul Office, Faizabad, District Faizabad, *khasra tarmimi abadi, Kot* Ramchandra, *Pargana Haveli* Awadh, District Faizabad, 1931.
25. Allahabad High Court, Lucknow Bench, Order on objections against Survey Commissioner's Report in Other Original Suit No. 4 of 1989 (Regular Suit No. 12 of 1961; Sunni Central Board of *Waqfs*, U.P. and others-Plaintiffs Versus Gopal Singh Visharad and Others-Defendants; Hon'ble Judges S.C. Mathur, Brijesh Kumar and S.H.A. Raza; dated 9.8.1991.
26. *Ibid.*
27. *Ibid.*
28. *Ibid.*
29. *Ibid.*
30. *Op. Cit.,* Nos. 12, 13, 17.
31. *Op. Cit.,* Nos. 14, 15, 24.
32. *khasra/khata khatauni/khewat* Records, *Kot* Ramchandra, *Pargana Haveli* Awadh, also Registration Deed, sub-Registrar's Office, Faizabad dated 29 April, 1986.
33. *Ibid.,* sub-Registrar's Office, Faizabad.
34. Daftar Sunni Central Board of *Waqf,* U.P., Lucknow, Faizabad, *Waqf* Papers.
35. *Ibid.*
36. *Ibid.*
37. *Ibid.*
38. *Ibid.,* Form Registry *Waqf* No. 38, U.P. Muslim *Waqf* Act, No. 13, 1936 A.D.
39. *Judgement of the Supreme Court of India*, the case of Gulam Abbas Vs. State of U.P., AIR 1981 SC 2196, pp. 2217-18, para No. 17. The Supreme Court declared that the claim of the Central Sunni *Waqf* Board that the 'Baburi *Mosque*' had been notified on 16.2.1944 as Sunni was "of doubtful validity and probative value".
40. *Op. Cit.,* No. 34.

8
Literary Sources

Apart from a source traceable to the late 17th/early 18th century, most of the works were produced in the post-1855 period. All the same, a few writers had lived under the *Nawabi* period and had been an eyewitness to the events and the position of *Janmasthan*/ Baburi *Masjid* during that phase.

The Muslim writers who were residents of Awadh and have written detailed accounts of the regional history of Awadh based on the past authentic contemporary sources of various nature, have unanimously stressed the fact that on the basis of Babur's order, the *Janmasthan* of Sri Ram Chandra at *Kot* Ram Chander, *Pargana Haveli, Awadh,* which comprised not only the private apartments (*mahal sarai*) of King Dashrath and Sri Ram but also a temple and a kitchen popularly known as *Sita Ki Rasoi* were demolished and a mosque constructed thereupon in 1528 A.D. under the guidance of the Commander Mir Baqi and a Muslim *faqir* named Sayed Musa Ashikan. Indeed, graphic descriptions have been provided by many historians in a significant manner. Of these the following deserve special mention:

(i) Early 18th century

Safiha-i-Chahal Nasaih Bahadur Shahi, written by the daughter of Bahadur Shah Alamgir during the late 17th century/ early 18th century. Out of the above *Chahl Nasaih* (forty Advices), twenty-five instructions were copied and incorporated in the manuscript entitled *Nasihat-i-Bist-o-Panjam Az Chahal Nisaih Bahadur Shahi* in 1816 A.D., which was preserved in the Library of Mirza Haider Shikoh s/o Mirza Suleman Shikoh. The text runs, "...the mosques built on the basis of the king's orders (ba *Farman-i-Badshahi*) have not been exempted from the offering of the *namaz* and the reading of the *khutba* (therein). The places of worship of the Hindus situated at Mathura, Benaras and Awadh, etc., in which the Hindus (*kufar*) have great faith—the place of the birth-place of Kanhaiya, the place of *Rasoi Sita,* the place of Hanuman, who, according to the Hindus, was seated by Ram Chandra over there after the conquest of Lanka—were all demolished for the strength of Islam and at all these places, mosques have been constructed. These mosques have not been exempted from *juma* and *jamiat* (Friday prayers). Rather it is obligatory that no idol worship should be performed over there and the voice of the conch should not reach the ear of the Muslims..."

Mirza Jan, the author of Hadiqa-i-Shahda, 1856, Lucknow, pp. 4-7 has reproduced the above text in Persian.

(ii) Ain-i-Akbari, 1598 A.D.

In the field of medieval historiography, Abul Fazl, the author of *Akbar Nama/Ain-i-Akbari* (late 16th century) is the earliest writer of the Mughal age to have categorically associated Awadh (Ayodhya) with the residential place (*banga*) of Sri Ram Chandra who during the *Treta* age was the embodiment of both the spiritual sovereign supremacy as well as the mundane kingly office. Abul Fazl also testifies that Awadh (Ayodhya) was esteemed as one of holiest places of antiquity. As in the *Ain-i-Akbari,* Abul Fazl is basically concerned with the institutional and administrative system of the Mughals (under Akbar). He does not provide any further detail.

(iii) AH 1271/1856 A.D.

Mirza Jan, *Hadiqa-i-Shahada* 1856, Lucknow, pages 4-7.

Even though written in the early second half of the 19th century, for his description on the construction of the Baburi *Mosque*, the author claims to have gone through various old sources. Mirza Jan in his own account says that the past Sultans encouraged the propagation and glorification of Islam and crushed the forces of the kafirs (*kufar*)-Hindus. Similarly, Faizabad and Awadh were also purged of this mean practice (of *kufr*). This (Awadh) was a great worshipping (religious) centre and was the capital of (the kingdom) the father of Ram.

Where there was a large temple, a big mosque was constructed and where there was a small *mandap*, there a small *kanati* masjid was got constructed. As such, the temple of *Janmasthan,* where there is the original birth-place (*masqat*) of Ram and adjacent to it is *Sita Ki Rasoi*—Sita is the name of his wife—at that site, a high and tall (*sarbaland*) mosque has been built by Babur Badshah under the guidance of Musa Ashikan.....That mosque is till date popularly known as *Sita Ki Rasoi*...., of all that only this portion remains and the Ram Darbar mosque was built by Fidai Khan, the *subedar*".

(iv) 1858 A.D.

Muhammad Asghar, *Khatib* and *Muazzan* of the Baburi *Masjid*, in his representation dated 30.11.1858, case No. 884, *muhalla Kot* Ram Chandra, Ajodhya, to the British Government in the complaint against the *Bairagis* of *Janmasthan* for alleged interference in the Baburi *Masjid* concedes the fact that in the outer space of the constructed mosque (of course, in the courtyard within the walled boundaries of the mosque) there had been *Janmasthan* lying desolate where the Hindus had been worshipping for hundreds of years thereupon. This is a frank admission of the fact that even though a major portion of the *Janmasthan* had been covered by the Baburi *Masjid*, the Hindus had been worshipping in the remaining open space for hundreds of years, *i.e.,* even during the Mughal and *Nawabi* periods and that they had never surrendered their claim of the entire *Janmasthan* area. Apparently, the controversy of the claim over *Janmasthan* by the Hindus *versus* Baburi *Masjid* was not a creation of the British 'Divide and Rule' policy.

(v) 1869 A.D. *Murraqa-i-Khusrawi*

Sheikh Muhammad Azmat Ali Alwi Nami, the author of *Tawarikh-i-Mulkh-i-Awadh* entitled as *Murraqa-i-Khusrawi* states that "Awadh was the capital of the father of Lachhman and Ram. (There) under the guidance of Saiyed Musa Ashikan, a magnificent Baburi masjid was constructed at the site of the temple within the premises of *Janmasthan*, which was popularly known amongst the Hindus as *Sita Ki Rasoi.* The date of construction can be reckoned from Khair Baqi...And a mosque was also constructed at the site of *Ram Darbar* by Fidai Khan, *subedar*, which was later on demolished and mitigated by the Hindus."

(vi) 1878 A.D.

Haji Muhammad Hasan, *Zia-i-Akhtar*, Lucknow, 1878, pages 38-39.

The author states that "the mosque which had been built by Saiyed Musa Ashikan in 923 AH in compliance with the order of Zahiruddin Badshah, Delhi, after demolishing the private apartments (*mahal sarai*) of Raja Ram Chandra and the *Sita Ki Rasoi* as well as the second mosque built by Muiuddin Aurangzeb, Alamgir Badshah, (in fact) both these mosques had developed cracks at various places because of the ageing character. Both these mosques have been gradually mitigated by the *Bairagis* and this very fact accounts for the riot. The Hindus have great hatred for the Muslims..."

(vii) Mirza Rajab Ali Beg, *Fasana-i-Ibrat*

(a) Rajab Ali, the author of *Fasana-i-Ibrat* describes "that during the reign of Babur *Badshah*, a magnificent mosque was constructed in Awadh at a place which is associated with *Sita Ki Rasoi*. This was Baburi *Mosque*. As during this period, the Hindus could not dare to offer any resistance, the mosque was constructed under the benign guidance of Saiyed Mir Ashikan. Its date of construction could be reckoned from (the words) *Khair-Baqi*. And in the *Ram Darbar*, a mosque was got constructed by Fidai Khan, the *subedar*."

(b) After further describing the construction of another mosque at Hanuman Garhi by Aurangzeb, the author states that later on, after the defeat of Nawab Shujauddaula at Buxar, the *Bairagis* occupied the latter place. The author, Rajab Ali asserts "that the above description has been provided in the historical works and the details which, along with the dates and years, etc., have been described in *Sahifa-i-Bahadurshahi* and anybody interested (in this) could verify..."

(c) "The *Bairagis* mitigated the mosque at Hanuman *Garhi* and constructed a temple (thereupon). And then, open prayers were henceforth offered (by the *Bairagis*) in the Baburi mosque comprising the site of *Sita-ki-Rasoi*. The (*Nawabi*) administration could do nothing about it."

(viii) Maulvi Abdul Karim, *Gumghasta Halat-i-Ajodhya Awadh* (The Forgotten Events of Ajodhya Awadh), *i.e., Tarikh-i-Parnia Madina Alwaliya* (in Persian), Lucknow, 1885 A.D.

The author who was also the *imam* of the Baburi *Masjid*, while giving description about the *dargah* of Hazrat Shah Jamal Gojjri states that "to the east of this *dargah* is *mahalla* Akbarpur whose second name is also *Kot* Raja Ramchandra Ji. In this *Kot*, there were few *burjs* (towery big halls). Towards the side of the western *burj*, there was the house of birth-place (*makaan-i-paidaish*) and the kitchen (*bawarchi khana) of* the above mentioned Raja. And now, this premises is known as *Janmasthan* and *Rasoi Sita Ji*. After the demolition and mitigation of these houses (*i.e., Janmasthan* and *Rasoi Sita Ji*), Babur Badshah got constructed a magnificent mosque thereupon."

(ix) Alama Muhammad Najamalghani Khan Rampuri, *Tarikh-i-Awadh*, 1909, Vol. II, vide abridged edition, Dr. Zaki Kakaurwi, pages 570-575.

(a) "In Ajodhya, where temple of *Janmasthan* of Ramchandra was situated, adjacent to it *Sita Ki Rasoi* is situated. Babur Badshah had built a magnificent mosque over there under the guidance of Saiyed Ashikan. Its date of construction is Khair Baqi (923 AH). Till date, it is known as *Sita Ki Rasoi.* By its side a temple exists. It is said that at the time of the conquest of Islam, there were still three temples, *i.e., Janmasthan*, which was the birth-place of Ramchandra Ji, *Swargadwar* alias Ram Darbar and the Thakur of *Treta*. Babur built the mosque after having demolished *Janmasthan*."

(b) "... In short, the turbulence (1855) reached such a stage that apart from the mitigated mosque at Hanuman Garhi, the Hindus built a temple in the courtyard of Baburi *Masjid* where *Sita Ki Rasoi* was situated..."

(c) " ...Ultimately, on *Zilqada* AH 1271/July, 1855, for the tenth or eleventh time, nearly two to three hundred Muslims gathered at Baburi *Masjid* which is situated inside the *Sita Ki Rasoi*..."

It is important to observe that the learned author used as many as eighty-one sources (manuscripts/books) covering the history of India/Awadh from the 17th to 19th centuries. It is a very comprehensive Bibliography-comprising mostly Muslim authors, though, a few Hindu and European writers have also been referred to.

(x) (Early 20th century) Maulana Hakim Sayid Abdul Hai, *Hindustan Islami Ahad Mein*

Maulana Hakim Sayid Abdul Hai (d. 1923), an eminent scholar on the history of Islamic culture and also the Rector of Nadwatul-Ulama, wrote on *India under Islamic Rule* in Arabic in the early 20th century which was later on published in Hyderabad in 1972. This was translated into Urdu along with a Foreword by his worthy son, Maulana Abdul Hasan Nadwi alias Ali Mian under the title *Hindustan Islami Ahad Mein* (Hindustan under Islamic rule) which was published by Nadwatul-Ulma, Lucknow, in 1973. An English version of the same book was published in 1977.

The book incorporated a chapter on "The Mosques of Hindustan" (*Hindustan ki Masjidein*) giving at least six instances of the construction of the mosques on the very sites of the Hindu temples demolished by the Indian Muslim rulers during the 12th-17th centuries. As regards Baburi *Masjid*, he writes that "This mosque was constructed by Babar at Ajodhya which the Hindus call the birth-place of Ram Chandra Ji. There is a famous story about his wife Sita. It is said that Sita had a temple here in which she lived and cooked food for her husband. On that very site, Babur constructed this mosque..."

(xi) Most of the above works are rather rare. However, it is very surprising that in some of the books which have undergone reprint in the post-1980 period, the portion relating to the destruction of *Janmasthan* temple and construction of the Baburi mosque by Babur on the same site has been deleted in the revised editions. This raises serious suspicion about the real intention in the post-1980 controversy over the issue of Ram Janmabhoomi/Baburi *Masjid*. This is borne out by the following instances:-

(a) It is significant to note that the author Maulvi Abdul Karim, the author of *Gumghasta Halat-i-Ajodhya* Awadh (vide No. VIII) was also the *Imam* of Babri *Masjid* and in his scholarly work has referred to numerous contemporary sources, from 16th to the 19th centuries. The same book was translated by his grandson, Maulvi Abdul Gufar, from Persian to Urdu and published in Lucknow in May, 1979 which retained the above mentioned description about the demolition of the temple at *Janmasthan* and construction of the mosque thereupon, vide page 40. But this portion has been omitted from the revised second edition in Urdu published in Lucknow, 1981, pages 53-54.

(b) Sheikh Muhammad Azmat Ali Nami's *Tawarikh-Mulkh-i-Awadh* entitled *Murraqa-i-Khusrawi's* manuscript, available at Tagore Library, University of Lucknow (U.P.), was for the first time published in 1986. In this version, the above mentioned portion relating to the construction of Baburi masjid on the site of the temple in the premises of *Janmasthan* as well as the portion relating to Amir Ali Shahid and the Hindu-Muslim riot of 1855 were deleted by the Fakhruddin Ahmad Memorial Committee under whose auspices the book was brought out. But Dr. Zakir Kakaurwi has published these portions separately under the title *Amir Ali Shahid Aur Marakha-i-Hanuman Garhi*, Lucknow, 1987, pages 9-11. The truth, once suppressed, thus prevailed.

(c) Similarly, certain additions/interpolations have been made in the Revenue Records as well. This is borne out by the comparison of the records available at the *Mahafaz Khana*, District Faizabad Vs. the Tehsil records of the Settlement Report of 1861. This is also confirmed by the fact that the *khasra kishtwar* of the second Revenue Settlement (1301 *Fasli*/1893 A.D.) do not carry such alteration/addition. These records still show the area on which Baburi *Masjid* had been earlier constructed and the adjacent area as *Sita Ki Rasoi* forming a part of the *Janmasthan* complex (vide *khasra* No. 163/5). In the records, there is no mention of any mosque and the land assigned to it in *muafi*. Similarly, there is an interpolation in the Revised *khasra* Records of the Nazul Department (*tarmimi khasra abadi*) of 1931 A.D. This is, however, a very serious matter, which requires further investigation in this regard.

9

No *Waqf* Associated with 'Baburi Masjid'

In the *Janmasthan* complex as recorded in the 1st regular Settlement Report (1861 A.D.), there is no plot/sub-plot which has been put as a *waqf* attached to 'Baburi *Masjid*.' At that time, Muhammad Asghar claimed himself to be *khattib* and *muazzan* (vide his representation to the British Government, case No. 884, *Muhalla Kot* Ramchandra, Ajodhya, dated November 30, 1858 A.D.) of the monument named as 'Baburi *Mosque*' situated at *Janmasthan*. According to the Muslim claim, this monument was registered as 'mosque' in 1860 A.D. only, *i.e.,* after the 1855 Hindu-Muslim riot and the tussle that followed. In his representation to the British Government, Mir Rajab Ali also designated himself as '*Khattib* Baburi *Masjid*' (vide Application No. 115, *Muhalla Kot* Ram Chandra, Ajodhya, dated November 01, 1860 A.D). All the same, in the *Hadbast* map appended to 1861 A.D. Settlement Report, the symbol of the 'Mosque' does not figure in the *Janmasthan* complex (*khasra kishtwar* No. 163/*abadi* plot No. 431-41).

As a matter of fact, both Muhammad Asghar and Mir Rajab Ali were residents of village Shahanwa (about three miles to the west of village *Kot* Ram Chandra/Ajodhya) and were petty zamindars/land holders/lambardars of village Shahanwa. The 1861 Settlement Report of village Shahanwa (vide No. *Hadbast* 571, village Shahanwa, *Pargana* Awadh, Tehsil/District Faizabad, available at the Tehsil Office, Faizabad) puts the revenues of the village under *khalisa* (government) and Muhammad Asghar, Mir Rajab Ali and Muhammad Afzal, etc., are shown as *pattidars* (vide **Exhibit No. 'A'**). Under the revenue system as inherited from the Mughal and *Nawabi* Governments, as *pattidars*/*maliks*/*lambardars*, etc., they were entitled to *nankar* (subsistence allowance) in the shape of *nankar/muafi* land in the same village. At the same time, they were landholders and their holdings etc., are recorded in the Settlement Report. But it is nowhere recorded that they enjoyed any *nankar/muafi* for the maintenance of the '*Mosque*' in *Kot* Ram Chandra, *Pargana* Awadh, Ajodhya, as *khattibs/muazzans*, etc. However, even though they could not furnish any documentary evidence to the British Government, they continued to claim that during the *Nawabi* period, their family had been getting the annual grant of Rs. 302/3/6 as *nankar* and *muafi* from the revenues of the village Shahanwa for its own maintenance and out of this income, they had been spending only a part of the amount for looking after some of the essential needs of the so- called 'Baburi *Mosque*' situated at *Janmasthan*, *Kot* Ram Chandra, *Pargana* Awadh, District Faizabad. After the First War of Independence in 1857 (mentioned as 'Mutiny' in the Report of the District Waqf Commissioner, Faizabad, dated 16.9.38), the British Government, apparently on political grounds, because of the loyalty and services rendered by the landlord/*pattidari* family of the village Shahanwa, continued the above mentioned amount in cash but from 1863-64 A.D. onwards, the British Government considered it expedient to commute this cash payment unto a conditional (*mashrut*) *muafi* land grant—a process which was completed by 1870 A.D. when, as explained further, the revenue-free land grant along with superior proprietary rights was bestowed on Mohammad Asghar and Mohammad Afzal Ali in the villages of Sholapur and Bhaharanpur but not in *Kot* Ram Chander where the *Janmasthan* 'mosque' stood. As such, all previous orders regarding the family grant to Muhammad Asghar/Muhammad Afzal Ali were superseded by the final order passed in 1870 under the authority of the Governor General in Council, whereby, a *sanad* for revenue-free land grant was issued by the Chief Commissioner, Awadh. On representation from the family, a decree to this effect was also given by the revenue authorities and entires were made in the revenue records accordingly during the same year (1870).

Later on when in 1938 A.D., controversy arose about the nature of the title to the land granted by the British Government for the maintenance of the '*mosque*', Pir Mir Taqi, the *khattib* and *muazzan,* while tracing the genealogy of his family, claimed that the Mughal king Babur built this 'mosque' situated on the site of *Janmasthan* and granted an annual amount of Rs. 60/- and some arable land in *madad-i-maash* in the village Shahanwa to Sayed Abdul Baqi, appointed as *khattib/muazzan* for his subsistence and the maintenance of the 'mosque'. Later on, after the fall of the Mughal Empire, during the *Nawabi* period, Nawab Saadat Ali Khan, king of Awadh, increased the annual grant to Rs. 302/3 as/6 pies. But as commented by the Waqf Commissioner, District Faizabad on 16.9.38 that in this regard, no written accounts were submitted by the *khattib/muazzan* family to the British Government for the continuation or bestowal of fresh grant for the same purpose.

It has already been observed that although Muhammad Asghar and Rajab Ali claimed to be direct descendants of Sayed Abdul Baqi, the first *khattib/muazzan* supposed to have been appointed by Babur, no reference of cash assignment or *madad-i-maash* land on hereditary basis can be traced in the first regular Settlement of the village Shahanwa in 1861 A.D. All the same, on repeated representations to the British Government by Muhammad Asghar and Rajab Ali, the British Government having discontinued the annual cash grant, granted afresh land in *muafi* in the village of Baharanpur and Sholapur in 1870 A.D. Later on, the *sanad* issued by the Chief Commissioner clarified that the cash *nankar* of Rs. 302/3as/6 pies received by Rajab Ali and Muhammad Asghar as rent-free tenure in village Shahanwa under the former Government (*Nawabi* Rule) was being maintained (as *muafi* land in the village of Baharanpur and Sholapur) under the authority of the Governor General-in-Council so long as the object for which the grant had been made was kept up on the conditions that the assignees would surrender all the (previous) *sanads*, title deeds, and other documents relative to the grant in question and above all, they and their successors would "strictly perform all the duties of land holders in matters of police and any military or political service that may be required of them by the Authorities... If any one of these conditions were broken by Rajab Ali or Mohammad Usgar or their successors, the grant will be immediately resumed". (vide **Exhibit No. 'B'**).

A serious controversy about the nature of the land grant in the village of Baharanpur and Sholapur earlier given by the British

Government to the assignees (*khattib/muazzans*) which was also in a way connected with the 'Baburi *mosque*' at *Kot* Ram Chandra, Ajodhya, arose in 1938 A.D. The District Waqf Commissioner, Faizabad (S.M. Omais), vide his decision dated 16.9.38, while interpreting the *sanad* earlier given by the British Government to the assignees (*khattib/muazzan*), maintained that even though the grant was conditional on the performance or duties of land holders in the matter of police, military or political service, etc., the object for which the grant was made was the maintenance of the '*mosque*'. He also stressed that the original object of the state grant of Emperor Babur and Nawab Saadat Ali Khan was also continued in the *sanad* by the British Government after the 'Mutiny', *i.e.,* for the maintenance of the 'mosque' and further that the *nankar* was to be enjoyed by the grantee for so long as the object of the grant, *i.e.,* the '*mosque*', was in existence. In view of this, the Commissioner gave a ruling to the effect "Clearly then the grant to Mohd. Zaki must be regarded as *waqf*, the purpose of which is the maintenance of the religious building known as the Baburi *Mosque*".

Muhammad Zaki, the *khattib/muazzan* (also *mutawalli* in case of *waqf*) raised serious objections to the decision of the Commissioner, Waqf Board. He maintained that the particular grant of land in Sholapur and Baharanpur had been made by the British Government which was a non-Muslim body and hence the grant could not be taken as Muslim *waqf*. Moreover, as per *sanad*, it was a conditional grant subject to the performance of military, police and other duties, etc., and in case of non-fulfilment of the latter services, the grant could not be regarded as a Muslim *waqf*. He contended that after the annexation of Awadh, the British Government, in lieu of cash *nankar* and *madad-i-maash* (as inherited from the *Nawabi* period), granted land to Muhammad Asghar and Muhammad Afzal and in the first Regular Settlement (1861), it was entered in the latter's *malkiyat* (ownership). Thereafter, on February 03, 1870 A.D., Muhammad Asghar and Muhammad Afzal got a decree in their favour whereby they were entered in the revenue records as superior proprietors and possessors in possession of the property (*malik-i-ala qabiz wa mutsarif jadaid*) and since then, their descendants have continued with the same status. As such, the property falling in the category of superior proprietorship (*malkiyat-i-ala*) did not fall in the definition of the Muslim *waqf*. He further contended, even though the descendants of Muhammad Asghar, etc., had been bearing the expenses for the essential items of expenditure for the maintenance of the 'Baburi *Masjid*', the family property was outside the jurisdiction of the Muslim waqf Act, No. 12, 1936 as the major amount of the income had been spent by them on their own subsistence as *madad-i-maash*, etc. This had always been recorded in the *khewat* records as such (vide **Exhibit No. 'C'**).

Apart from the above valid arguments, Muhammad Zaki always maintained that Sayed Abdul Baqi, the first *muazzan/khattib* of the 'mosque' appointed by Babur was a Shia and his descendents all through the ages, till date, belong to the Shia sect and could not be coerced to accept the spurious contention that the 'Baburi *Mosque*' might be put under the control of the Sunni Waqf Board. This position was taken by the *muazzan/khattib* family before the District Waqf Commissioner, Faizabad (1941). However, the latter's Report (dated February 08, 1941) simply reproduced and reiterated the position earlier taken by the District Waqf Commissioner in 1938 A.D. On the contrary, Muhammad Zaki and Malik Hussain, etc., the *muazzans/khattibs* vide their Application dated 26th September, 1943 A.D. serial No. 26, submitted to the Sunni Central. Board of Waqf, U.P, Lucknow, took a clear stand that there was no *waqf* for their properties in the villages of Buharanpur and Sholapur with total annual income of Rs. 528/14 as (Rupees Five hundred and Annas Fourteen only), *i.e.,* Rupees Three hundred fifty one and annas six (Rs. 351/6 as) from the village of Buharanpur and Rs. 177/8 as (Rupees One-hundred seventy seven and annas eight) from Sholapur. They contended that earlier they had been bestowed grant (*atiya*) by *Shahenshah* Babur and Nawab Saadat Ali Khan and in the present case (*i.e.,* land/income from Buharanpur/Sholapur) they were strictly governed by the *sanad nankar* granted by the British Government. They further maintained that the *khewatdars* (*i.e.,* the revenue authorities/records) did not recognise this as *waqf* and that it had been recorded in the revenue records only as *nankar muafi*. Of course, in the past they had been looking after the white washing, lighting arrangements of the 'mosque' and also making payment of the salaries of the *muazzans/*

Imams etc. Malik Hussain, s/o Syed Muhammad Zaki in his detailed letter No. 5607, dated 20.11.43/22.11.1943, (Vide **Exhibit No. 'D'**) in response to the Secretary, Sunni Waqf Board's communication vide No. 5272, dated 27th October, 1943, clarified his relation with the 'Baburi Masjid'. He categorically maintained (Vide para 5) that there was neither any *waqf* for the 'masjid' nor there had ever been a *Mutawalli* for it. Further, that his family has had *muafi* land (in the villages of Buharanpur and Sholapur) and being the *lambardar* (head) of the property and being (good) Muslims, it had been looking after the repair etc. of the same and that he, too, as *lambardar* had been discharging this obligation since 17 February, 1943. He stated that the expenditure incurred in this regard was from his family property which was in *muafi nankar* and not in *waqf* (Vide paras 8-9). In this letter, he also gave some details about the items of white washing, repair and floor carpet etc. relating to the '*masjid*' and some expenditure incurred in this regard since October, 1941. (Vide paras 2-3, 10-11). Notwithstanding all this, the legal tussle continued and in 1945 A.D., it was considered that the *muazzan/khattib* family (at this time Kalab Hussain, the brother of the deceased Muhammad Zaki) had been all through Shias.

It is equally important to note that during the 30s of the 20th century, as per statement of Muhammad Zaki, the *muazzan/khattib,* even though he was looking after some of the essential items of the maintenance of the '*mosque*' (*i.e.,* white-washing, lighting and flooring, etc.), from the income of the *nankar/muafi* grant held as *malkiyat* in perpetuity, he did not spend any money on the repairs of the 'mosque' in the aftermath of the riots in Ayodhya in 1934 A.D. The Collectorate and P. W. D. records of the District Faizabad bear out the fact that the entire expenditure for the repairs of the 'mosque' was met by the District Administration/P.W.D. Significantly, in the *waqf* records of the Sunni/Shia Boards of *waqf* or the Collectorate/U.P. Government Records, there is no mention of any *Mutawalli* or *waqf* from the income of which the structure of the 'Baburi *Mosque*' might have been rebuilt, as it ought to have been if there was any *waqf* with valuable revenue free grant of land held by Muhammad Zaki etc. in the villages Buharanpur and Sholapur, allegedly attached for the maintenance and upkeep of the same.

An elementary knowledge of the Mughal agrarian system/ *Nawabi* phase and the British administration in India as well as an understanding of the nature of the various categories of land grants for administrative purpose or to the religious institutions would clearly show that there has always been a basic difference between *nankar* (for personal maintenance) and *waqf*. In this regard, the contentions of the grantees, *i.e.,* Muhammad Asghar, etc. (19th century) and Muhammad Zaki/Kalab Hussain/Malik Hussain etc. (20th century) have been absolutely correct and tenable and that their properties in Shahanwa/Buharanpur/Sholapur could not be categorised as *waqf*. As such, they do not show any *waqf* relating to the alleged 'Baburi *Masjid*'. Even in the judicial records of the various suits pending before the Lucknow Bench of the Allahabad High Court, there is no registration of any *waqf* having any connection with the alleged 'Baburi Masjid' as per records of the Sunni Central *Waqf* Board.

After the above mentioned enquiry by the District Waqf Commissioner, his report as prescribed under the U.P. Muslims Waqf Act, 1936, along with the lists of the Shia *Waqfs* and Sunni *Waqfs,* was forwarded by the U.P. Government to both the Shia Central Board of Waqfs and Sunni Central Board of Waqfs as each of the two *Waqf* Boards were to publish the report alongwith their respective lists in the Official Gazette, under sub-Section (1) of Section 5 of the Act. In the Shia-Sunni legal tussle that followed, the Sunni Central Board of Waqf claimed that it was published as a Sunni 'Mosque' in the U.P. Gazette, dated 26.2.1944, even though in reality, the particulars of the 'Baburi Mosque' or the *qabristan* (graveyard) attached to it, do not find any place in the list of Waqfs published in the Government Gazette, dated 26.2.1944. As the Shia Board claimed it to be Shia *Waqf*, it filed a suit to get over the effect of the Waqf Commissioner's report on the assumption that the 'Baburi *Masjid*' had been notified to be a Sunni *Waqf* in the above mentioned Gazette notification, dated 26.4.1944, under section 5(1) of the U.P. Muslims Waqfs Act, 1936. In this suit No. 29 of 1947 between the Shia and the Sunni Central Boards of Waqfs of U.P., in his judgement dated 30.3.1946, the subordinate judge of Faizabad held the property in suit to be a Sunni *Waqf*. In the continued litigation between the above two parties, the Court of the Civil Judge,

Faizabad, which tried the case as preliminary issue, vide-judgement dated 21.4.1966 held that "no valid notification under Section 5(1) of U.P. Muslim Waqf Act No. XIII of 1936 was ever made" relating to the specific disputed property. As such, the Judge made it clear that the alleged notification of 26.2.1944 did not specify the property in suit as *waqf* property and that it was of no legal effect. This finding became final between the two parties. Later on, in the case of Gulam Abbas Vs. State of U.P. (vide A.I.R. 1981 & C 2196, pp. 2217-18, Paragraph 170 **Exhibit No. 'E'**), in the case between the Shia and the Sunni Muslims, the Hon'ble Supreme Court of India also found the above mentioned notification of the U.P. government, dated 26.2.1944, to be "of doubtful validity and probative value" and held it to be of no legal effect. As such, in view of the judgement of the Supreme Court, the said notification, dated 26.2.1944, was invalid and that the suit No. 29 of 1946 could not have been filed under Section 5(2) of the *Waqf* Act, with the result that the judgement in that Case, dated 30.3.1946 in that suit, is without jurisdiction and the findings recorded therein are of no legal effect. In fact, the above mentioned judgement of the Supreme Court has foreclosed the matter forever.

The earliest regular Settlement of 1861 A.D. as well as the later reports confirm the fact that these had been prepared taking into consideration the past records of the *Nawabi* period as well. As a matter of fact, as per the original documents, the entire complex of *Janmasthan* is covered under *khasra* No. 163 with 9 plots, with total area of 5 *bighas* and 4 *biswas*. However, under column No. 16 of *kaifiyat*, it is stated that in the area of *Janmasthan*, there is one *pacca* well, trees whose numbers is recorded in *khasra abadi* and *pacca* graveyard (*qabristan*). As distinct from the *khasra kishtwar*, in *khasra abadi* Nos. 431-441, (as recorded corresponding to No. 163 of the former) shows *abadi* (population) in this area. They do not mention the existence of any '*mosque*' though, in the *kaifiyat* they mention the prevalence of *pacca* graveyards *Imli* trees and *makans* (houses) etc. in the campus. For 4 *bighas* and 13 *biswas*, the superior ownership of the land has been declared in the name of Sarkar Bahadur Nazul (Government), and vide *khatauni* No. I, 1878 A.D., "*bighas* have been shown as *muafi* under mahal Azhar Hussain. However, in the settlement of 1301 *Fasli*/1893 A.D., in the *khasra kishtwar*, the same *khasra* number (163) remains, though the entire area is shown under 5 plots instead of 10 as previously in the 1861 Settlement Report. Both in the *khata khatauni/khewat,* the Hindu *Mahants* of *Janmasthan* have been shown with subordinate proprietary rights in *malikan-i-matahit* along with their respective shares. But later on, these numbers undergo a change during the *Fasli*/1344/45/1936-37 A.D. Settlement Report but the position of 1861 persists, even in later Settlement effected from time to time during the 19th and 20th centuries. It is also clear that the area on which the structure of the 'Baburi *Masjid*' stood is a part of the *Janmasthan* and under the subordinate ownership (*malikan-i-matahit*) of the Hindu *mahant.*

This position was inherited by the early British administration from the earlier records of the *Nawabi* and the Mughal periods. However, in the Settlement Record of 1861 of the *Mahafazkhana*, certain later alternations have been made wherein the name of *Jama Masjid* and the word *muafi* has been inserted. In plot No. 163/1 the words *Jama Masjid, muafi* and Azhar Hussain under columns Nos., 2, 3 and 4 respectively have been added (Vide **Exhibit No. 'F'**). But the copies of the same document prepared during the same year available at the Tehsil Office wherein only the word *Jama Masjid* has been added in column No. 2 but not *muafi* and Azhar Hussain in column Nos. 3 and 4 as against Muhafas Khanna Report clearly prove that the later additions are interpolations, done perhaps during the past few decades of the controversy (vide **Exhibit No. 'G'**). This is also confirmed by the fact that the *khasra kishtwar* records of the second Revenue Settlement effected in the year 1301 *Fasli* (1893 A.D.) do not carry out such alterations or additions (Vide **Exhibit No. 'H'**). These records still show the area on which 'Baburi Masjid' had been earlier constructed as *Sita Ki Rasoi,* forming a part of the *Janmasthan* complex and there is no mention of any 'mosque' nor any land assigned to it in *muafi*. It is evident that the interpolations in the Settlement Report of 1861 of the District Record Office (Muhafaz Khanna), Faizabad, have been done for a few other *khasra kishtwar* Nos. as well. All this needs a thorough probe on scientific basis.

As already stated, according to the revenue settlement effected in 1861 A.D., the total area covered by *khasra* No. 163 relating to *Janmasthan* has 10 distinct plots. There have been two more settlement operations since then. However, in the revenue settlements effected from time to time, the *khasra/khewat/khata khatauni* numbers as well as the numbers of plot undergo a change and there are also adjustments with the neighbouring plots. But, the table of equivalent past numbers and parts thereof, along with the current (*hal*) numbers (*Farad Mutabiqat*) is always appended and forms a part of the Settlement Report. In the latest revenue records of 1397-99 *Fasli*/1989-90, the erstwhile *Janmasthan* complex has been shown in four *khasra* Nos. *i.e.,* 159, 160, 146 and 147 R. The major portion of the *Janmasthan* complex comprising Ram Janmabhoomi, the so-called Baburi *Masjid* as well as the new *Janmasthan* falls under *khasra* Nos. 159, 146 (vide *khata khewat* No. 35) and 147 R wherein the names of the *Mahants* along with the areas in their ownership have been recorded. Only some portion of the complex falls under No. 160, which too is shown under *Mahal Nazul Sarkar*. In brief, *Janmabhoomi*/'Baburi *Masjid*' have been recorded under No. 159 and 160. The entire *khasra* No. 159 has been entered in the ownership of 'Shri Danesh Dhari Bhagwan Bara Asthan, Ajodhya' whereas some portion falling in *khasra* No. 160 has been recorded in the ownership of *Sarkar Nazul*. There is no *muafi/waqf* of any type associated with the '*mosque*'.

The entire Revenue Records dating from the first Settlement (1861 A.D.) have been examined. There is no record of any of 'Baburi Masjid', anywhere in the documents maintained by the Revenue Department of the Government of U.P. at the Collectorate and the Tehsil at Faizabad.

As distinct from the above mentioned revenue records, the Nazul Department of the District Faizabad, (U.P.) also prepared its own amended *khasra* records of the *abadi* settlements (*tarmimi khasra abadi*) in 1931 A.D. In there revised *khasras* of village *Ramkot*, both 'masjid' and *chabutra* indicating the temple at *Janmasthan* have been recorded in *khasra* No. 583. The 'mosque' has been shown in *waqf* under column 'Name of the present possessor' (*Nam Hal Qabiz*). At the same time, *Mahant* Charan Das in 1931 thereafter *Mahant* Raghu Nath Das in 1941 have been declared under-proprietors (*taliha matahit*) of the entire plot. Moreover, in these *khasra* records, *Arazi* No. 586 with an area of 11 *biswas*, 16 *biswansis* and 16 *kachwansis* (11-16-16) being in *abadi* is shown as graveyard (a *pacca qabristan* known as *Ganj-i-Shahidan*) and assigned in *waqf* (*waqf ahad Shahi*).

A note of caution is necessary with regard to the alleged *khasra* and map maintained by the Nazul Department in the Faizabad Collectorate which is relied upon by the plaintiffs of Suit No. 12 of 1961 (now O.O.S. 4 of 1989 before the Lucknow Bench of the Allahabad High Court). *Sunni Central Board of Waqf and others Vs. Gopal Singh Visharad and others.* The map maintained by the Nazul Department is not authenticated, nor prepared under any law, nor is it according to any ascertainable scale. The survey made on the basis of the *khasra abadi* and that map of the Nazul Department at the instance of the Plaintiffs in that Suit has been rejected by the High Court's Full Bench which is trying the case and a fresh survey has been ordered on the basis of revenue records in order to ascertain the exact situation of the land involved in that Suit. It is noticeable that the plot numbers given in the plaint of that Suit are based on the said *khasra abadi* of the Nazul department. There is no *Fard Mutabiqat* comparative table between the plot numbers given in the *khasra abadi* of the Nazul department and the *khasra abadi* maintained by the Revenue Department of the Government.

In fact, the purpose of the Nazul (Municipal) survey and the map prepared in 1931 A.D. was to identify the encroachments made on the Nazul property. Such as survey map cannot take precedence over the regularly conducted revenue settlement operations and the maps prepared thereupon, especially when the title to land is involved. In its order dated 10.1.1990, the High Court directed the Board of Revenue, U.P. State, to survey the site and make report with the assistance of the Municipal records and such other records which it considered to be useful and in its further order dated 23.5.1990 directed it to execute the commission and locate the plots with reference to documents on record only. The Commissioner, Shri J.P. Srivastava, appointed by the Board of Revenue for the purpose, submitted his report on 25.7.1990 wherein he had located the disputed property with references to the Nazul map of 1931, even though he conceded that the Nazul map and the settlement maps were on different scales and that it was not possible to juxtapose the two maps and prepare *Fard Mutabiqat* and correspond the Nazul *khasra* numbers with the settlement *khasra* numbers. Thereupon, the Hon'ble Court passed another order directing the Commissioner to submit supplementary report surveying and locating the property with reference to settlement maps of 1861 and 1937 A.D. The Commissioner submitted his supplementary report dated 8.2.1991 appended by 14 Annexures, to which serious objections were made by the Defendants.

In fact, the Commissioner, instead of surveying the land on his own, had just accepted the fresh map supplied by the Plaintiff, which in matters of details offered a completely inaccurate position in respect of *Janmasthan*/'Baburi *Mosque*', graveyards, the *shilanyas* site and various other plots. Such an act on the part of the Commissioner for having accepted the Plaintiff's map and adopting it as his own official map for submission to the court was characterised by the latter as "wholly unwarranted".

Having gone through the pros and cons of the entire case, the Hon'ble Court in its judgement on 8.8.1991, even though it refrained from calling the Commissioner's report as 'motivated', described it as "absurd". It refused to accept the Commissioner's view that correct map and report about *Kot* Ram Chandra were possible only with reference to Nazul map and that the Settlement Maps were not correctly prepared. In its judgement, it refused to keep the report of the Commissioner on record in the pending case.

As per revenue records, the *Shilanyas* site on which the foundation of the proposed construction of the Ram Janmabhoomi Mandir was laid by Shri *Ramjanmabhoomi Nyas* in November, 1989 with the consent of the then Government of India and *karseva* was performed on 30th October, 1990, does not fall in the disputed areas around *Janmasthan*/'Baburi Mosque' declared as such by the Injunction Order of the Allahabad High Court, Lucknow Bench on 14.8.1989 and subsequent order dated 7th November, 1989 for the maintenance of "status quo" and not changing the "nature of property in question" by the parties to the suit. The parties in suit are Sunni Waqf Board versus various *Mahants* in five suits registered since 1950, 1959, 1961 and 1989 but filed in 1989, at present pending for decision before the High Court. The *Vishva Hindu Parishad* is not a direct party to any of the above suits as the parties involved are the *Mahants* Vs. Sunni Waqf Board, U.P. and a few *Mahants* against each other. However, the *V.H.P.* has been supporting a couplet of *Mahants* from outside. All the same, the Muslim Personal Law Board Working Committee made statements to the effect (dated 6th and 8th December, 1990) that the *shilanyas* and *karseva* site chosen by Sri *Ramjanmabhoomi Nyas* was the property of the U.P. Waqf Board and that "the *shilanyas* on the disputed land surrounding the *Mosque* (Baburi) was illegal as the dispute is pending before the court and that the court has ordered the maintenance of *status quo* until the decision".

An examination of the official revenue records shows that the viewpoint of the Muslim Personal Law Board Working Committee and the U.P. Waqf Board that the *shilanyas* site claimed to be a part of the Nazul *khasra* No. 586 (stated in *waqf*) is a disputed one and that the performance of the *shilanyas/karseva* by Sri *Ramjanmabhoomi Nyas* in November, 1989/October, 1990 was in violation of the orders of the court is not tenable. A perusal of the records in respect of holdings in the village *Kot* Ram Chandra since the 1301 *Fasli* (1893 A.D.), even the Nazul Department's revised *khasras* (1931) and the third Regular Settlement of 1344 *Fasli* (1936-37) shows that there have been numerous mutations, even in respect of the desolate graveyards (*qabristan*) areas. All these amendments have to be discerned carefully as reflected in the relevant columns of the varying categories of the revenue records. It has already been stated that the High Court in its order dated 23.5.1990 held that the Commissioner's survey report based upon the Nazul records was defective and not according to law. In fact, for property issues, only the revenue records based upon the settlement reports are the proper records. Since the 1936-37 settlement, all amendments/mutations have been recorded in the yearly *khata khataunis* and *khewats*. The *shilanyas* site falls under *khasra* No. 865 and in July-December, 1981, the entries in the revenue documents stand in the name of *Mahant* Abi Ram Das. After the death of Abi Ram Das, as per the latter's will, the revenue entry was made in the name of his disciple, *Mahant* Dharam Das, who further bequeathed all his legal rights of the plots to Acharya Ram Nand of *Ramjanmabhoomi Nyas* under registered deed dated 29 April, 1986 as *Ramjanmabhoomi sthal* for the proposed construction of the temple. All this is clear from the revenue documents/registered deed in the sub-Registrar's court as well. Most significantly, when in October/November, 1989, *shilanyas* in the *Janmasthan* complex was laid by the *V.H.P.*, the then Home Minister (Sardar Buta Singh) under the Government of late Shri Rajiv Gandhi (Congress-I) got clarification from the Revenue Department and Advocate General of the then Congress (I)'s Uttar Pradesh Government, who observed that the site of '*Shilanyas*' was outside the limits of boundary in the site plan, which was a part of the Suit 12 of 1961, filed by the Central Board of Waqfs, U.P. and others, and that the site chosen for '*Shilanyas*' was at a distance of about 100 ft. from the boundary injuncted by the Court. This accounts for the repeated assertions on the part of the then Home Minister (Sardar Buta Singh) "that the site where *shilanyas* was performed last year was clearly outside the specifications given in the stay order on November 14, 1909 by the Full Bench of the Allahabad High Court. Subsequently, the stay order was taken up by the U.P. Government with the Court for certain clarifications... The Court had left no doubt whatsoever about the application of the stay order with the help of a map submitted to it by the Sunni Waqf Board..." and further "that the *shilanyas* site was out of operation of the stay order at that time and continues to be "even now". (dated December 6, 1990, New Delhi) Otherwise too, the entire hypothesis of the Central Board of Waqf, U.P., based upon the Nazul Record (1931) covering Nos. 586 and 583 is fallacious. A thorough study of the revenue documents from 1858-61 to 1991 A.D. shows that there was no *waqf* land associated with the 'Baburi Masjid' situated at the *Janmasthan* site and the *Janmasthan* complex.

Exhibit A (1st page)

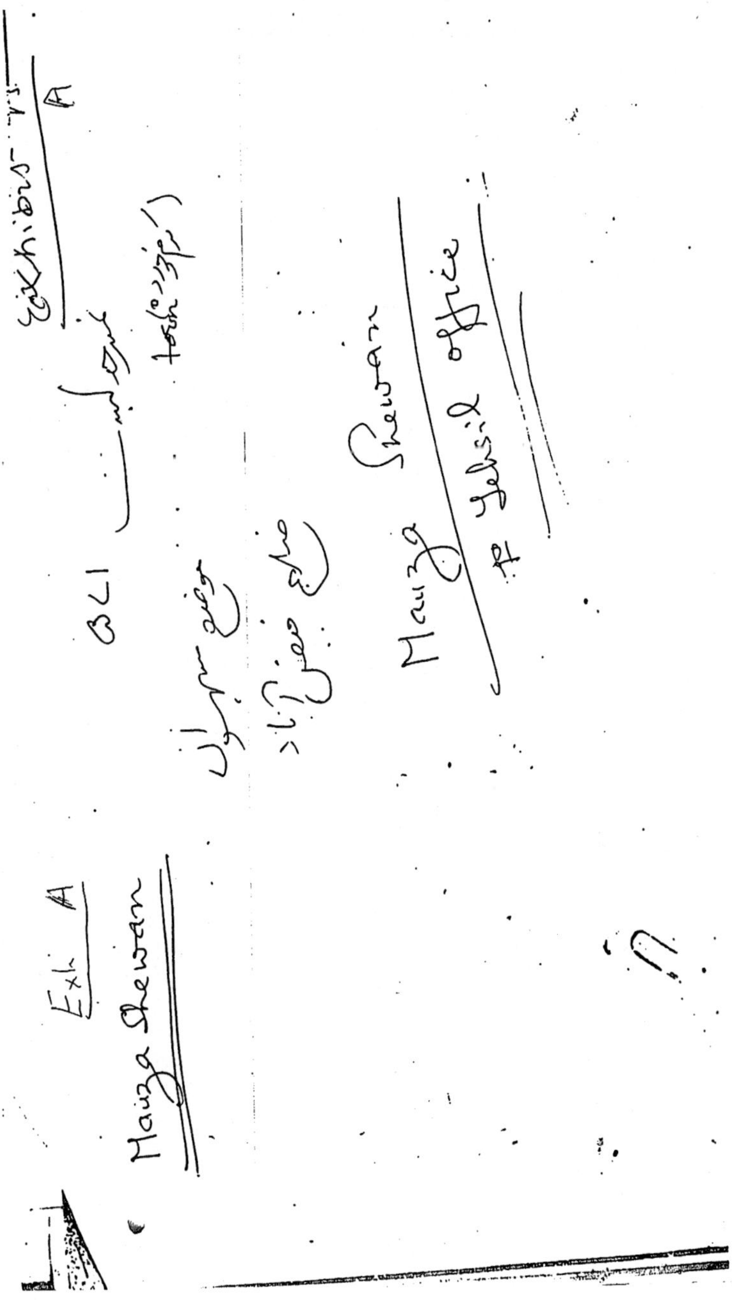
Exhibits A

Exh A

Mauza Shewan

Mauza Shewan

Tehsil office

Exhibit A (2nd page)

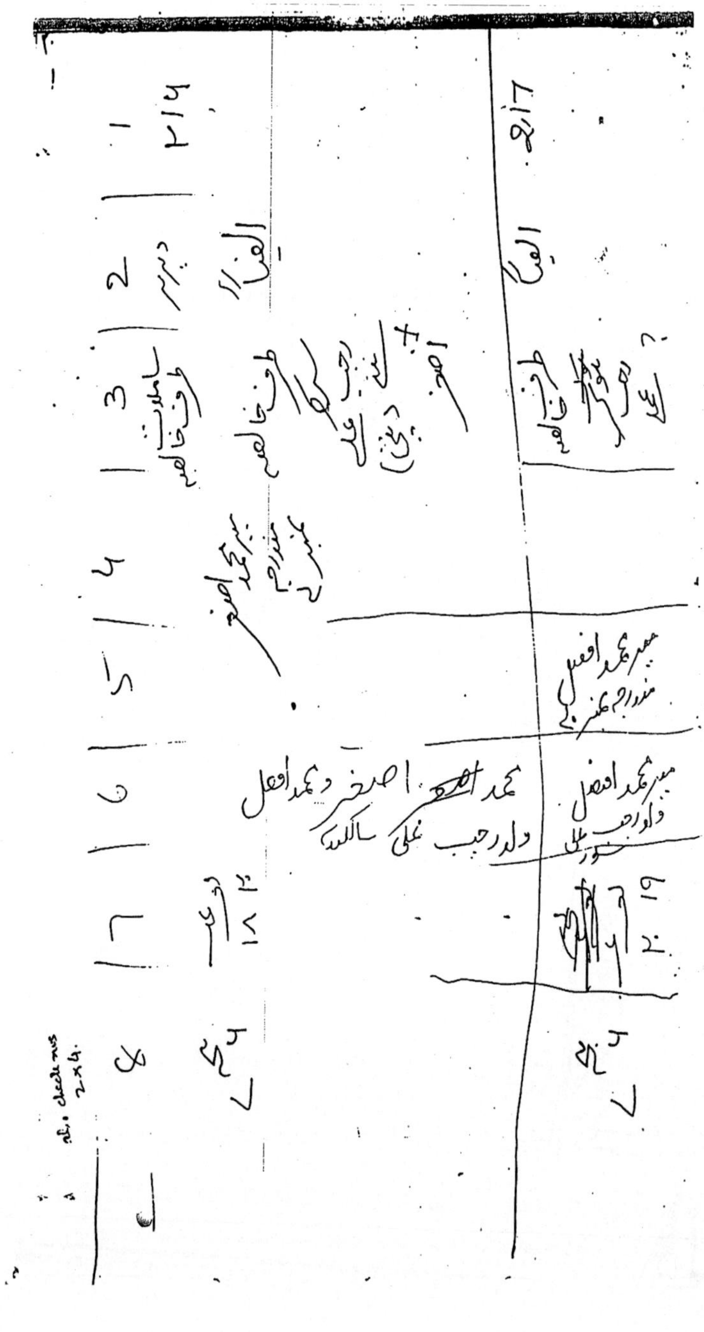

Exhibit A (3rd page)

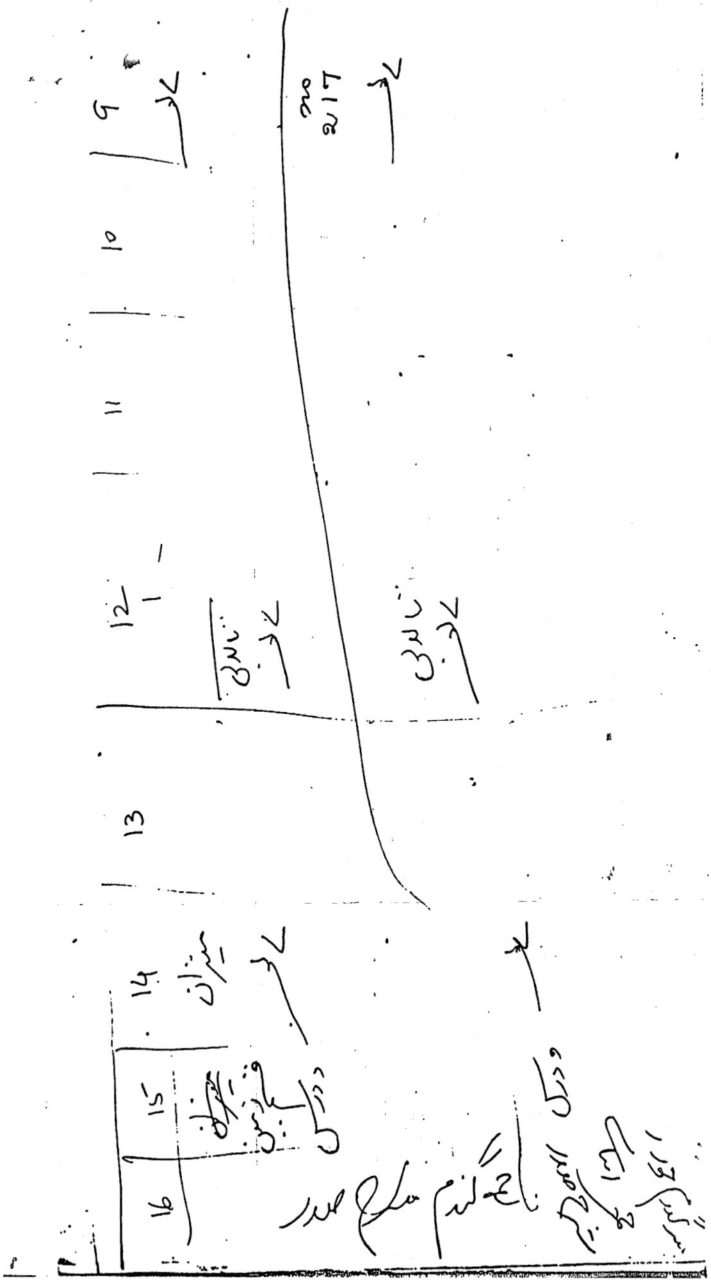

Exhibit A (4th page)

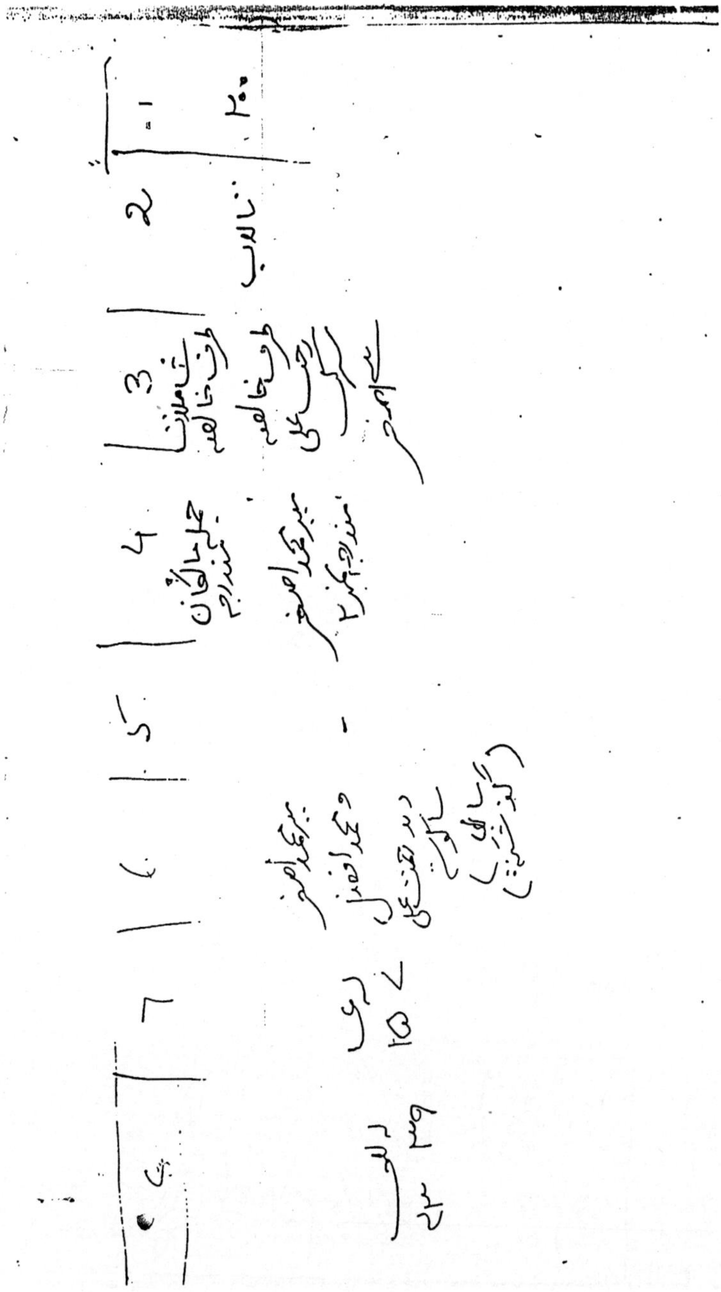

Exhibit A (5th page)

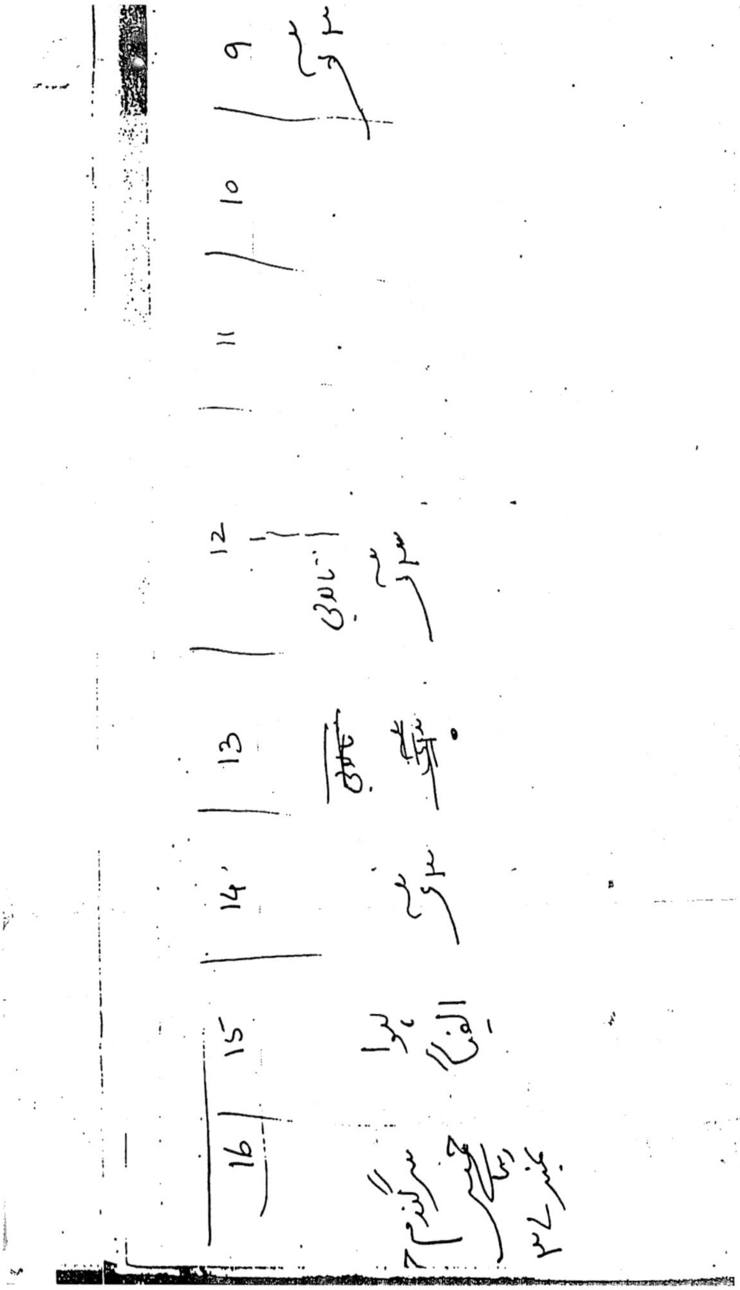

Exhibit B

Exhibit B

Exhibit B

Original

(Seal)
Chief Commissioner Oudh.

Sd. Elligible

Chief Commissioner

It having been established that after due enquiry that Rujub Ally and Mohammed Usgar received a Cash Nankar of Rs.302/3/6 Rupees three hundred and two, annas three annas and six pies from mauzah Shanwah Pr.Fyzabad in rent free tenure under the former Government. The Chief Commissioner under the authority of the Governor General in Council is pleased to maintain the tenure Grant for so long as the object for which the grant has been made is kept up on the following conditions. That they shall have surrendered all sunnuds title deeds, and other documents relative to the grant in question.

That they and their successor shall strictly perform all the duties of landholders in matters of Police and any Military or Political service that may be required of them by the Authorities and that they shall never fall under the just suspicion of favouring in any way the designs of enemies of the British Government. If any one of these conditions broken by Rujub Ally or Mohammed Usgar or their successors the grant will be immediately resumed.

True copy.

Exhibit C

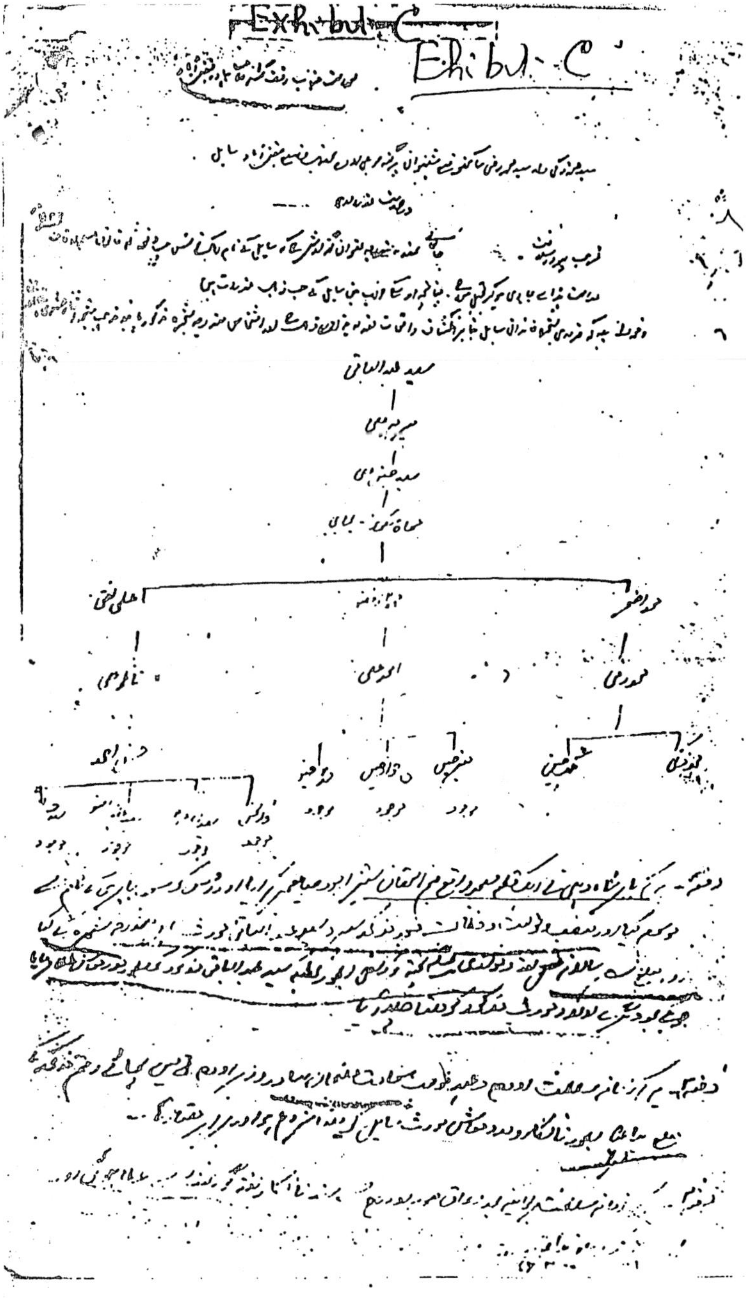

Exhibit D (1st page)

Exhibit No. D

[illegible]

No. 5607

File No.

Date 22.11.43

[illegible]

Exhibit D (2nd page)

Exhibit D (3rd page)

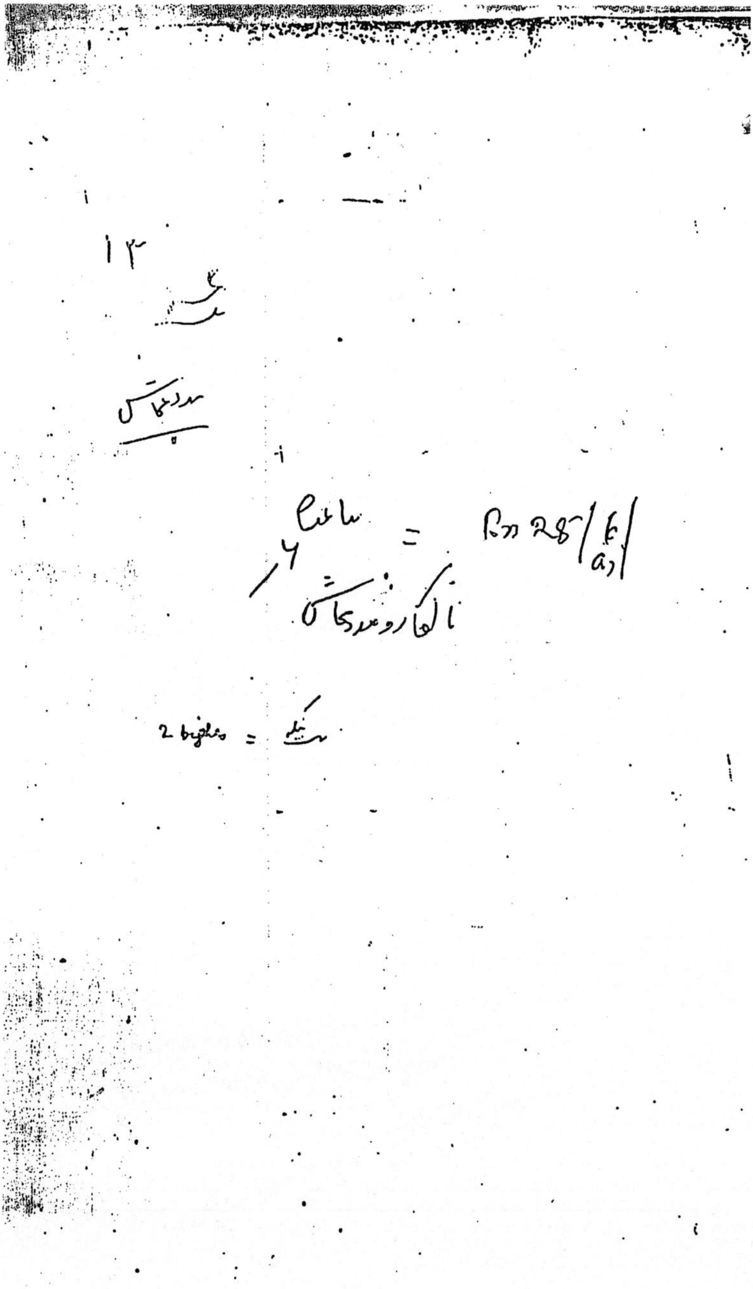

Exhibit D (4th page)

[illegible]

20 November, 1943 AD.

Syed Malik Husain s/o Syed Muhammad Zaki

Exhibit E (1st page)

THE

SUPREME COURT CASES

1982

Volume 1

Mode of Citation

(1982) 1 SCC

EASTERN BOOK COMPANY
LAW PUBLISHERS & BOOKSELLERS
34, LALBAGH, LUCKNOW—226 001

Exhibit E (2nd page)

Exhibit 'E'

column 'Name of Waqf' the entry reads 'Imambara and Masjid' suggesting as if only two properties were declared to be Shia Waqfs but at the foot of the Notification under Section 5 (1) there is a nota bene to the following effect:

"the details regarding property and other matters relating to the Waqfs are kept in the Board's office and can be inspected by any person who is interested in the matter."

It seems to us quite clear having regard to the six properties being specifically asked to be entered in the list of Shia Waqfs by Imam Ali Mahto in his application and the order made thereon, all the properties mentioned in the application must be regarded as having been entered in the list of Shia Waqfs by the Chief or Provincial Commissioner for Wakfs and the Notification under Section 5 (1) related to all those properties as having been notified to be Shia Wakfs, particulars whereof were stated to be available in the Board's office. The Nota Bene at the foot of the Notification, in our view amounted to sufficient particularisation of the properties notified as Shia Wakfs. Non-mentioning of those properties as Sunni Wakfs in Appendices VIII and IX sent to the Sunni Central Wakfs Board must amount to a notice to the Sunni Board and the Sunni Muslims that these had been enlisted as Shia Wakfs. Admittedly, no suit was filed either by the Sunni Central Board or any other person interested in those Wakfs challenging the decision recorded in his Report by the Chief or Provincial Commissioner for Wakfs within the time prescribed under Section 5 (2) of the Act and, therefore, the Chief Commissioner's Report together with the appendices X and XI thereto dated 28th/31st October, 1938, on the basis of which the Notification dated 15th January, 1954 was issued and published in Official Gazette on 23rd January, 1954, must be held to have become final and conclusive as between the members of the two communities. In this behalf we would like to refer to the decision of this Court in Board of Muslim Wakfs v. Radha Krishan, (1979) 2 SCR 148: (AIR 1979 SC 289) where one of us (Sen, J.) has analysed the scheme of the Wakfs Act, 1954 (a Central enactment) which is substantially the same as the scheme of the 1936 Act and we are in respectful agreement with the ratio of that case but here we are not concerned with any paramount title of any stranger (like the Maharaja) to any property declared as Wakfs and hence that part of the ratio of that decision will be inapplicable.

17. As against the aforesaid material respondents 5 and 6 and through them the Sunni community have relied upon a Notification dated 26th February, 1944 issued by the Sunni Central Wakfs Board under Section 5 (1) of the U. P. Muslim Wakfs Act, 1936 following upon the receipt of the Report of the Chief or Provincial Commissioner of Wakfs in respect of mosque in Doshipura showing the same as Sunni Wakf, copy whereof has been annexed as Annexure S-2 to the affidavit dated 6th February, 1980 of Mohd. Basir Khan filed on behalf of the Sunni Central Waqfs Board as its Pairokar. This Notification on which reliance has been placed by the Sunnis appears to us of doubtful validity and probative value for the reasons which we shall presently indicate. Though issued and published earlier in point of time than the Notification of Shia Central Waqfs Board, it is admittedly not based on Appendices VIII and IX annexed to the Chief Commissioner's Report dated 28th/31st October, 1938 but on the basis of some Registers of Waqfs (meaning lists of Waqfs) said to have been received by the Sunni Board from the Commissioner of Wakfs. Curiously enough the Sunni Central Waqfs Board has stated through two affidavits dated 6th January, 1980 and 9th January, 1981 of their Pairokar Shri Mohd. Basir Khan that along with the copy of the Commissioner's Report Registers of Waqfs were received but no appendices like Appendices VIII and IX were received from the Commissioner, that according to the Registers of Waqfs there were 245 charitable Sunni Waqfs in the District of Banaras which were covered by the 1936 Act and all such Waqfs were accordingly notified by the Sunni Board in the Government Gazette by issuing the Notification dated 26th February 1944 under Section 5 (1) of the Act. The original Report of the Commissioner does not refer to anything like Registers of Waqfs but, as stated earlier, it refers to Appendices Nos VIII, IX, X and XI and the endorsement

Exhibit E (3rd page)

on the slip under the signature of the Chief Commissioner shows that the former two appendices were sent to the Sunni Board and the latter two to the Shia Board. In face of this endorsement and having regard to the fact that the Shia Board had received Appendices X and XI along with the Commissioner's Report which that Board offered to produce, it is difficult to accept the statement of the Pairokar of the Sunni Board that no appendices were received by the Board along with a copy of the Commissioner's Report. It seems the relevant appendices, though received, are being withheld as their production would be adverse to the Sunnis. Apart from that aspect it is clear on their own admission that the Notification under Sec. 5 (1) of the 1936 Act was issued by the Sunni Central Waqfs Board not on the basis of Appendices VIII and IX which formed part of the Commissioner's Report but on the basis of some Registers of Waqfs said to have been received by it. The Notification regarding the Sunni Waqfs issued on the basis of material which did not form part of the Chief Commissioner's Report would be in Violation of Section 5 (1) of the Act which required issuance of a Notification thereunder 'according to' the Commissioner's Report and as such the Notification dated February 26, 1944 relied upon by respondents 5 and 6 and members of the Sunni community would be of doubtful validity. Secondly, the relevant entry in the Register of Waqfs is at Serial No. 224 and it pertains to "one quita mosque and land" of which the "present Mutawali" is shown as "Hayatullah resident of Doshipura, Banaras" and correspondingly the entry in the Notification dated Feb. 26, 1944 issued under Section 5 (1) of the 1936 Act is also at Sl. No. 224 which reads: "Masjid Doshipura — Hayatullah r/o Doshipura, Banaras — one quita mosque", but the petitioners have produced documentary and other material throwing doubt on the genuineness of the entry as being in relation to the mosque in question on Plot No. 246 (i.e. Municipal No. J-15/94), according to the affidavits of Dularey Mirza (the Peshkar of Shia Central Waqfs Board) dated 12th August, 1980 and 1st October, 1980 there were two Hayatullahs in Mohalla Doshipura, Varanasi, one was Hayatullah alias Hayatoo r/o H. No. J-15/125, Mohalla Doshipura, who had died in 1926 long prior to the Survey of Waqfs under the 1936 Act, that his son Abdul Shakoor, who was plaintiff No. 2 in suit No. 232/1934 admitted in his evidence in that suit that his father (Hayatullah) had expired 8 years before the filing of the suit and as such entry at Serial No. 224 which describes Hayatullah r/o Mohalla Doshipura as the "present Mutawali" (i.e. in 1944 when the Notification was issued) obviously could not refer to this Hayatullah father of Abdul Shakoor, while the other Hayatullah, who was known by the name of Moulavi Hayatullah r/o H. No. J-15/8 in Mohalla Doshipura was the father of Hakim Mahmood and Ali Ahmad, who are the present Mutawalis of a mosque in Mohalla Salarpura standing on Municipal No. J-18/108 and therefore, if the name in entry at Serial No. 224 refers to this Hayatullah who could be its "present Mutawali" in 1944 then the mosque would be the mosque in Mohalla Salarpura and not the mosque in question standing on Municipal No. J-15/94 (i.e. Plot No. 246) in Mohalla Doshipura and while making the entry by mistake Mohalla Doshipura was wrongly mentioned instead of Mohalla Salarpura as the two Mohallas are quite adjacent to each other; in other words, according to the petitioners if the entry at Serial No. 224 in the Registers of Waqfs or in the Notification dated 26th Feb., 1944 refers to Hayatullah father of Abdul Shakoor the entry is obviously wrong as it would be metioning a dead person as the "present Mutawali" of the mosque and in case the entry at Serial No. 224 is referable to Maulavi Hayatullah then the reference to the mosque being in Mohalla Doshipura would be erroneous. It is the petitioners' case that it was Maulavi Hayatullah who had as early as in 1944 submitted an application for registration of the mosque in Mohalla Salarpura standing on Municipal No. J-18/108 to the Sunni Central Waqfs Board but by mistake it was stated therein that the mosque was for the benefit of people of Doshipura and it was registered under his name under Serial No 224 in the Register of Waqfs maintained by the Sunni Board and by mistake that mosque was wrongly entered as being in Mohalla Doshipura; and in support of this reliance has been placed upon a Report dated 11th February, 1981 submitted by Inspector

Exhibit E (4th page)

Ashfaq Ali to the Sunni Board in which he had noticed and placed on record such mistake having taken place, copy whereof has been annexed as Annexure-I to the affidavit of Dularey Mirza (Peshkar of Shia Board) dated 13th February, 1980. in other words, the aforesaid material casts a serious doubt on the aspect whether the mosque mentioned in entry No. 224 in the Notification dated February 26, 1944 really pertains to the mosque in question standing on Plot No. 246 (Municipal No. J-15-94) in Mohalla Doshipura and as such the Notification will have no probative value. In this state of affairs Notice dated 11-4-1945 issued by Shia Board under Section 53 of the 1936 Act complaining about this entry at Sl. No. 224 relied upon by counsel for respondents 5 and 6 must be regarded as having been issued ex majori cautela. Thirdly, even if it were assumed for the purposes of argument that entry at Serial No. 224 in the Notification dated 26th February, 1944 refers to the mosque in question it cannot affect the customary rights of the petitioners and through them the Shia community to perform their religious ceremonies and functions over the other 8 plots and structures thereon which had been listed as Shia Wakfs under the Notification dated 15th January, 1954, especially when it is now common ground that the mosque on Plot No 246 is a public mosque constructed by general subscriptions and is accessible to members of both the sects for offering prayers and doing worship therein. Admittedly the Notification dated 26th February, 1944. does not refer to any other plots or the structures thereon at all We are, therefore, clearly of the view that the Notification dated 26th February, 1944 issued under Section 5 (1) of the 1936 Act by the Sunni Board is of no avail to the Sunnis for the purpose of defeating the customary rights of the Shias to perform their religious ceremonies and functions on the other plots and structures thereon

18. Apart from the finality attaching to the Chief Commissioner's Report (together with the Appendices X and XI annexed thereto) dated 29th/31st October, 1878, the petitioners have also claimed that the aforesaid plots and structures thereon had been registered as Shia Waqfs for performance of their religious ceremonies and functions under Section 38 of the 1936 Act by the Shia Central Waqfs Board after making full injury and following the procedure prescribed by that section as early as in 1952 and the Board had issued the requisite Sanads in that behalf. Reliance in this regard has been placed on five certificates issued by Shia Central Waqfs Board, Lucknow, bearing Certificate Nos 209, 210, 211, 214 and 21 all dated 22nd December, 1952 — first relating to Mardana Imambara (the Baradari) on Plot No. 247/1130, the second relating to Zanana Imambara on Plot No. 245, the third relating to Imam Chowk on Plot No. 247, being appurtenant to Baradari, the fourth relating to the entire Plot No. 602/1133 being appurtenant to the Baradari and the last relating to Sabil Chabutra Mardana on Plot No 246/1131 (Annexures VIII & VIII A to VIII-D to the Writ Petition) It may be stated that the petitioners have also produced a certificate of registration in respect of Purani Masjid of Doshipura as a Shia Wakf dated 3rd July, 1973 the registration being under the 1960 Act, but counsel for the petitioners fairly conceded that the mosque in question belongs to both the sects and no special rights are claimed by the Shias over it except those conferred on them under the decree in Suit No. 849 of 1878 by Shri Pramoda Charan Banerjee The registration in respect of the five properties mentioned above under Section 38 of the 1936 Act would be available to the petitioners and must prevail over the subsequent registration, if any, obtained by the Sunnis in respect of some of the properties under the 1960 Act; really speaking such later registration would be non est in the eye of law.

19. Apart from the Certificates of Registration issued by the Shia Central Wakfs Board on 22nd December, 1952 the petitioners are also relying upon yet another Notification issued by the Shia Central Wakfs Board under Rule 14 (viii) of the U. P. Shia Central Wakfs Rules, 1944 enlisting the Shia Wakf in question and published in the U. P. Government Gazette on 1st December, 1956. It may be stated that the Shia Board had framed rules called the U. P. Shia Central Wakfs Rules 1944 in exercise of powers conferred on it by Section 61 of the 1936 Act

Exhibit E (5th page)

and under Rule 54 (vii) the Board was required to notify a list of wakfs which had been registered during the year under report. It appears that a consolidated list of Shia Wakfs which were registered during the period 28th July, 1942 to 31st March, 1956 subsequent to the submission of the Report of the Chief Commissioner for Wakfs under Sec. 5 of the Act was published for the first time by the Shia Board under the Notification dated 1st December, 1956 issued under Rule 54 (vii); a copy of the relevant portion of that Notification is annexed as Annexure VII to the writ petition showing registration of Imambara-Baradari, Doshipura, at Serial number 152, Imambara Mutalik Purani Masjid, Doshipura at Serial No. 153, Mardana Imambara-Baradari at Serial number 155, Purani Masjid, Doshipura at Serial No. 157, Zanana Imambara, Doshipura at Serial No. 159, Imam Chowk, Doshipura at Serial No. 160 and Chabutra Mardana Sabil at Serial No. 161 as Shia Wakfs. This Notification issued by the Siha Board on 1st December, 1956, also supports the petitioners' case that the concerned properties had been registered as Shia Wakfs under Sec. 38 of the Act. It is thus clear that even on the second foundational basis the Shias have proved their existing or established entitlement to their customary rights to perform their religious ceremonies and functions on the concerned plots and structures thereon.

20. Much was made by Counsel for respondents 5 & 6 of certain documents on record showing derivative title of Sunni Muslims to a couple of plots in question and Counsel contended that whatever be the position with regard to three earlier documents (Patta of 1907, 1927 and 1930 about which the Courts have made observations in earlier litigation), there was yet one more lease of 20-4-1952, in respect of portions of three plots, namely, 602/1133, 247 and 245 in favour of Hafiz Mohd Yusuf and Akram-ul-Haq, two Sunni Muslims from the Maharaja whereunder they had acquired lessee's interest over the plots at an yearly rent of Rs. 3/- and they had dedicated the same to the Sunni community for use as graveyard and such subsequent title could not be affected by the decisions in earlier litigations. It must be stated that in support of this lease of 1952 no lease-deed nor any Patta has been produced, but reliance is placed on two documents (i) Extract of Register of Agreements (Agreement to Lease) dated 20-4-1952 and (ii) Receipt for payment of rent (curiously enough relating to three prior years July 1949, to June 1950, July 1950 to June 1951 and July 1951 to June 1952 = 1357, 1358 and 1359 Fasli), being Annexures 3 & 4 to the Counter-Affidavit of Respondent No. 5 dated 17-4-1979. At the outset we would observe that it is difficult to accept the claim that the three plots had been dedicated by the two Sunni Muslims to their community for use as graveyard, for, the Commissioners appointed by this Court for survey and spot inspection in December 1979, did not find any such use being made of plots Nos. 247 and 245 and merely noticed two graves and one in damaged condition on plot No. 602/1133 only — same plot with graves which was the subject matter of Maharaja's Suit Number 424/1931 in which a permanent injunction was issued restraining all Muslims (virtually all Sunnis) from using the said plot as any graveyard in future. Dealing with the aspect of derivative title put forward by counsel on behalf of the respondents Numbers 5 and 6 we have already made the position clear in the earlier part of our judgment that Shias' are claiming the rights to perform their religious ceremonies and functions on the plots and structures in question not so much on the basis of any title or ownership thereof but on the basis of customary exercise since time immemorial and they have been claiming such customary rights by prescription over the plots belonging to the Maharaja of Banaras as Zamindar and superior title-holder and the prescriptive rights have enured for the benefit of all the Shias notwithstanding such superior title in the Maharaja and if that be so they will also enure for their benefit as against any derivative title claimed by anyone under the Maharaja. Moreover, when these plots and structures, particularly these three plots were being registered as Shia Wakfs under the U. P. Muslim Wakfs Act, 1936 by the Shia Board and Sanads or Certificates of Registration in respect thereof were being issued in Dec. 1952, the two Sunni Lessees who are said to have obtained a Lease on 20-4-1952 did not raise

Exhibit F (1st page)

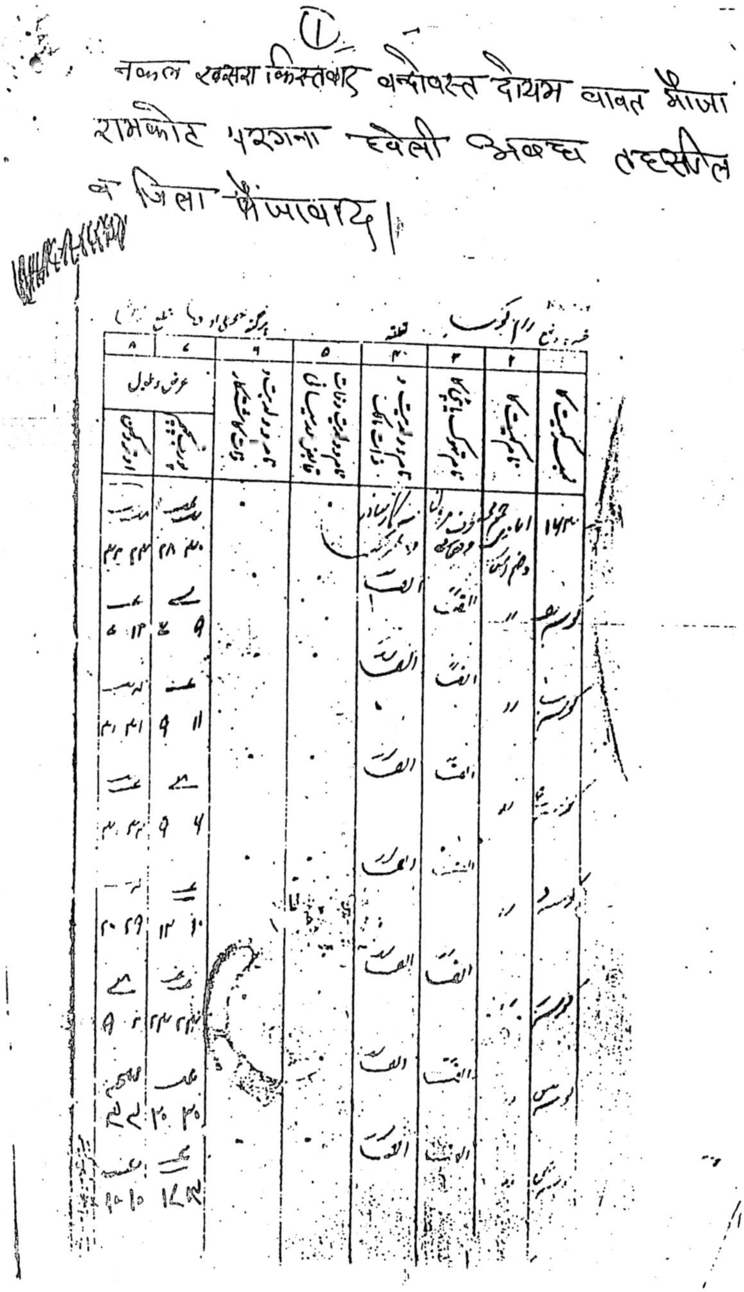

नकल खसरा किस्तवार बन्दोबस्त दोयम बाबत मौजा रामकोट परगना हवेली अवध तहसील व जिला फैजाबाद।

Exhibit F (2nd page)

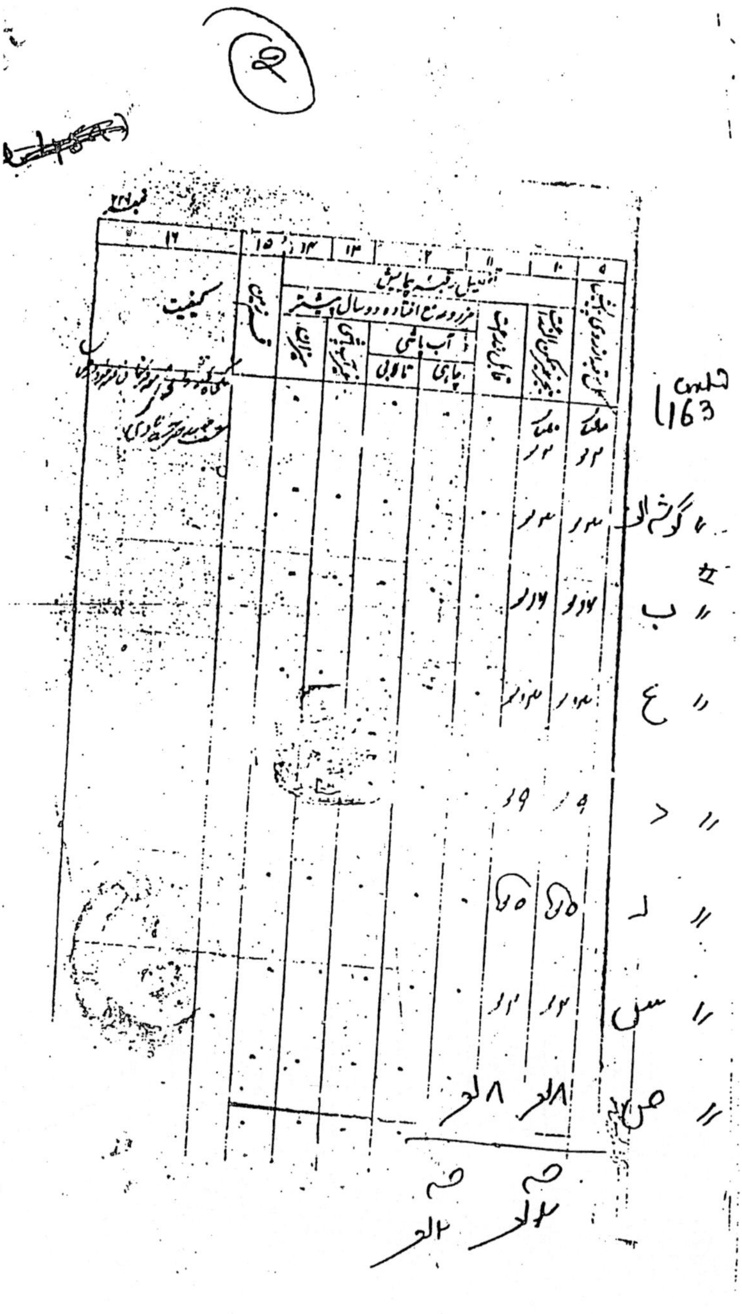

Exhibit F (3rd page)

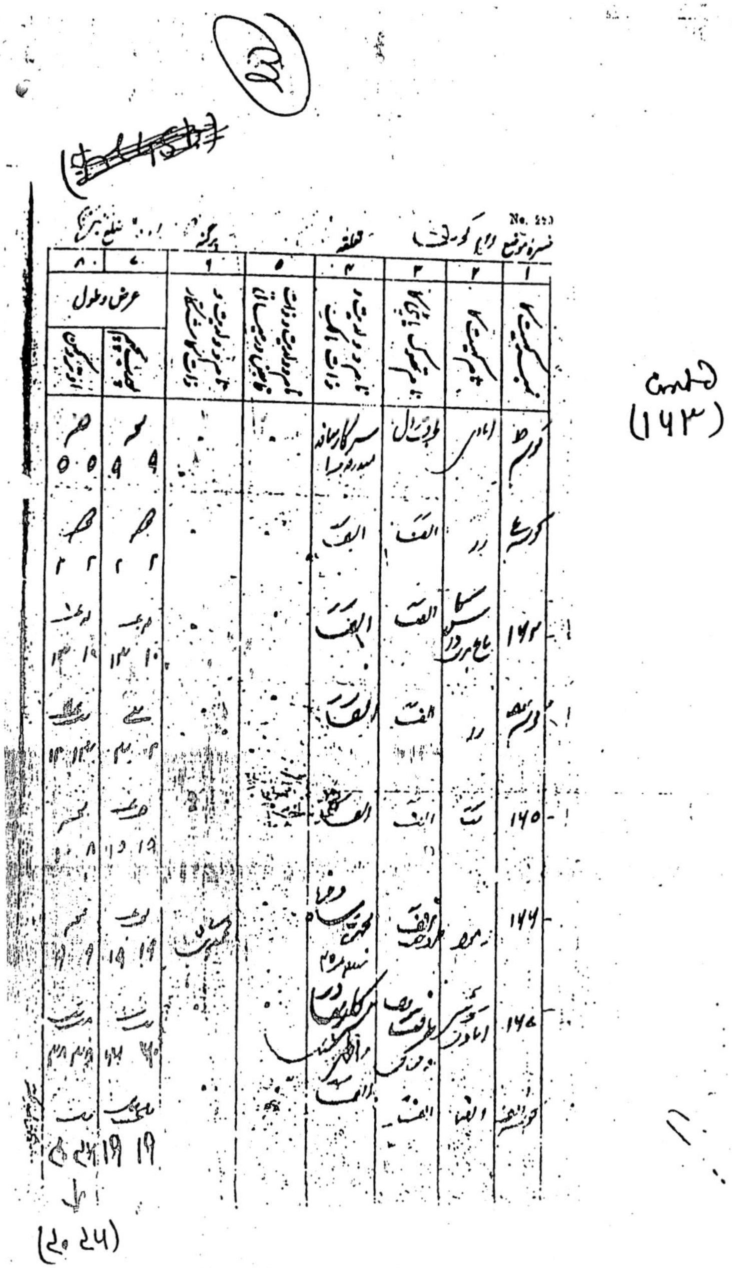

Exhibit F (4th page)

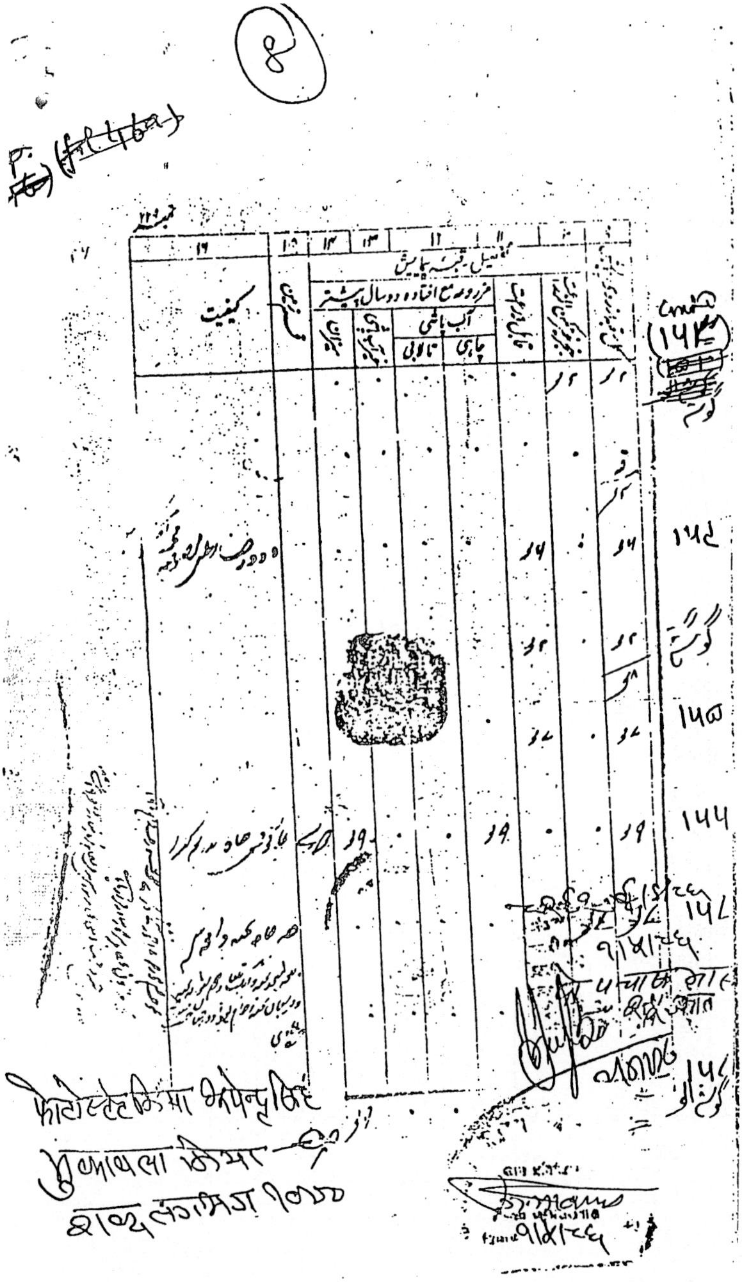

Exhibit G (1st page)

G

(Tehsil Office, Records Room)

Exhibit G (2nd page)

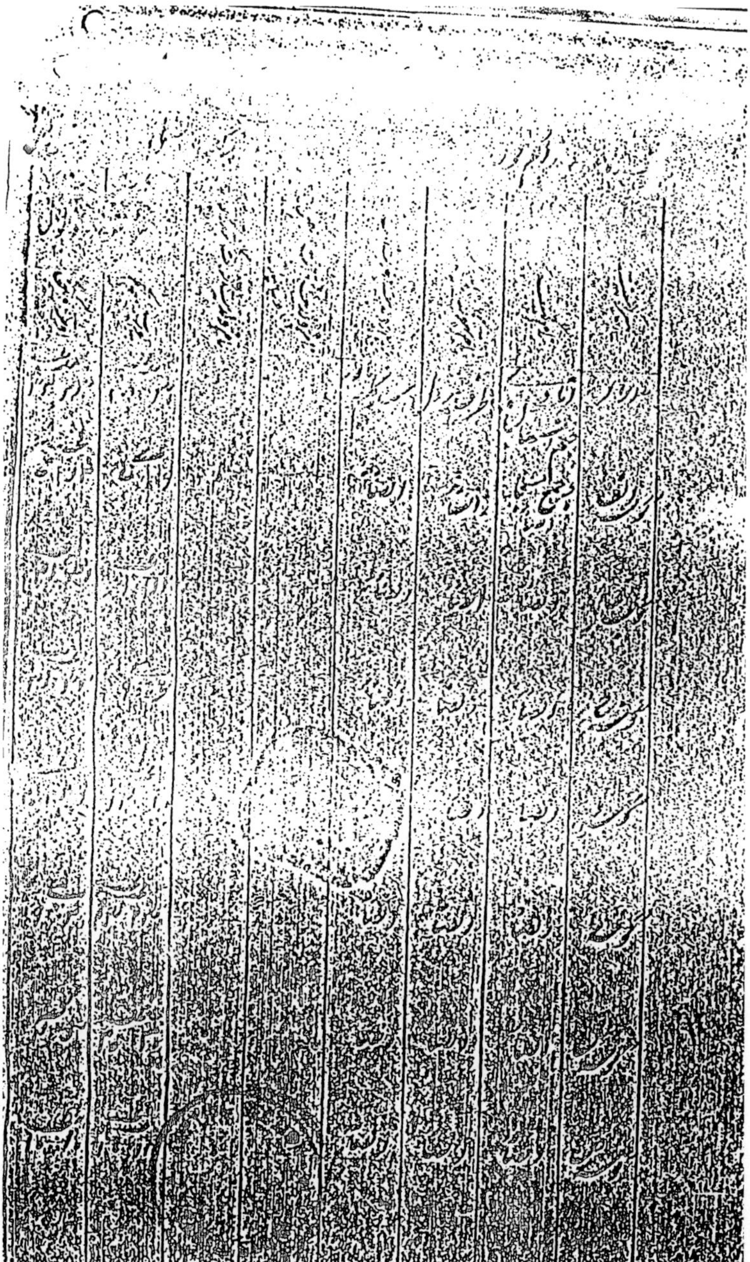

Exhibit G (3rd page)

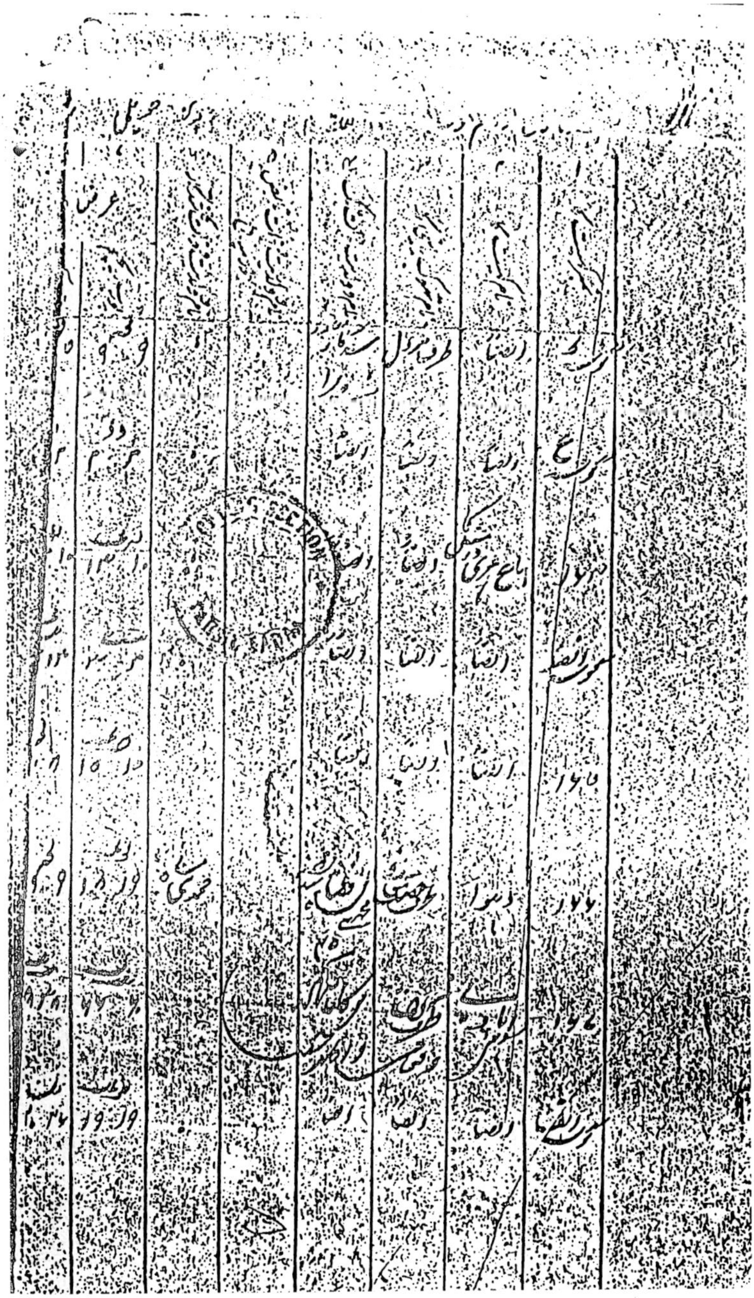

Exhibit H`

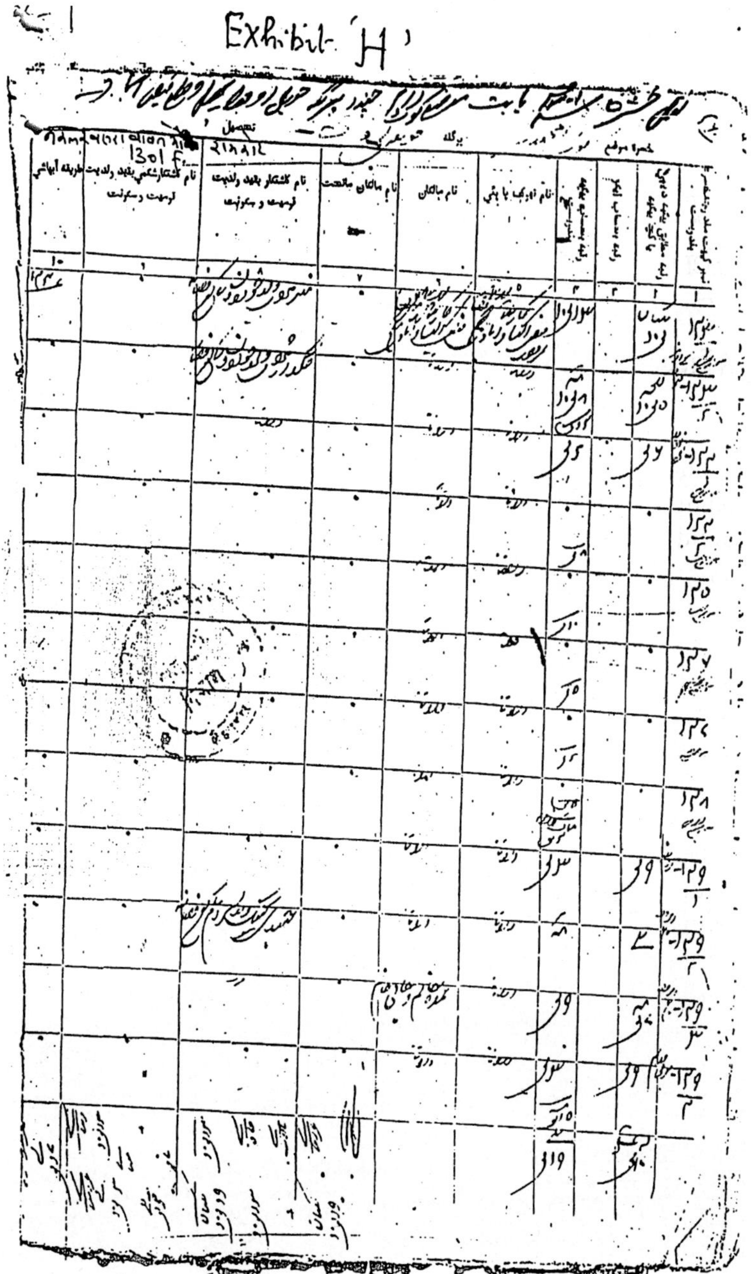
Exhibit 'H'

10

Prince Aurangzeb's Conversion of a Jain Temple at Ahmedabad into a Mosque and its Reconversion as Temple by Shahjahan, the Mughal Emperor, in the Years 1645-1648 A.D.

The devout Jain Shantidas, the great *Jawahari* (jeweller), commercial and financial magnate, *Nagarsheth* of Ahmadabad and his elder brother, Vardhaman, built a temple at *Bibipur*, now known as *Saraspur*, a *suburb* of *Ahmadabad in 1621-25 A.D.* In this temple called *Manatunga*, the image of Tirthankar was installed. The temple was dedicated to *Chintamani-Parshwanath*. The author of *Chintamani-Prasati*, a Sanskrit work (1640) calls it a magnificent temple of *Chintamani-Parshvanath*. A detailed account of the magnificence and nobility of the structure of the temple with the adornment of the vaults and black marble elephants at the entrance gate, cloisters with cells each containing a marble statue, in white or black, representing the Tirthankars of the Jain Pantheon is also provided by Albert de Mandelslo (1655 A.D.), a German traveller in Gujrat/Ahmadabad in 1638 A.D., *i.e.,* within twelve years of the completion of this temple. (vide Mandelslo's *Travels into the East Indies*, tr. J. Davies, London, 1662, p. 30).

In 1645, Prince Aurangzeb (*Shahzada* Sultan Aurangzeb Bahadur), the *subadar* (governor) of the Province of Gujrat ordered the desecration of the above temple and converted it into mosque named as *Quwat-ul-Islam* (vide Ali Muhammad Khan's *Mirat-i-Ahmadi*) written about 1761 A.D. Pers. Text, ed. S. *Nawabi* Ali, Pt. I, p. 220. As the *diwan* of the *Subah* of Ahmadabad, the author had an access to all the official documents of the Mughal age produced by him). This is fully borne out by Shah Jahan's *Farman* dated 3rd July, 1648, which refers to the fact that *Shahzada* Sultan Aurangzeb had constructed "in that place (temple) some *mihrabs* and given it the name of a mosque". Later on, the French traveller, M. de Thevenot, who visited Ahmadabad (1666 A.D.), gives an elaborate description of the fact that Aurangzeb had converted the "chief Pagod (temple) of Santidas" into a mosque and that "when he performed that ceremony, he caused a cow to be killed in the place, knowing very well that after such an action, the gentiles (Hindus-Jains) could worship no more therein..." and as the roof and the walls of the temple bore figures of men and beasts, Aurangzeb "caused the noses of all these figures, which had added a great deal of magnificence to that mosque, to be beat off". (vide *Travels of M. de. Thevenot*, tr. Lovell, London, Pt. III, p. 10). The taking over the possession of the Jain temple built by Shantidas by "the Muhammadans" and turning it "into a mosque" is equally confirmed by Jean Baptiste Tavernier, another French traveller who visited Ahmadabad not less than five times between 1641 to 1667 A.D. (vide J.B. Tavernier, *Travels in India*, Ed. Ball, I, p. 72).

It can be well imagined that Shantidas, the great financial magnate and *Nagarsheth* of Ahmadabad, the builder of the temple, would not pocket the insult inflicted by Aurangzeb, the Imperial Prince, to him as well as to one of the Supreme Souls of the Jain faith, without approaching the Mughal Emperor in this regard. This can be well premised from the *Farman* issued by Shah Jahan, dated 3rd July, 1648 A.D. which made a complete restitution to the Jain magnate. The *Farman*, apart from restoring the temple to Shantidas, refers to two significant matters, which otherwise are not known from any other source. Firstly, that earlier too, an order had been issued (by the Emperor) to *Umdat-ul-Mulk* Shaista Khan, the *Subedar* of Gujrat, who had succeeded Aurangzeb as the Governor for the restoration of the temple. This shows that immediate action was taken by the Emperor for *status-quo ante*. However, the *Farman* does not specify the reason for its non-implementation by Shaista Khan and for keeping the important matter in abeyanse. Secondly, most significantly, the *Farman* refers to a representation made by Mulla Abdul Hakim to "His Majesty that this building, by reason of its being the property of another person, could not be considered a mosque according to the inviolable Islamic Law..." As such, a Royal Order of His Majesty (Shah Jahan) was issued to the effect that as the (above) property (*makaan i.e.,* temple) was the property of Shantidas, the arch (*mihrab*) constructed thereupon by the *Shahzada* (Prince Aurangzeb) should be removed. Further, that the above mentioned person (Shantidas) should not be harassed (any more) and the afore-mentioned building (*makaan i.e.,* temple) should be handed over to him.

The above *Farman* dated 3rd July, 1648 A.D. (21st *Jamada* II, AH 1058) bears the *Tughra* (monogram) of the Emperor Shah Jahan and *Nishan* of Prince (*Shahzada*) Dara Shukoh, the newly appointed *subadar* of Gujrat. It has a separate distinct endorsement (apparently in Emperor Shah Jahan's own hand) below the *Tughra* and to the left of the seal of Muhammad Dara Shukoh, son of Shah Jahan, *Badshah Gazi*, to the effect that the administrators, (*hukam*) present and future, should act in accordance with the directions embodied in the *Nishan* (Order of Dara Shukoh). The *Farman* was issued on the same date that Dara Shukoh was appointed the *subadar* (Governor) of Gujrat in succession to Shaistah Khan who was transferred to the *subah* of Malwa (July, 1648). Even when appointed as Governor of Gujrat, Dara Shukoh was permitted to stay at the Royal Court and Baqir Beg bestowed with the title of Ghairat Khan was appointed as his deputy (*naib*) and sent to Ahmadabad for the governance of administration of the Province. As such, the *Farman* is specifically addressed to Ghairat Khan relating to the affairs of the above mentioned temple. It is stated therein that the earlier Royal Order issued to Shaista Khan while recognising this building (temple) as the property of Satidas (Shantidas), had directed the Governor (Shaista Khan) to remove the *mihrab* built by Prince Aurangzeb and hand over the building (temple) to Shantidas. But now according to this *Farman*, the *mihrab* was retained and a screen wall was to be made between the *mihrab* and the temple. However, complete possession of the temple was to be made over to Shantidas who could worship over there according to his creed. At the same time, the *Farman* orders that the *Faqirs* (medicants/destitudes/beggars, etc.) should be turned out of the premises and that the Boharas who had removed and carried away the materials of the temple were required to return the same to Shantidas and in case they (the Boharas) had used this material elsewhere, the price thereof may be recovered from them and paid to Shantidas. Finally, the *Farman* states that this order may be considered extremely urgent and that no deviation or disobedience may be shown in this regard.

Even though, in pursuance of Shah Jahan's *Farman*, the temple was restored (1648) to Shantidas, it fell into disuse and was virtually abandoned as at the time of its conversion into a mosque, Aurangzeb had slaughtered a cow in its premises. At the same time, it is reliably learnt from the author of *Mirat-i-Ahmadi* that having known about Prince Aurangzeb's order to convert it into a mosque, Shantidas buried underground two of the marble images, each weighing a hundred *man*, though it was given out that these would be destroyed. Nearly a hundred years later (in 1743 A.D.), during the reign of the Mughal Emperor Muhammad Shah, a period characterised by the above author 'marking the weakness of Islam and decline of religious zeal', the descendants of Shantidas, by means of a *douceur*, got permission to bring these images to the Ahmadabad city, which were installed in an underground temple having been in existence for a long time and where the Jains continued their worship secretly owing to fear of the Mussalmans.

The above mentioned *Farman* (3rd July, 1648) of Shah Jahan clearly bears out the fact that the 'mosque' constructed on the property and premises of a temple of another person/religious community cannot be considered a mosque according to "the inviolable Islamic Law". As such, any '*mosque*' constructed on the premises of a temple can be restored to the original owner/ religious community to which it belonged. So according to the Islamic Law as applicable in India during the Mughal age, re-conversion of the structure of a 'mosque' having been built or declared as such forcibly on the sacred premises/temple back to a temple of original religious community is absolutely valid. In the light of the above and the clear *Farman* of the Mughal Emperor Shah Jahan cited above, the assertion on the part of the All India Baburi *Masjid* Action Committee that in accordance with the Hanifa Law applicable in India, a Muslim *mosque* once dedicated to Allah cannot be surrendered as temple of another religious community is not tenable.

At the end, it many be observed that the Persian text of the above mentioned *Farman* of Shah Jahan is available in M.S.

Commissarit, *Imperial Mughal Farmans in Gujrat* (Reprinted from the Journal of the University of Bombay, Vol. IX, Part I, July, 1940) **(Appendix I).** Photocopies of the *Farman* vide Plate No. IX, p. 56 and its translation into English, pp. 39-41 are also enclosed. **(Appendix II).** The learned scholar M.S. Commissarit has also given a detailed account of the history of the above mentioned Shantidas's Jain temple and the English translation of Shah Jahan's *Farman* in his *Studies in the History of Gujrat*, Bombay/London, 1935, pp. 55-60; 62-63. **(Appendix III).** He has also dealt with it briefly in *A History of Gujrat*, Vol. II, *The Mughal Period from 1573 to 1758,* Bombay 1957, pp. 125; 129-31, 140-143. **(Appendix IV).**

The translation of the *Farman* from Persian to English is fairly correct and reliable. About twelve years ago, Professor Grover personally paid an official visit to the descendants of the family of Shantidas at Ahmadabad on behalf of ICHR, New Delhi, and examined the above *Farman* and other documents available with the family. He compared the photo plate provided by Commissarit in his book with the original *Farman* and found it completely authentic. (In case of any further need, fresh translation from Persian to English can be provided by me.)

Appendix I

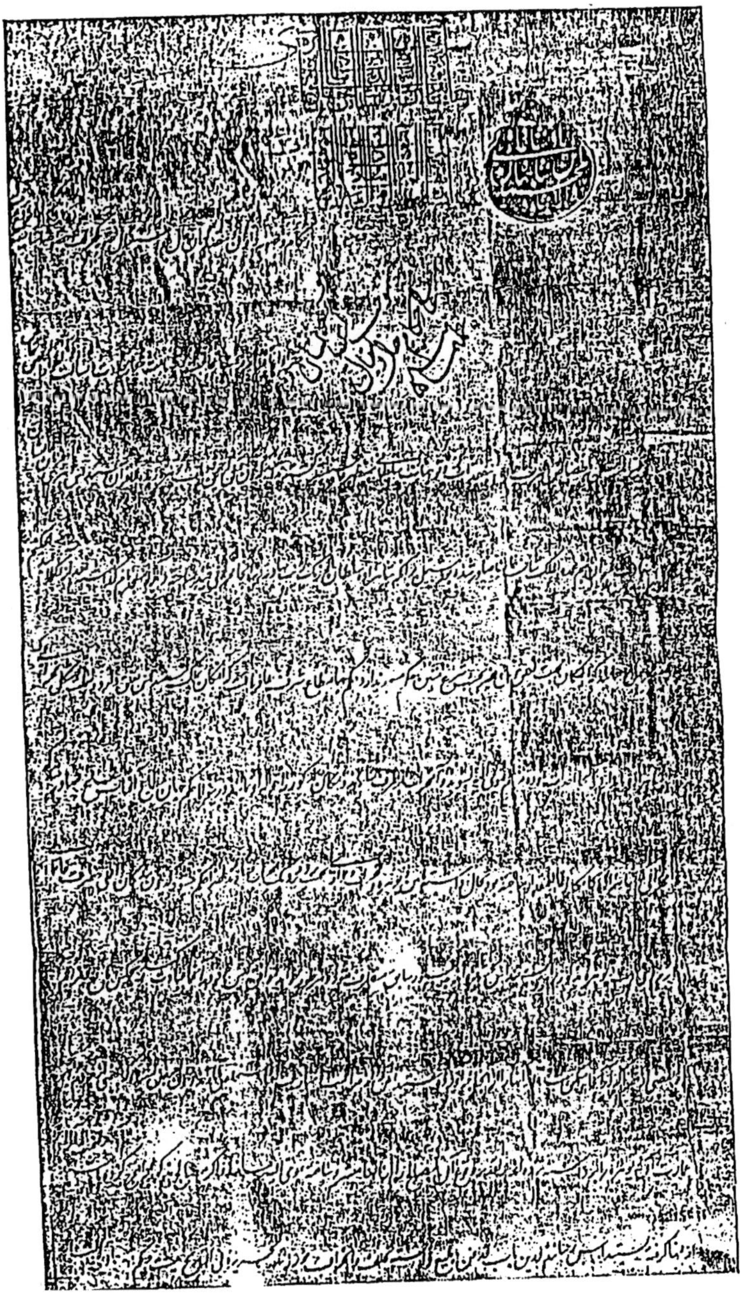

Appendix II

M.S. Commissariat, Imperial Mughal Farmans in Gujarat (Reprinted from The Journal of the University of Bombay, Vol. IX, Part 1, July 1940).

Plate IX: Farman of Shah Jahan, with the Nishan and Seal of Prince Dara Shukoh, directing Ghairat Khan, the Deputy Viceroy of Gujarat, and other officials of the province, to restore to Shantidas the temple of Chintamani which had been converted into a mosque by Prince Aurangzeb in 1645, and to make complete restitution for the damage done by the faqirs and the Bohras. Dated the 21st of Jumad-as-Sani, II, 1058 (July 3, 1648).[1]

(Tughra) 1. Farman-i-Abul Mazaffar Shihab-ud-din Muhammad Sahib Qiran-i-Tsani Shah Jahan Badshah-i-Ghazi.

2. Nishan-i-Alishan Dara Shukoh ibn Shah Jahan Badshah-i-Ghazi.

(Seal) As in Plate X.

Be it known to the governors, subahdars and mutasaddis, present and future, of the province of Gujarat, especially the one who has been worthy of various favours (here follow several honorific epithets), Ghairat Khan,[2] who has been reliant on and gladdened by royal favours, that formerly, in respect of the temple of the leading person of the time (zubdat al-akran), Satidas Jawahari, an exalted and blessed order had been issued to Umdat-ul-mulk Shahistah Khan[3] to this effect : 'Shahzada Sultan Aurangzeb Bahadur having constructed in that place some mihrabs (prayer-arches) had given it the name of a mosque; and, thereafter, Mulla Abdul Hakim had represented to His Majesty that this building, by reason of its being the property of another person, could not be considered a mosque according to the inviolable Islamic law; a world-obeyed order, therefore, obtained the honour of being burned that this building is the property of Satidas, and that because of the mihrab which the famous Prince had made in that place the above-mentioned person should not be harassed, and that the mihrab should be removed and the aforesaid building should be handed over to him'.

Now, at this time, the world-obeyed and illustrious order has been issued that the mihrab which the victorious and exalted Prince has constructed may be retained, and a wall be built near the same as a screen between the temple and the mihrab. Hence, it is ordained that, since his exalted Majesty has, as an act of favour, granted the aforesaid temple to Satidas, he should be in possession of it as before, and he may worship there according to his creed in any way he likes, and no one should obstruct or trouble him; and also that some of the Faqirs (beggars) who have made their abode in that place should be turned out, and Satidas should be relieved from the troubles and quarrels on their account. And since it has been represented to His Majesty that some of the Bohras have removed and carried away the materials of that temple, in the event of this being so, those materials should be got back from them and should be restored to the person referred to above (Satidas), and if the aforesaid materials have been used up, their price should be recovered from them and should be paid to Satidas.

In this matter, this order should be considered extremely urgent, and there should be no deviation from or disobedience to it. Written on the twenty-first of the month of Jumad-us- Sani in the year 1058 H. (July 3,1648).

References

1. For full details about the historical events connected with Shantidas's temple at Ahmadabad and its conversion into a mosque by Prince Aurangzeb, see Introduction, 14-16.
2. In H. 1058 (A.D. 1648), Prince Dara Shukoh was appointed by the Emperor Shah Jahan as the Viceroy of Gujarat, but he continued at the capital, while a trusted officer named Baqir Beg, who received the title of Ghairat Khan, was sent to this province as his Deputy to carry on the administration.
3. Shaistah Khan was an exalted noble of this time, being the brother of Mumtaz Mahal, the wife of Shah Jahan, and thus closely related to the Emperor. He was twice appointed Viceroy of Gujarat, viz.,in 1646-48 and again in 1652-54. The reference to him in this document relates to his first regime when in November, 1646, he succeeded Prince Aurangzeb as Subahdar of this province, and evidently received, according to this Farman, orders from the Emperor to undo the damage done by the Prince to the temple built by Shantidas. Shaistah Khan's rule in the province appears to have been harsh, and his attempt to monopolise indigo and other commodities was much resented by the English merchants at Ahmadabad (*Mirat-i-Ahmadi*, Pers. text, I, 224 ; W. Foster, English Factories in India (1646-50), 127, 161).

Appendix III

M.S. Commissariat, Studies in the History of Gujarat, Longmans, Green & Co, Ltd. (Bombay, Calcutta, Madras, London, New York and Toronto), 1935.

Shantidas Builds a Great Temple at Ahmadabad, 1621

The most important event in the early period of the career of Shantidas was no doubt the commencement in the year 1621 (Samvat 1678) of the magnificent Jain temple dedicated to *Chintamani-Parshwanath* in a suburb of Ahmadabad. The edifice must have been completed four years later in 1625, for in this year Shantidas is said to have formally installed therein the image of the Tirthankar. The temple is said to have been called Manatunga.[1] It was situated in the then flourishing suburb of Bibipur, which is now known as Saraspur, and the sacred monument was erected jointly by Shantidas and his elder brother Vardhaman. It is a matter for no small regret that while the great Muslim monuments of the fifteenth and sixteenth centuries at Ahmadabad still remain in almost perfect condition, this great Jain temple built in the seventeenth century, has practically disappeared owing to reasons which we shall describe later.

Prince Aurangzeb Converts the Temple into a Mosque, 1645

In 1645, Prince Aurangzeb, then Viceroy of Gujarat under his father Shah Jahan, ordered the beautiful temple built by Shantidas at the suburb of Saraspur to be desecrated and it was converted into a mosque under the name of *Quvvat-ul-Islam* (the Might of Islam).[2] The meagre refererence to this event in the *Mirat-i-Ahmadi* may be supplemented by a quotation from the French traveller M. de Thevenot, who visited Ahmadabad in 1666. He says:—

Thevenot's Account of the Desecration

"Ahmedabad being inhabited also by a great numbers of beathens, there are Pagods or idol-temples in it. That which was called the Pagod of Shantidas was the chief, before Aurangzeb converted it into a mosque. When he performed that ceremony he caused a cow to be killed in the place, knowing very well that, after such an action, the gentiles, according to their law, could worship no more therein. All round the temple there is a cloister furnished with lovely cells, beautified with figures of marble in relief, representing naked women sitting after the oriental fashion. The inside roof of the mosque is pretty enough and the walls are full of the figures of men and beasts; but Aurangzeb, who hath always made a show of an affected devotion, which at length raised him to the throne, caused the noses of all these figures, which added a great deal of magnificence to that mosque, to be beat off."[3]

Tavernier's Reference to the Temple

The famous French jeweller and traveller, M. Tavernier, who paid many visits to Ahmadabad in the course of his travels, is evidently referring to the Jain temple built by Shantidas when he says:—

"There was a Pagoda in this place which the Muhammadans took possession of in order to turn it into a mosque. Before entering it you traverse three great courts paved with marble, and surrounded by galleries, and you are not allowed to place foot in the third without removing your shoes. The exterior of the mosque is ornamented with mosaic, the greater part of which consists of agates of different colours, obtained from the mountains of Cambay, only two days' journey from thence."[4]

Shah Jahan Restores the Temple to Shantidas

It is not probable that so powerful a citizen and so devout a Jain as Shantidas would allow this insult offered even by an Imperial Prince to a monument built at such immense cost and dedicated to one of the Supreme Souls of the Jain religion to pass without making a representation to the Emperor. This may be premised from the grant of an Imperial farman, dated July 3, 1648, about three years after the Prince's viceroyalty, directing Ghairat Khan and other officials in Gujarat to restore the building to Shantidas and to make him complete restitution for all damage done. This most valuable historical document was in 1888 submitted by the then Nagarsheth Premabhai Hemabhai to the Superintendent of the Revenue Survey at Ahmadabad for his action.[5] But all traces of it were forgotten for about half a century till the author was able, after much labour, to locate it in the possession of Sheth Kasturbhai Manibhai, the grandson of Premabhai, at the end of 1932, in a long-neglected bundle containing several other valuable farmans.

Ghairat Khan as Deputy for Dara in Gujarat

This farman bears at its top the seal of Dara Shukoh and was granted on the 21st of Jumad-as-Sani of the Hijri year 1058 (July 3, 1648), being addressed to the officers of the Subah of Gujarat, and especially to Ghairat Khan, on whom special epithets of praise and regard are bestowed. The date is interesting, for we learn from the *Mirat-i-Ahmadi* that on this day the Emperor appointed his eldest son Dara as Viceroy of Gujarat in succession to Shaistah Khan who had been transferred.[6] But Dara's appointment was a nominal one, for he was allowed to remain at court and to carry on the government of his province by sending this Ghairat Khan as his naib or deputy to Ahmadabad. It is possible, therefore, that the farman was delivered to the latter on this day. As the farman has never been published before, we give below a full translation of the same :

Toghra (in golden ink): Farman-i- Abul Muzaffar Shihab-ud-din Muhammad Sahib Kirau-i-Sani Shah Jahan Badshah-i-Ghazi.

Nishan: Niskan-i-Alishan Shahzada Buland Iqbal Muhammad Dara Shukoh.

Seal (in black) Muhammad Dara Shukoh ibn Shah Jahan Badshah Ghazi.

Shah Jahan's Farman for the Restoration of the Temple, 3 July, 1648

'Be it known to the governors, subahdars aud mutasaddis, present and future, of the province of Gujarat, especially the one who has been worthy of various favours *(here follow various honorific epithets),* viz., Ghairat Khan, who has been reliant on and gladdened by royal favours, that formerly, in respect of the temple of the leading person of the time *(zubdat- al-akran),* Satidas Jawahari, an exalted and blessed order had been issued to Umdat-ul-Mulk Shaistah Khan to this effect: Shahzada Sultan Aurangzeb Bahadur had constructed in that place some mihrabs (prayer-arches) and had given it the name of a mosque; and after that Mulla Abdul Hakim had represented to His Majesty that this building, by reason of its being the property of another person, could not be considered a mosque according to the inviolable Islamic law; a world-obeyed order, therefore, obtained the honour of being issued that this building is the property of Satidas, and that because of the mihrab which the famous Prince had made in that place the above-mentioned person should not be harassed, and that the arch should be removed and the aforesaid building should be handed over to him.

'Now, at this time, the world-obeyed and illustrious order has been issued that the mihrab which the victorious and exalted Prince has constructed may be retained and a wall be built near the same as a screen between the temple and the mihrab. Hence it is ordained that, since his exalted Majesty has, as an act of favour, granted the aforesaid temple to Satidas, he should be in possession of it as before and he may worship there according to his creed in any way he likes, and no one should obstruct or trouble him ; also that some of the Faqirs (beggars) who have made their abode in that place should be turned out, and Satidas should be relieved from the troubles and quarrels on their account.

'And since it has been represented to His Majesty that some of the Bohras have removed and carried away the materials of that temple, in the event of this being so, those materials should be got back from them and should be restored to the person referred to above (Satidas), and if the aforesaid materials have been used up, their price should be recovered from them and should be paid to Satidas.

'In this matter, this order should be considered extremely urgent and there should be no deviation from or disobedience to it. Written on the twenty-first of the month of Jumad-as-Sani in the year 1058 H. (July 3, 1648).'[9]

Farman of 1629 about Jain Temple and Poshals

We may now refer to an imperial Mughal farman granted to Shantidas by Shah Jahan in the early years of his reign in which the Emperor makes certain grants which are different in their nature from those Palitana grants which are the subject of several well-known farmans of a later date. This farman, now in the possession of the firm of Sheth Anandji Kalyanji, was written on the 21st May of the Ilahi month of Adar in the second year of the coronation, i.e., in 1629-30. The document states that it had been brought to the notice of His Majesty that the temples of 'Chintaman' and 'Satrunja' and 'Sankhesara'[8] and 'Kesari'[9] were in existence long before the auspicious accession, and that there were three poshals[10] at Ahmadabad, four at Khambayat, one at Surat and one at Radkanpur in the possession of Shantidas. The order was, therefore, now issued to the effect that no one should put up at those places and houses for they had been granted to the Jains. The farman proceeds to add that the Sevras, 'who recite the books Sagar and Sarogun' were permitted to remain in the Subah of Gujarat and they are enjoined not to fight among themselves but to engage themselves in prayers for the continuation of the State.[11]

Evidently, Manekchand, who is mentioned in the *Mirat-i-Ahmadi* in some of the imperial farmans as the son of Shantidas, and who funneled, along with others, large sums of money to Prince Murad Bakhsh at Ahmadabad in 1658, was born after 1640 which is the date of the composition of the *Chintamani Prashasti.*

Appendix B

Description of the Temple of Shantidas given in the Chintamani Prashasti

'In S. 1678 (A.D. 1621), Vardhaman and Shantidas, who had reached the zenith of their fortune, who had taken the religious vow along with the members of their family, who had been leading a very pure life, and who had heard that building temples led to good luck, built a magnificent temple in the suburb of Bibipur (verses 45-49). On the arches of the temple there were statues of females resembling celestial nymphs, while at the door of the temple there was the Panchapatra for protection. The lofty steps of the temple indicated the way for the heavenward march of the devotees. There were six halls in the temple called Meghanada, Sinhanada, Suryanada, Rangarama, Khela and Gudhagotra. It had two turrets, four square temples around, and four underground shrines with idols of the Jina (verses 50-54).'[12]

Appendix C

Mandelslo's Account of the Temple of Shantidas at Ahmadabad in 1639 (Visit to the Temple of Shantidas)

Black Elephants at life size at Entrance

'At the entrance into the mosque there are two elephants of black marble done to the life, and upon one of them the effigy of the founder. The whole mosque is vaulted and the walls adorned with several figures of men and other living creatures. There was not anything within the mosque, save that at the further end of the structure there were three chapels or obscure places, divided one from the other by wooden rails, wherein might be seen statues of marble, like those we had seen in the cells, with this difference only that there was a lighted lamp before that which stood in the middle.

References

1. For the description of the temple given in the *Chintamani-prashasti* see Appendix B at the end of this chapter.
2. *Mirat-i-Ahmadi,* Pers. Text, ed. by Syed Nawab Ali, Part I.
3. *Travels of M. De Thevenot,* trasns. by Lovell, London, 1687, Part III, p. 10.
4. J.B. Tavernier, *Travels in India,* Ed. by Ball,I, p. 72.
5. *Jain Aitihasic Rasmala,* Ed., by Mohanlal D Desai, Part I, p. 30.
6. *Mirat-i-Ahmadi,* Pers. text, Ed. by Nawab Ali, Part I, p. 224.
7. The reverse of this Farman contains the following brief endorsement: 'through the humblest of servants, Biharimal.'
8. Sankheshvar is situated near Panchasar in the district of Munjpur, 24 miles south of Radhanpur in North Gujarat. It is still a famous place of Jain pilgrimage, but the present temples are modern and raised on the site of old buildings that have quite disappeared. *(Bombay Gazetteer,* V, 347) The *Mirat-i-Ahmadi* describes this temple as 'Sankh Parasnath, situated in pargana Munjpur, Sarkar Patan'. (Nawab Ali and Seddon, *Suppl.* 139).
9. The temple of Kesharianath, sacred to Adinath or Rishabhdev, is situated in the village of Dhuleva, about 36 miles from the city of Udaipur in the state of the same name.
10. A *poshal* is a place where a Jain stays when keeping his *posha* vow, one of the four disciplinary vows of the Jains (cf. *Sanskrit, Uposhatha-shala).*
11. A photographic facsimile of this Farman (marked E), as well as those of several others, with imperfect and faulty translations, will be found in a small book entitled "Memorial from...Sheth Anandji Kalianji the accredited representatives of the Jain community of India in reference to the grievances about their rights re: the Shatrunjaya Hill" (Bombay: *The Times Press,* 1925).
12. The Sanskrit text of the *Chintamani Prashasti,* which is corrupt, has been kindly rendered into English for the author by Prof. K. V. Abhayankar.

Appendix IV

M.S. Commissariat, A History of Gujarat, Vol II, The Mughal Period: from 1573 to 1758. Orient Longmans (Bombay, Calcutta, Madras, New Delhi and Hyderabad), 1957

Chapter XI

Prince Aurangzeb, Shaistah Khan amd Ghairat Khan as Viceroys, 1645-54

Desecration of Shantidas's Temple

In 1645, when he was in his 27th year, Prince Aurangzeb was appointed by his father to the responsible post of viceroy of Gujarat, and the events which happened at Ahmadabad during his brief viceroyalty are of special interest as showing how, even at this early age, his character manifested that religious intolerance and puritanical seal which subsequently led to events that embittered his life and paved the way for the decline of his Empire. Whether the Hindus at this capital gave any cause for offence to the young Prince is not known, for the historian simply states that the latter ordered the temple of Chintamani at Saraspur, a suburb of the city to the east, to be converted into a mosque under the name of *'Quvvat-ul-Islam'* (the Might of Islam).[1] This temple had been completed by Shantidas, the famous Jain jeweller, in 1625, and it has been fully described by the German traveller Mandelslo who visited Ahmadabad in 1638.[2] That this magnificent monument should have been desecrated and consequently abandoned for worship, and ultimately allowed to fall into ruin, cannot but be regarded as a misfortune. A direct reference to the slaughter of a cow in the temple at the time of its conversion into a mosque is also made by the French traveller M.de Thevenot who was at Ahmadabad in 1666.[3] In a later chapter, devoted to the career of Shantidas Jawahari, will be found a full account of the chequered history of this temple and its desecration.

References

1. *Mirat-i-Ahmadi,* I, 220.
2. See the author's Mandelslo's *Travels in Western India* (1931), pp. 23-25, and Appendix I.
3. *Travels of M. de Thevenot,* trans. by Lovell, London, 1687, Part III, 10.

****

The Order to Restore the Temple to Shantidas

The farman next proceeds to direct Ghairat Khan that, in modification of the above order to his predecessor, the mihrabs (i.e., prayer niches), 'constructed by the victorious and exalted Prince should he retained, and that a wall should be built up near the same so as to screen them off from the rest of the temple. Also that, since His Exalted Majesty had restored the aforesaid temple to Shantidas, the latter should be put in possession of it as before, so that he might worship therein according to his creed. The document contains some further orders relating to Faqirs and beggars who had made the building their abode, and to the Bohras who had pilfered materials from the temple.[1] That Shah Jahan, who never showed his father's or Akbar's toleration for Hindu shrines, should thus have so definitely reversed the action of his own son, and made such complete restitution to the Jain magnate, is ample proof of the personal influence of Shantidas with the Emperor, and of the honour and respect in which he was held at the royal court. But the grievous wrong done by the Prince to Shantidas and to the Jain religion and its votaries could not be undone even by the best efforts of the Emperor, and this great temple was doomed to decay and ruin. One unique feature of this *farman* is found in the fact that there is brief endorsement in the body of the document, near the first two lines, which was probably written by the Emperor himself in his own hand.

References

1. Vide the author's monograph on *Imperial Mughal Farmans in Gujarat,* in Journal of the University of Bombay, Vol. IX, Pt.I, July, 1940, pp. 39-41; also Plate IX (of the Persian text) and Plate XXII (for Prince Dara's Seal).

****

Chapter XIII

Shantidas Jawahari, the Jain Magnate of Ahmadabad

The Author's Memoirs on Shantidas

It is with a sense of satisfaction and some relief that one can turn aside for a while from political history in order to devote a chapter to the career and activities of the Jain magnate Shantidas Jawahari of Ahmadabad, who flourished during the reigns of Jahangir and Shah Jahan, whose great resources as a financier, and business connections as a jeweller, enabled him to enjoy considerable favour and influence at the imperial court at Delhi. The high social position he attained also helps to prove that the Hindu merchants and financiers of Gujarat during the 17th century, especially in the major towns of the province, enjoyed complete freedom to pursue their normal activities in trade and commerce, and to amass great wealth, even if they were debarred from the exercise of higher political and administrative functions. The career of Shantidas is also interesting for the fact that he was the first *nagarsheth* of Ahmadabad by popular voice, and that this title, with its attached status and conventional functions, was handed down in his family till recent times. Since the beginning of the present century, however, the great progress made in local municipal government, and other factors involving the decline of old institutions, have practically deprived the head of this family of almost all his traditional prestige and prerogative as the hereditary 'Mayor' of the city. A very full account of Shantidas, based on research extending over several years, has been published by the author in two separate works, viz., in his *Studies in the History of Gujarat* and in *Mughal Imperial Farmans in Gujarat.* It will suffice, therefore, to indicate here in outline the main episodes in his career.

Farman for its Restoration

Shantidas stood high in favour with the Emperor at this period, as may be judged from nearly a dozen royal farmans granted in his favour by Shah Jahan in the course of his long reign. It was not likely that he would allow this insult to his religion and his prestige, even though offered by an imperial Prince, to pass by without submitting a representation to the Emperor. Though we have no direct evidence for this, we may presume some such action to have been taken by him from the farman on this subject issued by the orders of Shah Jahan, bearing the nishan and seal of Prince Dara Shukoh, and addressed to Ghairat Khan. the deputy-viceroy of Gujarat. The details of this farman ordering the restoration of the temple to Shantidas have been given in a previous chapter. The great Emperor, be it said to his credit, had done what he could to make amends for the deep offence given to the Hindu magnate; but the mischief done was irreparable. No doubt, after the imperial orders, the building could no more be used by the Muslims as a mosque but for the Jain community also, it was forever desecrated, so that, as Thevenot says, 'according to their law, the gentiles could worship no more there.' Under these circumstances, it is not surprising that this superb monument fell early into disuse and disrepair, and today it has quite disappeared, its stones and materials having been for generations pilfered and carted away to build other structures.

11

Janmasthan (*Rama Janamabhoomi*) *Versus* 'Baburi *Masjid*'

The entire issue has to be examined in an objective and scientific manner. The approach should not be emotionally coloured by religious complexion. As India is a secular State, it is rather essential that communal harmony should be maintained and that differences amongst the different religious communities should be sorted out amicably.

For medieval Indian history, the historiography in post-independence period has undergone a radical change. Till, at least 1947, there was much less of a distinction between the 'Muslim historians' or 'Hindu historians' of the Mughal age so long as the works were written on the basis of the contemporary sources and in a scientific manner. Even the Muslim historians were very frank to make statements about the desecration of the Hindu temples and the construction of the mosques on these sites. May be their purpose was equally to highlight the glory of Islam and the triumphant nature of the Muslim rule in India. However, after 1947, there has been considerable camouflage by many Muslim historians to gloss over the real facts. The present day distinction between the 'Hindu testimony' and 'Muslim testimony' is rather arbitrary and unscientific in character.

For the history of Awadh, the 19th century works of the English writers have been rejected on the ground that they were biased as being based upon 'Divide and Rule' policy. This is, notwithstanding the fact that for their sources, most of their works referred to the earlier Muslim writers of the Mughal and later ages in a scientific manner. Not only that, even the historical works of the Muslim writers written during the period of the British rule in India or even earlier works of the *Nawabi* period, though based upon authentic contemporary sources, are being rejected simply on the ground they were published during the later half of the 19th century of the British regime in India. Such an approach, even though anomalous, has brought about a serious crisis in the Indian historiography posing a great challenge to objective and scientific historians, which has to be met with a dispassionate mind.

The issue as to whether the 'Baburi Masjid' was constructed on the same site where the earlier Hindu monument (temple) of *Janmasthan* (*Ramjanmabhoomi*) existed after the demolition of the latter and with more or less the same construction material or the mosque was constructed on an open plot unconnected with *Ramjanmabhoomi* or adjacent to the *Janmasthan* may be examined bearing in mind the following historical sources:-

(I) Literary, (II) Revenue records, (III) Judicial records, (IV) Archaeological evidence.

(I) Literary

The Muslim writers who were residents of Awadh and have written detailed accounts of the regional history of Awadh based on the past authentic contemporary sources of various nature, have unanimously stressed the fact that on the basis of Babur's order, the *Janmasthan* of Shri Ram Chandra at *Kot* Ram Chandra, *Pargana Haveli* Awadh, which comprise not only the private apartments (*mahal sarai*) of King Dashrath and Shri Ram but also a temple and a kitchen popularly known as *Sita Ki Rasoi,* were demolished and a mosque constructed thereupon in 1528 A.D. under the guidance of the Commander Mir Baqi and a Muslim *faqir* named Sayed Musa Ashikan. Indeed, graphic descriptions have been provided by many historians in a significant manner. Of these the following deserve special mention:—

(i) Mirza Jan, *Hadiqa-i-Shahada*, Lucknow, 1956, pp. 4-5; also vide Raise Ahmad Jafri, *Wajid Ali Shah Aur Un ka Ahad*, Lucknow, Chapter 9, pp. 244-247.

(ii) Haji Muhammad Hasan, resident of *qasba* Bijnor, District Lucknow, *Zia-i-Akhtar*, Lucknow, 1878, pp. 38-39.

(iii) Maulvi Abdul Karim, *Gumghasta Halat-i-Ajodhya Awadh* (The forgotten events of Ajodhya Awadh) *i.e., Tarikh-i-Parnia*

Madina Auliya (in Persian), Lucknow, 1885. It is significant to note that the author Maulvi Abdul Karim was also the *Imam* of Baburi *Masjid* and in his scholarly work has referred to numerous contemporary sources from 16th to 19th centuries. The same book was translated by his grandson, Maulvi Abdul Gufar, from Persian to Urdu and published in Lucknow in May, 1979 which retained the above mentioned description about the demolition of the temple at *Janmasthan* and construction of the mosque thereupon, vide page 40. But this portion has been omitted from the revised edition in Urdu, published in Lucknow, 1981, pp. 53-54.

(iv) Kamaluddin Haider Hasni al Hussaini al Mashhadi, *Kaiser ul Tawarikha Tawarikh-i-Awadh*, Lucknow, 1896, Vol. II, pp. 100-112.

(v) Sheikh Muhammad Azmat Ali Nami, *Tawarikh-i-Mulkh-i-Awadh,* entitled *Murraqa-i Khusrawi*. This manuscript available at Tagore Library, University of Lucknow, (U.P.), was for the first time published in 1986. In this version, the above mentioned portion relating to the construction of Baburi *Masjid* on the site of the temple in the premises of *Janmasthan* as well as the portion relating to Amir Ali Shahid and the Hindu-Muslim riot of 1855 were deleted by the Fakhruddin Ahmad Memorial Committee under whose auspices the book was brought out. But Dr. Zakir Kakaurwi has published these portions separately under the title, *Amir Ali Shahid Aur Marakha-i-Hanuman Gahri*, Lucknow, 1987, pp. 9-11.

(vi) Rajab Ali, *Fasana-i-Ibrat*, *Ibid.,* pp. 71-72.

(vii) Alama Muhammad Najamalghani Khan Rampuri, *Tarikh-i-Awadh,* 1909, Vol. II, vide abridged edition, Dr. Zakir Kakaurwi, pp. 570-575.

(viii) Lachmi Narain Sadr Qanungo and Munshi Maulvi Hashim, *Asrar-i-Haqiqat*, Lucknow, 1923, pp. 1, 64-67.

(ix) Muhammad Asghar, *Khatib* and *Muazzan* of the Baburi *Masjid* in his representation, dated 30.11.1958, Case No. 884 *muhalla Kot* Ram Chandra, Ajodhya, to the British Government in the complaint against the *Bairagis* of *Janmasthan* for alleged interference in the *Masjid* Baburi concedes the fact that in the outer space of the constructed *mosque*, of course, in the courtyard within the walled boundaries of the *mosque*, there had been *Janmasthan* lying desolate where the Hindus had been worshipping for hundreds of years thereupon. This is a frank admission of the fact that even though major portion of *Janmasthan* had been covered by Baburi *Masjid*, the Hindus had been worshipping in the remaining open space for hundreds of years *i.e.,* even during the Mughal and *Nawabi* periods and that they had never surrendered their claim of the entire *Janmasthan* area. Apparently, the controversy of the claim over *Janmasthan* by the Hindus versus Baburi *Masjid* was not a creation of the British 'Divide-And-Rule' policy.

Earlier, a European traveller, Joseph Tiffenthaler, a Jesuit Austrian (1710-1788) in his work entitled *Historich Geographische Beschereibung Von Hindustan,* (in German Language), 3 vols., 1785, 1787, 1788), has given a very graphic and meticulous account of *Janmasthan*, its demolition at the hands of Babur or Aurangzeb and a construction of mosque thereupon. This work was also translated into French entitled, *Geography De L' Indostan.* (vide details *La Province. D'Oude*). Joseph Tiffenthaler toured the Awadh region around 1766-71 A.D. As Joseph Tiffenthaler was a foreigner and relied upon hear-say, he was not sure whether the mosque was constructed by Babur or Aurangzeb. In this regard, it is significant to note that the author of *Zia-i-Akhatar*, as already mentioned above (vide Literary sources No. ii) states that in addition to the Baburi mosque, another mosque adjacent to the earlier one was also constructed by Aurangzeb, which in due course of time mitigated by the Hindu *Bairagis*.

So it is clear that the existence of the *Janmasthan* temple, its demolition during Babur's reign and the construction of a mosque is not a myth created by the British writers. It is equally authenticated not only by the Muslim writers of the British period, but the earlier *Nawabi* period as well. It is important to stress the fact that many of the above Muslim writers of the British period were highly critical of the British policy in Awadh and could not have bene influenced by the 'Divide-and-Rule' policy.

(II) Revenue Records

In the field of medieval historiography, Abul Fazl in his brief account of the *subah* of Awadh in the *Ain-i-Akbari* (Persian text, II, Lucknow, 1881, p. 78) provides the earliest reference to the association of Shri Ram Chandra with Awadh (Ayodhya). He states that Awadh "was the residential place (*bangha*) of Raja Ram Chandra, who during the *Treta* age was apparently the embodiment of both the spiritual sovereign supremacy as well as the mundane kingly office." As regards Awadh, he comments that at that time (16th century), it was one of the largest cities of India and was esteemed as one of the holiest places of antiquity. However, as the *Ain-i-Akbari* is basically an administrative manual (of the reign of Akbar), Abul Fazl does not provide any further detail.

For administrative purpose, the *subah* of Awadh under Akbar was divided into five *sarkars,* the *sarkar* of Awadh being one of them. Further, of the division of the *sarkar* Awadh into 21 *mahals* (for revenue administration), *Haveli* Awadh comprising two *mahals i.e.,* the proper city (*shahar*) and the suburban district was the headquarters of *sarkar* Awadh. As such, *Haveli* Awadh served as the capital of the entire *subah* of Awadh, the headquarters of the *sarkar* of Awadh as well as that of the proper Awadh *Pargana.*

The revenue documents of the *Nawabi* period and the British phase (from 1856 onwards) during the later half of the 19th and early 20th centuries have a direct linkage with the Mughal pattern of revenue administration. *Kot* Ram Chandra was one of the villages (*mauzas*) of the suburban *mahal/pargana* of Awadh and as per revenue records was quite distinct from the city (*shahar*) of Ayodhya. It was *Kot* Ram Chandra which was the residential headquarters of Shri Ram Chandra. As explained further, the *Janmasthan* (the name used both by the 19th century revenue records and literary sources) being a large complex comprising the palace, inclusive of the birth-place area of Shri Ram Chandra temple, kitchen (*Sita Ki Rasoi*) etc. was situated in *Kot* Ram Chandra.

The revenue records relating to village *Ramkot*, *Haveli* Awadh, District Faizabad, are extremely significant and clarify the factual proprietary position of *Janmasthan* vs. Baburi *Masjid.* As per land revenue procedure, they offer details of the numbered plots (*khasras*) of the entire village *Ramkot* in respect of the nature of land rights, their topographical position, the nature of soil along with the area of each plot with complete further details, whether inhabited with *abadi* (population) or a graveyard or arable land growing particular crops along with fruit bearing trees, if any, and paying land revenue or treated as *muafi* (exempted from revenue payment). The plots of land traditionally associated with *Janmasthan* complex are mostly shown as settled with *abadi* (population) and constructions thereupon. All these records are available at the District Record Office (*Mahafaz Khanna*)/Tehsil Office/Nazul Office, Faizabad. In fact, the records comprise various categories of revenue documents, *i.e.,* survey, *bandobast,* (settlement) *kishtwar khasra, abadi, khewats, khasra, khataunis* and maps etc. right from 1861 A.D. till date (1990).

A few records of Summary Settlements are also available for the years 1858-59 A.D. The earliest regular settlement of 1861 A.D. as well as the later reports confirm the fact that these had been prepared taking into consideration the past records of the *Nawabi* period as well (vide Basta Nos. 132 of 1861 pertaining to *khasra kishtwar, mauza Ramkot*, *Pargana Haveli* and Zilla Faizabad. Hose's Note, dated 1st April, 1905, No. 37, Nazul Office, Faizabad). As a matter of fact, as per the original documents, the entire complex of *Janmasthan* is covered under *khasra* No. 163 with 10 plots (vide 1st *khasra kishtwar* Settlement Report, 1861 A.D.) and the superior ownership of the land has been declared in the name of *Sarkar Bahadur Nazul* (Government). The *Mahants* of *Janmasthan* have been shown in the revenue documents with subordinate proprietary right (*malikan-i-matahit*). Such is the position not only in the 1861 Settlement Report but even later Settlements effected from time to time during the 19th and 20th centuries. It is also clear that the area on which the structure of the 'Baburi Masjid' stood is a part of the *Janmasthan.*

This position was inherited by the early British administration from the earlier records of the *Nawabi* and the Mughal periods. However, in the Settlement Record of 1861 of the *Mahafaz Khanna*, certain later alterations have been made wherein the name of *Jama Masjid* and *muafi* have been inserted in one of the plots but the copies of the same document prepared during the same year available at the Tehsil Office clearly prove that the later additions are interpolations, done perhaps during the past few decades of the controversy. This is also confirmed by the fact that the *khasra kishtwar* records of the second Revenue Settlement effected in the year 1301 *Fasli* (1893 A.D.) do not carry out much alterations or additions. These records still show the area on which Baburi *Masjid* had been earlier constructed as *Sita Ki Rasoi,* forming a part of the *Janmasthan* complex (Vide *khasra* No. 163/5) and there is no mention of any mosque and the land assigned to it in *muafi*.

Above all, most significantly, the map of the *Hadbast* of village *Kot* Ramchandra, *Pargana Haveli*, Tehsil and *Zilla* Faizabad, prepared in 1861 A.D., shows only the temple at *Janmasthan* in a significant manner and the Baburi *Masjid* is not even indicated. In another related map, it has been put in a most insignificant symbol. The revised *khasra* records of 1344-45 *Fasli* (1937-38) reiterate the same position as recorded in the earlier settlements excepting that in one of the plots, both *masjid* and *chabutra* indicating the temple at *Janmasthan* have been recorded. The *mosque* has been shown in *waqf* under the column 'Name of the Present Possessor' (*Nam Hal Qabiz*). At the same time, *Mahant* Raghu Nath Das has been declared as an underproprietor of the entire plot. Such a position occurs for the first time in the *khasra* records which had been regularly prepared since 1858-59 and 1861 A.D. Apparently, this change, even though anomalous, was effected by the British Government in the aftermath of the 1934 Hindu-Muslim riots over the *Janmasthan*-Baburi *Masjid* issue. However, this is not further reflected in the other related revenue documents available since 1937-38 A.D.

According to the revenue settlement effected in 1861 A.D., the total area covered by *khasra* No. 163 relating to *Janmasthan* has 10 distinct plots. There have been three more settlement operations since then. However, in the revenue settlements effected from time to time, the *khasra/khewat/khata khatauni* numbers undergo a change and there are also adjustments with the neighbouring plots. As per 1397 *Fasli*/1989-90 settlement, the erstwhile *Janmasthan* complex has been shown in four *khasra* Nos., *i.e.,* 159, 160, 146 and 147. *Ramjanmabhoomi* has been shown in two numbers, *i.e.,*

159 and 160. The name of the Baburi *Masjid* does not occur at all in any of these numbers. Of the combined numbers, most of the area has been put under *Nazul* whereas some portion has been shown in the ownership of the local *mahant*. The monument today named as *Janmasthan* to the east of Ram *Janmabhoomi/Baburi Masjid*, which earlier in the 1861 settlement operation had been combined with the latter, is shown in *khasra* Nos. 146 and 147R and is vested in the ownership of the Hindu *mahant*.

The plot of land erstwhile No. 586, where *shilanyas* was performed in November, 1989 for the proposed *Janmabhoomi* temple, has been shown as a part of *khasra* No. 160. It is equally clear from the mutations effected since 1930-35 A.D., that the erstwhile plot No. 586, the sub-plot now forming a part of No. 160A, has changed from the previous owners to a local *mahant*. It has been recorded in the *khata khewat* No. 23 of 160A, dated 1393-94 *Fasli*/1985-86 A.D. with an area of 3 *biswas* in the ownership of Sita Saran s/o Kewal Ram and Lachhman Prasad s/o Sita Ram whereas the rest of the area falls under *Nazul*. As such, as per revenue records, it is not a disputed plot of land even though in the present litigation pending before the High Court at Allahabad/Lucknow, it has been dragged as a 'disputed one' pending decision by the court.

(III) Judicial Records

(i) As regards the dispute between *Janmasthan* vs. Baburi *Masjid*, the earliest reference in the judicial proceedings, traceable so far, comes from Hafizullah, an official of the Faizabad Court, who in his note/brief submitted to the Court states in a categorical manner that "the mosque constructed by Babur was situated at the birth-place of Ram, son of Raja Dashrath, and was adjacent to the kitchen of Sita, wife of Ram (*i.e., Sita Ki Rasoi*)." This is also well acknowledged by Harbans Mukhia (vide Ayodhya dispute—Tool for Political Mobilisation, Hindu, Delhi, dated 7.9.1990). It is apparent that Hafizullah could not have submitted his opinion to the Hon'ble court unless he had relied upon the past judicial documents and allied sources in hand.

(ii) The main judicial records available at Faizabad and Lucknow from 1835 A.D. onwards cover as much of litigation between the Hindus *mahants* and the Muslim *imams* relating to Ram Janmabhoomi as between the Muslim Shia and Sunni sects over the management of the Baburi *Masjid.* They fully bear out the fact that the tussle between the Hindus and the Muslims over *Janmasthan* vs. Baburi *Masjid* existed during the *Nawabi* period and that it was not a creation of the British 'Divide-and-Rule' policy. The revenue documents appended to the judicial cases are significant enough tracing the tussle back to the 18th century, which may have been inherited from the earlier Mughal phase.

The judicial cases of the 19th century clearly record Baburi mosque located in *Janmasthan.* This is clearly borne out even from the representation made by the religious heads of the masjid to the British Government. In this regard, Muhammad Asghar, *khatib* and *muazzan* of the *mosque,* in his representation, dated 30th November, 1858, puts it as *Masjid Janmasthan* and in his representation, dated 21st January, 1870 puts is as *masjid Baburi Waqia Janmasthan.* Clearly, here, *Janmasthan* connotes a plot of land on which Baburi *Masjid* is situated (not any *muhalla* or street).

(IV) Archaeological Evidence

In an analysis of the historical facts, where the available literary sources relating to the medieval monuments are of a later phase than the contemporary period or are rather fragmentary, the most vital evidence is that of archaeological findings. In regard to the Ram *Janmabhoomi* vs./ Baburi *Masjid* problem, the following conclusions emerge based on archaeological evidence:—

(i) That a temple in the name of Shri Ram Chandra, which by the 19th century was popularly known as temple of *Janmasthan* and today known as Ram *Janmabhoomi,* was built during the 11-12 centuries.

(ii) That the temple was demolished in 1528 A.D. during the reign of the Mughal Emperor Babur and a '*mosque*' was constructed on the same site (of the temple) on the order of Babur's Commander, Mir Baqi.

(iii) That the date and genuineness of the inscriptions installed on the walls of the 'Baburi *Masjid*', both on the outer sides and inside walls of the structure need further careful examination. This is due to the fact that during the communal riots in March, 1934, the previous inscriptions were dismantled. The newly installed inscriptions after the riots were the supposed copies of the original ones and were not installed at the same places from where they had been reportedly removed and smashed. This is well confirmed by the fact that the most significant inscription according to which Mir Baqi built this monument (here it is not mentioned as a mosque) and the chronogram given therein, *i.e, Bawad Khair Baqi* (*i.e.,* 935 AH/1528 A.D.) is at present installed at the face of the outer wall of the mosque but according to Maulvi Abdul Karim, the *Imam* of the masjid in the late 19th century (vide *Gumghasta Halat-i-Ajodhya Awadh, op. cit.* No. (iii), Literary Sources), it lay installed below the pulpit (*mambar*) inside the mosque. Apart from it, earlier too, there had been communal riots when the 'mosque' had been severely damaged. At least, the riot of 1855 A.D. is on record when the Hindu *Bairagis* unfurled their own flag on the top of the dome of the 'Baburi mosque'.

Another inscription mentions the words 'Babar Qalander'. It is rather doubtful if the epithet of *Qalander* (a sufi *faqir* who renounces the mundane luxuries of life) was ever associated with Babur during his lifetime. At least, this is not borne out by any of the chronicles of the Mughal age.

12

The Rama Temple at Awadh (Ayodhya) and the Historical Records of its Destruction Based on the Testimony of the Muslim Scholars and Western Sources

(Comprising Sanskrit, Persian, Arabic, Chaghatay-Turkish, Urdu, Punjabi and English Sources)

Presented at World Archaeological Congress, Inter-Congress on Destruction and Conservation of Cultural Property held at Brac, Croatia, on May 3-7, 1998.

B.R. Grover & (Miss) Amrita Grover

During the last few years, stormy controversy has raged over the Ayodhya issue and copious literature comprising monographs and newspaper articles has been produced by historians, archaeologists and journalists on an unprecedented scale. A number of issues have been raised relating to the historicity or mythical character of Lord Rama, the dating of Valmiki's *Ramayana*, the identification of historic Ayodhya and its association with Lord Rama and even whether Ayodhya existed in Egypt[1] or Afghanistan or at Herat, and as to whether historical Rama is distinguishable from Rama, the Vishnu incarnate.[2] Even when conceded that Lord Rama was born in India at Ayodhya, the location of the ancient city of Ayodhya whether on the bank of the River Ganges or Sarayu and also the exact site of birth-place in the large presincts of the present day Ayodhya have become debatable[2a]. Controversy has also been raised about the period of the emergence of the 'Vaishnava' or Rama Cults, and also the fact whether a '*Vaishnava*' Rama temple existed during the early 16th century at *Janmasthan*, the birth-place of Sri Rama Chandra[3] when in A.D. 1528-29, Baqi Tashkandi (Mir

Baqi), the local *hakim* (commandar/administrator) of Awadh built a '*mosque*' over there under the orders of the first Mughal monarch, Zahiruddin Muhammad Babur (henceforth Babur). Also a question raised is whether the mosque was constructed on a vacant plot of land[4] or after the demolition of the temple, if any, on the site of *Janmasthan*[5].

Unfortunately, instead of judging these issues based on historicity and archaeological and epigraphic facts, the entire issue has been communalised and politicised. This poses a serious threat to the very concept of Indian historiography. Notwithstanding the aforementioned controversial aspects, the real issue which has finally emerged is "whether a Hindu temple or any Hindu religious structure existed prior to the construction of the *Ramjanmabhoomi*-Baburi *Masjid* (including the premises of the inner and outer courtyards of such structure) in the area on which the structure stood."[6]

Besides literary evidence, there is also ample archaeological evidence that Ayodhya was well-settled by about 800 B.C.[7] In fact, Valmiki in his *Ramayana* (4th-5th century B.C.) associates even the predecessors of Rama's Ikshvaku dynasty with Ayodhya which was the capital and the birth-place of Lord Rama[8]. Kalidasa, the poet laureate, in his famous poem *Raghuvamsa* has the same view[9]. By the 2nd century A.D., Rama had come to be recognised as the incarnation of God Vishnu which is indicated by epigraphic and numismatic data, viz., inscription on stone slab from *Kausambi* (modern *Kosam*, Allahabad district, Uttar Pradesh), coins from Mathura and copper plate from Bagh (Dhar district, Madhya Pradesh) discovered recently.[10] Ayodhya was held sacred especially by the *Vaishnavas* and those of the Rama Cult. As such, the earlier view of some historians that the Rama Cult became popular by the Gupta age (4th-5th centuries A.D.) has to be revised in view of these recent findings[11]. In fact, there are numerous Sanskrit texts comprising poems, dramas, prose, romance and *Champus, Ramayana, Purana, Upanishads, Panchtantra* works and various other religious texts which fully bear out the great antiquity and sanctity of Ayodhya and the veneration it commanded as the birth-place of Rama[12]. Most of these texts belong to the pre-16th century period. Above all, for the early medieval pre-16th century phase, the most clinching evidence for the existence and the geographical position of Rama's birth-place (*Janmasthan*) in Ayodhya is provided by the *Ayodhya Mahatmya Shlokas* which form a part of *Vaishnava Khand* of the *Skanda-Purana.*[13] Even though there is great divergence of opinion about the date of its writing varying from the 7th century A.D. to the 13th-14th centuries AD[14], the *Ayodhya Mahatmya* of the *Skanda-Purana* is mostly accepted as dated in the 13th century, and establishes the popularity of the *Janmasthan* of Lord Rama at Ayodhya having been in existence from the preceeding centuries.

In view of this, the contention that the Rama Cult of Ayodhya became popular from the 13th century onward and it gained ground with the Ramanandi Sect and composition of the Rama history in Hindi and became prominent in Ayodhya only in the 18th century A.D. when the Ramanandi *sadhus* settled and constructed a large number of temples therein[15] is based on completely mistaken observations without any positive evidence.

An authentic recension of *Ayodhya Mahatmya* provides only the direction for the location of *Janmasthan* in Ayodhya without giving distance based on a compass. It states "the *Janmasthan* is located to the east of Vighneshwara, north of Vashistha, and west of Lomash" and that this spot was worshipped especially on Rama *Navami* day (Rama's birthday)[16]. However, those who uphold that 'Babri *mosque*' was not constructed on the spot of Rama's *Janmasthan* temple after its demolition resort to a later recension of *Ayodhya Mahatmya* including unauthenticated and spurious compass locating Rama *Janmasthan* in relation to the shrine of Vighneshware[17] east and north-east which would put the *Janmasthan* site a couple of hundred yards away in the north-east from the actual site of *Janmasthan* replaced later by the 'Babri *Masjid*' in the 16th century. The addition of the two directional compass to the original manuscript of *Ayodhya Mahatmya* done in the 18th-early 19th centuries is apparently an interpolation which has been rejected by the scholars[18].

The presence of an ancient *Janmasthan* temple at the present site in the pre-Islamic era is well established by the latest archaeological discoveries made in June-July 1992[18a] when during the course of the digging and levelling operations by the Public

Work Department of the Uttar Pradesh State, India, towards the immediate east and south of the disputed structure of '*Ramjanmabhoomi*-Baburi *Masjid*', large floor areas of burnt bricks in pre-Islamic levels (5th to 12th centuries A.D.) were discovered. The floor covered with burnt-bricks spread over thousands of square meters, including the misnomered '*Janmasthan*' across the modern road. This road was built by the British Government after cutting the *Ramkot* mound, which in the pre-British period, formed an integral part of the *Janmasthan* complex. Apart from this, during the same levelling operations, huge burnt-brick wall of more than a dozen courses inclusive of the pre-Islamic levels running across the section of the eastern side of the disputed structure and even beyond it was discovered.

The ancient *Vaishnava* temple at *Janmasthan* (Rama's birth-place) destroyed in the early 11th century by the Turkish campaigns[19] was, as per inscriptional evidence available now, rebuilt around mid-12th century by Nyayachandra, the chief of the Saket *Mandalam* with headquarters at Ayodhya who, in fact, was the feudatory of the Gahadavala Kingdom of Kannauj[20]. However, during the 13th century, with the consolidation of the Turkish rule in North India and decline of the Gahadavala rulers of Kannauj, the Awadh (Ayodhya) chief assumed direct vassalage of the Turkish Sultanate of Delhi.

The viewpoint that *Janmasthan* (*Ramjanmabhoomi*) temple at Awadh (Ayodhya) had already been demolished and replaced by a 'mosque' on the same site by either Sultan Ibrahim Sharqi of Jaunpur (1402-36), during the interregnum Sharqi rule over Awadh (A.D. 1399-1479) or Sikandar Lodhi (Sikandar *But Shikan,* the iconoclast 1489-1517) and that Mir Baqi simply carried out the repairs[21] is not at all correct. There is no direct evidence in this respect in any of the Persian chronicles and such a version is also contradictory to the text of the inscriptions installed on the 'mosque' as stated further, which clearly put the date of the construction/ completion of the 'mosque' in the year A.D. 1528-29.[22]

Another viewpoint that the disputed mosque over *Janmasthan* site was constructed by the Sharqi ruler, Hussain Shah in A.D. 1467-68 /AH 872/2 August 1467-21 July 1468 on a vacant plot[23] of land and that Mir Baqi merely renovated it on the basis of Babur's orders is equally erroneous. This version is, in fact, based on the misinterpretation of an Arabic inscription earlier available on the wall of the '*mosque*' recorded by Francis Hamilton Buchanan (1813-14) and is absolutely a mistaken one. Buchanan equally confirmed that there was another Persian inscription on the wall which clearly stated that the structure was constructed by Mir Baqi in A.D. 1528-29 on the basis of Babur's orders. Obviously on the same structure, there could not be two inscriptions, one in Arabic and another in Persian, installed simultaneously with two different chronograms with the supposed date of AH 872/A.D. 1467-68 A.D. and AH 935/A.D. 1528-29 respectively. Besides this, as explained later, the Arabic inscription found to be of doubtful character was removed in the course of the 19th century. It is significant to observe that even the afore-mentioned Persian inscription has been misread by some scholars.

The fact that *Janmasthan* (*Ramjanmabhoomi*) temple in Awadh (Ayodhya), a venerable religious place of pilgrimage for the Hindus having been in existence prior to its demolition by Babur (A.D. 1528-29), is also borne out by the visit of Guru Nanak Dev, the founder of the Sikh Panth, to this holy place in (VS 1562/A.D. 1505). A few authentic *Janm Sakhis* depicting the life and *udasis* (itineraries) of Guru Nanak Dev specifically mention that Guru Nanak Dev made pilgrimage to Awadh Puri (Ayodhya) in A.D. 1505 and that after having taken bath in the River Sarayu had *Darshan* of Lord Rama in the aforesaid temple[24]. It was the present-day Ayodhya and River Sarayu that he visited and worshipped over there. He stayed at a place, now marked as *Brahma Kund Gurudwara*, just one quarter of a kilometre right at the back and western side of *Janmasthan*, then situated on the bank of the flowing River Sarayu.

The continued existence of the *Janmasthan* (*Ramjanmabhoomi*) temple built around the mid-12th century to the beginning of the Mughal era can be well-explained on political grounds. It is known from the contemporary Persian accounts that during the Sultanate period, the Rajas of Awadh (Ayodhya) like the Rajas of Kangra (Punjab hills), Tirhut (Bihar) and Gorakhpur (U.P.) were powerful chiefs and even defied the Delhi Sultans many a time by evading payment of the revenues (*kharaj* and *jizya*) to the state,[25] a potential weapon in the hands of the Hindu chiefs. The chiefs of Awadh (Ayodhya), Gonda, Bahraich and Gorakhpur wielded considerable economic, political and military power. Moreover, despite all mutual political rivalries, the sense of unity on the part of the Hindu chiefs in the territories of Awadh and neighbouring regions for the protection of the *Janmasthan* temple at Ayodhya was quite marked. However, it was not possible for the local chiefs to have met the challenge of the powerful military machinery with fire power of various categories and artillery along with the superior art of warfare of the Mughals who emerged on the political scene of India during the early 16th century.[26] This accounts for the fact that the *Janmasthan* (*Ramjanmabhoomi*) temple of Ayodhya constructed in the mid-12th century continued to exist through the Sultanate period (both Delhi Sultanate and *Sharqi* kingdom of Jaunpur) till it was razed to the ground in the early 16th century (A.D. 1528-29) by Baqi Tashkandi (Mir Baqi), the *hakim* of Awadh (Ayodhya) appointed by Babur.

It has been suggested by some scholars that the Mughal monarch Babur never visited Awadh (Ayodhya) proper[27] for conducting the affairs of the state. This notion is completely misconceived as according to Babur's own statement, in his march towards the eastern districts to finish the hostility of the Afghans, after having crossed the River Sarayu, he camped at the junction of the River Ghaggar (Gogra) and Sarayu (28 March, 1528/7 *Rajab* AH 934), a place just two or three *krohs* (four to six miles) from Awadh (Ayodhya) proper[28]. He stayed there for at least six days, if not more, and thereafter there is a sudden break in Babur's Memoirs w.e.f. 3rd April 1528 to 17th September 1528. This accounts for the gap in the details for the various instructions and measures adopted for the administration of Awadh.

All the same, it is clear that it is at this stage that Babur entrusted the administration of Awadh to Baqi Tashkandi (alias Baqi Shaghawal/Mir Baqi) as the *hakim i.e.*, administrator cum commander who, in fact, was present at the camp at the time of this appointment. During this period or a little later, Baqi Tashkandi alias Mir Baqi demolished the Hindu *Janmasthan* temple and constructed 'mosque' on the same site, even re-using the same materials.

According to the inscriptions installed on the walls, the 'mosque' was constructed by Mir Baqi in A.D. 1528-29 AH 935 on the basis of Babur's orders[29]. The inscriptions do not give any indication, whatsoever, that the 'mosque' was constructed on the same site of *Janmasthan* after the latter's demolition. Nor does Babur in his Memoirs makes any statement either about the demolition of the *Janmasthan* temple at Ayodhya or even about the construction of the 'mosque' over there in accordance with his orders. However, the absence of inscriptional evidence on the monument that it stood on the earlier demolished Hindu temple is by no means an evidence that it was constructed on a vacant plot of land. With the exception of the *Quwwatul-Islam mosque*(1192-98) at Delhi, which still bears an inscription of its having been constructed on the site and with the material of the demolished temples[30], several instances could be quoted to show that many Hindu temples including those considered most sacred by the Hindus were destroyed and mosques, or at times, even mausoleums were constructed at the very sites of the erstwhile holy shrines but these monuments do not bear any inscription on their walls to this effect.

The latest addition to the numerous Hindu temples converted into mosques during the medieval Indian period is afforded by the Bijaya Mandir, Vidisha, near Bhopal, Madhya Pradesh[30a]. The excavations conducted by the Archaeological Survey of India in 1973-74 have brought to light an 11th-12th century Hindu temple at Vidisha, erstwhile Bhelsa state in Madhya Pradesh, converted into a mosque during the medieval age. According to the report of the Archaeological Survey of India, most likely the temple was converted into a mosque by the Mughal Emperor Aurangzeb (1658-1707). Even till date, the pillars of the temple contain two Sanskrit inscriptions. One of the inscriptions names the Parmar King Nar Varman and the second inscription mentions it as temple of Charachika on which the mosque was constructed. There is no inscription installed on the monument which states that the mosque was constructed on the earlier site of a temple. In the middle of the temple hall, there still stand the steps of pulpit (*mambar*) from which *Namaz* was offered. Stone boulders at the back of the temple and other sides are being removed by the Archaeological Survey of India to bring the pillars to the purview. About two hundred and fifty Hindu deities have already been discovered, which speak eleoquently about the magnificent temple on the site converted into a mosque.

The latest inscriptional evidence discovered in the aftermath of the demolition of the disputed structure on 6th December, 1992 at Ayodhya bears out the fact that around mid-12th century, Nyayachandra, the chief of the Saket *Mandalam* with headquarters at Ayodhya, who was the feudatory of Govindachandra (1114-1154), the ruler of the Gahadavala kingdom, built the *Vaishnava* temple at this site[31]. It was this temple which was demolished by Mir Baqi for the construction of a 'mosque' at the same place. Even though *w.e.f.* 3rd April 1528, for nearly four and a half months, *i.e.,* till 17th September 1528, there is an abrupt break in Babur's Memoirs, it is as well known that when Babur again visited the eastern districts, *i.e.,* Jaunpur territory, etc., next year in May-June 1529, the period for which there is no break in his Memoirs, Baqi Tashkandi (Mir Baqi) came from Awadh along with army to pay obeisance to him on 13th-17th June 1529.[32] However, Babur does not mention about the construction of a '*mosque*' at Awadh (Ayodhya) on the basis of his earlier orders and, least of all, the construction of a 'mosque' on the site of the demolished Hindu temple. It is clear that Babur deliberately observed complete silence about the destruction of the Hindu *Vaishnava* temple at Awadh (Ayodhya) and construction of a 'mosque' thereupon[33].

There is no evidence of any kind that the temple could have been destroyed during the course of any conflict with the Afghans or the local chief of Awadh (Ayodhya)[34]. As such, the demolition of the Hindu *Janmasthan* temple at Ayodhya and its replacement by a 'mosque' was a sheer act of vindictiveness and vindication of the supremacy of Islam over heathenism (*kufr*), so dear to Zahiruddin Muhammad Babur.

Babur's bigotry is reflected in his own Memoirs when during his war against Rana Sanga (27th March 1527, Battle of Kanwa), he called his own army as the army of Islam waging a crusade (*Jihad*) and his victory as "the up-bearer of the standard of Islam against the infidels and absurd (*batil*) Hindus[35]". Such was the extent of Babur's bigotry that even though during the course of his marches towards the eastern regions and return to Agra, he spent numerous days on the bank of the River Ganges and crossed it at least four times, he never used its water as he contended, that the River Ganges was considered sacred and worshipped by the infidels (Hindus) and, as such, it was not good for him (and other Muslims) to use it[35a].

In their effort to re-appraise Babur's character and personality and with a view to publicising Hindu-Muslim and Shia-Sunni amity, with political motivations some scholars have quoted a "Secret Will" of Babur (*Wasiyat-nama-i-makhfi*) giving instructions to his son Humayun (on I *Jumada* AH 935/A.D. 11th January, 1529) a little less than two years before his death (30th December 1530), for the cow protection and non-desecration of the temples and places of worship of any community and overlooking the differences between the Sunnis and the Shias[36] in order to show that such a monarch could not have demolished *Janmasthan* Hindu temple for the construction of a 'mosque'. However, this "Secret Will" is fake and has already been discarded as such by some eminent scholars[37]. The text of the 'Will' is doubtful and a scrutiny of the transcript would reveal that there are a number of spelling mistakes of the words in the *Tughra* (Invocation) and the text. Besides this, the so-called advice given by Babur to Humayun, as stated in the 'Will' for cow protection is contradicted by Babur's own daughter, Gulbadan Begum, who in her work entitled *Humayun Nama* states that cow meat was a regular part of the food supplied by her mother to the functionaries at the makeshift tomb (*mazar*) of Babur at Agra for about two and a half years[38]. In fact, the entire "Will" was purposefully concocted by someone to give Babur the image of a secular monarch.

That Babur was far from a secular or judicious monarch is confirmed by the eyewitness account of Guru Nanak Dev (a Saint, 1469-1537) who described his plundering activities as marauder and called Babur *Yama* (messanger of death) having burnt down the Hindu temples, whereby even the adjoining mosques were also destroyed[39]. In fact, Guru Nanak Dev's particular hymns about Babur's atrocities and carnage termed as 'Babur *Vani*' stand included in the sacred Sikh *Adi Granth* (1604).

Similarly, another eyewitness account about the destruction caused to the cultural heritage in the Dibalpur, Punjab, around Delhi

(1521-26) and Jaunpur-Awadh's territories (1528-29) given by the Muslim Saint Shaikh Abdus Qaddus Gangoi was recorded by his disciple Shaikh Rukuddin in *Lataif-i-Qaddusi* (AH 944/A.D. 1537-38).[40]

Abul-Fazl, the well known author of late 16th century work *Ain-i-Akbari,* which forms a part of *Akbar Nama,* considered the fact that Ayodhya, a sacred place of the Hindus, was among the important places of pilgrimage of India. He also held Awadh and Ayodhya as synonymous. He stated that Awadh (Ayodhya) was the residence of Sri Ramachandra during the *Treta* age and *Rama Navami* (Rama's birthday) was celebrated here, being one of the holiest places of antiquity[41]. Abul-Fazl also commented that the vast territories to the extent of 40 *krohs* (80 miles) in the east and 20 *krohs* (40 miles) to the north-south of the famous pilgrimage place of Ayodhya were regarded sacred and worshipped during the month of *Chait* (*Chaitra*—March-April) of the years[42]. He also regarded Sarayu as one of the sacred rivers of the Hindus.

In the *Ain-i-Akbari*, Abul Fazl was silent not only about the destruction of the temple (of *Janmasthan*), he does not even refer to any 'mosque' constructed in the city of Awadh (Ayodhya) during the reign of Babur. But for that matter Abul Fazl did not either say a word about the destruction of the Somnath temple by Sultan Mahmud of Ghazni in his account of the *subah* of Gujrat, even though he referred to the capture of the fort of Junagarh by Sultan Mahmud-I and the construction of another fort there. Could it be presumed that Abul Fazl's complete silence in this regard was deliberate or due to the non-availability of the source material in this regard?

Sahifa-i-Chihil Nasaih Bahadur Shahi written in the early 18th century (in Persian language), is the oldest known account of the destruction of *Ramjanmabhoomi* for the construction of Baburi 'Mosque', and its author is none other than Aurangzeb's grand daughter. The work of Theology (*Shariah*) comprising forty counsels was written by the daughter of Bahadur Shah (*ibn*) Alamgir (Bahadur Shah—A.D. 1707 to 1712). The text of the (relevant) 25th counsel (*nasihat*) taken from the above mentioned manuscript copy was reproduced by Mirza Jan, the author of *Hadiqa-i-*

Shuhada (1856)[43]. This passage provides clear evidence of the fact that despite the demolition of the Kanhaiya (Kesava Deva) temple at Mathura (1669), *Sita Ki Rasoi (Janmasthan)* temple at Ayodhya (1528) and *makaan Hanuman (Hanuman Garhi)* temple at Ayodhya and construction of the 'mosques' on the very respective sites, the Hindus continued to perform image worship and even blew conch shells and the Friday prayers were not being performed by the Muslims in these '*mosques*'.

Some biased historians have expressed doubt about Mirza Jan's accuracy of reproduction of the passage in Persian from *Chihil Nasaih Bahadur Shahi* or even the authorship of the latter book by a daughter of Bahadur Shah (son of Aurangzeb), the Mughal Emperor, as this title is not traceable in any of the catalogues published in the United Kingdom[44]. However, these scholars ignore the fact that there are numerous medieval manuscripts, even anonymous, extant in the Indian libraries which have not been so far listed or catalogued by C.A. Storey and D.N. Marshal in their bio-bibliographical/bibliographics surveys[44a]. Of course, numerous important manuscripts which find description in the medieval Persian chronicles having been lost apparently do not find place in the modern bibliographical works.

The authenticity of the afore-mentioned textual source of *Chihil Nasaih Bahadur Shahi* was confirmed by Nawab Ali Naqi Khan, the Prime Minister of Awadh when in A.D. 1855, while discussing the position of the Ayodhya riots with Major General Outram, the resident of the English East India Company at the Court of Awadh, he referred to the text of the book generally known as 'Forty injunctions' written in about A.D. 1707 during the reign of Bahadur Shah 1st (son of Aurangzeb)[45]. Ali Naqi Khan further asserted that this book, available in the Awadh Royal Archives, clearly mentioned the existence of the mosques at Mathura and Ayodhya, built at the Hindu temple sites. As such, the text of the *Chihil Nasaih Bahadur Shahi* from which Mirza Jan reproduced the 25th counsel in his work *Hadiqa-i-Shuhada*, is the same one referred to as 'The Forty injunctions' (*Chihli Nasaih*) by Nawab Ali Naqi Khan, the Prime Minister of Awadh, and further testified by the latter to have been written in the reign of Bahadur Shah (about 1707 A.D.), son of the Mughal Emperor, Aurangzeb.

Ever since Indian independence (1947), there has been no problem for the Indian society more controversial than the "Mandir-*Masjid*" Ayodhya issue. This has polarised the historians and has caused a deep crisis in the Indian historiography. The irony is that all through the 19th-20th centuries and till at least around A.D. 1980, the Indian historians, both Muslims and Hindus, unanimously upheld the view that during the reign of Zahiruddin Muhammad Babur, the first Mughal Emperor, on the basis of his orders, his local administrator cum commander (*hakim*) at Awadh (Ayodhya), Mir Baqi demolished the Hindu temple of the 12th century situated at *Kot* Rama Chandra on the birth-place of Sri Rama Chandra, and constructed a mosque thereupon in A.D. 1528-29. This structure came to be known as *Masjid Janmasthan* or "*Masjid Waqia Janmasthan*" *i.e.,* mosque situated on the site of *Janmasthan.*[46] The *Janmasthan* site has continued to be claimed by the Hindus ever since then all through the Mughal rule, (1528-1722) , the *Nawabi* kingdom (1722-1856) as well as the British regime (1856-1947) in Awadh and Hindus have continued to worship at the site. But as the movement for restoring the disputed place to the Hindus became intense, the particular passages in the writings referring to the destruction of *Janmasthan* temple and building of the mosque at the same site were expunged in the revised editions of many a work which was motivated[47]. Besides this, the unholy alliance between the pseudo-secular historians and Muslim fundamentalism has tried to set aside the 19th-20th centuries writings on the pleas that they reflected the British "Divide-And-Rule" policy and that the Muslim writers wrote with a sense of 'bravado' and for the 'glorification of Islam[48]. These are no grounds for setting aside facts of history.

The records of the *Nawabi* rule in Awadh show a long drawn tussle between the Hindus and the Muslims as well as the Shia-Sunni Muslims amongst themselves over the possession of the *Janmasthan* "Baburi *Masjid*" site. The intermittent references to the statements of the Qazis of Faizabad for the years A.D. 1735, A.D. 1825 are very clear on this issue.[49] A significant note submitted by Hafizullah, the *darogha* of Faizabad court to the Awadh Royal Court (1825) clearly states that the 'mosque' constructed by Babur was situated at the birth-place of Rama, son of Raja Dasharath, and adjacent to the Kitchen of Sita, wife of Rama (*i.e., Sita Ki Rasoi*).[50]

Mirza Jan, in his book entitled *Hadiqa-i-Shuhada* (Orchard of Martyrs-A.D. 1856), made a categorical statement that the way the past Muslim Sultans cleared the rabble of infidelity in Mathura and Benaras, in the same manner they purged "Faizabad-Awadh (Ayodhya), a great place of worship and the capital of Rama's father, from the filth of the false belief. Its temples were destroyed and no stone or idol was left intact. Thereafter, where there was the large/main (most sacred) temple, a big mosque was built thereupon, and where there was a small temple (*mandap*), there a small (*kanati*) mosque was constructed. As such, on the site of the *Janmasthan* temple situated on the purified birth-place of Rama (*butkhana-i-Janmasthan arghin maskancras* Rama) and the adjacent *Sita Ki Rasoi*, Sita being name of the latter's (*i.e.,* Rama's wife), a lofty mosque was constructed by Babur Shah under the guidance of Saiyed Musa Ashiqan"[51].

As a matter of fact, apart from the above mentioned scholars, a number of other eminent writers during the 19th and 20th centuries gave the same version of the demolition of the *Janmasthan* temple (on the birth-place of Rama), adjacent of *Sita Ki Rasoi* and construction of the "Baburi *Masjid*" by Babur on the same site, though, of course, with different writing style and emphasis. Barring a few who used Persian or Arabic as medium, they all wrote in vernacular Urdu language. There scholars comprise Rajab Ali Beg Surur (1787-1867) the author of *Fasanah-i-ibrat*[52]; Shaikh Muhammad Azmat Ali Kakorawi Nami, the author of *Tarikh-i-Awadh/Muraqqa-i-Khusrawi* (1869)[53]; Kamaluddin Haider Hasani Al Mashhadi alias Saiyad Muhammad Mir Lucknowi (1794-1881), the author of *Sawanahat-i-Salateen-Awadh* (in two volumes, 1879).[54] Its second volume, reprinted in 1896, was also entitled *Kaiser-ut-Tawarikh*); Haji Muhammad Hasan, the author of *Zia-i-Akhtar* (1878)[55]; Maulavi Abdul Karim, the *imam* of Babri *Masjid* and the author of *Gumgashtah-i-Halat-i-Ayodhya Awadh* (in Persian)[56]; Najmulghani Khan Rampuri, the author of *Tarikh-i-Awadh* (in five volumes, 1909-19)[57] and Maulana Hakim Saiyed Abdul Haye (d. 1923), the author of *Al-Hind-u-Fial-Ahd al Islam* (Arabic) *i.e., India Under Islamic Rule.*[58] In addition to these,

Nizamuddaulah, the resident of the Government of Kashmir at the Court of Awadh (1876) after intensive investigation had come to the same conclusion[59].

Even though being reputed scholars, all of them based their accounts on the past historical records; of these Rajab Ali Surur. Shaikh Muhammad Ali Kakorawi Nami, Maulavi Abdul Karim and Najmulghani Khan Rampuri claimed to have utilised past authentic sources. Rajab Ali also made reference to *Sahifa-i-Bahadur Shahi,* the authenticity of which had already been confirmed by Nawab Ali Naqi Khan, the Prime Minister of Awadh (1855). Rajab Ali further stated that this manuscript was still available (1867) and could be consulted by any one who wished to do so. Significantly, he also remarked that during the 1855 communal riots at Ayodhya, open prayers were offered by the Hindu *Bairagis* in the 'Baburi *mosque*' comprising the site of *Sita Ki Rasoi* and that the *Nawabi* administration could do nothing about it.[60] Shaikh Muhammad Azamat Ali Kakorwai in *Muraqqa-i-khusrawi* claimed that his statements were based upon the past historical accounts. He further maintained that ever since the triumphant occupation by Saiyed Salar Masud Gazi (1028-32), the previous Muslim Sultans had built mosques, hospices (*khankahs*) and travelling lodges on the sites of the Hindu places of worship and also had propagated the Mohammadi faith (Islam) through the *muezzins* (prayer-callers) and school teachers and destroyed the practice of heresy (*bidat*) and conch-blowing practice (at the temples). As such, the way Mathura-Vrindaban were cleared of heresy (*bidat*) ,in the same manner the *Janmasthan* temple which was the main worshipping place in Faizabad (Awadh) located at the capital (seat of throne) of the father of Lakshman and Rama having been demolished, a lofty Baburi *Masjid* was erected on the advice of Musa Ashiqan and that it was still known as *Sita Ki Rasoi* amongst the Hindus. The author clarified that henceforth the Hindus built their own temple (*Ram Chabutra*) in the courtyard of the Baburi *Masjid*, where Sita kitchen (*Sita Ki Rasoi*) had been located but it was not liked by the Muslims [60a].

Maulavi Abdul Karim being himself the *Imam* of Baburi *Masjid*, in his work on *Gumgashtah-i-Halat-i Ayodhya Awadh*, having referred to various medieval and 19th century sources, particularly the *Sufi* literature, gave detailed descriptions of the tower halls (*burjs*) and identified the western tower hall (*burjs*) as the birth-place of Rama, which along with *Sita Ki Rasoi* was demolished by Babur for constructing a mosque thereupon[61]. Saiyad Kamaluddin Haider Mushhadi, a reputed 19th century historian in his scholarly work entitled *Sawanehat-i-Salateen-i Awadh* (Its Part II also named as *Kaiser ut Tawarikh*) has reproduced a copy of the written statement of Hafizullah, the *darogha* of the court of Faizabad to the effect that during the regimes of the past (Muslim) kings, all the temples of the city of Awadh were converted into mosques whereby at the sites of the big temples, Jamai *Masjids* were constructed whereas for the (other) mosques constructed on the sites of the smaller temples, *muezzins* (prayer-callers) and sweepers were appointed. As such, the grand and magnificent Jamai *Masjid* was constructed by Babur Badshah on the site of *Janamasthan, i.e.,* the birth-place of Rama, son of Raja Dasharath, adjacent to the building (*makaan*) named as *Sita Ki Rasoi*, the latter being the wife of Rama. In fact, the complex was popularly known as *Sita Ki Rasoi*[61a].

Similarly, another elegant *masjid* was erected at Ram Ghat on the bank of the River (Saryu) at the site of the demolished Hindu temple, of which a part of the wall was still in existence. Similarly, Najmulghani Khan Rampuri produced his work *Tarikh-i-Awadh* after having consulted about eighty past authentic sources (listed in the Introduction) in Persian, Urdu and English, and manuscripts of the 17th-19th centuries comprising mostly the Muslim authors along with a few Hindu and European writers as well as original documents in Persian since the time of Nawab Safdarjang (early 18th century)[62]. However, it may be observed that in the afore-mentioned works, the chronogram deduced from the inscription on the wall of the 'Baburi Masjid' as 'Khair Baqi' (AH 923) is erroneous which should have been 'Bavad Khair Baqi' (AH 935/A.D. 1528-29).

Apart from these literary scholars, Mr. Akhtar Ashan Naqvi, a Muslim Civil Judge, Faizabad, in a regular suit of 1945 between the Shia Central Board of *Waqf*, U.P. V/s. Sunni Board of *Waqf*, U.P. having examined the historical issues of the construction of Ayodhya mosque, based on an analysis of Babur's Memoirs, the First

Settlement Report of Faizabad and the District Gazetteers, reaffirmed the fact that Babur destroyed the *Janmasthan* temple (1528) and on its site built a mosque using largely the materials of the old structure[63]. He further commented that unless disproved by superior evidence, these works must be accepted as containing a correct history of the subject mentioned therein.

It is significant to observe that the manuscript of the afore-mentioned *Tarikh-i-Awadh/Muraqqa-i-Khusrawi* (1869) of Muhammad Azmat Ali Kakorwi Nami, available at the Tagore Library, University of Lucknow, was published for the first time in 1986 but in this edition, the portion relating to the construction of 'Baburi *Masjid*' on the site of the temple in the premises of *Janmasthan* and the Hindu-Muslim riot of 1855 were delected by the Fakhruddin Ali Ahmed Memorial Committee under whose auspices the book was brought out. But recently, these two portions have been published under a separate title.[64] Similarly, when the earlier work of Maulavi Abdul Karim, written in Persian entitled *Gumgashtah-i-Halat-i-Ayodhya Awadh* was translated by his grandson, Maulavi Abdul Guffar, into Urdu and published in 1979, it retained the description about the demolition of the Hindu temple of *Janmasthan* at *Kot* Ram Chandra—Ayodhya by Babur and construction of a *'mosque'* on the same site but later on in the revised 1981 edition, the portion about the demolition of the temple at *Janmasthan* and the construction of mosque was deleted.[65]

Apparently, the afore-mentioned deletion from the earlier published texts was done with a guilty conscience and motivation and is tantamount to suppression of historical evidence and distortion of history. As such, the fact of the demolition of the *Janmasthan* temple in Babur's reign and the construction of a mosque upon is well-authenticated by the Muslim writers not only of the colonial period but the previous *Nawabi* regime of Awadh as well. In fact, many of the above Muslim writers were highly critical of the British policy in Awadh and could not have been influenced by the "Divide-and-Rule" policy.

The western sources comprise the European travellers to India, the British administrator-scholars and historians, and the British Officers who worked in India in various capacities as well as the archaeologists of the Archaeological Survey of India and a few judges of the District Civil Court at Faizabad.

Of the travellers, during the early 17th century (1608-11) of the Mughal rule (Jahangir's reign), William Finch,[66] who visited Ayodhya, has not mentioned the existence of any mosque or 'Baburi masjid' over there. On the other hand, in his account he confirmed the existence of the ruins of Rama Chandra's castle and houses where the Indians (Hindus) believed he had incarnated thousands of years back. He further remarked that certain Brahmins who lived in these ruins recorded the names of all such Indians (Hindus) who took bath in the river running thereby. Thus William Finch's confirmation of the still existing ruins of *Janmasthan* where only the Brahmans lived (for worship, etc.) and lack of any reference to the existence of any 'mosque' is significant.

Another European traveller, Joseph Tieffenthaler[67], an Austrian priest, who visited various places in India (1766-71) and stayed in Awadh of which he has left an account in his book originally written in Latin and later translated both in German and French for which the title in English may be put as *History and Geography of India,* regarded Ayodhya as a very ancient city and maintained that its fortress of *Ramkot* comprising the birth-place temple of Rama was destroyed by Babur (or Aurangzeb) and on this site a '*mosque'* with three domes was constructed. Tieffenthaler also commented that of the fourteen columns of the ancient temple re-used in the *mosque*, twelve of these supported the inside arcades of the '*mosque*' and two were placed at the door of the cloister. He further emphasised that the Hindus refused to give up this place and despite the 'Mughals' efforts to prevent them, they were coming to this place for worship. They had also constructed *Ram Chabutra* in the courtyard of the *'mosque'* which they called *Bedi* meaning a crib, where they used to circumambulate thrice and then prostrated on the ground. Tieffenthaler is emphatic that the Hindus practised their religious ceremonies at both the places, *i.e.,* at *Ram Chabutra* and inside the *'mosque'* as they considered that this was the place with a house where Vishnu (*Beschan*) took birth in the form of Rama. Tieffenthaler also referred to a famous place called *Sita Ki Rasoi*, adjacent to the city at the centre on a higher ground on which, in fact, the afore-mentioned *Ram Chabutra* was built near

Rama's birth-place whereupon the *'mosque'* was constructed. He also mentioned that the Hindus had continued celebrating *Ram Navami* (birthday of Ram) on 24th of the month *Chait* (*Chaitra*) and people gathered at this famous fair from all over India. The authenticity of Tieffenthaler's description about the worship by the Hindus at *Ram Chabutra* and the adjacent site within the disputed structure of *Ramjanmabhoomi*-'Baburi masjid' being the birth-place of Rama is well-confirmed by still an earlier 18th century revenue Map of Ayodhya around A.D. 1717 which depicts *Janmasthan* along with various other religious places of Ayodhya and the River Sarayu[68].

Francis Hamilton Buchanan, the British administrator who undertook the survey of India (1807-14), surveyed Ayodhya (1813-14) as a part of the survey of Gorakhpur district was the first person to have noted the inscriptions, both in Persian and Arabic, on the walls of the disputed structure of *Janmasthan*/'Baburi Masjid'[69]. Buchanan also emphasised the Persian inscription which states that on the order of Babur, this structure was erected by Mir Baqi in the year 935/A.D. 1528-29, 'Bavad Khair Baqi', as clearly indicated in the inscription being the chronogram.

Apart from this, there is a Persian document of Aurangzeb's reign (later half of the 17th century) also bearing the *tughra* in Arabic in the praise of God appended to the unpublished Buchanan's papers which narrates the version that Babur demolished the sacred Hindu temple on the advice of the Muslim *darwesh* (*fakir*) and a mosque was constructed on this site by Mir Baqi (popularly mentioned as Mir Baqaullah Khan)[70]. The English translation of this document was reproduced by Buchanan in his own handwriting. Quite significantly, in the survey records of Buchanan, the disputed site has been marked as *yanmasthan, i.e., Janmasthan.*

As Francis Hamilton Buchanan's afore-mentioned original Survey Report (1807-14) remained unpublished, its edited version was published by Montgomery Martin in 1838 under the title *The History, Antiquities, Topography and Statistics of Eastern India*[71]. It is clear from the relevant passages that Buchanan fervently believed in the great antiquity of Ayodhya as well as the historicity of Rama as he remarked that from his very name,

Ramgarh, he was inclined to think that it was a part of the building actually built by Rama. He also discussed various popular beliefs as to whether the ancient temples at Ayodhya were built by Vikrama, the elder (of Ujjain in about 1st century B.C.) or the later Vikrama of the 11th century and as to whether the temples were destroyed by Aurangzeb or had been destroyed earlier. A minute reading of the text of the report would show that Buchanan was inclined to accept that the ancient Ayodhya temple had been built by the later Vikrama and also thought that the Hindu tradition that these temples were destroyed by Aurangzeb was 'ill-founded' as he mentioned that the particular mosque having black-stone pillars with Hindu images, as per inscriptional evidence on it was built by Babur five generations before Aurangzeb. Some scholars hold Buchanan 'found the temple —destruction theory to bc very ill-founded,[72] which in fact is a complete misreading of the text. Buchanan further commented that the pillars with Hindu images installed in the mosque had been taken from a Hindu building and most likely were taken from the ruins of the palace. Read in the background of the description of the temples built in the past and their subsequent destruction, the reference to a 'Hindu building', would essentially imply a Hindu temple, and the use of the term 'palace' as a substitute for Ramgar (fortress) itself comprising the Hindu temple as well. As such, when the entire text is read between the lines and property interpreted, it becomes clear that Buchanan accepted the version that the old Hindu temple of the birth-place of Rama was demolished and on its very site Babur built a mosque in which the black-stone pillars of the erstwhile Hindu temples were re-used. Later on in A.D. 1854, Edward Thornton in his *Gazetteer of the Territories under the Government of the East India Company* not only referred to fourteen columns with elaborate workmanship having been taken from the old Hindu temple and re-used in Babur's mosque, but equally asserted that the Hindu pilgrims worshipped on the *Ram Chabutra* which was believed to be Rama's cradle[73].

It is significant to note that unlike the literary sources, after the British Government took over the Awadh administration, the official documents (both in vernacular and English) did not put the disputed structure as 'Baburi masjid' but simply either as *Janmasthan* or '*Janmasthan*' mosque or '*masjid waqia Janmasthan*', *i.e.,* masjid situated on *Janmasthan*. In the post-1857 period, C.U. Aitchinson, Under Secretary to the Government of India, with the Governor General in his correspondence (1863) with the Chief Commissioner of Awadh used the terms *Janmasthan, i.e.,* '*Janmasthan* mosque'[74] for the so-called Baburi masjid. The very use of the terms *Janmasthan* as a substitute for the 'mosque' or *Janmasthan* mosque or '*masjid waqia Janmasthan*' suggests that it was all through well-acknowledged that the 'mosque' had been constructed on the very site of *Janmasthan* (Ram's birth-place) or else why such terms should have been used for this *'mosque'*?

During the second half of the 19th century British administration in Awadh, both the legal and expert archaeological opinions confirmed the fact that the *Janmasthan* 'mosque' located in the *Janmasthan* complex was built by Babur at the very site of the sacred Hindu temple after the latter's demolition. In a landmark judgement in 1886 in Civil Appeal # 27 of 1885 against the earlier judgement in the suit # 61/280 of 1885 of *Asthan Janmasthan* Vs. the Secretary of State for India and Mohammad Asghar, the District Civil Judge, Faizabad, Col. F.E.A. Chamier recorded, "I visited the land in dispute yesterday in the presence of all parties. I found that masjid built by Emperor Babur on the border of the town of Ayodhya, that is to say to the west and south it is clear of habitation. It is most unfortunate that a masjid should have been built on land specially held sacred by the Hindus. But as the event occurred 356 years ago, it is too late now to remedy the grievance..."[75]

The said Judgement was followed by an equally important expert opinion on the archaeological aspect by E.A. Fuhrer of the Archaeologial Survey of India in 1891. E.A. Fuhrer concluded that on the eve of the Muslim conquest, there were three important temples at Ayodhya, *i.e.,* the *Janmasthan* (birth-place temple of Rama), the *Swargadwar* and the *Treta ke Thakur*. On the *Janmasthan* site, Mir Khan (Mir Baqi) built a masjid during the reign of Babur and used therein many of the black-stone (*kasauti*) columns. Later on, mosques were constructed on the site of other two afore-mentioned temples by Aurangzeb.

The criticism by some biased historians that E. A. Fuhrer based his conclusions merely on local affirmation and tradition is not justified. A careful and critical reading of his report on Ayodhya

(Faizabad district), would show that for the historical account comprising past history, topography and monumental structures, both Brahmanical and Jain temples, Fuhrer well-utilised the *Ramayana*, the *Ain-i-Akbari*, General Cunnigham's report and the other past archaeological reports. The very fact that as a parallel case of the destruction of another temple at Ayodhya, *i.e., Treta Ke Thakur*, later destroyed by Aurangzeb for the construction of a mosque on the same site, Fuhrer relied upon the foundation-stone inscription (in Sanskrit) dated *Samvat* 1241/A.D. 1184 discovered from the ruins of the dilapidated mosque clearly shows that for archaeological analysis of the monuments, Fuhrer did not bank upon mere tradition[76a.]

P. Carnogy, Settlement Officer and Officiating Commissioner, Ayodhya, Faizabad, in his work entitled *Historical Sketch of Tehsil Zila Fyzabad, with the old capitals Ajudhia and Fyzabad*, while going through his past history of *Janmasthan* / and other temples in Ayodhya is also emphatic on the aspect that in A.D. 1528 Emperor Babur built the mosque on the very site of *Janmasthan*, *Ram Kot* (Ayodhya) *denoting* birth-place of Shri Ram Chandra and after the demolition of Lord Rama's birth-place (*Janmasthan*) temple, a fine temple, many of its *Kasauti* columns carved with different devices, still in existence, were re-used in the construction of the Baburi *mosque*[77]. Most significantly, according to P. Carnegy, who was the first Settlement Officer of District Fyzabad (1861) and had first-hand knowledge about the events of his own official tenure and a few years preceding him, till 1855 when the Hindu-Muslim riot took place, the possession of the *Janmasthan* premises inclusive of the site of the 'mosque-temple' structure in the *Janmasthan* premises was vested with the Hindus. But during 1855 riots, the Muslims took forcible possession of this structure for some time and claimed it as 'mosque' situated at *Janmasthan* (*masjid waqia janmasthan*). However, they were evicted by the Hindus through bloody conflict in the third round and when the British annexed Awadh (January-February 1856), the possession of the *Janmasthan* premises was with the Hindu *Bairagis* and *Mahants*. Carnegy noted that until 1855 both the Hindus and the Muslims worshipped alike in the 'mosque-temple'. But the British Government in order to prevent dispute, divided the courtyard of the *Janmasthan* site into inner one for the 'mosque structure' and outer portion for the Hindu platform. This was done by putting up a railing in the courtyard dividing the 'mosque structure' from the outer courtyard whereupon the Hindus who had been worshipping there for centuries raised a platform (*Chabutra*) for making their offerings. Still after Carnegy's observations, later on in 1873, a doorway was provided in the wall which in front was divided from the '*Janmasthan* masjid' by a railing. An appeal against this order of Deputy Commissioner Faizabad (dated 10 November 1873) lodged by Mohammad Asghar on behalf of '*Janmasthan mosque* at Ajodhia' was rejected by the Commissioner, Faizabad in 1877 (13 December 1877). As a matter of fact, according to the eyewitness accounts and enquiry report (A.D. 1855/AH 1271) submitted by Maulavi Nihaluddin *amin* and Maulavi Muhammad Hafizullah, *darogha* of the Faizabad Court on the 1855 riot, even earlier on the order of the King Nawab Wajid Ali Shah, a railing (*kataira/chabutra*) dividing and demarcating the boundaries of the Baburi *Masjid*/Jamai *Masjid* and *Sita Ki Rasoi* compound comprising Hindu worship place was built in 1853 but this was gunned down into pieces by Hindu *Bairagis*. Apart from this, Carnegy may be credited for having rightly noted the construction of the new *Janmasthan* temple in neighbouring part of the same *khasra* plot of land (now across the road) in the early 18th century. In fact, the first Report of Settlement of Land Revenue of Faizabad district by A.F. Millett, Officiating Settlement Officer (published in 1880)[78] for historical portion, virtually reproduced from the earlier historical sketch given by P. Carnegy.

The assertions made by P. Carnegy are also reiterated and confirmed by the *Gazetteer of the Province of Awadh* (1870). Later on, H.R. Neville, the editor of *Barabanki District Gazetteer* (1902)[79] as well as that of *Faizabad District Gazetteer* (1905) gave more or less the same version.[80] While tracing the history of the Faizabad District and basing his conclusions on the study of the medieval Persian chronicles as well as archaeological evidence, Neville categorically stated that "in 1528 Babur built the mosque at Ajodhya on the traditional spot where Rama was born". He further spelt out that the *Janmasthan* in *Ram Kot* was marked by the birth-place of Rama and in 1528, Babur having halted around Ayodhya for a week destroyed the ancient temple and on its site built a mosque, still known as Babur's mosque. Neville commented that from the archaeological viewpoint it was quite discernable that the materials of the old structure were largely employed and many of the columns comprising close-grained black-stone, called by the natives *Kasauti* and carved with various devices were still in good preservation. Having described the dimension and shape of the columns, Neville pointed out the existence of two inscriptions in Persian dated AH 935/A.D. 1528 installed on the mosque, one on the outside and the other on the pulpit. Neville also remarked that the desecration of the most sacred spot in Ayodhya caused great bitterness between Hindus and Musalmans and on many occasions, the feeling led to bloodshed and in 1855 after an open fight, the Musalmans forcibly occupied *Janmasthan*. Later on, the Hindus made a counter-attack and having stormed the *Janmasthan* reoccupied it. As the Hindus had never surrendered their claim, they had continued to worship in the same building. But since the 'Mutiny' (1857 war of Independence), after the Hindus had been forbidden by the British Government an access to the inner yard of the mosque, they had put up an outer enclosure and a platform in front of the mosque for making their offerings.

Mrs. A.S. Beveridge who translated Babur's Memoirs (*Babur Nama*) from the Chagatay-Turkish Text into English, having accepted H.R. Neville's viewpoint on the destruction of the ancient temple (marking the birth-place of Rama) by Babur for the construction of a mosque on its site during the course of his stay near Awadh (Ayodhya) for a few days (at least w.e.f. 28 March to 02 April, 1528) for the settlement of its affairs[81] further commented that "presumably during his afore-mentioned stay at Ayodhya, having been impressed by the dignity and sanctity of the ancient Hindu shrine, and being an obedient follower of Muhammad, he was intolerant of another faith, would regard the substitution of a temple by a mosque dutiful and worthy, - the mosque was completed in 935 AH A.D. 1528-29 but no mention of the completion is in the *Babur Nama*"[82].

In the recent years, as already discussed, the Dutch scholar, Hans Bakker, well-equipped with the knowledge of Sanskrit for the study of the ancient multifarious texts and having personally examined the *Ramjanmabhoomi*-Baburi *Masjid* structure during his stay at Ayodhya accepted that an old *Vaishnava* temple, situated on the holy spot of Rama's birth, (*Ramjanmabhoomi temple*) which being in existence in the 12th century was destroyed by Babur and replaced with the 'now-existing *mosque*' (in 1984).[83]

Koenraad Elst, a Belgian scholar has taken keen academic interest in the Ayodhya controversy since 1989-90 and has produced two monographs on the subject[83a]. Even though he has personally visited and examined the location and physical aspects of the disputed structure (*Ramjanmabhoomi*-'Baburi *Masjid*') for the analysis of the entire issue in historical perspective, he has basically relied upon the sources comprising a few published works related to the subject, articles, letters and statements of the scholars both pro-*Janmasthan* temple and anti-*Janmasthan* temple, journalists and politicians published in the daily newspapers, especially the Indian Express and a few weekly newspapers and magazines. All the same, having claimed internationally accepted standards of methodology and inference in scientific history-writing and looked into the problem in historical perspective, in regard to the *Janamasthan* temple at Ayodhya, he concluded "that all the indications available from the traditional belief consensually held by the local Muslims as well as the Hindus, was that the 'Baburi Masjid' was built in replacement of a Hindu temple where Rama worship used to take place."

Koenraad Elst, having examined the position of Ayodhya and Rama worship during the ancient and early medieval pre-Babur era and effectively met with the arguments of the anti-*Janmasthan* scholars, maintains that the debate over Ayodhya is really a footnote to the fundamental ideological debate about the nature of Islam. He has well argued that so long as the claim that a temple was demolished to make way for the "Baburi *Masjid*" is accepted, it is besides the point that Babur or Mir Baqi could be personally absolved from the charge of being fanatical as the demolition of the temple structure by them is traditionally said to have taken place under pressure from a local Muslim fanatic cleric, Fazl Abbas alias Musa Ashikan. However, due to his reliance on the study of the literary sources in Urdu or Persian by some other scholars without coordination with the 19th century archaeological and land revenue documents and maps, Koenraad Elst in matters of detail has been inhibited in methodological approach like the scholars on whom he has mostly relied. As such, he has not appreciated the fact that the structure to the north of the disputed structure of *Ramjanmabhoomi*-'Baburi *Masjid*' being quite distinct from the latter and popularly known as '*Janmasthan Sita Rasoi*' or 'New *Janmasthan* Temple' was built only in the early 18th century while the intervening road which separated the two monuments was constructed in the late 19th century. The erstwhile pre-Mughal structure on this site forming a part of the larger *Janmasthan* complex was also demolished in Babur's reign along with the other structures of the entire *Janmasthan* complex. In fact, this controverts the diversionary tactics of the scholars and politicians who regard the 18th century monument named or *Janmasthan Sita Rasoi'* or 'New *Janmasthan'* as the real birth-place (*Janmasthan*) of Lord Rama.

It is well borne out by the British Revenue Officers and the original land revenue records of various categories by the British Settlement Officers that in continuation of the past *Nawabi* regime during the British period (1856 onwards) as well, the title to the land of the *Janmasthan* complex in *Kot* Rama Chandra, inclusive of the disputed structure of *Ramjanmabhoomi*-'Baburi *Masjid*' remained vested with the Hindu *Mahants* and *Bairaghis*.[84] Since A. D. 1861, there have been three regular land revenue settlements, *i.e.,* A.D. 1861, 1893-94 and 1936-37 under the supervision and charge of the English Settlement Officers.[85] For all proprietary rights, the last, *i.e.,* the third settlement (1936-37) is still in vogue till date. As per all the three settlements, the ownership of the plots/sub-plots of the *Janmasthan* complex has remained vested with *Sarkar Nazul* and Hindu *Mahants* as subordinate land owners (*malikan-i-matahit*) exempted from the payment of any rent (*lagaan*). No plot or sub-plot comprising the disputed structure of *Ramjanmabhoomi*-'Baburi Masjid', has been shown in Waqf.[86] Most significantly, the appended maps to the Settlement Reports of *Kot* Ramachandra, especially the Boundary Map (Hadbast)[87] and the settled population (*Abadi*) map of 1861 settlement duly attested by the Settlement Officer and the subsequent Revenue Maps till 1936-37 and thereafter show only *Janmasthan* (birth-place of Rama) and do not indicate any 'mosque' in the *Janmasthan* complex[88].

All the afore-mentioned western scholars being professionally specialists in their respective fields exhibited an objective and scientific approach to the contentious Ayodhya issue. As such, it cannot be maintained that they were in any way influenced or motivated by the imperialist 'Divide-and-Rule' policy as alleged by some.

References

1. M.V. Ratnam, *Rama, the Greatest Pharaoh of Egypt*, Rajahmundry, 1934, pp. 88-95.
2. Shyam Narain Pande, 'Historical Rama distinguished from God Rama', a Paper read at Ancient India Section, Indian History Congress, 58th Session, Bangalore. November 14-16, 1997. It was also reported in the Press under the titles "Ram Lived in Afghanistan: Historian", Indian Express, Bangalore, November 19, 1997; "Ayodhya Existed in Afghanistan: Historian," The Times of India, New Delhi, November 23, 1997. The afore-mentioned report of the Indian Express that Pande's Paper was supported by R.S. Sharma who said, "Dr. Pande's view was correct. The truth that the U.P. Ayodhya was not the birth-place of Rama cannot be denied." This view expressed by R.S. Sharma is contradictory to his earlier opinion that Rama's Ayodhya existed on the bank of the River Ganga rather than on the bank of River Sarayu. (See details vide R.S. Sharma, Reference No. 15). The above mentioned viewpoint of S.N. Pande and R.S. Sharma were rebutted with cogent arguments in a rejoinder by B.R. Grover, published under the title "Historian demolishes claims of Rama's birth-place being in Afghanistan". Indian Express, Bangalore. November 22, 1997.

2a. For details of controversy, see Reference Nos. 15, 21, 27 versus Nos. 5, 83, 83a. Also D.P. Dubey, 'Ayodhya: Where History Stands Abused,' *Pilgrimage Studies, Sacred Places, Sacred Traditions*, (ed. D.P. Dubey), Allahabad, 1955, pp. 251-74.

3. *Ibid.*
4. *Ibid.*, also Reference No. 23.
5. For details, see Reference Nos. 22, 24, 31, 37, 43, 49-65, 67-70, 73-83a; specially, B.R. Grover vide Reference Nos. 31, 50 and 68. Also Aziz Ahmad, *Studies in Islamic Culture in the Indian Environment*, Oxford, 1964, p. 88.
6. *White Paper on Ayodhya*, Government of India, February 1993, p. 107. This was also the Reference made by the President of India to the Supreme Court (of India) under Article 143(1) of the Constitution of India on 7th January, 1993 for its opinion.
7. B.B. Lal "Was Ayodhya Mythical City", *Puratattva,* No. X, 1978-79, pp. 45-49.
8. The *Ramayana, Bal-Kanda,* 5, 7-23, S.C.D., 'Historicity of Ramayana and the Indo-Aryan Society', Delhi, p. 157; B.B. Lal, 'Ayodhya of the Valmiki

Ramayana: An energizing debate on its identification', *Puratattva,* No. XVI, 1985-86. Earlier A. Cunningham, vide *The Ancient Geography of India* (Varanasi edition, 1979, pp. 341-342), while discussing the dimensions of the ancient Ayodhya, capital of Rama, considered that the present-day Ayodhya along with the neighbouring city of Faizabad constituted just one-half of the "probable size of the ancient capital of Rama". It has also been well argued that at least upto the 5th century A.D., the city of Ayodhya and Saketa (Saketa Nagar) being identical, constituted the ancient capital of Raja Dasharatha and his son Rama, and later on too was the capital of Kosala kingdom. However, later on Kalidasa (Gupta age, 4th-5th centuries A.D.), in *Raghuvamsa* (VI), 71 and XI-1 puts Ayodhya as the capital of North Kosala. Some scholars place Kalidasa in the 1st century B.C.

9. For details, A.M. Shastri, 'Ayodhya and God Rama', *Puratattva*, No. 23, 1992-93, p. 36.

10. S. Kelkar has translated into English, *History of Indian Literature*, Calcutta, 1927, pp. 500-517, which provides all evidences in this regard. Also, A.M. Shastri, *Op. cit.* No. 9, pp. 35-39.

11. A.M. Shastri, *Op. cit.* Nos. 9 & 10, pp. 36-37, having reviewed the earlier works, *i.e.*, *Collected Works of R.B. Bhandarkar*, IV, Pune, 1929, p. 67 and *Materials for the study of the Early History of the Vaishnava Sect,* second edition, Calcutta, 1936, p. 174, and the further evidence provided by J. Allen, *Catalogue of the Indian Coins in the British Museum, Coins of Ancient India,* London, 1936, pp. CX, 179-81, pl. XXIV, 5-14 as well Ramesh K.V. and Tewari S.P., *A Copper-plate of the Gupta period from Bagh, Madhya Pradesh,* New Delhi, Mysore, 1990, p. 1, text lines, 1-5; Introduction, pp. VII-VIII, came to the conclusion that the Rama Cult could be ascribed to the second century A.D. and that by the third quarter of the 4th century A.D., Rama had been completely identified with Vishnu.

12. For details, *Evidence for the Ramjanmabhoomi Mandir*, *Vishwa Hindu Parishad*, New Delhi, pp. 2-8, *History Versus Casuistry, Evidence of the Ramjanmabhoomi Mandir presented by the Vishva Hindu Parishad to the Government of India in December-January 1990-91;* Voice of India, New Delhi, 1991 (henceforth *History Versus Casuistry*), pp. 5-12; Also *Padmapuran*, Bombay, 1927, V, 28, 49; 37.29-30, VI 242, 41-42; *Bhagavata Purana,* ed. J.L. Shastri, Delhi, 1983, IX, 8, 17-19, *Visnudharmottara Purana*, Bombay, 1912, 1.13.1-2; *Vamana Purana* and *Narada Purana* No. 38/62 and 1.34/138 respectively.

13. *Ayodhya Mahatmya, Skandapurana: Vaishnava Khanda*, ed. K. K. R. Shreshthi, Bombay, 1910, *Shloka* No. 19.

14. The scholars of the Puranic studies put varying dates of the composition and compilation of the vulgate called *Skandapurana*. For example, Acharya Baldev Upadhyay (in *Purana Vimarsha*, p. 158) having used a manuscript of Darbar Library, Kathmandu, Nepal, places it in 7th century; P.V. Kane, *History of the Dharma Shastra* puts it between 7th and 9th centuries; R.C. Hazra, *Studies in Upapuranas*, I (*Sura* and *Upapuranas*), Calcutta, 1956 and *Studies in the*

Puranic Records on Hindu Rites and Customs, Delhi, (1940), 1975, pp. I, 19, 54, 157-66, II, 197-204 as well as Lallanji Gopal put it about 10th century; V.S. Pathak puts it in 11th-12th centuries and above all, Hans Bakker, *Ayodhya*, (in Three Parts, Egbert Forsten, Groningen, 1986), I, pp. 129-130 is inclined to accept "the close of the 13th or (beginning of) the 14th century as the most plausible date of the reduction of the a-type-of-text and its insertion in the *Vaishnava Khand*" by which time the Rama Cult was well established in Ayodhya. Also, Hans T. Bakker, 'The History of Hanumat Worship in Ayodhya' vide *Pilgrimage Studies, Text and Context*, Falahari Baba Commemoration Volume, Editors-Lallanji Gopal, D.P. Dubey, Allahabad, 1990, pp. 127-35. Here the author holds the 12th century *Agastyasamhita*, one of the earliest Rama Worship manual, and the *Ayodhyamahatmya* included in the *Vaisnavakhanda* of the *Sikandpurana* dating 13th century which describes the centre of Ayodhya, evidently the area that later became known as Ramdurga or *Ram Kot*.

15. R.S. Sharma, *Communal History and Rama's Ayodhya*, New Delhi, 1990 (henceforth R.S. Sharma), pp. 14-17, 25-27 and 31.
16. *Op. cit.,* No. 13
17. R.S. Sharma, M. Athar Ali, D.N. Jha and Suraj Bhan, *Ramjanmabhoomi-Baburi Masjid, A Historians' Report to the Nation*, New Delhi, 1991 (henceforth R.S. Sharma and Others), pp. 5-8. These historians have relied on *Vaishnava Khanda* of the *Skandapurana* as set out by A.B.L. Awasthi in *Studies in Skandapurana*, Pt-III, Vol. I, Lucknow, 1983, pp. 75-83, which also provides two compass directions for the *Ramjanmasthan* in relation to the shrine of *Vighnesvara*, east and north-east. It also uses varying terms for Rama's birth-place, four times as *Janmasthan*, once as *Ramajanma* and once as *Ramajanmasthan*.
18. The additional *Shlokas* in the recension vide *Op. cit.,* No. 17 have been found to be interpolations and unwarranted. Even Hans Bakker, *Op. cit.* No. 14, Part-II, pp. 143-46 having critically examined the topographical location of *Janmasthan* based on the comparative study of the varying texts of the *Vaishvna Khand* of the *Skandapurana* found the additional three "*slokas* in MS P" with compass directions, as quoted by Awasthi, to be of spurious character.

18a. This discovery was made by B.R. Grover (the co-author of the present paper) during his camp at Ayodhya (4-18 July 1992) who also released three reports of his findings to the Press. As the discovery was of great significance, later on the archaeologists, *i.e.,* Dr K.M. Srivastava also visited the spot on 22-23 July 1992 and confirmed the revolutionary findings. (Also published in *Ramjanmabhoomi: Ayodhya, New Archaeological Discoveries,* New Delhi, 1992, pp. 1, 11-12).

19. Based on the Persian sources, it can be well maintained that the ancient *Janmasthan* temple at Ayodhya was destroyed by Saiyed Salar Masud Ghazi, the nephew of Sultan Mahmud Ghazni. It was during the years 1029-1032 that Salar Masud accompanied by Malik Fazal carried out the militant Islamic

campaign (*tabligh* and *Jihad*) around Benaras, in Jaunpur and Awadh (Ayodhya) and desecrated the Hindu holy shrines. The Jain literary sources confirm the fact that some of the Jain temples of Ayodhya were also desecrated and destroyed by Salar Masud who remained in its occupation for some time.

The conquest and occupation of Awadh (Ayodhya) by Salar Masud Ghazi is further confirmed by the fact that Maulavi Abdul Karim, while giving details about the tombs and mosques in Ayodhya, in his book *Gumgashta-i-Halat-i-Ayodhya Awadh* (vide Ref. No. 56, pp. 13 & 24) also traced the tomb of *Bakshi* of Salar Masud Ghazi within Ayodhya and three other tombs of martyrs of the latter's army near Ayodhya towards the Faizabad road. Besides, the details about the campaigns of Salar Masud Ghazi in territories of Kannauj, Awadh and Bahraich have been provided by Qutubddin Ahmad in *Tarikh Saiyed Salar Masud Ghazi*, Lucknow, 1887, pp. 21-24, 43-60. Also, Muhammad Naim Ullah Khayali Humayu, *Tarikh-i-Masudi*, Lucknowi, 1953, pp. 144-146. Apart from various other medieval sources, the latter author has extensively quoted from *Mirat-i-Masudi* (manuscript in Persian) written by Abdur Rehman Chisti in the early 17th century in Jahangir's reign.

20. For details see Ref No. 31.
21. R. Nath, *Architecture of the Baburi Masjid of Ayodhya*, Jaipur, 1991, p. 38, R. Nath's argument that Mir Baqi was too occupied with the military affairs to have found time for the demolition of the *Janmasthan* temple and that for fighting against the Afghan rebels, he could ill-afford to offend the religious susceptibilities of the Hindus is based upon unfounded assumption. It is clear from Babur's Memoirs that Baqi Tashkandi, *i.e.,* Mir Baqi remained posted at Awadh for at least for a year and three months, if not more (vide Ref No. 32) and that the Afghan menace in the proper Awadh territories had been practically eliminated for the time being. Moreover, far from being solicitous towards the Hindu religious feelings, he destroyed the *Janmasthan* temple. As per the inscriptional evidence, on Babur's orders he built a 'mosque' at this site where "the angels descended". The hypothesis of repairing the already existing dilapidated mosque constructed earlier on this site for winning the sympathy of the local Muslims against the rebellious Afghan chiefs is equally imaginary and unreliable. However, there is no denying that from the architectural viewpoint, as correctly pointed by R. Nath (*Ibid.* pp. 19-20), the 'mosque' represented the Jaunpuri style rather than the Mughal features as reflected in the monuments built during Babur's reign at other places, *i.e.,* Agra, Sikri and Dholpur. As a matter of fact, in the initial stages of the Mughal rule, the continued impact of the local traditional style of architecture was inevitable. Apart from the afore-mentioned 'mosque' built by Mir Baqi there are a few other monuments at Ayodhya, still extant, which were built during the earlier phase of the Mughal rule with marked Jaunpuri style of architecture. Similarly, the mosques built in Babur's reign at other places in North India, *i.e.,* Palam (Delhi), Panipat and Rohtak (Haryana) bear the continued features of the Lodhi architecture as well as the impact of traditional style of architecture.

Of course, from the period of Sultan Ibrahim Sharqi (1402-36) to the end of the Sharqi rule in Jaunpur in 1479, the chiefs of Ayodhya/Awadh territories accepted the suzerainty of the Jaunpur Sharqi rule and paid tribute to the latter. The Sharqi domination equally affected the local architecture of the Awadh territories. This also accounts for the fact that like the Atala *Masjid*, *Masjid* Khalis Mukhalis and Jhanjiri *Masjid*, all the three mosques built by Sultan Ibrahim Sharqi (1402-36) in Jaunpur on the sites of the demolished Hindu temples, the 'mosque' built by Mir Baqi (1528) in Babur's reign at the site of the erstwhile *Janmasthan* temple at Ayodhya, did not have any minarets attached to it. Otherwise too, parallel architectural features in respect of main gates, ceilings and *mehrabs, dalans* and re-used temple materials could be traced in the above mentioned 'mosques'.

21a. For details of conversion of the afore-mentioned Hindu temples unto mosques at Jaunpur by Sultan Ibrahim Sharqi and the structural character of the mosques without minarets, Maulavi Khairuddin, *Jaunpur Nama*. (Ms. in Persian), Jaunpur, 1833, second edition published, Jaunpur, 1899, p. 42. Also Maulavi Nuruddin Zaidi, *Tajali Nur*, (Ms. in Persian), Jaunpur, 1905, Vol. III, pp. 182-83; Mir Ali Zamin Sahib Tarandi, *Chiragh-i-Nur* Jaunpur, 1932, p. 138. This has been reproduced in the Geography of Jaunpur (*Geographia-i-Jaunpur*), Jaunpur Part 1, 1872. According to these writers, the temple of Atala Devi originally built by Raja Vijyachandra was partly destroyed by Firuz Tughluq in 1364-76. But due to stiff resistance on the part of the Hindus, some portion was retained as the temple while foundation of the mosque was laid on the demolished portion. However, due to chaotic condition after the death of Firuz Tughluq, the mosque could not be fully constructed. But the Sultan Ibrahim of the Sharqi dynasty demolished even the remaining portion of the temple and completed the mosque on the entire plot, in the premises of the Jaunpur fort.

According to the afore-mentioned sources viz. *Jaunpur Nama, Geographia-i-Jaunpur*, p. 50, *Chiragh-i-Nur*, p. 139, another temple built by Vijayachandra, the Gahadavala ruler was converted by Ibrahim Sharqi into Jhanjiri *Masjid* (named so after beautiful Jhanjarian, also named as Zanjiri *Mosque* by Cunningham). Similarly, according to the same sources, the *Khankah* (hospice) Shirazi as well as the *Masjid* Khalis Mukhlis named after the brother of the Sultan were built on the site of the demolished temple earlier constructed by Vijayachandra. Also see Reference No. 58 as per description provided by Maulana Hakim Saiyad Abdul Haye. Still another *mosque* claimed to have been built by Sultan Mahmud Shah in AH 860/A.D. 1455-56 at Jaunpur named as *Masjid* Lal Darwaza (or *Masjid Namaz Gha*) even now bears the name of Raja Vijayachandra.

22. See for details, Ref. No. 29.

23. Mrs. Surinder Kaur and Sher Singh, *Archaeology of Babri Masjid-Ayodhya*, New Delhi, 1992, pp. 11-13; 38; 144-162. For their hypothesis that the disputed mosque at Ayodhya was built by Hussain Shah Sharqi of Jaunpur in AH 872 (2nd August 1467-21st July 1468), the authors have relied on the manuscript of Francis Hamilton Buchanan (1807-1814) No. Eur D 91, pp.

113-122, Vol.1). From the Arabic inscription provided by Buchanan, the above mentioned authors have deduced the chronogram dating (AH) 872 from the words "Maimoon alaihe bakhate". A proper scrutiny of this inscription would reveal that though it mentions the name of Fateh Muhammad Ullah, the scribe of the inscription, it by no means provides any chronogram which is otherwise given in another Persian inscription of Babur's reign installed on the wall of the 'mosque' as quoted by Buchanan. Mrs. Surinder Kaur and Sher Singh have derived the chronogram from the inscription in a very arbitrary manner. Also, the reading of these authors of the afore-mentioned Persian inscription which provides the chronogram, is completely wrong. In the last line of this inscription, they have substituted the words 'Bavad Khabar Baqi' for 'Bavad Khair Baqi'. A careful reading of the last line would reveal that the word used in the inscription is 'Khair' which in Persian has clearly two dots and *zer* under it. These authors have read this word only with one dot below it and have also ignored the *zer* put under it. Moreover, the words 'Bavad Khair Baqi' given in the last line of the inscription are the same as recorded in the preceding line which runs as 'Bavad Khair Baqi Basal-i-Banaish', implying that the monument was constructed in the year AH 935/A.D. 1528-29 as deduced from 'Bavad Khair Baqi'. Also see details vide Ref. No. 29.

As distinct from afore-mentioned version, Sushil Srivastava in his work, *The Disputed Mosque*, (vide Reference No. 27) and the excerpts published in *Sunday,* dated 6.1.1991 and his Paper 'The Ayodhya Controversy: where lies the Truth' (vide RJB-BM' ed. Mishra and Singh, New Delhi, 1991, pp. 94, 86-111) makes unwarranted statement that 'probably' the structure which came to be known as 'Baburi *Masjid*' was constructed during the late 14th century during the regime of Khawaja-i Jahan (Khwaja Jahan Malik Sarwar, 1393-1402) who on the decline of the Tughluq dynasty established the kingdom of Jaunpur (1393-1479). Sushil Srivastava has indulged in speculation in an unscientific manner and without any evidence in hand underlining his statement as 'probable'.

24. Bhai Mani Singh's (Diwan of Guru Govind Singh, late 17th/early 18th century) *Pothi-Janm Sakhi* vide edition V.S. 1947/A.D. 1890, Lahore, p. 213), provides clear testimony to this pilgrimage. Another important *Janm Sakhi* entitled *Guru Nanak Bansh Prakash* by Baba Sukh Wasi Ram Bedi written in 1886 VS/A.D. 1829 offers details (vide *Chhand* No. 1000-1001) about Guru Nanak's visit to Ayodhya in the company of Mardana, a bath in the Sarayu River and finally homage to Rama (*Darshan Ram Nihar*). Similarly, *Janm Sakhi*, known as *Bhai Bala Wali Janm Sakhi* edited in 1940 VS/A.D. 1883 accounts for Guru Nanak Dev's pilgrimage to Awadhpuri (Ayodhya) on the ground that Guru Nanak identified this city (*Nagri*) with Sri Ramachandraji, the *Avtar*. Also Rajendra Singh, *Sikh Itihas Mein Sri Ram Janmabhoomi*.

25. Zia-al-Din Barani, the author of *Tarikh-i-Firuz Shahi* (Persian text, edited Syed Ahmad Khan, Calcutta, 1860, pp. 571-72, 587), as well as the anonymous author of *Sirat-i-Firuz Shahi* (Persian M.S. available at Khuda Baksh Library, Patna) provide details about the position and role of the Awadh (Ayodhya)

Chief and other Chiefs at the time of the accession of Firuz Tughluq to the throne in A.D. 1351, the reconciliatory policy of the latter who in A.D. 1353 equally sought the help of these powerful chiefs to checkmate the aggressive designs of the ruler of Bengal.

26. For fire power of the army of Babur used in the battles of Panipat (1526) and Kanwa (1527), see details, Zahiruddin Muhammad Babur, *The Babur Nama*, Chagatay Turkish Text, Hyderabad Manuscript (Codex), Salar Jang Collection, Hyderabad, India (henceforth B.N. Chaghatay-Turkish, Hyderabad Codex). For Battle of Panipat, fols. 264a-267b; Battle of Kanwa, fols. 309a-325a. Also Translation, A.S. Beveridge [1921], 1989, New Delhi (henceforth B.N. tr. Ms. Beveridge), pp. 468-75 and 546-76 respectively. Also translated, edited and annotated by Wheeler M. Thackston under the title *The Babur Nama Memoirs of Babur, Prince and Emperor*, 1996, New York, (henceforth B.N. tr. Thackston), pp. 323-27 and 370-87 respectively. Also Iqtidar Alam Khan, 'The Indian Response to Firearms (1300-1750)', Presidential Address, Indian History Congress, November, 1997, Bangalore, pp. 10-18. Apart from these, the eyewitness accounts of both Guru Nanak Dev (in Punjab) and Abdus Qaddus Gangoi (for Dibalpur, Punjab, neighbourhood of Delhi, Jaunpur and Awadh) stress the fire power of the army of Babur which caused havoc in the armies of the adversaries. (For details, Ref. No. 39 and 40).

27. Only a few instances may be cited. R.S. Sharma, *Op. cit.* No. 15; Same Article circulated by him, p. 18; Romila Thapar, S. Gopal and others, (25 historians), *The Political Abuse of History: Baburi Masjid-Ramjanmabhoomi Dispute*, J.N.U. New Delhi, Nov., 1989, Section-III of the pamphlet; slightly shortened text also published in the Times of India, Nov. 06, 1989; S. Gopal, ed; *Anatomy of a Confrontation, the Baburi Masjid-Ramjanmabhoomi Issue*, New Delhi, 1991, Introduction, pp. 11-21; also other Articles by various scholars therein, pp. 22-218; Sushil Srivastava, 'The Ayodhya Controversy: Where lies the Truth? vide *Ram Janmabhoomi Baburi Masjid, Historical Documents, Legal Opinion and Judgments*, ed. V.C. Mishra, P. Singh, the Bar Council of India Trust, New Delhi, 1991 (henceforth 'RJB-BM' ed. Mishra and Singh), pp. 86-111; also, *The Disputed Mosque—A Historical Survey*, New Delhi, 1991, pp. 67-112. Saiyed Shahabuddin Abdur Rehman, ed. *Babri Masjid* (Urdu), 3rd edition, Azamgarh, 1986 (henceforth Abdur Rehman, 'Babri *Masjid*); A few letters of Syed Shahabuddin published in monthly *Muslim India*, 7/89: also Indian Express, dated 08.3.90 and 09.4.90; Irfan Habib; 'Peoples Democracy', April 14, 1991, p.7E, also Gyanendra Pandey, *The Construction of Communalism in Colonial Northern India*, Oxford University Press, New Delhi, 1990.

28. B.N., Chagatai-Turkish Text, Hyderabad Codex fols. 337b-339a; John Leyden and Williams Erskine, *Memiors of Zehir-Ed-Din Muhammad Babur, Emperor of Hindustan, written by Himself* in the Chagatay Turki, tr. Vol. II, London, 1921, pp. 332-33; B.N. tr Ms. Beveridge pp. 600-602; B.N. tr. Thackston pp. 400-402; Also *Zahiruddin Muhammad Babur Mirza, Babur Nama, Chaghatay Turkish Text with Abdur Rahim Khankhanan's Persian Translation and English translation* by W.M. Thackston, tr., Sources of Oriental Languages

and Literatures, 18 Turkish Sources XVI Part-III, Department of Near Eastern Languages and Civilisations, Harvard University, 1993, pp. 718-721. The translation of the passage by the above authors from Chagatay-Turkish into English is rather too general and not very apt. A more appropriate translation, both in letter and spirit, has been provided by the present authors in the text.

28a. *Ibid.*

29. Maulvi Ashraj Hussain, "Inscriptions of Emperor Babur", Epigraphica Indica-Arabic and Persian Supplement, 1965, Delhi, 1966, pp. 58-62. Ashraj Hussain has quoted three inscriptions in Persian vide Plate No. XVII (b) with two inscriptions with three couplets each and Plate No. XVII (c) with eight couplets along with the name of the scribe as well. Also S.K. Banerji, 'Babur and the Hindus,' The Journal of the United Provinces Historical Society, Vol. IX, July 1936, Part II, pp. 70-96. Banerji has reproduced the two Persian inscriptions, one inside and the other outside the mosque as well as the English translation as rendered by Ms. Beveridge in *Babur Nama.* (Vide Reference No. 81). However, the second inscription considered incomplete (with only three verses) by Ms. Beveridge was reproduced in toto (comprising even the name of the scribe) by Banerji, along with his comments. The first inscription clearly mentioned that the mosque was constructed on the command of Babur whereas the second noted Babur as *Qalandar* (not attached to money, power and worldly pleasures), Mir Baqi (Isfahani?) as the builder of the mosque and the fort as well as the date of construction in words as nine hundred and thirty five (*Hijri, i.e.,* AH 935/A.D. 1528-29).

Even though Banerji did concede the fact that the "Jami *Masjid* at Ajodhya was built in Babur's time on a site sacred to the Hindus as Rama's "birth-place", he held that the destruction of the temple at *Janmasthan* was an act of Mir Baqi who, in fact, "was responsible for the demolition of Rama's temple and obtaining sanction, afterwards, for the erection of this *Masjid*, from the Emperor". Banerji considered that Babur was quite "magnanimous towards the people of the country, most of whom were Hindus" and 'that Babur was not actuated by any iconoclastic zeal" which is borne out by his visit to the Hindu temples at Gwalior and the "Secret will" (*Wasiyat-nama-i-makhfi*) addressed to his son Humayun. As a matter of fact, Banerji's" analysis is deficient in many a respect. Mir Baqi was not merely the Superintendent who destroyed the temple and constructed *mosque* on it in AH 935/A.D. 1528-29 while passing through Ajodhya in pursuit against the Afghans, he was, in fact, the regular *hakim* (administrator-commander) of Awadh. (see details vide Reference Nos. 28, 28a-29). Moreover, as per inscriptional evidence, Mir Baqi/Baqi Tashkandi built the mosque at Ayodhya on the basis of Babur's orders. At the same time, in his plea to show the considerate attitude of Babur towards the Hindus and his non-involvement in the destruction of the *Janmasthan* temple, Banerji's appeal to the unauthentic document of the so-called "Secret Will" of Babur is rather too far-fetched (See details vide Reference No. 37). Similarly, all these comments are equally applicable to Radhey Shyam who in his work (*Babur*, Patna, 1978, pp. 368-72, 457-60, 487-94 and 505-507) has followed Banerji's line of thought so as to exonerate Babur and hold Mir Baqi responsible for the destruction of the *Janmasthan* temple at Ayodhya and the construction of the Jami *Masjid* on its site.

Of the two inscriptions installed on the walls inside the 'mosque' available till 6 December, 1992, it was the inscription installed on the left to the pulpit (*mambar*) which mentioned that Mir Baqi built it on the orders of Babur in AH 935/A.D. 1528-29. As a matter of fact, there was no person by the name of Mir Baqi in the court of Babur. This accounts for the fact that some scholars have failed to identify this person. (R.S. Sharma, *Op. cit.* No. 15 comments that "identity of Mir Baqi is not known from any source."). The real name of this person was Baqi and the scribe used the designation of Mir out of regard for him. The name Baqi was very common in Central Asia. In his Memoirs, Babur mentions six different persons whose names were Baqi, though with different surnames or designations. In fact, it was Baqi Tashkandi who was appointed administrator/commander (*hakim*) of Awadh in September 1528 and he has been twice specifically mentioned by Babur for the years AH 934-935/A.D. 1528-29 commanding the army of Awadh (Ayodhya). As Babur was very fond of using various titles for the same person, he calls Baqi Tashkandi (*i.e.,* hailing from Tashkent) as Baqi *Mingbashi* (*i.e.,* head of thousand troops) and also as Baqi *Shaghawal* (as supreme of *qazis* and *mullahs*) and Baqi Beg (*i.e.,* with the title of a Beg). Also, B.N. tr. Ms. Beveridge, *Op. cit.* No. 26 index, p. 742. It has already been stated above that Baqi Tashkandi (alias Mir Baqi) was present with Babur on 28th March-2nd April, 1528, when he was appointed as the *hakim* of Awadh (vide Op. cit. Nos. 28 and 28a). However, for another inscription on the wall, Shahabuddin Abdur Rehman, *Babri Masjid, Op. cit.* No. 27, p. 123 has misread the word Asaf *Saani* (the just, Asaf the second) as Isfahani and the name of the person as 'Mir Baqi Isfahani', which is completely wrong as the same Baqi could not hail both from Tashkent (Central Asia) and Isfahan (Iran).

30. A.G. Page, *Memoirs of the Archaeological Survey of India*, No. 22, *An Historical Mandir on the Qutb;* Delhi, Calcutta, 1926, pp. 29-33, with plates No. 3-10.

30a. Vidisha was an important town of *Pargana* Bhilsah, *sarkar* Raisen, *Subah* Malwa. Bhilsa served as silver minting place during the reign of Aurangzeb and its name was changed to Alamgirpura. The co-author of this Paper (B.R. Grover) visited the site on 4th November, 1996 and the afore-mentioned description has been given based on personal observation and inspection of the site.

31. This is also supported by an archaeological evidence. After the demolition of the disputed structure (*Ramjanmabhoomi*-'Baburi *Masjid*') at Ayodhya on 6th December, 1992, three dedicatory inscriptions in the Devnagri script along with other artefacts were discovered (6th-7th December, 1992) from the rubble which had been earlier hidden in the walls of the structure. Of these three, one Hari-Vishnu 12th century inscription of 20 lines engraved on a thick slab of buffstone (5' x 2' x 2.5') in Sanskrit written in the Nagri script which mentions that the temple of Vishnuhari was built by Nyayachandra, the chief

of Saket Mandalam who was the feudatory of Govindachandra (the Gahadwal king of Kannauj, A.D. 1114-1154). The detailed inscription written by the scribe named Ayushachandra, (son of Alhana, a grandson of king Sallakshana) in its fifth verse clearly refers to *Janmabhoomi* of Sri Rama as it pays homage to the holy spot (*dhama*), the birth-place of that incarnation (of Vishnu) who did great glorious deeds and was the killer of "Dashaanan" (the ten- faced demon, *i.e.,* Ravana), viz. Dasharath's son, Rama. For details, A.M. Shastri, *Op. cit.* No. 9, p. 37-38; T.P. Verma, 'Palaeographic Evidence of the Ayodhya inscriptions'; G.C. Tripathi and D.P. Dube, 'A Short Note on the Vishnuhari Temple inscription of Ayushyachandra, vide *Itihas Darpan*, Bhartiya Itihas Sankalan Yojana Samiti, Delhi, Vol. III, No. *2,* December 1996, pp. 62-73; B.R. Grover, 'Seminar on Distortion of History—The Current Experience (December, 1995, Calcutta). A Critique', *Itihas Darpan* Vol. III, No. 1, 1996, pp. 35-41, 47-51.

As such, the discovery of the afore-mentioned inscription which marked the dedicatory foundation tablet of the 12th century Vishnuhari temple hidden in the walls of the '*mosque*' along ith other artefacts clearly establishes that Mir Baqi built the '*mosque*' on the very site of the *Janmasthan* (of Rama) after the demolition of the former temple.

32. B.N. Chaghatai-Turkish Text, Hyderabad Codex, fols. 379a-b, 380a; B.N. tr. Ms. Beveridge, *Op. cit.* 26, pp. 684-85. Also B.N. tr. *Thackston*, pp. 443-44.

33. Babur's deliberate silence over certain delicate issues is further confirmed by the instance of the destruction of the Hari temple of the Hindus at Sambhal in December 1526 and construction of a mosque on the same site out of the debris of the demolished temple by his General, Hindu Beg. Even though for this period, there is no break in Babur's Memoirs, the inscription on the mosque, dated 1 *Rabi* AH 935/6 December, 1526 mentions that it was built by Hindu Beg on the orders of Babur. Nor does the inscription record that it was built on the site of a demolished Hindu temple with the re-used material which is otherwise fully supported by internal archaeological evidence.

34. There is no record to show that any resistance was ever offered by the local Ayodhya chief or the regional chiefs to save the *Janmasthan* temple from destruction. However, according to indigenous and traditional Hindu sources, Shyamanand, the head priest along with other Brahmins offered stiff resistance for about 17 days before they were overpowered leading to the demolition of the *Janmasthan* temple.

35. Chagatai-Turkish Text, Hyderabad Codex, fols. 316a-317a; 323b-325a; B.N. tr. Ms. Beveridge, *Op. cit.* 26, pp. 558-60, 572-75; B.N. tr. Thackston, pp. 378-80, 385-87, Also E. Denison Ross, *A Collection of Poems (Turki text) by the Emperor Babur, with Introduction*, Calcutta, 1910. Plate No. XV of *Diwan-i-Babur Padshah*, p. 39.

35a. Shaikh Rizq Ullah Mushtaqui, *Waqiat-e-Mustaqui*, Tr and ed. Iqtidar Husain Siddqui, ICHR, New Delhi, p. 117. The author (1495-96 to 1581-82) was contemporary of Babur.

36. Abdur Rehman, *Baburi Masjid, Op. cit.* No. 27; p. 7 which also quotes Rajendra Prasad, *India Divided,* 3rd edition p. 39; Document No. 21. B/2, vide list No. 111 submitted by All India Babri *Masjid* Action Committee to the Ministry of Home Affairs, New Delhi in 1991: R. Nath, *India as seen by Babur* (1504-1530), New Delhi, 1996, pp xi, 2-3, 22; Surinder Kaur, Sher Singh, *The Secular Emperor Babar—A Victim of Indian Partition*, New Delhi, 1991, pp. 63-65. However, the latter scholars, p. 66, based on a Persian inscription reproduced from A. Fuhrer's Report (Archaeological Survey of India-New Series, Vol. 1, North-Western Provinces of Sindh, Oudh, 1889 A.D., pp. 67-68) think that the mosque was constructed in AH 930/1523-24) during the reign of Ibrahim Lodhi. According to Fuhrer, the word *hijra* as written in Persian had been misread as *panch* (five) whereby the very date of construction of the mosque in AH 930 had been misread as AH 935. But this inscription is quite different and contradictory to the inscription quoted by Francis Hamilton Buchanan (1807-14, vide Reference No. 23) and does not find any place amongst the three inscriptions found later on (Details vide Reference No. 29). Apparently, if in existence, it was removed at some later stage. However, based on the afore-mentioned inscription as recorded by Fuhrer, the statement of Surinder Kaur and Sher Singh that the 'masjid' was built in AH 930/A.D. 1523-24 during the reign of Ibrahim Lodhi is in contradiction with their earlier stand (vide Reference No. 23) that this disputed mosque was constructed by Hussain Shah Sharqj of Jaunpur in AH 872/ 1467-680.

37. S.R. Sharma, *Religious Policy of the Moghul Emperors*, (1942), Asia Publishing House, Bombay, 1962, pp. 74, 93-95. Prof. Sharma, even before the Partition of India (1947), traced the history of the finding of this document by N.C. Mehta from Bhopal and also published by the latter in 1936. It was exhibited in the meeting of the Indian Historical Records Commission. Prof. Sharma has also provided its Persian text which was on various valid grounds found by him to be an unauthentic document.

    In fact, varying versions are current in respect of the fake "Will". A thorough examination of the text of the so-called Babur's "Secret Will" (*Wasiyat-nama-i-makhhfi*) meant for (his son) Humayun being publicised by pro-Baburi *Masjid* scholars when compared with the photocopy of the same, available at the National Archives of India, New Delhi, has been found defective in many respects. It does not have the correct spelling of invocation, '*AL Hamdu Lillah*' nor does it put any date which otherwise is recorded as 11th January, 1529 (1 *Jumada* I A.H 935) in the latter photocopy. This transcript carries three to four spelling errors. However, the transcript of the National Archives of India is equally defective with wrong spellings of some words, and spurious *tughra* (invocation). Of course, Gulbadan Begum (vide Ref. No. 38) does refer to a verbal 'Will' expressed by Babur at his deathbed (26th December, 1530) wherein he said that he had bestowed everything that he owned (*i.e.,* crown, territories) to Humayun and required all those (courtiers) present not to deviate from Humayun's welfare and having trust in God, he hoped that Humayun would treat all his subjects well. Except for this, no other Will has been quoted by Gulbadan Begum or any other Mughal source.

As a matter of fact, N.C. Mehta (I.C.S.), a bureaucrat was shown this document by His Highness, the Nawab of Bhopal in the Hamida Public Library, Bhopal. As stated by Mr. Mehta, the document "embossed with an earlier Royal seal, dated 933 Hijri was written on a thin gold-sprinkled hand-made paper in a small but beautiful handwriting." Mr. Mehta called it the "Imperial farman" and "a document of unique importance for the history of India". According to the Nawab of Bhopal, this was one of the heirlooms of the Bhopal State even though it was unknown as to from where and at what stage it reached the afore-mentioned Library. However, with the courtesy of the Nawab, Mr. Mehta published its text (in Persian) along with its literal translation in English and Commentary in the Journal,' '*The Twentieth Century*', January, 1936, pp. 339-44 under the title 'An Unpublished Testament of Babur—A Unique Plea for Tolerance'. The same document supposed to be Babur's "Secret Will" has also been reproduced by R. Nath, *India as Seen by Babur (1504-1530),* New Delhi, 1996, pp. 18-22.

The document, after the praise of God, bearing a seal dated AH 935 (October 1526-September 1527) of "Zahir-ul-Din Muhammad Babar Badshah Bahadur Ghazi" covers the so-called "Secret Will" (*Wasiyyat nama-i-makhfi*) of "Zahiruddin Muhammad Babur Badshah Ghazi" conveyed to (*ba*) "Nasiruddin Muhammad Humayun—may God prolong his life." Keeping in view the stability of the Sultanate, Babur wrote to his son Humayun that as God had bestowed upon the latter the sovereignty of the country of Hindustan having different religious faiths, it was proper to keep his heart free from religious bigotry, to administer justice in accordance with the practice of every community, especially to avoid the cow-slaughter to win the hearts of the people and to render the subjects (*raiyat*) of this country bound to the kingdom through obligations, not to desecrate the temples and places of worship of any community under the royal allegiance and rather should adopt ways of administration of justice so that the king (*Shah*) and the subjects (*raiyat*) should mutually benefit from each other as the progress of Islam rests on the 'sword of kindness' than 'the sword of persecution', to overlook the differences between the Sunnis and the Shias which is a cause of weakness of Islam and above all to harmonise the subjects (*raiyat*) with different convictions (*qalub*-hearts) like the four Elements so that the body-politic of the Sultanate remains safe from different diseases, and finally to emulate the great deeds of Hazrat Amir Timur *Saheb Qirani* for strengthening the measures of the state administration. The document ends with a verse from the Quran, 'Nothing rests on us but to deliver the message'. Dated 1 *Jamada I*, AH. 935/A.D. 11th January, 1529.

Apparently, keeping in view the need for communal harmony, the afore-mentioned document was forged by somebody in the late 19th or the early 20th century during the phase of struggle for Freedom against the British rule in India so as to portray the Islamic rule in India, even of Babur, as liberal. In fact, quite prior to Mr. Mehta's afore-mentioned article, this document available at the Hamida Library at Bhopal had been brought to light by Colonel Laurd, the founder-administrator of the Bhopal State Library. According to the latter, at the time of the collection of MSS for building the library through advertisement, this document (5"x8") had been purchased from an indigent Tonk Mussalman who stated that originally having obtained from Delhi, it had been with his family for some time. In order to verify its genuineness, Mr. Laurd referred it to the Royal Asiatic Society. This was examined by experts in literary technicalities *i.e.,* A.G. Ellis, Ghulam Yazdani, Sir T. Arnold, L.D. Barnett, Abdul-Majid Belshah, E. Edwards and Sir E.D. Ross. Based on the data supplied by these scholars, Ms. A.S. Beveridge published her comments, 'Paternal Counsels Attributed to Babur in a Bhopal Ms. (Dec. 1922)—The Bhopal *Wasiyat Nama-i-Makhif* in the 'Journal of Royal Asiatic Society of Great Britain and Ireland,' Vol. 55, 1923, pp. 78-82. Ms. Beveridge pointed out various technical flaws with regard to the invocation, seal, the legend on the seal, the way Babur's name has been put, some linguistic flaws and the date of writing of this document. Even though Ms. Beveridge's objections are quite valid, she considered the script of the manuscript as that of the 18th century rather than 16th. In fact, as already stated, it could be well contented on the basis of the language and contents that the document with all the technical flaws and ignorance of the gaps in Babur's Memoirs, was prepared during the late 19th or early 20th century.

Having noted the observations made by Ms. Beveridge, Radhey Shyam (vide Reference No. 59, pp. 458-590, 487-94), without any documentary evidence, concluded this was only a 'rough draft' of the "Secret Will" (*Wasiyat nama*) got prepared by Babur at Dholpur on 11th January, 1529 and that Babur "hardly got an opportunity to go through the draft and correct the linguistic error etc."

Even though the number of the available *Farmans* issued by Babur as ruler of Hindustan (1526-1530) is very few, a comparison of the invocations (*tughra*) of these documents with the "Secret Will" in hand clearly brings out the ingeniousness of the latter document. The seals of the other genuine *Farmans* bear the legend as 'Zahiruddin Muhammad Babur *ibn* Umar Shaikh Kurgan' rather than Zahiruddin Muhammad Babur Badshah Bahadur Ghazi' wherein the word 'Bahadur' is as put by Ms. Beveridge 'an anachronism' since Babur had already assumed the title of *Padshah* in A.D. 1505. Moreover, it is evident from the *Babur Nama* that all letters written by Babur to other persons or even to Humayun in his own hand, dated AH 13 *Rabi* I 935/26 November, 1528 (vide B.N. Chaghatay Turkish, Hyderabad Codex, fols no. 348a-349b; tr. Ms. Beveridge, pp. 624-27, tr. Thackston, pp. 412-14) were in Chaghatay-Turkish language and the way Babur had addressed Humayun had a different format than in the present document relating to "Secret Will" written in the Persian language.

It may be well observed that on 2 *Jumada* I AH 935/11th January, 1529, the day on which the afore-mentioned Babur' "Secret Will" is supposed to have been written, Humayan was in Samarqand and Babur himself was camping at the Lotus-Garden of Dholpur (28 *Rabi* II AH 935/9th January, 1529 to *Jumada* I/14th January, 1529) for the construction of Hot-bath and reservoir etc. Of these days that Babur spent at Dholpur, there is a gap in the *Babur Nama* in respect of description of the events for two days, *i.e.*, 1st and 2nd *Jumada* I AH 935/(Tuesday-Wednesday) 10th-11th January, 1529. (For details, B.N. Chagatay-Turkish, Hyderabad Codex, fol. 356 a; B.N. Tr. Ms. Beveridge, p. 639, B.N. tr. Thackston, pp. 420-21). It is also well known that the description of the events of the gap years or months or days in the Memoirs of Babur were not available even to Abdur Rahim Khanakhana when in A.D. 1589, he translated Babur's Memoirs (*Waqiyat-i-Baburi*) from Chaghatay-Turkish into Persian and even to Abul Fazl when he wrote the *Akbar Nama* (1595) after having sifted all the source-material of Babur's reign available to him and they are not traceable in any of the manuscripts of *Babur Nama* available in Europe or Asia in any of the Libraries or private collections. Then, how come, this single document of Babur's "Secret Will" (*Wasiyat-nama makhti*) unknown to the scholarship world all through the centuries since A.D. 1530 (Babur's death) appeared all of a sudden in the early 20th century when a Tonk Muslim claimed that his family had acquired it from Delhi and sold it to the Hamida Public Library, Bhopal (India). What a wonderful discovery? R.Nath, *Op. cit.* No. 36, pp. 18-22, reproduced a copy of letter dated 11.2.1921 addressed by B. Ghoshal, the curator of the library to Sir (syed) Ross Massod, Hyderabad, who further passed on the Papers to Professor H.K. Sherwani. The "Will" was examined and transcribed by the latter. R. Nath has also reproduced a facsimile copy of the "Will" in Persian, its transcription and its translation in English. Without critical examination of the "Will", and considering it a genuine document, R. Nath considers that "Babur was against demolition of temples or any other iconoclastic measures in the name of Islam and he classified them under tyranny (*zulm*)." Such a statement is absolutely contrary to the facts as known from Babur's own reign and nature of his rule in Hindustan. Mohibul Hasan in his work, *Babur-Founder of the Mughal Empire in India*, 1985 ed., p. 184, has toed S.K. Bannerji" version in a slightly modified manner. He thinks that the Rama temple at *Janmasthan* was pulled down by one of Babur's overzealous officials during one of the crises of his reign without sanction from the Emperor.

38. Gulbadan Begum, *Humayun Nama* (Persian text), ed. Rashid Akhtar Nadwi, Lahore (Pakistan), 1968, p. 177, Also tr. (Urdu), pp. 43-44.

39. *Shri Guru Granth Sahib*. tr. (in English), Gurbachan Singh Talib, Patiala, 1988, Vol. II, *Raga Asa*, pp. 769, 883-85.

40. *Lataif-i-Qaddusi* (Persian text), ed. Hafiz Muhammad Usman, Delhi, AH 1310/A.D. 1893, *Lataif* No. 75-92; pp. 62-73.

41. Abul Fazl, *Ain-i-Akbari* (Persian, A.D. 1598), Vol. II Lucknow, 1881 A.D., *subah* Awadh, p. 78; tr. (English), Jarrett and J.N. Sarkar, Calcutta, 1949, II, p. 182. Henceforth, for Reference Nos. 41-43, 45-46, 49-62, 64-86, also see *History Versus Casuistry*, pp. 13-34 pertaining to Documentary Evidence : Muslim Testimony, Evidence from the Revenue Records and some other portions written by one of the present authors (B.R. Grover) for *Evidence for the Ramjanmabhoomi Mandir V.H.P., New Delhi*, 1990-91. These portions have been verbatim reproduced in *History Versus Casuistry.*

42. *Ain-i-Akbari* (Persian), Ms. (17th century) No. 55.73/1369, National Museum, New Delhi, folios unnumbered; tr. Jarrett and Sarkar, III, Calcutta, 1948, p. 335.

43. Mirza Jan, *Hadiqa-i-Shuhada*, Lucknowi, A.D. 1856, p. 6-7. Even though the author wrote the book in Urdu language, he reproduced the Persian text of the 25th Counsel from *Sahifa-i-Chihil Nasaih Bahadur Shahi*, the transcription of which having been completed on 15 *Shaban*, AH 1231 /11 July 1816 was deposited with the Library of Mirza Haider Shukoh *ibn* (son of) Mirza Sulayman Shukoh. The passage runs, "...The places of worship of the infidel Hindus (*musharkin Hindu*) situated at Mathura, Benaras and Awadh, etc., which the 'wicked and worthless' infidels (*kufar-i-nabkar*), according to their own belief and faith consider these (places) as the birth-place of Kanhaiya (Lord Krishna), the place (*muqami*) of *Rasoi Sita* (pertaining to *Janmasthan* of Ramachandra), the monument (*makaan*) known as the seat of Hanuman, who according to the Hindus was installed by Ramachandra over there after the conquest of Lanka), were all demolished for the might of Islam, and at all these places mosques have been constructed. They (the rulers) should not keep these mosques free from the Friday congregational prayers (*juma we jamait*). Rather it is obligatory that no open ceremony of idol worship should be performed over there and the sound of conch shall could not reach the ear of the Muslims...." (Translated by B.R. Grover, the co-author of this paper).

    In the text, Mirza Jan also mentions the forty Counsels were copied by the original author, daughter of Bahadur Shah (1st) from *Sahifa-i-Shahi*. Later on, Ali Naqi Khan (A.D. 1855) the Prime Minister of Awadh who had this book in the Awadh State Archives called it by the title of the 'Forty Injunctions' (*Chihil Nasaih*) vide Ref. No. 45 and still later Rajab Ali Surur in *Fasanah-i-ibrat* (vide Ref. No. 52 and 60) called it *Sahifa-i-Bahadur Shahi*.

44. R.S. Sharma and Others, *Op. cit.* No.17, pp. 21-23.

44a. C.A. Storey, *Persian Literature A Bio-Bibliographical Survey*, Luzac Co. London, 1927, Section I and other Vols; Vol II, Pt. I, London, 1972; Pt. 2, London, 1971; Pt. 3, Leiden, 1984; Also, D.N. Marshal, *Mughals in India, A Bibliographical Survey,* 2 Vols; Vol I-Manuscripts, Asia Publishing House, Bombay, 1967.

45. National Archives of India, New Delhi (N.A.I.), Foreign Department, Political Proceeding, Fort William, 28th December, 1855, Consultations F.C. No. 450, pp. 429-36.

46. Muhammad Asghar, the *Imam* (*khatib* and *muezzin*) of the 'mosque' in complaint against the *Bairagis* of *Janmasthan* addressed to the British Government, dated 30th November, 1858, called it '*Masjid Janmasthan*' (*Janmasthan mosque*) vide Abdur Rehman, Babri *Masjid, Op. cit.* No. 36; Also Ref. No. 51.

47. See Ref. No. 64 and 65.

48. Irfan Habib, "Interview of the Week', Sept. 07, 1986. The Sunday Observer; Article in Peoples Democracy, *Op. cit.* No. 27. Also R.S. Sharma and Others, *Op. cit* No.17, p. 21.

49. N.A.I. *Op. cit.* No. 45, No. 355, para No. 5, *Purcha* from Nawab Wajid Ali Shah, the king of *Oudh* to Major James Outram, the British Resident, dated 12th August, 55 (1855).

50. For details, B.R. Grover and S.P. Gupta, "RJB-BM", ed. Mishra and Singh, *Op. cit.* No. 27, p. 157-58. This is also quoted by the author of *Muraqqa-i-Khusrawi*, Ref. No. 53. This is further acknowledged by Harbans Mukhia vide 'Ayodhya Dispute-Tool for Political Mobilisation', *Hindu*, dated 07.9.1990.

51. *Op. cit.* No. 43, pp. 2-7.

52. Rajab Ali Beg, *Fasanah-i-Ibrat* (1860), Lucknow, 1884, pp. 71-73.

53. Shaikh Muhammad Azamat Ali Kakorawi (1811-93), *Muraqqa-i-Khusrawi* alias *Tarikh-i-Awadh*, 1869, Ms. Tagore Library, University of Lucknow (4954.5 M 70 MK 46339), fols. 230b-231a. As such, the way Mathura-Bindra Ban were cleared of heresy (*bidat*), in the same manner the *Janmasthan* temple which was the main worshipping place in Faizabad (Awadh) located at the capital (seat of throne) of the father of Lachman and Rama having been demolished, a lofty Baburi *Masjid* was erected on the advice of Musa Ashiqan and that it was still known as *Sita Ki Rasoi* amongst the Hindus. The author further clarified that henceforth the Hindus built their own temple (*Ram Chabutra*) in the courtyard of the Baburi *Masjid*, where earlier Sita's kitchen (*Sita-ki-Rasoi*) had been located but it was not liked by the Muslims.

    The above section of the manuscript was first published in 1896 and later in 1989 was incorporated in Zaki Kakorawi's *Amir-Ali Shahid Aur Muraqqa-i-Hanuman Garhi* (henceforth Zaki Kakorawi) Lucknow, 1987, pp. 71-73.

54. Saiyad Kamaluddin Haider Hasani Al Mashhandi alias Muhammad Mir Lucknowi (1794-1881), *Sawanehat-i-Salateen-Awadh* (Urdu) in two Volumes, Lucknow (1879), 1896, Vol. II, 1896, pp. 111, 117; Reprinted at Cawnpur in 1907, Vol. II, p. 117. The author clarifies that the Jamai *Masjid* built by Babur Badashah was located at *Janmasthan* (*Masjid Jamai Banai Babur Badshah Waqia Janmasthan*). The afore-mentioned title was also popularly known as *Tarikh-i-Awadh* or *Brief History of Oude in Two Volumes*.

    As a matter of fact, Saiyad Kamaluddin Haider had completed his above work by A.D. 1859-60 but was for the first time published only in A.D. 1879 under the patronage of Sir Raja Dig Vijya Singh of Balrampur with an Introduction by the latter himself (Vol. I, pp. 2-4). It is claimed that without an Introductory part, the book in two volumes was translated from Urdu into English as well by Col. Chamberlain, magistrate, Lucknow, 1859. Apart from the afore-mentioned historical work, Saiyad Kamaluddin Haider also translated Samuel Johnson's novel, *The History of Rasselas Prince of Abissinia,* from English into Urdu. For details about the life and works of Kamaluddin Haider, see Ashfaq Ahmad Azami, *Tawarikh-i-Rasselas, Shahzada Habsh*, tr. Saiyad Kamaluddin Haider alias Muhammad Mir Lucknowi, Azamgarh, 1983, pp. 5-71.

55. Haji Muhammad Hasan, *Zia-i-Akhtar*, Lucknow, 1878, pp. 38-39, dedicated to the king of Awadh, Wajid Ali Shah. Here, the author has given credit to

Saiyed Musa Ashiqan (the Sufi *faqir*) who on the orders of Babur got the mosque built after having completely mitigated the women's private apartment of Raja Ramchandra and Sita's kitchen.

56. Maulavi Abdul Karim (AH 1235-1308/A.D. 1820-1891), *Gumgashta-i-Halat-i-Ayodhya* Awadh (The forgotten events of Ayodhya Awadh), *i.e., Tarikh-i-Parinah Madinatu L-Auliye* (Persian) written most likely in the second half of the 19th century, tr. Urdu, Maulavi Abdul Gaffar, Lucknow [1979] and 1981; 1979 edition, p. 40.

I am obliged to Maulavi Ishtiaq Ahmad, the *Imam* of the Alamgiri *Mosque* in Ayodhya who gave me the 1981 Urdu translated version of the above-mentioned book in January 1990, a photocopy of which I gave to Harsh Narain, the author of "Focus on Muslim Sources", Delhi, 1993. Apart from various other misinterpretations regarding other 'Muslim Sources,' Harsh Narain's acceptance of the viewpoint that Babur visited Ayodhya as a young boy in disguise (vide pp. 30-37) is erroneous. In this regard, his reference to a later source, Abdullah's *Tarikh-i-Daudi* (written in Jahangir's reign) is of little relevance as these are only anecdotes quoted by Abdullah. On the contrary, it is clear from Babur's Memoirs that he crossed the River Indus for the first time and entered the territories of Hindustan on 15th February, 1519 even though he had always cherished in his heart to possess Hindustan. Babur also maintains that he entered Hindustan after having made proper military arrangements at the base from Kabul to the River Indus. Thereafter he has given details about the Salt Rauge (*Koh Jud*) and the territories of Bhira and Khushab which he claimed as his ancestral properties since the olden days of Amir Timur (the Turk). Similarly, later on at the time of the 5th and last expedition of Hindustan in AH 932/A.D. 1525-26, and more especially after his victory over Ibrahim Lodhi and entry in the palace (*manzil*) of the latter in Agra (10th May, 1526), Babur again provides details of his earlier attempts and the final conquest of Hindustan which clarify the entire position and contradict any supposed visit on his part earlier to A.D. 1519. For details, B.N. Chagatay, Turkish Text, Hyderabad Codex, fols. 222a-232a, 251b-270a; B.N. tr. Ms. Beveridge, pp. 377-93; 445-80; B.N. tr. Thackston, pp. 274-85, 311-30.

Regarding A.R. Khan's statement in Indian Express, March 17, 1990, even though his viewpoint about Babur's visit to Ayodhya in September 1528 is quite correct, his doubt about the historicity of Musa Ashiqan or Saiyad Mir Ashiqan (Fazl Abbas Musa Ashiqan) is unfounded. It is clear from the Sufi literature that both the Muslim Sufis, *i.e.,* Shah Musa Ashiqan and Shaikh Jamal Gojra were in Awadh during the early 16th century. (Abdur Rehman Chisti, *Mirat-ul-Israr*, Ms. No. 4539/69.72, Allamah Shibli Noamani Library, Maktaba Nadwatul-Ulama, Lucknow, India, pp. 258-59, 305-6), However, the demolition of the *Janmasthan* was Babur's own decision which was implemented by Mir Baqi (Baqi Tashkandi).

57. Muhammad Najmul Ghani Khan Rampuri, Tarikh-i-Awadh, Lucknow, 1919, Vol. V, pp. 200-01. While discussing the mosques in Ayodhya, the author

stresses the fact that Babur after having mitigated the *Janmasthan* temple located on the birth-place of Maharaja Sri Ramchandraji built a mosque over it using the ornamented *Kasauti* stones of the same temple in his mosque which was there till date (1919 A.D.).

58. Maulana Hakim Saiyad Abdul Haye (former Nazim, Nadawatul Ulama, Lucknow, d- 1923), *Al-Hind-u-Fial-Ahd al-Islam* (Arabic), Hyderabad, 1972. Translated into Urdu by Maulavi Shams Tabrez Khan (Member, Academy of Islamic Research and Publications, Nadawatul-Ulama, Lucknow, India) with an Introduction (*muqadama*) by Maulana Abdul Hasan Ali Nadawi (*i.e.*, Ali Main, son of the author of the book and is at present Nazim (Rector) of Nadawatul-Ulama, Lucknow) under the title *Hindustan Islami Ahd Mein*, Academy of Islamic Research and Publication, Lucknow, 1973, p. 141. (The book is also available at Allamah Shibli Nomani Library, Nadawatul-Ulama, Lucknow, vide No. 1631/41994, Preserved Section). The author confirms the fact that Baburi *Masjid*, Ayodhya, was built by Babur on the site claimed by the Hindus as the birth-place of Ram Chandraji. He further maintains that it was said and as was well known that (adjacently) over here that was Sita's temple where she used to live and cook food for her husband (Rama). The Baburi *Masjid* covered both these areas. Even though in the first sentence, the author is categorical about the construction of the mosque on the site of Rama's birth-place (*Janmasthan*), in the second sentence, he narrates a version based on popular belief that adjacent to the birth-place (*Janmasthan)*, there was Sita's temple where she used to live as well as cook for her husband. The assertion on the part of some scholars that the author, Abdul Haye, himself considered that the version of Babur's mosque having been built on Rama's birth-place (*Janmasthan*) on mere tradition (*i.e.*, "it is said") is wrong interpretation of the statement made by *the author*. It is were so, there would have been no attempt at an interpolation as stated further. It is not only Baburi *Masjid* at Ayodhya, the author also makes categorical statements for a few other mosques as well built during the Islamic Rule to the effect that the *Masjid* Quwwat ul-Islam at Delhi built in AH 587/A.D. 1191-92/AH 592/A.D. 1197 by Qutbu-d-din Aibak on the order of Shahabuddin Gauri (the first Turkish ruler of Delhi Sultanate), the Atala *Masjid* at Jaunpur built by Ibrahim Sharqi (1402-36) and the Jamai (*Masjid*), Attawa, also built by the Sharqi Sultans, the *Masjid* Alamgir, Benaras, at the sacred place of *Vaishnava* temple as well as the masjid at Mathura at the place of Gobind Dev temple built by Alamgir (the Mughal monarch Aurangzeb) were all constructed on the very sites of the Hindu temples after their demolition and in some cases, even with their ornamental material being re-used. (For details, Tr. Urdu, pp. 136, 139-140, 146). However, as a footnote to the afore-mentioned Urdu translated title, Ahmad Azmi on 11th November, 1986, added in his own handwriting and light blue ink that the author's (Abdue Haye) statement based on historical research was incorrect as it had been well confirmed by the research based writings of both Muslim and non-Muslim historians that the Baburi *Masjid* could not be established as a temple and nor was there any temple prior to the construction of the Baburi *Masjid*.

This footnote is not printed and is not a part of the book. This is rather an unauthorised interpolation and is not an integral part of the afore-mentioned translated version entitled *Hindustan Islami Ahd Mein*. As a matter of fact, an English version of this book was published in 1977. But for this paper, the Arabic and Urdu versions have been relied upon by the authors. However, based on English version, also see Arun Shourie, 'Hideway Communalism' vide *Hindu Temples, What Happened to Them: A Preliminary Survey,* New Delhi, 1990, pp. 1-11.

59. *Op. cit.* No. 56, p. 20 vide Nizamuddaulah's statement in 'Awadh Akhbar', dated A.D. 1876. Also reproduced in Maulavi Abdul Karim, "*Gumghasta Halat-i Ayodhya Awadh, Op. cit.* No. 56, pp. 20-22.

60. *Op. cit.,* No. 52.

60a. *Op. cit.,* No. 53

61. *Op.cit.,* No. 56.

61a. *Op. cit.,* No. 54.

62. *Op. cit.,* No. 57, Vol. I, Lucknow, 1919, pp. 10-12.

63. Judgement of Akhtar Ahsan Naqui, Civil Judge, Faizabad, dated 30.3.1946 in Regular suit No. 29 of 45, Shia Central Board of Waqf, U.P. Vs. Sunni Board of Waqf, U.P., pp. 7-10.

64. Zaki Kakorawi, *Op. cit.,* No. 53.

65. The passage is available in the 1979 Urdu edition, p. 40. Here the author comments that Babur built a mosque on the very birth-place building (temple) of Ram and Sita's kitchen situated on the western side of *Kot* Ramchandra after having demolished the latter. Thereafter an inscription was installed on the pulpit (*mambar*) when Babur ordered the construction of the mosque. The above description excepting the construction of the mosque on Babur's order was omitted in the 1981 edition.

66. Report of William Finch (1608-11) vide William Foster, ed: *Early Travels in India*, 1583-1619, London, 1921, p. 176.

67. Joseph Tieffenthaler's account was originally written in Latin. It was translated into German language under the title *Historich Geographische Bescherailhung Von Hindustan*. It was also translated into French by A. Anquetil Du Perron, M. Jaques Rennell and Mr. Jean Bernouli, under the title *Description Historique ET Geographique De L' I'nde*, Berlin, 1786, (*History and Geography of India*). It has a portion on *La Provinca D' Oude* (Province of Oudh) along with sketches of monuments vide pp. 250-260. Shri A.K. Chatterjee, I.A.S., has provided me with its English translation from the afore-mentioned French version of *History and Geography of India* for which I am extremely obliged to him.

68. G.N. Bahura and C. Singh, *Catalogue of Historical Documents in Kapad Dwara Jaipur No. 2 Maps and Plans*. His Highness' Secretariat, Jaipur, p. 36, Serial No. 179, also *Kapad Dwara Documents*, Private Collection Series, N.A.I., New Delhi. For details, B.R. Grover, 'An Analysis of the Revenue Documents Relating to *Janmasthan* (*Ram Janam Bhoomi*) Versus 'Baburi

Masjid' At *Kot* Ramchandra, Awadh (Ayodhya) in Historical Perspective' published in *Ayodhya, History, Archaeology and Tradition* (Papers presented in the Seminar held on Feb. 13-15, 1992), ed. Lallanji Gopal, Varanasi, 1994, pp. 338-354. (Henceforth B.R. Grover, 'An Analysis of Revenue Documents Relating to *Janmasthan...*)

The map shows rectangular plan of the complex, with the structure of the main *Janmasthan* '*masjid*' on the western corner of the fort (*i.e., Kot* Ramchandra) along with crenellad rampart (*parkota*) while towards the east of the main structure, with some gap is an open courtyard on the side of which is a *Chabutra* (raised platform) marked '*Janmasthan*'. Figures representing the visiting pilgrims are shown circumambulating and worshipping the *Janmasthan Chabutra*. Tieffenthaler's description along with sketches practically tallies with the same.

Also, R. Nath, *Op. cit.* 21; *Architecture and site of the Baburi Masjid of Ayodhya (A Historical Critique),* 1991, Jaipur, Rajasthan, *Ibid.,* 'Ram-*Janmasthan* of Ayodhya in 1717 A.D., A Reaffirmation', 1991; Sawai Jai Singh had acquired Ram *Janmasthan* in 1717 A.D.; Business and Political Observer, 6-7, 1993.

The viewpoint held by R.S. Sharma and Others, *Op. cit.,* No. 17, p. 28 and statement in The Hindustan Times, 14th May, 1991 that Tieffenthaler's description making the initial phase of creation of a tradition for treating the 'mosque' and its surroundings with Rama's crib as sacred and that hitherto there was no tradition of a temple having existed in Rama's "fortress" or "palace" is completely hypothetical and betrays complete ignorance of the other indigenous sources from the afore-mentioned *Kapad-Dwara Collection of Records*, Jaipur (Rajasthan). Moreover, as clearly stated vide *Op. cit.*, Nos. 43-44, pp. 21-23, their whole argument about the unauthentic character of the text of *Sahifa-i-Chihil Nasaih* (early 18th century) is erroneous which, otherwise, as explained earlier specifically mentions the existence of a temple (*Sita Ki Rasoi*) over here.

69. India Office Library and Records, London, Francis Hamilton Buchanan's unpublished Manuscript, Mss. EUR. E 73 relating to Ayodhya (1813-14). I am extremely obliged to the authorities of the India Office Library, London, for having supplied me the Photocopy of the same in 1992 through Shri K.V. Ruparelia, Gen. Secy., V.H.P.—U.K.

70. *Ibid.* This inscription also seems to have been installed on the 'Baburi *Masjid*' during Aurangzeb's period or later which was recorded by Buchanan (1814). However, either having been found of doubtful validity, it was removed during the course of the 19th century, or smashed in the 1855 communal riots in Ayodhya as it is not traceable in any of the accounts of the British regime in Awadh (from 1856 onwards) and was not recorded by E. A. Fuhrer (1891) either. (vide Reference No. 76).

All the same, the fact that Buchanan got this inscription translated into English and reproduced it in his own handwritting without any comments on it shows that he, at least, did accept the viewpoint of the destruction of the

Hindu temple on Rama's birth-place and construction of a mosque thereupon by Mir Baqi on Babur's orders. However, as already discussed vide Op. cit. No. 23, this inscription has been completely misconstrued and distorted by Mrs. Surinder Kaur and Sher Singh in an amateurish manner.

71. Montgomery Martin, *History, Antiqiuities, Topography and Statistics of Eastern India,* Vol. II, p. 335-36.

72. R.S. Sharma and Others, *Op. cit.,* No. 17, pp. 20-21.

73. Edward Thorton, *Gazetteer of the Territories under the Government of the East India Company,* 1854, pp. 739-40.

74. Old Oudh Records, Office of the Board of Revenue, United Provinces, for the years 1858-90, Oudh General, Faizabad District, Foreign Dept. General, File No. 529; From C. U. Aitehison Esqr., Under Secretary to the Government of India with the Gov. Gen. to the Chief Commissioner of Oudh, No. 582, Simla, 15th August, 1863, and No. 2482, dated 25.8.63 to Commissioner, Faizabad.

75. District Record Office, Faizabad, (Judicial Branch), Judgement of F.E.A. Chamier in Civil Appeal No. 27 of 1885, dated 28th March, 1886.

76. E. A. Fuhrer, *The Monumental Antiqiuities and Inscriptions in the North-Western Province and Oudh,* Archaeological Survey of India, Allahabad, 1891, pp. 295-97.

76a. *Ibid.*, p. 297.

77. P. Carnegy, *Historical Sketch of Tehsil, Zilla Fyzabad, with old Capitals Ajudhia* and Fyzabad, Lucknow, 1870, pp. 5-7. 19-21.

77a. *Murraqa-i-Khusrawi* alias *Tarikh-i-Awadh* (1869), Ms. *Op. cit.* No. 53. fol. No. 235a; Saiyed Kamaluddin, *Swanehat-i-Salateen-i-Awadh*, Its Vol. II also entitled *Kaiser-ut-Tawarikh* (1896), *Op. cit.* No. 54, p. 112; 1907 Edition, pp. 118-19.

77b. District Record Office, Faizabad, U.P., Appeal of Mohd. Asghar in Mic. Appeal No. 56 decided on 13.12.1877 by the Commissioner Faizabad Division in re Mohd. Asghar Vs Khem Das.

78. A.F. Millet, *The Report of Settlement of the Land Revenue, Faizabad District*, Allahabad, 1880, paragraphs No. 618-19, 666-69.

79. H.R. Neville, *Barabanki District Gazetteer*, Lucknow, 1902, pp. 168-169.

80. H.R. Neville, Fyzabad, A Gazetteer, Vol. XLIII of the *District Gazetteers of the United Provinces of Agra and Oudh*, Allahabad, 1905, pp. 153, 173-79.

80a. *Ibid.*

81. B.N. tr., Ms. Beveridge, *Op. cit.* No. 26, p. 656.

82. *Ibid.* Appendix U-The Inscriptions of Babur's *Mosque* in Ayodhya (Oudh), pp. IXXVII-IXXIX.

83. Hans Bakker, *Op. cit.,* No. 14, and 18, Pt. I, pp. 44, 54, 125, 129-30; Pt. II, pp. 143-46.

83a. Koenraad Elst, (i) Ram Janmabhoomi Vs Baburi *Masjid*, A Case Study in Hindu Muslim Conflict, New Delhi, 1990 (Title No. 1) and (ii) Ayodhya and After, Issues Before Hindu Society, New Delhi, 1991 (Title No. 2) (iii) '*Ramjanmabhoomi* Vs Baburi *Masjid*: Some Political observations' RJB-BM, ed. Mishra and Singh, pp. 36-72. In Title No. I, pp. 3-90, Koenraad Elst covered the anti- *Janmasthan* views of the Jawahar Lal Nehru University twenty five historians (*i.e.,* S. Gopal, Romila Thapar, Bipan Chandra, Harbans Mukhia, K.S. Chaudhry and others) published in a six-page booklet—(see Reference No. 27), the versions of Surinder Kaur and Sher Singh (see Reference No. 23), Syed Shahabuddin, Abdur Rahman, R.S. Sharma, Gyanendra Pandey and Mohammad Abdul Rahim Qurashi versus the pro–*Janmasthan* temple scholars viz Harsh Narain, B.B. Lal, S.P. Gupta, Arun Shourie, A.K. Chatterjee and A.R. Khan who were involved in the cross-fire debate in the Indian Express, a daily newspaper. Also Koenraad Elst, Title No. 2, pp. 1-19. However, as explained in the text, Koenraad Elst's reliance on Harsh Narain that the earlier structure standing on the present misnomered *Janmasthan* was not demolished in Babur's reign is highly misplaced.

84. For details, B.R. Grover, 'An Analysis of the Revenue Documents Relating to *Janmasthan...*', *Op. cit.* No. 68, pp. 343-347.

85. District Record Office, Faizabad, Faizabad (U.P.), *Basta* No. 132 of 1861; *Khasra Abadi*, 1861; *Bandobast* 1301 *Fasli*/A.D. 1893; *Bandobast* 1344/45 *Fasli*/A.D. 1936-37 (all in Urdu).

86. *Ibid.*, Also, B.R. Grover, '*Waqf* Not Attached To Baburi *Masjid*', The Statesman, New Delhi, 15th November, 1992.

87. *Hadbast-Map* (Boundary Demarcation Map) of the village *Kot* Ramchandra, *Pargana Haveli*, *Awadh,* Tehsil and District Faizabad, incorporated in the Settlement Report (1861) vide Basta No. 132 of 1861.

88. *Abadi* Map (Map of Settled Population) of village *Ramkot*, *Pargana Haveli, Awadh,* included in the 1861 Settlement Report vide *Basta* No. 132 of 1861. Also, the field map (*Khasra Kishtwar Map*) of 1936-37 Settlement which clearly mentioned the disputed structure as *Janmabhum*. This confirms the fact that till 1937-38 A.D., in the Revenue documents, the structure and its premises (comprising both the inner and outer courtyards) was named as *Janmabhum* (*i.e., Janmasthan*) and not as 'Baburi *Masjid*'.

13

Judgements of The Lucknow Bench of Allahabad High Court on the Ayodhya Issue with Special Reference to *Rama Janamabhoomi* versus 'Baburi *Masjid*' during the 19th and 20th centuries

The judicial records of the 19th and 20th centuries bear our the fact that the disputed structure named '*Ramjanmabhoomi*-Baburi *Masjid*' at Ayodhya was constructed in the reign of the first Mughal king, Babur (in 1528 A.D.) on the very site of the Hindu holy shrine– the birth-place (*Janmasthan*) of Shri Ram Chandra after the demolition of the latter. They equally emphasise that there was continual tussle regarding the legal title as well as the possession of the site of the disputed structure not only between the Hindu *Mahants* and the Muslims but also between the *Shia* and *Sunni* Muslims communities.

The earliest reference to the judicial proceedings, traceable so far, was made during the pre-British *Nawabi* regime in 1822 A.D. by Hafizullah, the *darogha* of the Faizabad Court, who in his Note submitted to the Royal Court categorically stated that the 'mosque' constructed by Babur was situated at the birth-place of Ram, son of Raja Dashrath, popularly known as the '*Sita Rasoi*'.

It is also borne out by the contemporary British Reports that when the Hindu-Muslim riots took place in 1855 A.D. over the supposed demolition of a 'mosque' at the premises of the Hanuman Gharhi, the possession of the 'mosque-temple' structure in the *Janmasthan* premises lay with the Hindus. But during the 1855 riots at Ayodhya, the Muslims took forcible occupation of this structure claimed as 'mosque' situated at *Janmasthan* (*masjid waqia janamsthan*). They were ultimately evicted by the Hindus through bloody conflict and in 1856 A.D. when the British annexed Awadh, the possession of the premises lay with the Hindu *Bairaghis* and *Mahants*. However, the British Government in order to prevent disputes put up a railing in the Courtyard dividing the 'mosque' structure from the outer courtyard whereupon the Hindus who had been worshipping here for centuries raised a platform (*Chabutra*) for prayers and making their offerings. In 1873 A.D., in order to give a separate entrance on fair days to *Janmasthan,* the District administration opened a doorway in the wall which in front was divided from the *'Janmasthan Masjid'* by a railing. An appeal against this decision was made by Mohammad Asghar but the Commissioner of Faizabad Division, vide his Order dated 13.12.1877, rejected the appeal in case of Misc. Appeal No. 56 in re. Mohd. Asghar Vs. Khem Das.

The next judicial landmark is the Suit No. 61/280 of 1885 of *'Asthan, Janmasthan'* V/s. The Secretary of State for India and Mohamad Asghar. The report of the *Amin* Commision, dated 6.12.1885 filed in the afore-mentioned suit, is of immense significance which shows that *Sita Rasoi, Chabutra, Janmasthan* and the *Chhapar* (enclosurement) of the disciple (*Chela*) of the *Mahant* are all situated within the boundary wall of the site where the so-called *masjid* stood. Above all, beyond the boundary wall and just adjacent to it is the deep depression path-way on all the four sides (*parikarma*) of the pilgrims (*Khai Parikarma Har Chahar Taraf*) as of old. The fact is that the entire site enclosed by the *parikarma* is the *Janmasthan* of Lord Rama which was embellished by the construction of the so-called *mosque* by the Muslim invaders not only to destroy the holy place of pilgrimage of *yore* of the Hindus but to humiliate them. Even though the sub-judge Faizabad Pandit Harkrishan, in order to avoid communal tension did not permit the Hindu *'Mahant'* to build a temple in 'the *Chabutra*'. He commented, "the place where Hindus worship is in their possession, can not be questioned." In further appeal against the judgement, Mr. F.E.A. Chamirs, the District Judge, Faizabad, did not accept the appeal but in his judgement made important reflections on the historicity of the vital issue of the construction of the '*mosque*' on the Hindu place of worship and commented....... "It is most unfortunate that a *masjid* should have been built on land specially held sacred by the Hindus."

Later on, there was *Shia-Sunni* tussle over the nature of the *waqf,* that was supposed to have been granted in favour of 'Baburi *Masjid*' and the latter having been gazetted as a *Sunni mosque.* In the Regular suit No. 29 of 1945 between *Shia* Central Board of *Waqf* Vs. *Sunni* Board of *Waqf,* U.P., Lucknow, even though Mr. Akhtar Ashan Naqvi, Civil Judge, Faizabad, gave judgement in favour of *Sunni Waqf* Board, having examined the historical issue, he reaffirmed the fact that Babur during his one week's sojourn at Ayodhya (1528), "destroyed the *Janmasthan* Temple and on its site built a mosque using largely the material of the old structure." However, later on Shri P.S. Shukla, Civil Judge, Faizabad, in his judgement on 21.4.1966, set aside the earlier judgement of 1945 on the ground that "No valid notification under Section (5)1 of U.P. Muslim *Waqf* Act (XIII of 1936) was ever made so far relating to specific disputed property" and the Gazette's notification of that suit was not valid notification and of 'no avail to them." Lastly, the Hon'ble Supreme Court of India, in the case of Gulam Abbas Vs. State of U.P. in 1981 A.D., declared that the claim of the Central *Sunni Waqf* Board that the 'Baburi *Mosque*' had been notified on 16.2.1994 as *Sunni* was of doubtful validity and prohibitive value."

The installation of the idol of Bhagwan Shri Rama Lala under the central dome of the disputed structure on 23.12.1949 by Hindu *Mahants* who claimed it to be Shri *Ramjanmabhoomi* led the *Sunni Waqf* Board in 1961 to file a suit in the court of the Civil Judge, Faizabad, *viz., Sunni* Central Board of *Waqfs* U.P. and others Vs. Gopal Singh *Visharad* and others. In the meantime, temporary injunctions were issued in the suit No. (2) of 1950 by the Court of the Civil Judge, Faizabad, restraining the removal of the idols from the building and any interference into *puja* by the Hindus. As other suits had also been filed, in respect of *Ramjanmabhoomi,* on 18.12.1961, the four suits were consolidated and suit No. 12 of 1961 was made the leading suit. On 1.2.1986, the District Judge, Faizabad, in Misc. Civil Appeal No. 8 of 1986 issued order for opening the locks on the gates of the enclosures of the disputed structure and removed all hurdles in the performance of *puja* and *darshan* on the part of the pilgrims. Later on, the Allahabad High Court while allowing the two applications, case No. 29 of 1987 and case No. 11 of 1989, withdrew all the five suits from the District Judge's court for original trial by the full Bench of the High Court. Later when after the demolition of the disputed structure at Ayodhya on 6.12.1992, the Government of India made a Reference under Article 143 (1) to the Hon'ble Supreme Court of India as to whether a Hindu temple or any religious structure existed prior to the construction of the *Ramjanmabhoomi*-Baburi *Masjid* in the area on which the structure stood, all the suits before the Allahabad High Court abated. But after the Supreme Court declined to answer the Reference vide its judgement on 24.10.1994, they were again referred to the Lucknow Bench of the Allahabad High Court. Issues have been framed afresh and the suits are being tried by a special Bench of the Allahabad High Court at Lucknow.

Apart from the above suits, the discovery of the archaeological artefacts and the 12th century Sanskrit Inscription from the debris of the demolished structure confirming the existence of the Hindu *Vaishnava* Temple at the disputed site before its demolition in 1528 A.D. has added another significant dimension to the judicial suits pending before the Lucknow Bench of the Allahabad High Court. The orders of the Allahabad High Court, dated 1st Jan. 1993 and that of the Supreme Court dated 21.9.93 regarding the safety and preservation of the archeological remains discovered at site on 6.12.1992, are already on record for implementation. At the same time, the issue of getting the afore-mentioned Sanskrit Inscription is under adjudication as per law.

14

Note on Omissions in The Government of India's White Paper on Ayodhya, dated February 1993

In October, 1992, I submitted the documents relating to *Ramjanmabhoomii*-'Baburi *Masjid*' issue but these have not been listed in the White Paper on page 19 (Resumption of Negotiations) in any of the paras 4.8 to 4.13; pp. 3-4, paras, 1.11 to 1.16 wherein the Documents submitted by *V.H.P.* have been described. The unlisted documents are as follows :—

(i) "Prince Aurangzeb's Conversion of a Jain Temple at Ahmedabad into a *mosque* and its reconversion as temple by Shahjahan , the Mughal Emperor, in the years 1645-1648 A.D.; 6 pages along with 4 Appendices comprising a copy of the original *Farman* of Shahjahan (in Persian) dated 3rd July, 1648 and its translation into English and other related sources listed on page 5 of the Paper submitted to the Ministry of Home Affairs on 12th October, 1992.

(ii) A note on "No *Waqf* Associated with the 'Baburi *Masjid*'" comprising 21 pages alongwith 6 Annexures relating to the Revenue Documents and the judgement of the Hon'ble Supreme Court dated 1981 regarding the issue of the registration of the 'Baburi *Mosque*'/ *Waqf,* submitted to the Ministry of Home Affairs on 20th October, 1992.

(iii) A Note on the Proposed Memorandum of Understanding between the All India *Shia* conference and *Vishwa Hindu Parishad*/Shri *Ramjanmabhoomi Nyas*, dated January, 1989 regarding the transfer of the building known as Shri *Ramjanmabhoomi*/Baburi *Masjid*, Ayodhya, in accordance with the Jafri Sect', 6 pages along with an Appendix comprising a copy of the proposed Memorandum of Understanding, 3 pages, submitted to the Ministry of Home Affairs on 21st October, 1992.

In this regard, I may further state that the Document No.1 relating to the conversion of the Jain Temple at Ahmedabad by Prince Aurangzeb, the Provincial Governor and its re-conversion as the erstwhile temple on the orders of Shahjahan, the Mughal Emperor, was written in September, 1992 as the Government of India at that time was anxious to have an instance from medieval Indian history where such re-conversion of a mosque unto an erstwhile temple had taken place. It was around mid—September, 1992 that I, in my personal capacity as historian, was approached by the Ministry of Home Affairs, on behalf of the Hon'ble Prime Minister, to suggest source-material in this regard. Though having gathered some references from the National Archives of India, New Delhi, I did supply some material, thereafter, I made a trip to Ahmedabad and collected the relevant original documents on the subject. It was on the basis of these documents that I prepared a regular Note along with Annexures, which later on I submitted during the course of the *V.H.P.*/A.I.B.M.A.C. dialogue in October, 1992. This rebuts the theory that 'once a *mosque* is always a *mosque*'. It is a pity that such a significant document could not find place in the list of Documents of the White Paper.

As regards No.(ii) (No *Waqf* Associated with 'Baburi *Masjid*'), I may state that this was initially submitted to the Ministry of Home Affairs on 10.1.1991 during the course of mutual dialogue between *V.H.P.* and A.I.B.M.A.C. Later on, when at the time of resumption of the mutual negotiations on 16th October, 1992, the Special Cell on Ayodhya, Prime Minister's Office, distributed the documents of *V.H.P.*/A.I.B.M.A.C. of the earlier phase in December, 1990-January, 1991, except for a stray paper of an Annexure of my above mentioned Paper, I did not find either the text or the Annexures attached to Paper in the material circulated to us. I immediately pointed out this lapse during the course of the meeting. However, I was asked by the Chairman to resubmit the paper, which I did on 20th October, 1992. Notwithstanding the importance of the Paper with great bearing on the Waqf issue, it has not been listed in the White Paper.

The third Paper was on the proposed Memorandum of Understanding (January, 1989) drafted after tripartite negotiations between the Government of India (under late Shri Rajiv Gandhi), the *V.H.P.*/Shri *Ramjanmabhoomi Nyas* and the All India *Shia* Conference, which claimed to be the real 'inheritors' of the structure of the '*Shia* Baburi *Masjid'* and agreed to its shifting to another place in Village Sahanava (where Mir Baqi's *Mazar* is situated) after having obtained a regular *Fatwa* from the head of the Jafari sect of the *Shias*. This brings out the genuine efforts on the part of the Government and the concerned parties for an amicable solution of the disputed issue. But that was not to be due to an external pressure exerted by the A.I.B.M.A.C./A.I.B.M.M.C. and some other bodies of the *Sunni* community. The blackout of such a significant event, which forms a part of the proceedings of the Ministry of Home Affairs itself, from the White Paper is inexplicable

II. (a) A White Paper by the Government is supposed to deal with the subject in a dispassionate manner, not only with regard to the role and policy of the present Government but even the previous Governments, regardless of the party in power. On the Ayodhya issue, it was during the regime of late Shri Rajiv Gandhi that apart from the Government's negotiations with different contending parties, as explained in detail in the above mentioned Paper (iii), a regular Memorandum of Understanding between the *V.H.P.*/Shri *Ramjanmabhoomi Nyas* and the *Shia* Muslims was proposed in January, 1989 but this fizzled out due to opposition on the part of the A.I.B.M.A.C./A.I.B.M.M.C.

(b) The next phase started with the former Prime Minister, Shri Chandra Shekhar, who involved the *V.H.P.* and the A.I.B.M.A.C. in mutual negotiations for peaceful settlement of the issue. Though the White Paper. (vide Chapter I, p.1, para 1.4) does refer to this aspect having been started in December, 1990, it offers only a summary assessment of the Government's dialogue with the contending parties though in fact, the negotiations were initiated in November, 1990. It was on 20th November, 1990 that the Hon'ble Prime Minister, Shri Chandra Shekhar invited the *V.H.P.* and the A.I.B.M.A.C. separately in the forenoon and afternoon respectively for discussion on the subject. As I was also officially invited as expert-historian on behalf of *V.H.P.*, I personally handed over a detailed Paper entitled "*Janmasthan* (*Ramjanmabhoomi*) Versus 'Baburi *Masjid*'" to Shri Chandra Shekhar, who was kind enough to go through it on the spot and put it on record with his office/Ministry of Home Affairs. Surprisingly, I find that this paper too has not been listed in the White Paper.

(c) It was only after the meeting on 20th November, 1990 that the Government initiated the policy of mutual dialogue and exchange of historical documents by *V.H.P.* and the A.I.B.M.A.C. In a joint meeting of the *V.H.P.* and A.I.B.M.A.C. held on 10th January, 1991, under the Chairmanship of the then Minister of State for Home Affairs, Shri Subodh Kant Sahay, I was again invited as expert-historian to represent the case of *V.H.P.* I made nearly one hour's Presentation which is on record with the Ministry of Home Affairs. This aspect is well confirmed by the fact that a summary of my Presentation has been produced from the official minutes of the meeting by the 'BJP's White Paper on Ayodhya,' The Ram Temple Movement', Bharatiya Janta Party, April, 1993, pp. 64-65, para 6.5. In fact, this should have been listed in the Government's White paper which is completely silent in this regard. It was during the course of this meeting, on the basis of my Presentation as well as the Historical Documents already submitted by me to the Hon'ble Prime Minister on 20th November, 1990, referred to above, that my suggestion for dividing the source—material into four broad categories, *i.e.,* Historical, Revenue, Legal (Judicial) and Archaeological Evidence was officially accepted for the examination of the records.

(d) During the course of the meeting on 10.1.1990, apart from my unlisted Paper, I also submitted a Note along with an English translation of the Persian text of the 25th Counsel (*nasihat*) embodied in *Sahifa-i-chihal Nassaih Bahadur Shahi* written by the grand daughter of the Mughal Emperor, Aurangzeb, in the late 17th/early 18th century. Since this Note, along with English version of the text, did not form a part of the *V.H.P.*'s documents circulated on 16th October, 1992, I pointed out this lacuna and was asked to resubmit the same. Consequently, I personally handed over its copy to Shri Vinod Dhall, Joint Secretary, Ministry of Home Affairs, in his office in October, 1992. But unfortunately, even this Paper has not been mentioned in the White Paper vide the Documents submitted by

V.H.P., in October, 1992. In fact, this is a separate Note with English translation of the full Persian text than the earlier document, a mere excerpt, which, of course has been listed in the *V.H.P.*'s documents submitted in December, 1990 in the White Paper.

(e) The White Paper has listed not only the Documents submitted by the A.I.B.M.A.C. but has even recorded the correspondence and the request made by the latter for the procurement of more documents by the Government of India for it (vide p. 54 Nos. F, F.15, G, G. 1 to G. 3). However, contrary to this, the request/correspondence made on behalf of the *V.H.P.* for the acquisition of copies of Documents/Maps/ Books etc. find no mention in the White Paper. This is an invidious discrimination made in this regard.

In January 1991, I approached the Ministry of Home Affairs to procure copies of the Revenue Documents from the District/Tehsil/ Nazul Office, Faizabad (U.P.), as well as books from the Islamic Libraries / Centres, which otherwise have been mostly suppressed or withdrawn by the latter in the past few years, so that these could be put up before the Joint *V.H.P.*/A.I.B.M.A.C. meetings to be held on 24-25, January and 5th February, 1991. A copy of the letter dated 16th January, 1991 was delivered personally to the Joint Secretary (O.S.D.), Ministry of Home Affairs, along with the list of the Documents and Books requested for procurement. Little later, I further wrote to the letter on 21st January, 1991 for procuring a copy of the so-called Babur's Last Testament (so called *Wasiyat Nama Mukhfi* of Zahiruddin Muhammad Babur Badshah) available at the National Archives of India, New Delhi, so that it could be perused by the members of the Joint Committee meeting to be held on 24th-25th January, 1991. However, none of these letters/appended Documents requested for procurement on behalf of *V.H.P.* have been listed in the White Paper whereas in a parallel case to this, the A.I.B.M.A.C. demand has been duly listed. What an impartial way of recording? I had, of course, to manage to procure the required Documents/Books through my own resources to prepare the material for the subject in hand.

B.R. Grover

Chapter 15

Final Report of Profesoor B.R. Grover on the Materials Dug Out while levelling the ground by the Government

During the course of digging and levelling operation in the eastern and southern sides of the Ramjanambhoomi/'Babri Masjid' barbed-wire structure, a big hoard of about a dozen and a half of fragmentary pieces of sculpture and architectured structures were found on 18.6.92 (Photographs enclosed). As these findings at the Ramjanambhoomi/'Babri Masjid' complex were of great national importance in the context of the ongoing controversy, the Historians Forum, New Delhi, appointed an expert committee of archaeologists and historians to examine their nature and linkage with the erstwhile ancient Ramjanambhoomi temple and structure. Led by Professor B.B. Grover (Former Director, Indian Council of Historical Research, New Delhi), the committee comprised Dr. Y.D. Sharma, Dr. K.M. Srivastava, Dr. S. P. Gupta (archaeologists), Professor Devendra Swarup Agrawal, Dr. Sardindu Mukerji (University of Delhi), Professor K.P. Nautiyal (Vice-Chancellor, Avadh University, Faizabad) and Dr. Sudha Malaya (Bhopal).

After an analytical examination, the committee found that these beautifully carved buff sand-stone sculptural and architectural pieces belonging to the 11th-12th centuries AD, comprise *amalaks*, pieces of door-jambs, carving curved *Gandi* (facade) of *Shikhara*, pieces of mouldings and capitals of pillar in semi-lotus petals. A detailed examination made it patently clear that these pieces belong to a Hindu stone temple of the 11th-12th century A.D. Of the noticeable carving techniques, these are of regular relief type of ancient and early medieval Hindu art as well as the sinking of unwanted surface introduced during the 11th-12th centuries A.D. having been influenced by the early Islamic architectural decoration - examples of which can be seen later on in the Qutab Complex (early 13th century AD) at Delhi. Above all, the buff sandstone pieces found here are similar to those used in the wall of the present Ramjanambhoomi/'Babri Masjid' structure. The committee also found that of the section of the dug up area by the side of the barricaded barbed-wire towards the east and south, the section facing the south is closest to the area, earlier excavated by Professor B.B. Lal from where a series of pillar bases were found.

The members of the committee left for Delhi on 3.7.92 leaving behind Professor Grover, who had even earlier studied the complex in 1990-91 A.D. long before the present digging operation, to keep an eye on any further significant finding relating to the Ramjanambhoomi/'Babri Masjid' structure and also to see that such findings were extracted carefully, without any damage. During the digging operation, the above mentioned sculptural and architectural pieces, typical of the Nagara style prevalent in North India during the 10th-12th centuries A.D., had been found as debris in the pit of the dug up area of a wall in the east-south of the Ramjanambhoomi/ 'Babri Masjid'. Moreover, a long single piece beam decorated with one fully opened flower in the centre and two half-open lotus flowers at the two ends, typical of the 11th-12th century A.D., apparently fixed as a part of the entrance gate to the *janmasthan* (Ramjanambhoomi) structure, were also traced. Considering that these fragments belonged to the demolished Hindu temple, and that the entrance gate of the temple should be on the ground around this area, Professor Grover thought that the ground on which the gate stood must be pacca. So on 6.7.92, when the tractor was plying for further unearthing and leveling purpose, he walked around this area and felt that there was hard ground underneath. At about eleven feet below the main level of the eastern wall, in order to avoid any damage to the hard ground, further digging through tractor was stopped and Professor Grover, with a shovel in hand, personally dug up the rest of the earth about one foot and found that about 12' below the main wall, there was a regular layer of burnt-bricks. After further digging in a similar fashion at various other places on the eastern and southern sides of the barbed-wire walls of Ramjanambhoomi/'Babri Masjid' structrure, it was found that there was a regular layout of the floor of burnt-bricks (vide F at the sketch map) belonging to the early medieval times.

As a matter of fact, as per Reports of the Archaeological Survey of India, the burnt-bricks found in the Ganga Valley could be traced to 4th-5th century B.C. The excavations conducted at Kosambi, Hastanpur, Sringaverapor, Hulas pertain to the Sunga (2nd-1st centuries B.C), Kusanas (late 1st-3rd centuries A.D.) and the Gupta (4th-6th centuries A.D.) periods. The big bricks, in particular, belong to the Kusana sites. As such, ever since ancient times, the tradition of manufacture of bricks continued uninterrupted in the Ganga Valley all through the Maurya (4th-3rd centuries B.C.), Sunga, Kusana, the Gupta periods and early medieval times. The use of big burnt bricks remained common only up to the advent of the Turkish rule (i.e. late 12th - early 13th centuries A.D.) i.e. the 'Muslim period' and not thereafter. Henceforth, mostly the *Lakhauri* burnt-bricks were used, more so, during the Mughal age and the Nawabi rule in Awadh. The burnt-bricks used in the flooring of the recently discovered *Janamasthan* complex pertain to the period not later than early medieval period i.e. 11th-12th centuries A.D. and are in conformity with the ancient Indian tradition.

This floor of bricks to the east and southern side of the walls of the standing Ramjanambhoomi/'Babri Masjid' structure runs into hundreds of square yards and covers the area even around the present site of *shilanyas* and beyond, both on the eastern and southern sides. All this courtyard made of burnt-bricks was part and parcel of the stone built Hindu temple demolished by Mir Baqi, the Avad commander/administrator of the first Mughal Emperor, Zahiruddin Mohammad Babur in 1528 A.D. The use of the floor bricks of the earlier time at the time of construction of the temple and the floor in the 11th-12th centuries A.D. also indicates that the temple seems to have been reconstructed and improvised from time to time by the Hindu rulers and as per adopted practice, the previous bricks were equally used for the purpose of the construction of the floor.

A further digging and survey of the complex was made on 7th-9th July, 1992. It was found that the above mentioned bricked layout and the flooring of the courtyard does not form a flat ground. It is of uneven nature, with slightly higher level in the north, a little lower in the east, rising higher again towards the side of *Sita Koop* i.e. with higher level in the east, rising higher again towards the side of *Sita Koop* i.e. with higher level in the south, thereafter running as flat ground for a considerable portion towards the recently constructed enclosed wall (*Ram Deewar*) in the south and finally with lower downward trend in the west. The unevenness may be due to heavy weight of earth dumped thereupon and the depressions in the flooring may have teen caused at some places in the course of over four and a half centuries since early 16th century (1528 AD) when the Hindu temple was demolished or due to seepage of rain-water through the earth down to the single brick-flooring of the courtyard. On the other hand, if this uneven level is structurally the same as constructed *abnitio*, it may be ascribed to an uneven nature of the ground situated at higher level of Kot Ram Chandra. However, a possibility of still an underground layer of earlier burnt-brick-flooring/structure cannot be ruled out, which, of course, could be ascertained only by further regular digging and excavation at certain chosen places by archaeologists of the Archeological Department of the Uttar Pradesh State or Archaeological Survey of India or any other independent organization.

On the 13th-15th July, 1992, after a proper survey, a tentative measurement of the brick-floored area around the Ramjanambhoomi/'Babri Masjid' structure was done and photographs of the same at different specimen places in varying directions were taken. For the sake of convenience, the briok-floored area may be divided in three portions i.e. (i) the plot between the eastern wall of the main structure of Ramjanambhoomi/'Babri Masjid' and the opposite *Ram Deewar* from the north to the south till the point facing the eastern wall when the latter takes turn to the south of the structure; (ii) plot of land from this point towards the mid-gate of *Ram Deewar* on the Manas Bhawan side to the south covering the brick-flooring area as well as the southern side of the main structure outside the baricaded wired and bamboo pillars till the *Ram Deewar* on the south-west side; (iii) and lastly the western side of the standing Ramjanambhoomi/'Babri Masjid' structure outside barbed-wire barricades which is in a triangular shape. The area of the land within the barbed-wire barricade at the back/West of the structure has not been measured as it is not permissible to enter this portion of the premises. Even though the measurement has been done separately in respect of each of the above plots, the total brick-flooring area of the entire complex around the main structure of Ramjanambhoomi/'Babri Masjid' comes to approximately 16,296 sq. metres. It practically comprises most of the area of 2.77 acres acquired by the Uttar Pradesh State and enclosed by the *Ram Deewar*.

All this can be further compared and ascertained from the areas recorded in the relevant *khasra kishtwar* plot of the revenue documents. Significantly, the brick-floored area as well as the measured land under the main structures, covers the total area of Ramjanambhoomi/*Janmasthan* complex records since the 1st Regular Settlement (1861 AD) of Kot Ram Chandra, comprising 5 bighas and 4 biswas. As per Settlement Report and map of 1936-37 A.D., with revised *khasra* numbers and necessary reshufflings and clubbings with the neighbouring plots since the previous Settlement operations of 1861 and 1893 A.D., and which is still operative and adopted in the revenue records of rights prepared in 1990-91 A.D., the Ramjanambhoomi/'Babri Masjid' complex, where at present the digging is going on, falls under the *khasra kishtwar* plot Nos. 159 and 160 and parts (*minjumla*) of *khasra* plot Nos. 161-163, 170-172 enclosed by the recently constructed *Ram Deewar*. The proper Ramjanambhoomi/'Babri Masjid' structure with barbedwire-enclosure falls under *khasra* plots No. 159 and 160, the main portion being in plot No. 159. The *shilanyas* site, also forming a part of large sized *khasra* plot No. 160 with an area of 5 *bighas* and 13 *biswas*, being in Nazul as well as the ownership of three other underproprietors, is not attached to any waqf. As the road (*Khasra* No. 158) dividing the proper *Janmasthan* (Ramjanambhoomi)/'Baburi Masjid' area was constructed during the late 19th century under the British Raj, the present so-called *Janmasthan*/misnomered *Sita Rasoi* falls under *Khasra* plot Nos. 146 and 147. Earlier in the ancient and early medieval ages, the entire complex comprising the present Ramjanambhoomi (*Janmasthan*)/'Babri Masjid'area as well as the present so-called *Janmasthan*/*Sita Rasoi* built during the 18th - 19th centuries, was one complex and was named as *Janmasthan*.

This is well borne out by the First Regular Settlement Report (1861) and the appended map. Burnt-brick flooring has been traced both in the western sectors of the present Ramjanambhoomi/'Babri Masjid' as well as in the present *Janmasthan* and the east of *Janmasthan's Sita Rasoi*. Though the measurement of the brick-flooring, as mentioned above has been done only for the complex of Ramjanambhoomi, the conducted survey shows that during the ancient/early medieval ages, the brick-flooring covered the entire present Ramjanambhoomi/*Janmasthan* complex.

In the annals of Indian history and culture, there have been a few landmarks which speak of the cultural glory of the ancient and early medieval ages. After Mohenjodaro/Harappa/Lothal/Ropar, Dvaraka (under Sea) excavations, both during the colonial and Free India's periods, the latest discovery of the vast burnt-brick flooring of the courtyard forming an integral part of Ramjanambhoomi/ *Janmasthan* temple complex of ancient and early medieval ages constitutes a further landmark of multi-dimensional significance.

On the 11th-13th July, 1992, earth from the walls to the east and south of Ramjanambhoomi/'Babri Masjid' was got removed. Most significantly, it was found that both the walls are laid with burnt-bricks at various portions, especially in the mid-lower half, and at the bottom strata (where burnt-brick flooring is traceable) with height of 12' each. The top of the eastern wall is laid with two hard rammed floors of *chunam* and *kankar*, one above the other, with an apparent conspicious break between, but over and above the layers of the brick-wall. The southern wall is in a more ruinous condition with large pit from where the recent sculptural and architectural fragements have been discovered. All the same, this wall too has a layer of coarses of bricks on the eastern-southern portions at the height of about 3' to 7' as well as a regular layout of the bricks at the lower portion and the bottom running all through on the southern side. Of course, the extreme southern portion of the wall assumes ruinous state before taking turn to the west. Both on the eastern and the southern walls, large pits and brick debris have been located. These are clearly depicted in the photographs taken. All this bears out the utter destruction and ruination caused even to the eastern and southern brick-walls at time of the demolition of the Hindu temple.

The burnt-bricks used in the eastern wall belong to different early medieval and ancient Indian periods. A close view of a section of the wall before taking turn to the southern side reveals several structural remains as well as a huge brick-wall of 16 courses and floors of different periods. On the north-eastern side, as well, the 12' brick-wall has also been laid with multiple courses of bricks from the bottom to top. Similar position can be discerned from the mid-eastern wall. The southern wall, because of the cavity around the mid-portion and the pit from which architectural and sculptural fragments have been recently discovered, is comparatively in a dilapidated condition. All the same, after scraping, it has been found that the south-east section is intact and exhibits similar layout of the multiple courses of bricks from the bottom to the top (here around 10') as in the case of the wall (12') on the eastern side of the structure. The south-west portion of the southern wall, although in a dishevelled state, apart from structural remains, also comprises multiple courses of burnt bricks at the bottom. A little more digging than 10' on the southern side, from where the sculptural and architectural pieces have been found, has shown that the burnt brick-wall penetrates further down with several courses of burnt-bricks. This is equally true of the dug up section covering the eastern burnt-brick wall of Ramjanambhoomi/'Babri Masjid'. Photographs of both the eastern and southern walls with burnt-bricks structure at different portions have been taken.

As regards the western wall at the back of the Ramjanambhoomi/'Babri Masjid' structure, it was not possible to examine it because of the barbed wire-fencing and lack of entry facility. However, it is significant to observe that on the western sector, excavations were carried out by the Archaeological Survey of India and the published Report in this regard is available (see Indian Archaeology - A Review - 76-77 and 79-80.) In the earlier excavations carried out at Ayodhaya at the back of the Ramjanambhoomi/'Babri Masjid' structure, a culture sequence starting from 6th-7th century B.C. upto early medieval times was encountered. The burnt-brick structures were noticed right from the 4th-5th century B.C. upto early medieval times through the Mauryas (4th-3rd centuries B.C), Sunga (2nd-1st centuries B.C.), Kusanas (late 1st-3rd centuries A.D.) and the Guptas (4th-6th

centuries A.D.). As these excavations were conducted by Professor B.B. Lal under the project of the Ramayana and the Archaeological Survey of India under Dr. K.V. Sundarajan and Dr. K.N. Dikshit (at present Jt. Director General, Archaeological Survey of India), these experts will be in a better position to assess the situation. All this clearly shows that the present Ramjanambhoomi/'Babri Masjid' structure with courtyard in the front within the barbed-wiring was fortified on all the four sides, i.e. by the burnt brick walls on the eastern and southern sides and as is already known, by burnt-bricks/stone-slab walls on the western and northern sides, the latter two being in a dilapidated condition.

As regards the southern wall, nearer to the end of the eastern side wall, from the pit of which the above mentioned pieces of sculpture and architectural fragments have been found from 3' to 7' above the present ground level, there is a regular lay out of burnt-bricks running into the courtyard of the main structure which clearly indicates that the structure of the erstwhile Hindu temple still exists in a demolished form and lies burried under the inner wall end the existing structure of Ramjanambhoomi/'Babri Masjid' raised above the ruins of the Hindu temple.

The discovery of the sculptural pieces, architectural fragments of the demolished Hindu temple with burnt-brick walls in the east and south as well as the burnt-brick court-yard forming a part of the temple offer irrefutable archaeological evidence about the existence of the Hindu temple and its outskirts at this site. Apart from its artistic value, it reveals the vastness of the brick-flooring of the courtyard with rare monumental layout which bears testimony to the grandeur and glory of the temple. It throws a challenge to the All India Babari Masjid Action Committee/Babari Masjid Movement Coordination Committee and other such organisations which deny the existence of the Hindu temple over here before it was destroyed by Mir Baqi, the commander of Babur, the first Mughal Emperor, for the construction of the mosque thereupon.

It may be further observed that the discovery of the burnt-brick walls on the eastern and southern sides of the main structure as well as the burnt-brick flooring around the complex rules out the possibility of the seepage of the rainwater into the foundation of the Ramjanambhoomi/'Babri Masjid', as feared in certain quarters.

It is as well borne out by the revenue records that the enclosure wall (*Ram Deewar*) constructed by the Uttar Pradesh State around the Ramjanambhoomi complex does not in any way violate the *status-quo* orders relating to the disputed area issued by the Hon'ble Court of the Lucknow Bench of the Allahabad High Court. At the same time, as per revenue records, the site on which the *shilanyas* was laid in November, 1989, does not constitute a part of the disputed area and is clearly outside specifications given by the Special Bench of the Allahabad High Court in their Injunction Order dated 14.8.1989 and clarification dated 7th November, 1989 for the maintenance of *status quo* and for not changing the character of the property in question by the Parties to this suit.

At the end, it any added that during the course of further digging of earth, and levelling operation, on the eastern side of the Ramjanambhoomi/'Babri Masjid' structure, on 16.7.92, a few *ashta'dat* and earthen articles along with one rusted iron-blade and a stone-slab have been found. Of those, the most significant is one small sized two faced figurine having height of 2" and 6 centimetres in the middle, made of *ashta'dat* (a combination of eight metals) with the figures of Hanuman on one side and Gavun on the other along with a *mukat* (head-gear) on the top having two circled lines below it. It is at present in the possession of Mahant Narayana Chari of Dant Dhawan Kund, Achari Mandir, Ayodhaya. The other articles comprise a large sized earthen vessel (*matka*), 1.23 metres high with 1.86 metres in circumference in the middle; 2 pieces of *pacca* stone made, slightly pinkish, *belana* type skin rubbers; one full sized and the second broken in two parts; 2 pieces of ware like *kalas*, one complete in form and the other broken; one piece of sprinkler (water container) and one piece of iron small axe (*talab*) without wooden handle. The exact location of the above mentioned discovered articles is about 15 metres to the east from the northern end of the eastern wall dug up so far, near the barbed wire-pole. These have been found at about 10' below the main eastern wall of the structure of Ramjanambhoomi/'Babri Masjid'. With complete digging operation at this portion done during the last three days, the burnt-flooring at this side of the courtyard is also very clear. A lined stone-slab like the earlier ones discovered on 18.6.92 has also been found at this place. Photographs of all the articles inclusive of the brick-flooring and the stone slab have been taken.

Of all the above mentioned articles, the findings of the double-faced Hanuman/Gavun *ashta'dat* and the large sized earthern vessel are rather significant. The above mentioned *figurine* is in addition to the two images of Hindu deities found on 18.6.92 in the debris around the southern wall of the structure of Ramjanambhoomi/ 'Babri Masjid' and which, at present, are in the custody of the local Police Department. Of these two pieces of sculpture, the fragment of a stele of Vishnu image showing significantly a *Chakrapurush* i.e., a youthful male standing; *tribhanga* and holding vertically at the palm of the right hand the characteristic wheel of *Chakra* of Vishnu. On the right side, there are three subsidiary small panels which show Parashurama holding cup of wine supporting the canopy of serpent-hood, below him Balarama, the elder brother of Lord Krishna and thirdly at the bottom the image of Maitri Devi (Mother Goddess) in a sitting posture. The second sculptural piece is a fragment of image of Shiva-Parvati, which is largely broken.

The large sized vessel is reminiscent of such vessels found in some of the ancient sites in India. It was usually used for the purpose of storage of grain etc. Though the exact date of the earthern vessel can be determined only after a scientific analysis, it seems that it belongs to the late ancient or early medieval age. All the articles discovered on 16.7.92, seem to be pertaining to the premises of the nearby demolished structure inclusive of the Hindu temple. Of course, all the above mentioned articles need a thorough scientific examination.

B.R. Grover

Chapter 15 (a)

Supplementary Note dated 9th July 1992

After submission of the Report on 6th July '92, further revealing information has been gathered in respect of the dug up area with burnt-brick flooring in the east of the present structure of Ramjanamhoomi/'Baburi Masjid' as well as the southern dug up wall (about 10') outside the barbed wire enclosure of the structure.

(i) A further excavation and survey has shown that the burnt-brick layout and flooring (Referred to in the Report dated 6.7.92) does not form a flat ground. It is of an uneven nature, with higher level in the north, a little lower level in the east and again slightly higher level in the south of the floored compound. It may be due to the fact that with heavy weight of earth as well as the seepage of rainwater downwards, depressings in the single-brick flooring may have been caused at certain places in the course of the centuries since the early 16th century (1528 AD) when the Hindu temple was demolished. On the other hand, if this uneven level is structurally the same as constructed *abnitio*, it may be ascribed to an uneven nature of the ground situated at a higher level of kot Ram Chandra. At the same time, there is possibility that there is still an underground layer of earlier brick-flooring/structure which only further digging and excavation at certain chosent places by the expert archaeologists can throw further light in this respect.

(ii) Of the eastern side of the dup up wall, on the discovered brick-flooring at a distance of about eight metres in the north-east (marked 'C' in the sketch-map) there is small platform (*chabutra*, 4'x3') made of stone slabs joined by small stone *kankars* with the help of lime of that age. That such lime was used for joining disjointed stone-slabs was known during the early medieval age is evident from many other monuments of the 12th-14th centuries A.D. constructed in North India. It seems in the context that this small platform may have been used by the Hindu Priests for offering *Puja* or addressing the gathered pilgrims (*Yatris*) in the vast floored courtyard of the temple or it may even be a portion of an earlier still larger *garun asthamb*.

(iii) During the last two days (7, 8 July 1992), the dug up wall on the eastern side of the structure of Rama janamabhoomi 'Baburi Masjid' has been scraped end layers of earth debris have been removed from it. This has clearly brought to our purview a regular layer of the burnt-brick wall of about 12' above the brick-flooring of the courtyard. The top of the wall is laid with two hard rammed floors of *Chunam* and *kankar*, one above the other, with an apparent conspicous break between but over and above the layers of the brick-wall. This clearly indicates the utter destruction and ruination caused even to the brick-walls at the time of the demolition of the Hindu temple. Similar is the position of the wall stretching towards the southern side of the Ramjanamhoomi/'Baburi Masjid'. A further scientific scraping of the above mentioned brick wall is needed to determine the exact position of the Gate to the temple, of which *amalakas*, carving curved *Gandi* (facade) of *Shikhara*, pieces of door-jams etc. have been recently found. An indication in this regard has already been made in the Analysis Report of the sculptures submitted on 3.7.92.

(iv) At the end, it may be mentioned that a thorough survey of the complex around the Ramjanamhoomi/'Baburi Masjid', area based upon the authentic Revenue *Khasra* records/maps shows that the boundary wall (*Ram Deewar*) constructed by the Uttar Pradesh State is undoubtedly outside the disputed *khasra* Number of plots and does not in any way violate the status-quo orders of the Hon'ble High Court. Nor does the site on which *Shilanyas* was laid in November, 1989 under the Congiees (I) regime form a part of any disputed area in contravention of the orders of the Hon'ble High Court.

(v) With the digging of the ground below 10', there has been absolutely no danger of any future accumulated rain water seeping into the foundations of the Ramjanamhoomi/'Baburi Masjid', as feared in certain quarters. Now that a burnt brick-floored area along with a burnt-brick wall as mentioned above have been traced, any rain water seeping into the underneath temple structure or the present Ramjanamhoomi/'Baburi Masjid' premises is out of question.

Dated 9th July, 1992

Appendix V

Masjid groups could not dispute the fact of demolition recorded by Aurangazeb's grand-daughter, or the finding that Babur's will (which says he was secular) was a forged document

6.5. The minutes of the meeting of 10th January, 1991, contains the presentation made by Prof. B.R. Grover. The points made by Prof. Grover which were not rebutted at the meeting by anyone are summarised below:

"It is very unscientific and unjust to label this belief of Ram Janmabhoomi as of recent origin. A vast mass of historical and archaeological evidences is there to prove that the Hindus have regarded it as the birth-place of Lord Ram for centuries. It is a different matter whether these writings have been labelled either imperial or partisan.

"Whether Ram was a historical figure or a myth is not a relevant question. The moot question is whether there was a temple at the disputed site prior to the construction of the mosque or not.

"I have examined relevant revenue records for two months and found that there has been a tampering with the revenue records. He gave some instances. He claimed that even the tamperings can be detected by proper scrutiny.

"We have classified evidences into four categories (a) historical (b) archaeological (c) revenue and (d) legal. Then he went on citing documentary evidences from the evidences submitted earlier. He told that the earliest reference is in Abul Fazl's book, *Ain-e-Akbari*. He called Abul Fazl a secular scholar.

"Oudh is the name of both province and the town. The first reference of Babri Masjid is that of 1855. In 1861, Ayodhya was outside Ram Kot.

"Babar went to Ayodhya twice. There is one direct reference when he says that he visited Oudh and was to go for Shikar. But immediately thcrefier the pages are missing since the time of Babar. Another visit is inferred from the reference of Buxar.

"I don't claim that Babar went to Ayodhya to demolish the temple. But certainly he had dialogue with local people.

"I have examined and found that the place is called Ram Janmabhoomi after 1949. Earlier it was called Janmasthan; prior to that it was known Sita Ki Rasoi the temple which was demolished and the mosque was constructed.

"Then he gave the testimony of Aurangzeb's grand-daughter. She was scholarly. She was the daughter of Bahadur Shah I. Bahadur Shah was 62 years old when Aurangzeb died. So (he age of Bahadur Shah's daughter can be well assessed. She made it clear the offering of the namaz in the recently converted mosques including those at Mathura, Kashi and Ayodhya was sacred. She writes this temple [was] Sita Ki Rasoi temple. This was known by the name at the time.

"Then he read some other testimonies from the evidences already submitted. He cited the Imam's accounts. How Muhammad Asghar, Muazzan of the Babri Masjid filed a representation in 1858 in which he alleged that the Hindus had temporarily occupied the mosque and how they have been struggling for occupying the Janmasthan which was having a mosque built over it. Then he cited the Kazi's verdict, his peshkar's version and Wazid Ali Shah's decision. Then he cited Muslim writers testimonies and made it clear that they are based on numerous writings of earlier period and hence they are to be relied upon.

"Then he narrated how there has been a deliberate attempt to suppress the testimonies of Muslim writers. Four such instances have been given in the main evidence submitted earlier. Many more can be added. Then he gave the account of Joseph Tieffenthaler which makes it abundantly clear that the Ram Janmasthan temple was different from the birth place of Lord Ram. It was the place where the mosque was constructed and the Hindus had not forgotten this site. He further said that there was no road before the 20th century separating the present structure from the present Janmasthan temple. The entire area was one complex known as Ram Kot.

"The architectural style of the mosque is Jaunpuri. There is no minar in the mosque.

"In 1934 Bairagis threw [away] the main plaque during the riot. This plaque was earlier in the mimbar; but now it is not fixed at the old place. In the riot of 1855 also, the Hindus tried to capture the mosque. He suggested that Babar Kalandar was different from Babar, the Mughal Emperor. He further said that the so-called Babar's will has been found to be a forged document.

"Then he dealt with revenue records at length. He said that when khasra, khata, khatauni records are scrutinized and maps of all the four bandobasts are examined, it is clear the proprietory rights are in the names of the Bairagis and their disciples. Though many of these records have already been tampered, no further tampering should take place. The question of this land belonging to the waqf arose from 1935 onwards. Earlier it was not the waqf property. The grant had been given to an individual by the Britishers for hoping them. The testimony of Md. Asraf proves this point."

No one disputed the points presented by Prof. Grover, except that in regard to tampering which also was not denied.

Appendix VI Exhibit 1

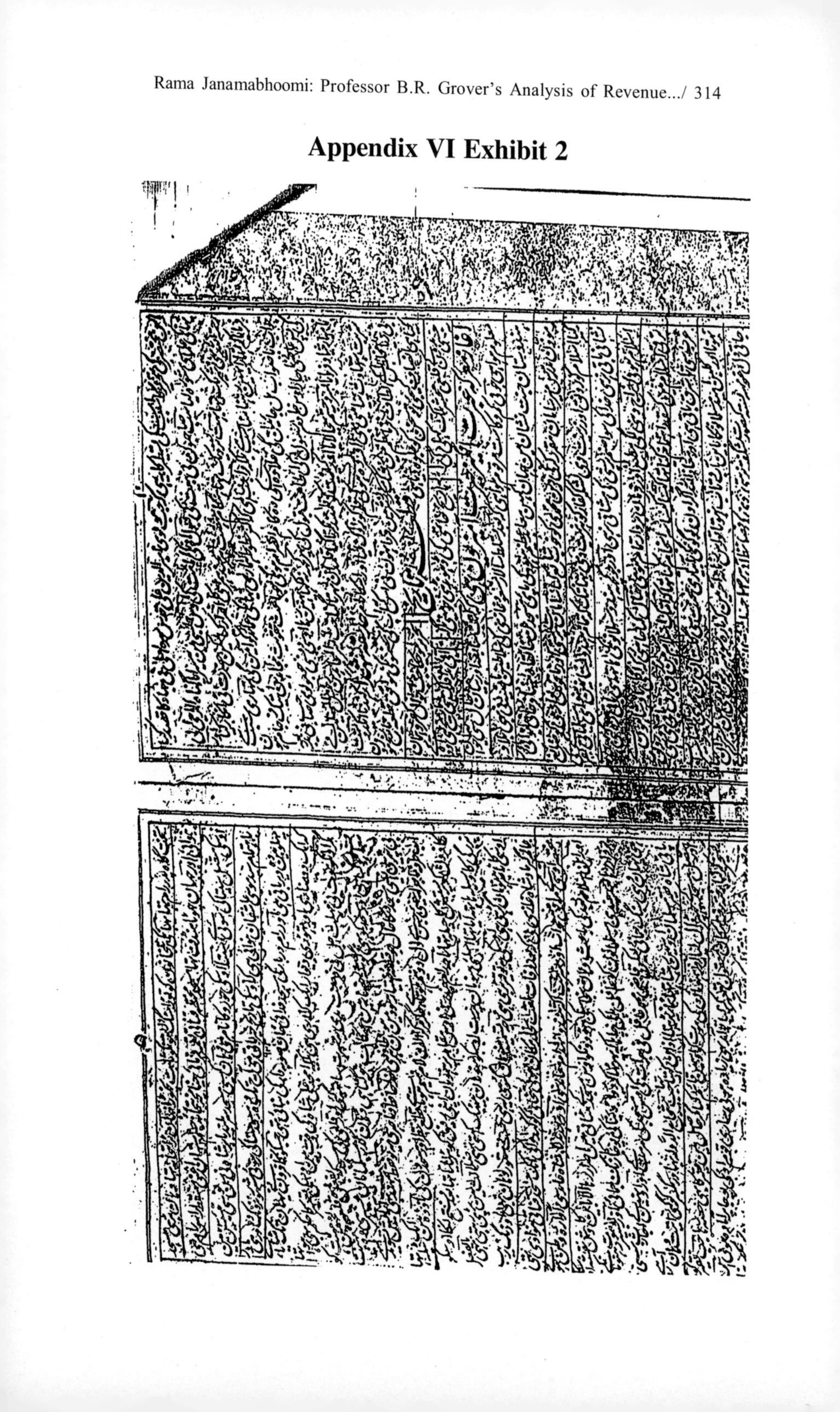

Appendix VI Exhibit 2

Appendix VI Exhibit 3

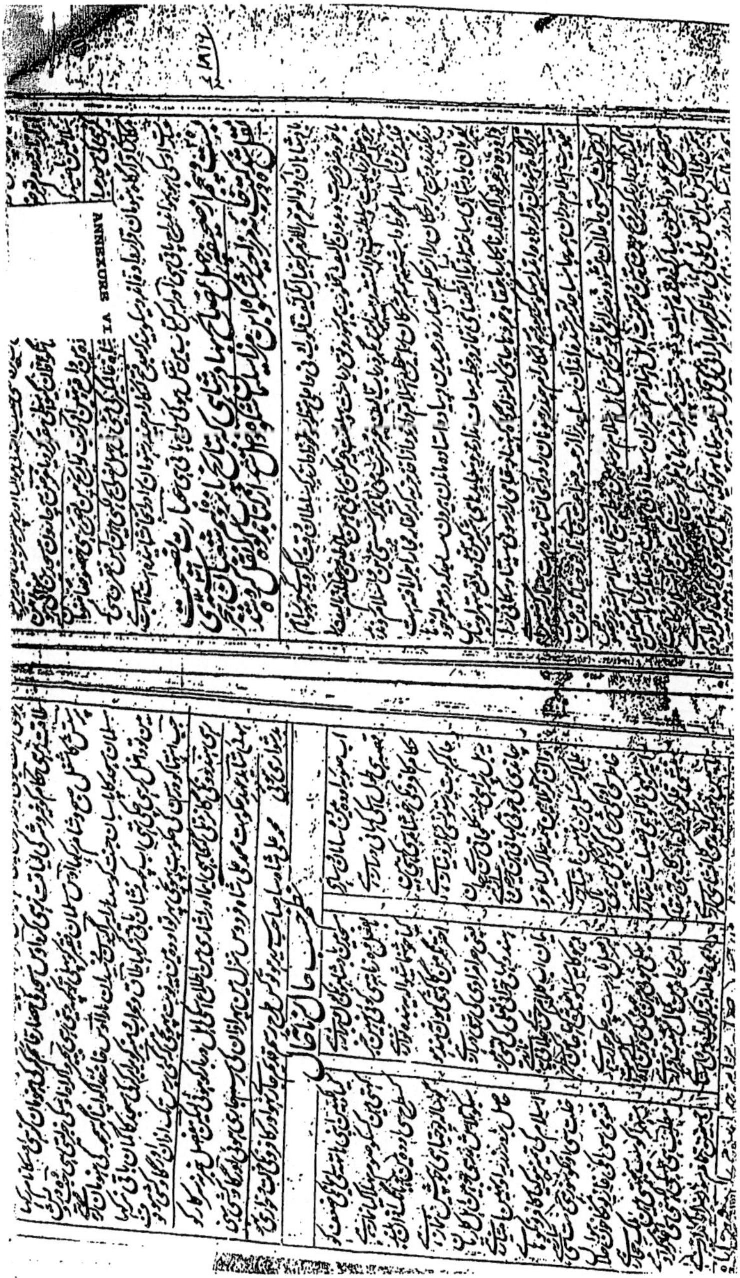

Translated from Persian text into English by Professor B.R. Grover and submitted to the Ministry of Home Affairs on 10.1.1991 by B. R. Grover

Sahifa-i-Chihal Nasaih Bahadur Shahi, written by the daughter of Bahadur Shah (*ibn*) Alamgir during the late 17th century/early 18th century.

The work entitled *Sahifa-i-Chihal Nasaih Bahadur Shahi* (comprising forty counsels) was written by the daughter of Bahadur Shah (*ibn*) Aiamgir (Bahadur Shah I - 1707 to 1712 A.D.) A copy of this work, the transcription of which was completed on 15th *Shaban* A.H. 1231/11th July, 1816 A.D. was deposited with the Library of Mirza Haider Shukoh ibn Mirza Sulayman Shukoh-The text of the (relevant) twenty fifth counsel (*nasaihat*) taken from the above manuscript copy is being reproduced appropriately.

Sahifa-i-Chihal Nasaih Bahadur Shahi is the oldest known account of the destruction of Ram Janambhoomi for – construction of the Baburi mosque, and its author is none other than Aurangzeb's grand-daughter.

Mirza Jan, the author of *Hadiqa-i-Shahda* 1856, Lucknow, has reproduced the above text in Persian on pp. 4-7 of his book. The text runs as follows:

"It behoves the great and august kings that they should care for the heart-felt desires (i.e., welfare/happiness) of both the low and the high because it is incumbent upon the ruler of the time to look into the difficulties of the people. Without confronting the hearts of the people (i.e., without their happiness), the progress and brightness (i.e., prosperity) of the State and the regime is impossible. That is why the great rulers have always regarded the comfort of the people as the most important ingredient of the State and its administration and (they) still regard it so. But as regards any such considerate attitude towards towards the non-muslims (*ghair mushrib*), there need not be any relaxation on the part of Islam. Keeping in view the night and sway of Islam, (the rulers) should keep all the infidels (*mushrikan*) under the domination of Islam and they should also not ignore the lawfully realizable *jizya* from the non-believers (*kufar*). They should also not exempt the various *Rajghan* (Hindu Rajas) from the order requiring the latter to be present on the days of Ids and standing on feet (as *piyadas*) outside the mosques built in their (respective) jurisdictions on the basis of the royal order. They (the Hindu *Rajghan*) have to be present in this position till the (offering of) *nemaz* and the reading of the *khutba* is over. The places of worship of the infidel Hindus (*musharkin* Hindu) situated at Mathura, Banaras and Awadh, etc., which the "wicked and worthless" infidels (*kufar-i-nabkar*), according to their own belief and faith consider these (places) as the birth place of Kanhaiya (Lord Krishna) the place (*muqami*) of Rasoi Sita (pertaining to Lord Rama), the monument (*makan*) known as the seat of Hanuman, who, (according to the Hindus) was installed by Ram Chandra over there after the conquest of Lanka - were all demolished for the might of Islam, and at all these places mosques have been constructed. They (the rulers) should not keep these mosques free from the Friday congregational prayers (*juma wa jamait*). Rather it is obligatory that no open ceremony of idol-worship should be performed over there and the sound of the conch shell should not reach the ear of the Muslims. In the same manner, they (the rulers), should enjoin the *Sheikhul Islam*, in particular, to realise that the propagation of the strong faith and the might of the people of Islam depends upon all this action and he should not show the slightest negligence in this matter.

Appendix VII
Guru Nanak's Visit to Ayodhya: Taken from 'Sakhis' of Guru Nanak

ਸਾਖੀ ਗੁਰੂ ਜੀ ਅਜੁਧਿਆ ਕੋ ਗਏ

ਸ੍ਰੀਗੁਰੂਨਾਨਕਜੀਕਹਿਆ ਭਾਈ ਬਾਲਾ ਏਹਭੀ ਨਗਰੀ ਸ੍ਰੀਰਾਮਚੰਦਜੀ ਕੀਹੈ ਏਥੇਸ੍ਰੀ
ਰਾਮਚੰਦਰਜੀ ਅਵਤਾਰ ਧਾਰਕੇ ਚਰਿੱਤ੍ਰਕੀਏਹੈਨ ਸੋਦੇਖਦੇਹੀਚਲੀਏਰੇਤਾਂਸ੍ਰੀਗੁਰੂਜੀ
ਸਰਜੂਨਦੀਦੇਕਿਨਾਰੇਪਰਜਾਇਬੈਠੇਤਾਂਓਥੋਂਦੇਲੋਕ ਚਰਨੀਂ ਆਇਲਗੇ ਤਾਂਭਾਈਬਾਲੇ
ਕਹਿਆਸ੍ਰੀਰਾਮਚੰਦਰਜੀਤਾਂ ਨਗਰੀਕੋ ਸਾਥਲੇਗਏਸਨ ਏਹਕਹਾਂਸੇ ਆਈ ? ਤਾਂਓਥੋਂ
ਪੰਡਿਆਂ ਆਖਿਆ ਸ੍ਰੀਬਾਬਾਜੀ ਜੇਹੜੇ ਘਰਸਨ ਓਹ ਤਾਂਨਾਲਨਹੀਂਸੇ ਪੈ ਗਏ ਅਤੇ
ਸ੍ਰੀਰਾਮਚੰਦਰ ਦਾ ਦਰਸ਼ਨ ਕਰਤੇਥੇ ਅਰਜੋਉਨਕਾਨਾਮਜਪਤੇਥੇ ਸੋ ਬੈਕੁੰਠਕੋ ਜਾਇ
ਪ੍ਰਾਪਤਭਏਹੈਨ ਤਾਂਸ੍ਰੀਗੁਰੂਜੀਕਹਿਆ ਭਾਈ ਤੁਸੀਂਵੀ ਸ੍ਰੀਗੁਰੂ ਨੂੰ ਮਿਲਕਰਪਰਮੇਸ਼ਰ
ਕਾ ਨਾਮ ਜਪੋ ਪੂਰਨਗੁਰੂਕਾਧਿਆਨਧਰੋ ਤੁਸੀਭੀਬੈਕੁੰਠਕੋ ਪ੍ਰਾਪਤ ਹੋਵੋਗੇ ਤਾਂਉਨਾਂ
ਪੰਡਿਆਂਕਹਿਆਮਹਾਰਾਜਾਜੀ ਗੁਰੂਕਿਤਨੀਤਰਾਂਦੇਨਹੈ ਤਾਂਗੁਰੂਜੀ ਕਹਿਆ ਗੁਰੂਤੀਨ
ਤਰਾਂਦੇਹੁੰਦੇਹੈਨ ਪ੍ਰਿਥਮੇਤਉਗੁਰੂਪੰਡਿਤ ਹੋਤਾਹੈ ਪਰਪੰਡਿਤਗੁਰੂਔਰਲੋਕੋਂਕੋ ਉਪਦੇਸ਼
ਕਰਤੇਹੈਂ ਪਰਆਪਨਹੀਂ ਕਮਾਵਤੇ ਤਿਸਕਉਮਿਲਨੇਕਾ ਪੁੰਨ ਹੋਤਾਹੈ ਗਤੀ ਨਹੀਂ ਹੁੰਦੀ
ਅਵਧੂਤਗੁਰੂਹੈਂ ਸੋ ਉਨਾਂਦੇਵਿਦਿਆਰੂਪੀ ਹਾਥ ਪਾਉਂ ਨਹੀਂ ਹੋਤੇ ਕਿਉਂਕਿ ਕਿਸੇਸੰਤ
ਮਿਲਕੇ ਗਿਆਨਪ੍ਰਾਪਤਹੋਯਾਹੈ ਸੋ ਆਪਣਾ ਉਧਾਰਕਰਲੈਂਦੇ ਹੈਨ ਪਰ ਦੂਸਰੇ ਕਉ
ਨਹੀਂਪਾਰਕਰਸਕਤੇ ਔਰਜੋਮਹਾਂਪੁਰਖ ਗੁਰੂਹੈਨ ਸੋ ਆਪਤੇਮੁਕਤਰੂਪ ਹੈਨ ਅਰ ਜੋ
ਕੋ ਮਿਲਤਾ ਹੈ ਸੋ ਉਸਕਉ ਸਤਨਾਮ ਦੇਕਰ ਤੁਰਤਹੀ ਉਧਾਰ ਕਰ ਦੇਤੇ ਹੈਨਏਹ
ਨ ਸ੍ਰੀ ਗੁਰੂਜੀਕੇ ਸੁਨਕਰ ਅਜੁਧਿਆਵਾਸੀ ਸਭ ਸ੍ਰੀਗੁਰੂਜੀਕੇ ਚਰਨਾਉਪਰ ਢਹਿ
ਅਤੇਅਰਜ਼ਲਗੇ ਕਰਨ ਹੇਨਿਰੰਕਾਰਜੀਸਾਨੂੰ ਸੰਸਾਰਦੇ ਦੁਖਾਂਪਾਸੋਂ ਬਚਾਉ ਜੀ ਅਤੇ
ਜੀ ਕਲਿਆਣਕਰੋਜੀ ਆਪਮਹਾਂਪੁਰਖਹੋ ਤਾਂਸ੍ਰੀਗੁਰੂਜੀਕਹਿਆ ਭਾਈ ਤੁਸੀ ਜਗਤ
ਤ ਜਾਣੋ ਤੇ ਆਏ ਸਾਧਦੀ ਸੇਵਾ ਕਰੋ ਮਨਕਰਕੇ ਪਰਮੇਸ਼ਰਦਾਜਾਪਕਰੋਦੇਖਾਵੇ

Appendix VIII Page I

अयोध्या का विष्णु-हरि मन्दिर शिलालेख
(अपूर्ण पाठ)

1. ॐ नमः शिव [ा य] ।

... सुविक्रमतजो सतां समन्ताद्दिशां प्रांशुत्वेन निश्चर्व्वषो ।

2. ... सतमुद्देशां र[वा] मनस्तागुम् ॥1॥

संवर्त्तप्रमदोद्धरः कुलगिरिः....

ग्रामाहारकणद्...

ब्रह्माण्डं करसंपुटेन विबुधाम्वो [यो?] ऽ न्या ...

... भ्मार्ग्गव विभ्रता नवद् वन्धो ऽ वतंसो भुवः ॥2॥

यस्मिन्ना

3. [ज्ञि/जनि?] लक्ष्मि (= मी) चिरस्थायिन्य [?नी]

देवद्विजकृत्यवाञ्छो [सो/धो] पचिते (पवित्रे?)

पश्चार्थवेदनाबद्ध (वन्ध्य/रन्ध्र) नम्र.. जज्ञिरे ॥3॥

ते चण्डीपति चण्डताण्डव वलत् (चलत्) चूडा...

ब्रह्मण्डोच्चकपालरन्ध्रसरणिप्रस्थायि [स्वत्-] कीर्तयः ।

वीरास्तत्र कुले जनिं जगृहि

4. रे यैः भार्गवीया ऽऽ हव-

क्षीणक्षत्रिय से [शे] ष रक्षण विधौ बद्धो नियोगग्रहः ॥4॥

वन्ध [ा ?] देवकुलमाकुलतानिवृत्ति-

निर्व्यूढना प्रतिमवि [ग्रह] जन्मभूमिः ।

यत्रातिसाहससहस्रसमिद्धधामा

धामे ऽ जनिष्ट जगदिष्टतमोत्त-

5. म श्रीः ॥5॥

मा मे दया न वपुषि द्रविणेषु तृष्णा

निष्णाति [?] रम्यविरसा सरसेन्द्रियार्थो [र्थाः]।

Appendix VIII Page II

इत्युद्गृणन्ननुदिनं स क्षिरसवासा (?)

मामैषणा स जगदे जगदेक [वीरः] ॥6॥

युद्धकेलिदलिता ऽखिल मेद [= दिनि] भिल्लपल्ली सहस्र वनितासु निकुञ्जगासु।

उत्कण्ठा

6. काचिदपि नो विट-विष्टि दालितेषु स्तनेषु व्रण[णि] तेषु [जघनेषु?] मुहुर्लिखतः ॥7॥

पुरा कीर्त्या न्यस्तं तदनु तनुना ऽध्यासितुमना

मनस्वी स्वर्लोकं परिणतिमुपेतः [प्र] शमिनीम्।

स सर्वस्वं क्षत्रं [क्षात्रं?] ...भुवि (वर्यति?) सल्लक्षणसुतः [ते]

श्रिया सार्द्ध दध्रे हुतभुजि तिवा

7. श्चा निरमहः ॥8॥

तद्धाम निःसीमममोघमन्यो र्धन्यो च सा [?] कांचन दानशक्तेः।

अमानुषं पौरुषमाविरासीत् सल्लक्षणे विश्वविलक्षणं तत् ॥9॥

युद्धः [शुद्धः?] श्री क ... [ब] लाधिकरणं बाहुर्महावाहिनी

कीर्तिः वंधत [?] चकार (प्रकार?) विधये ते.. यदं

8. शन सज्जो [मैः] नापि बिना निजोपकरणान्येतानि निःकण्टकं

यः (ये?) साम्राज्यपरिच्छदं विदधिरे चिन्तावितानोज्झितम् ॥10॥

सम [स्त] जितराजो[ज्य] स्य

चिरं निस्त्रिंश पठसः [?मानसः?]

... पि धृतो मूर्द्धना

यो जहारांशु जीवतम् ॥11॥

पालय [मलय?] वलयस्यान्ते शान्ते

9. वियत्तटिनीतटे

हिमगिरिगुहागेहद्वारे दरी विसौ [विषमौ?] षधिम्।

प्रथमलिखितां सिद्धैर्यस्य प्रशस्तिपदावलीं

पठति निपुणं स्त्रैणं मोदान्नभःस्थलचारिणाम् ॥12॥

कैलासाचल [मेख] लासु मलयप्रान्तेषु मेरोःशिरो-

भागे सर्व [=स्वर्ग] तरंगिणी-तटभुवि

10. स्थानेषु चान्येष्वपि।

कृत्वा तर्प्पण (चार्च्चन?) शिल्पजां प्रतिकृतिं वृद्धो-पदेशात् पति-

Appendix VIII Page III

प्राप्त्यै खेचरकन्यकाभिरनिशं यद्वाहुरभ्यर्च्यते ॥ 13 ॥
रज्यद्धारा पेशलैरिष्टसिद्धि
प्राप्त्यै गायद्भि वस्यं [?]....जगद्भिः।
गेहे यस्य श्रीविलासाभिरामे
[ऽ] न्या
11. गा [?] दुच्चैः गीयते कारणौ..[?] [कन्यकाभिः?] ॥ 14 ॥
अमरपुरपुरन्ध्री बन्धुतामव्यलीकां
भजति सुकृतवासे तत्र सल्लक्षणाख्ये।
प्रति पुरि न तस्य प्राप्य सद्योऽनवद्यं
सुतमुदित विवेकं शोकमौ [ज्झत्] लं तव ॥ 15॥
अल्हणः प्रणयपेशलः सतां
गर्ज्जतां क्रकच
12. कोटिरुद्भटः।
आनिनाय नयनिह्नवे नयः [य-, यं?]
प्रह्वतां प्रकृतिचञ्चलां श्रियम् ॥ 16॥
लोकोत्तरः स खलु कोऽपि यदाभिमुख्यो
ऽ हंकारराशिरगलच्चिरसंभृतो ऽ पि।
संसार पाशभि ... दृशैव यस्य
जाताः श्लथाः सुकृत-दुःकृतकं ... शु ॥ 17 ॥
13. पौरुष प्रतिरं [ब?] धीति पुरन्ध्रीति च विन्यताम् [?]
येन लोकानुरुद्धापि प्रतिषिद्धा नगो [मो?] न्नरिः [?] ॥ 18॥
तस्यानुजो जगति [जयति?] **मेघसुतः** श्रुताढयः
श्रीमानभूद [त्] नयचन्द्रपदाभिलप्यः।
गोविन्दचन्द्रधरणीन्द्रगुरुप्रसादात्
साकेतमण्डलपतित्वम
14. लाभि येन ॥ 19॥
शश्वत् संगररंगनामितरिपुस्कन्धेन युद्धोद्धुरां
वीरास्तेन न केवलं बलवता दोर्दुर्म्मदा[न्] मोचिताः।
अप्युद्दाम वसुप्रदाननिरतस्वान्तेन चैकान्ततो

Appendix VIII Page IV

दूरारूढ़धनान्धतामदमसौ कल्पद्रुमस्या जितः ॥20॥
टंकोत्खात,
15. विशालशैलशिखरश्रेणीशिलासंहति
व्यूहै विष्णुहरे र्हिरण्यकलशश्रीसुन्दरं मन्दिरम् ।
पूर्वैरप्यकृतं कृतं नृपतिभिर्येनेद[मि]त्यद्भुतं
संसाराण्णर्वशीघ्रलंघनलघू [न्] पादान्धिया ध्यायता॥ 21॥
गोविन्दचन्द्रक्षि तिपालराज्य
16. स्थैर्य [•र्याय/र्येण] निस्तन्द्र भुजार्गलस्य ।
अथ प्रपेदेऽस्य पदं कनीयान्
आयुष्यचन्द्रो ऽल्हणसूनुरेव ॥22॥
न साहसांकेन न शूद्रकेण
तस्योपमानं विदधुः कवीन्द्राः ।
कृतं भिया यस्य पुरो न कामाद्
अन्येन मन्ये धनुराततज्यम् ॥23॥
17. उद्दामसौधविबुधालयनीमयोध्याम्
अध्यास्य तेन नयनिह्नुतवैशसेन ।
साकेतमण्डलमखण्डमकारि कूप-
वापीप्रतिश्रयतडागसहस्रमिश्रम् ॥ 24॥
नित्यं निरोध विधये [निधये?] निजवल्लभानां
हेमा [चला] मल शिलातल तला [=ताल]
18. लीनाः ।
कस्तूरिकैणतरुणीश्रवणोपभोग-
योग्यं जगुः सरभसं सरसं यशो ऽस्य ॥25॥
अविमुक्तविशालाक्षी ललिता नन्दिता सदा ।
काशीवद[य]स्य देहश्रीःसतां निर्वाणकारणम् ॥ 26॥
अब्धि [मृ] चितयन् [?] हिरण्यक
19. सि[शि] पुं संयम्य वाणं [?] रणे
कुर्व्वाणो बलिराज बाहुदलनं कृत्वा बहून् विक्रमान् ।
कुर्व्वन् दुष्टदशानन व्यसनम [नस्य निधनं?] ......

Appendix VIII Page V

को ऽप्यन्यः स दशाधिको ...... ॥27॥

पुण्यावता ...... ॥ 28॥

अत्र सुरादिन्त [त्त?] वने

20. ...... तो निहन्ति

पाश्चात्यभीतिमपि भीषणबाहुदण्डः ।

तेजः प्रभावमहतां महनीयमेव

पूर्व्वापरा ि[=दि] ...... ॥29॥

... प्रजानां परिणामवद्भिः ।

ख्याते क्षितौराज ... वं **श्रीआयुष्यच [न्द्रः]** ...... ॥30॥

नोट : उपर्युक्त पाठ डॉ० जी० सी० त्रिपाठी एवं डॉ० डी० पी० दूबे के संयुक्त प्रयास पर आधारित है।

Appendix IX

A Short Note on the Vishnuhari Temple Inscription of Āyushyachandra

This inscription is written on a buff sandstone-slab (1.10x56m) recovered from the ruins of the controversial structure which was demolished on the 6th December 1992 in Ayodhya. The slab was embedded in the lower portion of a wall some three to four feet above the ground. It contains 20 lines in all and is composed in chaste Sanskrit. The palaeography of the script unmistakably indicates that it was inscribed in the Nāgāri characters which were in vogue sometimes during the 12th century.

It seems that a part of the inscription continued on a second stone-slab as well which has unfortunately not yet come to light. The inscription was got written by one *Āyushyachandra*, son of *Alhana* and a grandson of king *Sallakshana*. The name of the father of *Sallakshana* was perhaps also indicated in one of the verses in the beginning but since the initial portion of the inscription is highly damaged, it is now difficult to reconstruct this name.

The inscription consists of some 30 verses in Sanskrit composed in different metres. It opens up with an obeisance to Lord Siva, probably the family deity of the royal dynasty. The first verse which has come down to us in a mutilated form, refers to the exploits of the Dwarf incarnation of Vishnu. Verses 2 to 4 refer to a particular dynasty of the rulers whose name is not available but they are eulogised and glorified in such high terms that a very important dynasty (Raghuvamsa ?) seems to be meant. The rulers of this dynasty, very great in number, were the ornaments of this earth; they were steadfast and strong like high mountains. They had immense riches and their treasury was never depleted. They were sensitive to the problems and difficulties of their people and were munificent towards the *Brahmanas*, also pious and religious. To them goes the credit of performing great rituals and of building temples for gods with the result that their fame ascended right up to heaven and reached even the outer shell of the Universe.

The fifth verse is very important and refers to the Janmabhumi of Shri Rama. The poet pays his respect to the holy spot (*dhāma*) which is the birth-place of that incarnation (of Vishnu) which possesses the highest and the most desirable glory in this world and whose splendour was constantly enhanced by performing thousands of brave deeds. He was also one who was instrumental in abating the anxieties and worries of the family of gods.

Verses 6 and 7 refer to some king in this family who was totally unattached to this world, even though a king, and was disinterested in its pleasures including wealth and women. In the verse 8 he is said to have coronated his son *Sallakshana* before going to heaven. Verses 9 to 15 sing the glory of this king. He was very strong and powerful but at the same time kind and liberal. Instead of taking recourse to weapons and army, he usually tried to solve the problems of people with peaceful means. His kingdom comprised a large part of the mountain-tracks of the Himalayas where the monuments erected by him are still said to exist. A number of maidens of Himalayan region dreamt of having this king as their husband. When he died, his elder son Alhana took over and soon became a powerful monarch capable of shattering the pride of many an adversary.

According to verses 16 to 19, after his death his younger brother (i.e. cousin) named *Nayachandra* who was a son of *Megha*, obviously the uncle of *Alhana*, ascended the throne. This Nayachandra, it seems, for the first time, got the suzerainty of the Saketa region by the grace of Gahadawal king Govindachandra (1114-1154 A D.). In other words Govindachandra was pleased to cede the territory of Saketa to Nayachandra and made him his vassal or feudatory. Verse 20 makes a mention of the valour and prowess of the king as well as his extraordinary liberality and munificence.

The next verse, i.e. 21st, makes an unmistakable reference to a temple of Vishnuhari which the king Nayachandra constructed after having brought solid boulders from the mountain peaks which were chiseled out by his orders. The stone-slabs were arranged to form a unique temple the like of which had not yet been constructed by any other previous king. The temple was crowned with a golden Kalaśa (copula) lending great beauty to the temple.

The king was succeeded by *Ayushyachandra* who is the son of *Alhana*. This Ayushyachandra was also a protege of king Govindachandra and was so meritorious that he seems to supersede in qualities even the ancient kings like Vikramaditya and Śudraka. He had his royal seat in the city of Ayodhya which was full of high rising temples and structures. He was of non-violent nature and was given to philanthropic acts of constructing wells, step-wells, tanks and residences for the poor and needy.

Verses 25 to 30 glorify the deeds of Āyushyachandra. He had his kingdom extended upto Himalaya where the women singing melodious songs in his glory attracted the female musk-deer. He was a handsome man of wide eyes and of jolly temperament.

Verse 27 compares him with Vishnu and discovers better qualities in him than in the ten incarnations put together. The next verses which are available in highly mutilated form refer to his royal authority, his capability to check inimical forces coming from the East and the West as well as his genuine concern for his subject.

The inscription is incomplete.

NOTE : *The estampage of the inscription preserved in the Hon'ble High Court is obscure and illegible at a number of places. These lacunas could be filled up and a better reading obtained if one studies the original.*

- G. C. Tripathi and D.P. Dube

(Reprinted from *Itihas Darpan*, Vol. III, No. 2, 1996)

List of Original Revenue Records and Books

1. Bando Bast Report, 1822 AD.

   District Records Office (Muhafaz Khanna) Faizabad (U.P.)

2. Settlement Report of 1861 AD- Bastna No. 132 of 1861 AD. pertaining to Khasra Kishtwar, muaza Ramkot, pargana Haveli and Zilla Faizabad.

   (a) Available at District Records Office (Mushafaz Khanna), Faizabad.

   (b) Available at Tehsil Office (Record Room), Faizabad.

   (c) Appended Maps to the village.

3. Settlement Report of 1861 AD- Basta No. 132 of 1861 AD vide F. No. Had Bast 571, Village Shanawh, pargana Awadh, Tehsil/District Faizabad.

   Available at the Tehsil Records Room (Tehsil Office) Faizabad.

4. Settlement Report 1301 Fasli/1883 AD

   (i) Khasra Kishtwar, mauza Kot Ram Chander, pargana Haveli, Tehsil and Zilla Faizabad.

   (ii) Khatauni mauza Kot Ram Chander, pargana Haveli Tehsil and Zilla Faizabad.

   Available at District Records Office (Mahafaz Khanna), Faizabad.

5. Hose's Note dated 1st April 1905 AD, No. 38, Nazul Office, Faizabad.

6. Record of the Nazul Department, 1931 AD

   Tarmimi Khasra Abadi, mauza Kot Ram Chander, Ayodhya pargana Haveli Awadh, Tehsil and Zilla Faizabad, 1931 AD. Available at Nazul Office, Faizabad.

7. Settlement Report 1344 Fasli/1936-37 AD.

   (i) Khasra Kishtwar, mauza Kot Ram Chander, pargana Haveli Awadh, Tehsil & District Faizabad. Village Shanawh, pargana Awadh, Tehsil/Distt Faizabad.

   Available at the District Records Office (Mahafza Khanna), Faizabad.

(ii) Khewat, mauza Kot Ram Chander, 1344 Fasli/1936-37 AD.

(iii) Khatauni, mauza Kot Ram Chander, 1344 Fasli.

(iv) Appended Maps of mauza Kot Ram Chander.

8. Settlement Report, 1397 Fasli/1989-90 AD, mauza Kot Ram Chander, pargana Haveli, Tehsil & District Faizabad.

   a) Khasras

   b) Khewats

   c) Khata Khatauni

   d) Appended Maps.

List of Books

1. Mirzan Jan, *Hadiqa-i-Shahada*, Lucknow, 1856 AD. may be available at university library/Private collection libraries.
2. Mirza Rajab Ali Beg Suru, *Fasana-i-Ibrat*, Lucknow.
3. Shaikh Mohammad Azmat Ali Kakorawi, (*Tawarikh-i- Mulk-i-Awadh entitled Murraqa-i-Khusarawi*).
4. Dr. Zaki Kakorawi, *Amir Ali Shahaur and Markah-i-Hunuman Garhi*, Lucknow, 1987. Available at Lucknow.
5. Haji Muhammad Hassan, Zia-Akhtar, Lucknow, 1878. Available at Maulana Azad Library, A.M.U. Aligarh.
6. Maulvi Abdul Karim, *Gumgashte Halat-i-Ajodhya* Awadh i.e. *Tarikh-i-Parnia Madina Alwaliya* (in Persian), Lucknow, 1885.
7. -Ditto- Revised and Translated into Urdu by Maulvi Abdul Gafar, Lucknow, 1879. Available at Lucknow.
8. Kamaluddin Haider Hasni al Hussaini al Mushhadi, *Kaiser ul Tawarikh Ya Tawarikh-i-Awadh*, Lucknow, 1986, Vol. 1 & 2. Available at Lucknow.
9. Alama Muhammad Najamalghani Khan Rampuri, *Tarikh-i-Awadh*, 1909, Vols available at State Library Rampur.
10. –Ditto-Abridged Edition, Vols 1 & 2 by Dr. Zaki Kakarwi. Available at Maulana Azad Library, A.M.U. Aligarh.
11. Luchmi Narian Sadr Qanungo, *Asrar-i- Haqiqat*, Lucknow, 1932.

    Available at Lucknow, University Library, Private Collection Libraries.
12. Maulana Habim Saiyad Abdul Hai *Al Hind F. Alhad al Islami* (in Arabic) i.e. India Under Islamic Rule.
13. -Ditto-

    Translated into Urdu by Maulana Abdul Hasan Nadwi, alias Ali Main, Nadwatul-u-lma, Lucknow, 1973.
14. -Ditto- English Translation 1977.
15. *Malfuzal-i-Shah Abdul Haq*, may be available at Oriental Library Tonk, Rajasthan, Lucknow/Aligarh.

16. *Tarikh-i-khandan-i-Hazrat Muss Ashiqan*: Sabzposh Press, Gorakhpur, (U.P.).
17. *Tawarikh-i-Sabri*, Nawal Kishore Press, Lucknow (U.P.).
18. *Malumat-i-Shah Hali*, Sabzposh Press, Gorakhpur (U.P.).
19. *Halat-i-Khandan Shah Murad Ullah*, Bahraich, (U.P.).
20. *Khandan-i-Hazrat Shah Fateh Ullah*, Awadh, Sabzposh Press, Gorakhpur, (U.P.).

Inscriptions and Images Found While Digging

1. A stone-tablet Vishnu-Hari Temple **Inscription** of 20 line text composed in Sanskrit language and written in Nagari script of llth-12th century style. It is securely dated in the first half of the 12th century A.D.
2. An eight line fragmentary **inscription** on a stone pillar, composed in Sanskrit language and written in Nagari script of llth-12th century A. D. style. It is precisely datable to mid-to-late 12th century A.D.
3. A two-line fragmentary Sanskrit **inscription** engraved, on a stone pillar in Nagari script. It is precisely datable to mid-12th century A.D. on palaeographic grounds.

Images

1. A standing image of Vishnu wearing a long *vanamala*. Highly weathered. Engraved on a *dvara-shakha* or door-jamb. Datable to 10th century A.D.
2. A head of Shiva Bhairava with tall *jata-juta* hair-do, covering the head, wide open eyes and two protruding teeth. Datable to the early 12th century A.D.
3. A severly damaged image of a standing deity in *tribhanga* pose, possibly Ganesha with a rishi (?), seen from the back, under a narrative panel raised and supported by a yaksha. Datable to early 12th century A. D.
4. A long frieze of garland-bearer couples (*vidyadharas*). Datable to early 12th century A.D.
5. A fragmentary frieze of *vidyadharas*. Datable to early 12th century A.D.

Architectural Pieces

1. *Ddvara-shakha* (door-jamb) with four parallel vertical friezes showing floral motifs. Datable to 10th century A.D. with Vishnu image.
2. A top-stone of the *jala* decoration of the *shikhara* showing floral designs. Cut in stencil technique. Datable to 12th century A.D.

3. A large fragment of the ceiling, bluish dark stone, showing meandering creepers with two *kirtimukha* figures large eyes and horned head arranged in concentric rectangles. Datable to 12th century A.D.
4. A section of frieze showing flowers and leaves in interconnected roundels, with upper and lower borders of closely placed beads, the bottom has running Us. The deeply cut crevices are found indifferently filled with *chunam* or lime plaster. It is a most telling and convincing evidence of the fact that the stones like this were fixed in the walls of the 'mosque' with sculptured face turned inside the core of the wall. Datable to 12th century A.D.
5. Some half-a-dozen pillars of buff sandstone with curved brackets. Datable to 12th century A.D.
6. Three *amalakas*, each on these had topped the *karna shikharas* or corner spires of the temple. Datable to llth-12th century A.D.

Persian Inscription

1. There is a large fragment of the Persian inscription which was once fixed on the top of the main entrance of the central domed chamber. Datable to early 16th century A.D.
2. Central piece of the ceiling of the dome decorated with fully opened flower and iron chain. Datable to 16th century A.D.
3. A *vitana* stone or lintel, once found fixed on the main entrance of the 'mosque'. It bears lotus motifs of Hindu sacred symbols. Datable to 11th-12th century A.D.
4. A *chhadya* stone. Datable to 11th-12th century A.D.